THE
STORY OF RELIGION
IN AMERICA

ISBN: 0-8010-8019-3
Copyright 1930, 1939, 1950 by Harper & Row, Publishers
Reprinted 1973 by Baker Book House Company
by arrangement with Harper & Row Publishers, Inc.

Second Printing, October 1975

PHOTOLITHOPRINTED BY CUSHING - MALLOY, INC.
ANN ARBOR, MICHIGAN, UNITED STATES OF AMERICA
1975

CONTENTS

v

PREFACE TO THE REVISED AND ENLARGED EDITION

TWENTY years have elapsed since the appearance of the first edition of this book in 1930. In 1939 an enlarged edition was published in which the latter part of the volume was entirely rewritten and two additional chapters added in the interest of a more adequate coverage of the period since 1880. Previous to the appearance of the first edition relatively little research had been done in American church history by trained historians. Since that time numerous Master's and Doctor's dissertations have been prepared by graduate students in many of our most distinguished universities, ranging over the whole field of the history of Christianity in America. The present revised and enlarged edition has leaned heavily upon these researches, and some hundred titles have been added to the Bibliography. Corrections and additions have been made throughout the volume and an additional chapter added covering the period since the outbreak of World War II,—ten confused and difficult years.

The development of the field of American church history during the past twenty-five years has been a coöperative enterprise of an increasing number of scholars and it is gratifying to those of us who have shared in its cultivation that it has now become a recognized field of research and teaching in an increasing number of our leading theological seminaries, colleges and universities. This volume may have had some part in this growing interest, and it is hoped that this new revised and enlarged edition will help continue its development.

CHAPTER I

✜ ✜ ✜

CREATIVE FORCES IN AMERICAN RELIGION

THE last census of religious bodies reveals the fact that there are in the United States more than three hundred denominations of Christians, presenting a more complicated religious pattern than exists among any other people in Christendom. What are the forces which have been responsible for such seeming confusion? Is there a common thread which runs through the three hundred years of American religious history binding these divergent elements into a whole? It is the purpose of this introductory chapter to point out some of the outstanding factors which have been responsible for the distinctive trends in the history of American religion, and to find, if possible, that magic strand which brings understanding out of confusion.

One element which has contributed to this seeming religious chaos is the fact that American religious history has been written by the denominational historian and in denominational terms. The history of each denomination has been told as a complete story in itself, taking little account of other denominations, or of economic, social and political influences. Too frequently it has been written in a denominational spirit, for the purpose of exalting the denomination or of praising its leaders. But facts relating to one denomination are not enough. Taken by themselves, all the incidents which go to make up the life of a denomination do not mean much in gaining an understanding of the total religious life of the nation. Indeed, the history of one church, taken by itself, may be actually misleading. To gain complete understanding it is needful to take into consideration what all the churches have done, as well as every other influence which has entered into the moral and religious life of the people.

1

The pioneer is always an independent individualist, determined to go his own way in religion as well as in politics, and therefore the frontier was fruitful in the multiplication of new sects. Denominations such as the Dunkers and Mennonites, which were of European origin, when transplanted to America divided and redivided as they moved westward into the undeveloped frontier, and recent studies have shown that the multiplication of the small sect since 1880 has been largely confined to the Middle and Far West. Good examples of the division of the larger churches caused by frontier conditions are those which resulted in the formation of the Disciples and the Cumberland Presbyterians. In both instances it was frontier liberalism contending against the narrow control of the older settled regions.

The multiplication of small colleges under church control is another result of frontier conditions. Indeed, most of the American colleges have been founded on a frontier. The general poverty of a new country made it impossible to send young men east for their training; therefore, the only alternative was to bring education to the ministerial student on the frontier. The same process of college founding has characterized practically every American frontier, from the founding of Harvard and Dartmouth to the establishment of the newest college in Montana and Wyoming. Besides these far-reaching influences the frontier supplied that challenge to the heroic without which Christianity seems never to have been able to perform its best work. It was the need of the frontier, also, which when brought to the knowledge of the East was largely responsible for the beginning of the modern Missionary interest, which has supplied one of the chief influences in the life of the American churches.

III

The most important and far-reaching of the schisms in the American churches were caused by Negro slavery, and the effects of that bitter contest in the churches are still with us. This fact has given to the history of American Christianity a peculiarity all its own, and any attempt to understand American church history must of necessity give large attention to the institution of slavery. Apart from its moral and religious aspects, nowhere can there be found a better example of the influence exerted upon organized Christianity by economic conditions than is furnished by a study of the relation of the churches to slavery. Parties in the churches for and against slavery did not begin to form until cotton growing had developed into a vast industry. It was not until church members had become wealthy cotton growers, that the churches ceased to denounce the institution. At the adoption of the Constitution all the churches were unanimous in their opposition to slavery; by the opening of the Civil War the churches had become a bulwark of American slavery.

Since the Civil War numerous attempts to heal the slavery schisms have been made, but, with one notable exception, in vain. Failure seems to have been largely due to such causes as memories of former bitterness and denominational and sectional pride, while Negro membership in white churches has led to complications. The rapid rise of large Negro churches since the Civil War has been a development peculiar to the United States and must be studied in connection with the slavery background.

IV

Up until the third decade of the eighteenth century the lower classes in the American colonies were little influenced by organized religion and only a small percentage of the population were members of the colonial churches. On the other hand, in the nations of western Europe, where state churches commonly existed church membership came about as a matter of course. Even in the Puritan colonies only a comparatively small proportion of the total population were members of the church, while in Virginia at the opening of the eighteenth century not more than one in twenty were church members, and the proportion was undoubtedly smaller in the other southern colonies. Thus there came to be more unchurched people in America, in proportion to the population, than was to be found in any country in Christendom. It was this situation which made necessary the development of a new technique to win people to the church, and this new method, peculiar to America and to other newly settled areas, was revivalism. The Great Awakening was the first religious movement which made any serious impression upon the common people of the American colonies, and marks the beginning of an aggressive American Christianity.

From that time until the end of the nineteenth century revivalism has manifested itself at frequent intervals in America. In its earlier phases revivalism grew largely out of frontier conditions, and performed

CHAPTER II

✢ ✢ ✢

THE EUROPEAN BACKGROUND

IT WAS long the custom of Protestant ministers in the United States to speak of the discovery and colonization of North America as a providential event. The facts seemed perfectly clear. Just twenty-five years after Columbus made his famous voyage of discovery, Martin Luther nailed his ninety-five theses to the church door at Wittenberg. Thus the beginning of Protestantism and the discovery of America were contemporaneous events. In other words, God appeared to have saved America for Protestantism. To them it seemed that a divine wisdom and a controlling providence had kept the very existence of America a secret until the fullness of time. But whether providential or not, it is a significant fact that these two great historic events, taken together, ccntain the key which explains to a large degree the establishment of the English colonies in America.

England was more than a century behind Spain and Portugal in founding colonies. At the opening of the period of discovery the majority of Englishmen were little interested in establishing an England beyond the seas, and as late as the opening of Queen Elizabeth's reign (1558) there were, perhaps, not more than a few hundred Englishmen outside the British Isles. But within a hundred years, following the close of that long reign, English trade had gone out in every direction, and English colonies were to be found in America, in Africa, in Asia and in the islands of the sea. England had succeeded Spain as the mistress of the seas and the foundations of the British Empire had been permanently laid. All this was the accomplishment of the sixteenth and seventeenth centuries. The sixteenth was the century of English pioneering on the sea; in the seventeenth every English colony in

America was planted except Georgia. These were also the centuries *par excellence* of the English trading companies. But what were the reasons which made these centuries a period of such feverish activity on the part of Englishmen? The economic historian would attempt to explain it by saying that a new set of economic forces were at work, while the political historian would mention the political rivalries between Spain, France, Holland and England as the most important contributing factor. But neither of them, nor both together, can explain adequately the establishment of the majority of the English colonies in America. It is true that economic stress was, very probably, responsible for bringing the majority of colonists to America during the whole period of the colonies, but religion was responsible for the *founding* of more colonies than any other single factor.

To understand this sweeping statement it will be necessary to examine the religious situation in England and also in the several European countries which contributed so largely to the peopling of the English colonies. It is, therefore, the purpose of this chapter to explain the European conditions out of which came the several groups of religionists which migrated to America in the sixteen and seventeen hundreds, and were responsible for laying the foundations of the American churches.

The first English colonies in America were founded by Englishmen, and throughout the whole period of colonization colonists from the British Isles made up the largest part of every colony. We will, therefore, first consider the religious situation in England, Scotland and Ireland, which accounts for the coming of the Puritans, the Cavaliers, the Quakers, the Catholics and finally the Scotch-Irish. Out of these groups came Congregationalism, the Established Church, the English Catholic Church, the Baptists, the Friends and the Presbyterians. These were the most important of the colonial churches, though the Dutch and German elements in the middle colonies particularly were not far behind in numbers and influence. From these elements came the Reformed Churches, the Dutch and German, and the Lutherans, besides the Mennonites, the Dunkers and the Moravians.

"England passed through the Reformation without a Civil War, yet no country in Europe found greater difficulty in coming to a religious equilibrium after that change." Led by the strong-minded Henry VIII —motivated largely by personal ends—and taking advantage of a strong nationalistic movement already under way against foreign control,

Englishmen. No liberty of worship, whatever, was permitted, and any clergyman who deviated from it was liable to be treated as a criminal, while all nonconformists might be excommunicated and were liable to be imprisoned.

By the death of Queen Elizabeth the Anglican had become the national church in a sense in which it had never been before. At the beginning of her reign the people of England, religiously speaking, were a fluid mass, ready to change from Catholicism to Protestantism and back again, at the bidding of their sovereign. But now a new generation had grown up, which knew no other religion, and the fact that it had the authority of law gave Anglicanism a patriotic sanction which no other church possessed. But in spite of these strong urges toward the national church, it failed to obtain the allegiance and affection of all of the English people. There were, first of all, the Catholics, a small group, it is true, but made up of many wealthy and influential people, the type which generally holds to the old and is slow to take up with the new. Their religion was outlawed, because Catholicism was considered the deadly enemy of the Elizabethan state, although the queen had no antagonism to Roman Catholicism as such, and long lists of anti-Catholic laws were placed upon the statute books by the English Parliament. Such laws were not only passed during the reign of Elizabeth; but even in the reign of James I—from whom the Catholics had expected more lenient treatment because of his Catholic mother, Mary Queen of Scots—the severity of anti-Catholic legislation was increased, because of the fright the king experienced over the Gunpowder Plot, at the very opening of his reign. During the reign of Charles I the Catholics received better treatment, but from 1640 to 1660, the period of the triumph of extreme Protestantism under the Commonwealth, the Catholics were bitterly persecuted.

All this would seem to indicate that there would be a large Catholic exodus from England, yet few Catholics left England, and no English colony remained Catholic for any length of time. Perhaps the chief reason for this fact has already been suggested. The English Catholics were not of the emigrating class. They represented the nobility and the landed gentry, and the conservative tendency which held them to the old religion would hold them to the old home. Then, being of the higher class, they had a better chance to escape the severity of the laws, and we know that the laws against them were largely unenforced, and they were never so badly treated as the anti-Catholic legislation might indicate. Nor were they ever without hope of a bettering of their condition, while toleration in the colonies was always as uncertain as in the homeland.

Of far greater importance, from the standpoint of English colonization of America, was the second group of Englishmen who were dissatisfied with the newly established Church. These were the Puritans. It has been suggested that if the English government had not interfered, England would have divided naturally into two religious camps—the Catholic on the one hand and the Puritan on the other. The Anglican system was the artificial medium between the two extremes.

Throughout Elizabeth's reign the Puritan party was growing in influence and numbers. During the first two decades to 1578, they were particularly concerned about purifying the English Church of all its Catholic practices, such as the use of vestments by the clergy, the using of the sign of the cross in baptism, the celebration of saints' days, kneeling to receive the communion, and the use of certain formulas in the service. Failing to accomplish their ends in Convocation, many Puritan ministers began to disregard the law prescribing these formulas and practices, and changed the service to suit their puritanical taste, while some resigned their pastorates. It was at this time that the term "puritan" came into use as a term of opprobrium, signifying those who insisted on an ultrapure ritual. The next stage in the development of English Puritanism began about 1570, and took the form of agitation to change the government of the church. In 1572, in their "Admonition to Parliament" they declare that "the names archbishops, archdeacons, lord bishops, chancellors, etc., are drawn from the Pope's shop, together with their offices, so the government which they use . . . is anti-Christian and devilish, and contrary to the Scriptures." The system of church government which they advocated was the Presbyterian, which had been introduced from Scotland by the Book of Discipline of 1560. So strong was the movement in this direction that it appeared, for a time, as if the Church of England would be reorganized along Presbyterian lines, but through the stern opposition of the queen and the rigorous administration of the Archbishop of Canterbury, Whitgift, the movement was held in check. Toward the close of Elizabeth's reign the Puritans were emphasizing such matters as strict Sabbath observance, and attacked the immoralities and extravagances of the times.

was in Lincolnshire that the Massachusetts Bay Company was born, formed by wealthy and influential Puritans of the region. The New England leaders were Cambridge men. Thus it was but natural that the first Puritan college in America should be located in the village which they named Cambridge, since their infant institution was modeled after one of the colleges at Cambridge University, and named after a young Puritan minister, a graduate of Cambridge, John Harvard. It was mainly from this region that some twenty to thirty thousand of England's strongest and most intelligent citizens left, between the years 1628 and 1642, to make their homes in the New England across the sea.

By 1642 Puritanism in England was completely triumphant. Seven years later the king was beheaded, and for the next decade England was governed without a king or a House of Lords. The Anglican Church was now under a cloud. The Puritans in turn became persecutors, and the Anglicans, who had fought, during the Civil Wars, on the king's side, began to leave in great numbers for Virginia, Maryland and the Carolinas. They came to escape conditions at home just as intolerable as those which had caused the migration of the Puritans to Plymouth and Massachusetts Bay.

The period of the Commonwealth was one of religious disintegration in England. The breaking down of the old organizations and the disappearance of the old authority presented a glorious opportunity to the individual religious leader, and as a result numerous small religious bodies began to appear. Among the better known of these were the Anabaptists, the Millenarians, or Fifth Monarchy men, who went about preaching the millennial kingdom of Christ on earth and the Friends, or Quakers. From the standpoint of their importance in the colonization of America, the Quaker was by far the most interesting and significant of these individualistic religious movements of the seventeenth century.

Fortunately there have always been mystically-minded people. Such an individual was George Fox, a weaver's son and an apprentice to a shoemaker, with little book learning beyond the Bible, but blessed with spiritual insight. After years of inner struggle, during which he wandered about through the Midlands of England, Fox became by 1647 an apostle of a new reformation. He rejected all the conventional beliefs and taught that there was direct illumination from God within every man's inner being; that there was no need for a priest or minister, since religion is something that begins in the soul of man, and is not primarily concerned with books, creeds or institutions. In the propagation of these ideas Fox met with abuse and violence. Sixty times was he brought before magistrates, and was imprisoned eight times, for longer or shorter periods. By 1652 others began to join his movement, especially in the northern counties, where Swarthmore Hall became the center of their increasing activities. By 1654 there were sixty people proclaiming the principles of the Quakers, some of them women, and by 1659 there were probably thirty thousand Quakers in England.

This rapid increase in numbers, and the enthusiasm with which they preached their peculiar notions, together with their intrusion into the churches, where they denounced the paying of tithes, the taking of oaths, and every other practice which they disapproved, brought down upon them such harsh treatment as only seventeenth century England knew how to impose. They were ridiculed by the clergy, fined and imprisoned by the magistrates and subjected to every indignity by their jailers. Nor did the coming of Charles II to the throne in 1660 relieve their distresses. The Church of England, now once more restored to its place of influence, asserted its despotic power as vigorously as in the time of Laud. By 1662 more than four thousand Quakers were to be found in the jails of England, and in the homeland there seemed no immediate hope for better treatment.

Meanwhile conversions to Quakerism were going on apace. At first the appeal had been largely to people of the lower middle class, but now they began to gain converts from among those of family and fortune. In 1667 William Penn, the son of Admiral William Penn, was "convinced" and soon became one of the most active champions of the persecuted sect. The claim of 16,000 pounds against the king, which was a part of the considerable fortune which Penn inherited from his father, was repaid by Charles II in the shape of a great land grant in America, toward which the tide of Quaker emigration soon set in, and within an incredibly short time a great Quaker commonwealth was created. From 1656 to the end of the colonial period Quakerism was an expanding force in America, for the New World presented favorable opportunities for the carrying out of the Quaker ideals of life which were not to be found in the mother country. There is evidence that America had a prominent part in the thoughts and plans of George Fox almost from the inception of his movement, for the New World presented to him what seemed a providential field to be won for his truth.

had been built up in North Ireland with the coming of the Scottish colonists, with an efficient ministry, trained largely in Scottish universities. These stanch Presbyterians, supporting their own churches voluntarily, were, in addition, compelled to pay tithes for the support of the Church of Ireland, an Anglican organization, which represented only a small minority of the people. By 1750, it has been estimated that 100,000 people of this racial group had found homes in America.

So far the English, Scottish and Irish background of the American religious groups has been traced; it remains to discuss the Dutch, German and French background.

When the Reformation began, the Low Countries were linked with Spain, under the rule of Charles, the grandson of Ferdinand and Isabella. Since the Netherlands were thus united to the most Catholic country in Europe, it was but natural that vigorous attempts should be made to keep out Lutheran ideas from the beginning. Proclamation followed proclamation, edict followed edict, forbidding open or secret meetings, against printing unlicensed books, against the reading of the Scriptures. Long lists of prohibited books were posted while the penalties for the violation of these prohibitions became increasingly severe. But in spite of all these precautions the number of heretics rapidly increased. Persecution followed, attended by harrowing atrocities, and it is estimated that 30,000 people had been put to death in the Netherlands when Charles abdicated the throne in favor of his son in 1556.

If Charles V had scourged the reformers of the Netherlands with whips, Philip II lashed them with scorpions. For four years Philip remained in the Netherlands to administer the edicts against the heretics, but heresy continued to spread in spite of all he could do. Even the Catholics of the Netherlands opposed the enforcement of the most severe edicts, or "Placards'" as they were termed, and sent a petition to Philip asking for a change of policy allowing a degree of religious freedom. To this the king responded by introducing the Spanish Inquisition (1565), which only served to increase the number of Protestants within the provinces. Finally, two years later, open rebellion broke out. The Duke of Alva, of dreadful memory, came with his veteran troops, his unlimited powers and "Council of Blood," and 10,000 more victims were added to the already long list of martyrs for conscience sake, while Dutch and Walloon refugees, estimated at 400,000, were to be found in England and southern Germany. William Prince of Orange, himself a Catholic, and recognized as their leader by both Dutch Catholics and Protestants, led the revolt against Spanish rule, and one by one the cities drove out their Spanish governors and placed themselves under his banner. In 1576 came the Pacification of Ghent, in which Holland and Zealand and the fifteen southern provinces agreed to unite to expel the Spaniards. Three years later, after the southern, French-speaking provinces had returned to Roman Catholic uniformity, the Union of Utrecht was formed, uniting the seven northern provinces, which three years later renounced allegiance to the King of Spain and constituted themselves an independent republic. Religious toleration was one of the glories of the new Republic of United Netherlands, for one of the provisions of their union was that no one should be questioned on the subject of divine worship.

The long bitter struggle against the Spaniard had intensified Dutch Protestantism, and it was in the midst of their terrible trials that their churches were organized. Luther, Zwingli and Calvin, all had their followers in the Netherlands, but in the end the Calvinist influence proved the stronger, and the Dutch Church became Calvinistic in discipline and doctrine. Both the Lutheran and Zwinglian systems were closely related to the civil government, but when the Dutch churches were deciding on their form of government, the Duke of Alva was the ruler of the Netherlands and thus the favor of government was entirely out of the question. The Presbyterian system, therefore, which had been the form of government adopted by the Church in the early centuries, when it was under the ban of the Roman Empire, seemed the form best suited for a "Church under the Cross."

The first one hundred years following independence were the greatest in the history of the Dutch people. In the long struggle against the Spaniard the *Sea Beggars* had played a prominent and heroic part. Again and again they had routed the clumsy Spanish ships, and whenever the *Beggars* appeared, the Spaniards had learned through bitter experience that the best thing to be done was to flee. The terrible struggle through which they had come, instead of exhausting their energies, seemed but to have awakened them to a more vigorous life. Having achieved independence, they became at once one of the great commercial and maritime powers of Europe, and Dutch ships were soon finding their way into every port. Those were great years in the history of the Dutch people. Rubens was engaged in painting his glorious pictures; Hugo Grotius was writing his matchless treatises on the freedom of the seas, laying the foundation for international law; while Dutch trading companies, both east and west, were establishing the foundations of the Dutch colonial empire.

The Dutch colonies, wherever founded, were primarily trading centers. The Dutch people did not migrate in great numbers to their colonies, largely because the population of the mother country was small, having been sorely depleted by the long, bloody wars. But those who did settle in America were of such sturdy stuff and the institutions they established, including their church, were so highly developed that they continued to exercise an influence far larger than their actual numbers would seem to warrant.

It has been estimated by painstaking students that in 1750 at least 100,000 Germans were to be found in the English colonies in America. The largest share of them were in Pennsylvania, where they numbered perhaps 70,000, though Germans were also to be found in New York, in the western counties of Virginia and the Carolinas and in Georgia.

To account for this large migration of Germans to the New World it will be necessary to recall some of the effects of the Thirty Years' War (1618-1648). There is little doubt but that this war was one of the most cruel and brutal in modern history. Seventy-five per cent of the population throughout Germany were killed, while the property loss was even greater, and it is an accepted fact, based upon carefully gathered statistics, that the war set back German material development by two hundred years. Southern Germany, or the Palatinate, was the region which suffered most. But so fertile was the soil and so great was the recuperative power of the people, because of their industry and agricultural skill, that soon after each invasion the country was transformed from a desert into a garden, only to attract other plunderers. But as though the sufferings of the Thirty Years' War were not enough, Louis XIV of France, on three different occasions (1674, 1680, 1688) in the last quarter of the seventeenth century, sent his armies into the Palatinate to burn and to plunder. The greed and the cruelty of the French, we are told, exceeded even that of the "Landsknechte" of the Thirty Years' War, who drove nearly 500,000 Palatines from their burning houses and devastated fields.

Added to the terrible conditions produced by the wars and invasions were the religious persecutions. The Treaty of Westphalia (1648), which marked the end of the Thirty Years' War, provided for some degree of toleration. Catholics, Lutherans and Reformed were to have equal rights in the Empire, though the individual princes could still restrict the religious freedom of their subjects. But neither Catholics, Lutherans nor Reformed respected the rights of the small sects, such as the Mennonites, Dunkers and German Quakers. Thus religious persecution, the tyranny of petty rulers, destructive wars and general economic distress produced the background out of which came German emigration to the American colonies.

In 1671 and again in 1677 William Penn visited the continent and the lower Rhine region. Penn's sympathies were aroused by the distresses of the Palatines, and when he had become the possessor, a few years later, of his great American province, he appointed agents to solicit settlers from among the Palatines. Penn's pamphlet, "Some Account of the Province of Pennsylvania in America" was translated into German in 1681, the first of a series of pamphlets and tracts by which the people of the Palatinate and the regions outside were made acquainted with the "Holy Experiment" which William Penn was fathering in America. And one may well imagine the joy with which these simple people read Penn's essay on "Religious Liberty" which was appended to his advertisements.

Still another group of persecuted Germans, some of whom eventually found their way to the English colonies in America, were the Salzburgers. These were German Lutherans, driven from the Austrian archbishopric of Salzburg by the fanatical zeal of the archbishop in 1731. More than 30,000 of them were exiled from their native land, and the cruelty of their sufferings soon aroused the indignation of all Protestant Europe. Seventeen thousand of them eventually found homes in Prussia, where they were received by the king, Frederick William I. Just at this time the colony of Georgia was being planned by a group of philanthropic Englishmen, and they, coöperating with the Society for the Promotion of Christian Knowledge in London, provided a haven for some of the most daring of the Salzburgers on the soil of the new colony of Georgia. Their first settlement in America was called Ebenezer—the stone of help—for, said they, "hitherto hath the Lord helped us" (I Sam. 7:12).

It only remains, in this chapter, to recount the background which brought to the American colonies the religious exiles driven from

France by the revocation of the famous Edict of Nantes—the French Huguenots. While they did not come to America in great numbers, yet in proportion to their numbers no single group made so rich a contribution to the English colonies.

The period of the Wars of Religion in France was from 1562 to 1598. There were, all told, eight separate wars during these years. They were ferocious wars indeed, for both Protestants and Catholics were imbued with an extreme fanaticism. Both sides drew allies from the outside. Massacres and assassinations characterized the long struggle; the massacre of St. Bartholomew (1572); the assassination of the Guises (1588); and finally the assassination of Henry III (1589) brought Henry of Navarre, the leader of the Protestant forces, to the throne, as Henry IV. As the only means of bringing peace to his distracted kingdom, Henry resolved to become a Roman Catholic. By this act conditions all over the kingdom changed as if by magic. Nobles, provinces and towns now came forward with offers of their allegiance, and the long wars were at last at an end.

The laws against Protestants, however, were still in force, but the king had given his word to his former companions in arms that all would be well with them. The French Protestant Church was now well organized, with a General Assembly, meeting year by year, and they were demanding equal rights with their Roman Catholic fellow subjects. The king was true to his word and out of the negotiations, carried on by delegates representing the Protestant party, there came finally the Edict of Nantes (1598), the charter of French Protestantism. This granted liberty of conscience throughout the kingdom, state payment for their ministers, while they were given equal entry to all schools, universities and hospitals, and all public offices were open to them.

For nearly a hundred years after the issuing of this famous edict the French Protestants lived under its protection and did their part in resuscitating "the corpse of France." Under Louis XIII, by the aid of his crafty minister Richelieu, France became the ascendant nation in western Europe. It was during these years of returning greatness and wealth that France began the establishment of her colonies in the New World. The early attempts to establish colonies as places of refuge for Huguenots, as in Florida and Brazil, were all failures, while the later colonies founded in the valley of the St. Lawrence, under the administration of Richelieu, were all orthodox Roman Catholic.

Finally in 1685 came the revocation of the edict. This was preceded by twenty years of persecution and forced conversion of the Protestants, and the revocation was but the culmination of a policy of suppression and "jesuitical interpretation of the terms of the edict." Such are the causes for the great migration of French Huguenots which set in toward the close of the seventeenth century and continued until France had lost a large proportion of her best people.

The desire of Louis XIV was not to drive the Huguenots away, but to force their conversion, and for this reason emigration was prohibited. Soldiers were quartered in their houses, but some of them left their homes in the night, "leaving the soldiers in their beds," and abandoning their homes with the furniture. Every wise government in western Europe was eager to offer them a refuge, for they brought with them an industrial skill which represented the best that Europe had to offer. Thus they introduced manufacturing in north Germany, a suburb of London was filled with them, while the Prince of Orange soon had regiments of soldiers recruited from among them. Many went to the Dutch colony in South Africa, while every colony in America, from Massachusetts to South Carolina, extended them a welcome.

CHAPTER III

✣   ✣   ✣

ESTABLISHED CHURCH BEGINNINGS IN AMERICA

IN LIEU of cargoes of gold and silver for which the early Virginia colonists diligently searched but failed to find in the bays and inlets of the Chesapeake, the ships of the Virginia Company were loaded with ship timbers, cedar, black walnut and clapboards. For Jamestown, the first permanent English colony in America, was the child of a commercial company and was established as a commercial enterprise. Much of the hardship endured by the Jamestown colony was due to the fact that most of the early colonists were gentlemen, unaccustomed to such hard labor as was required to obtain such cargoes. Though primarily concerned with trade the members of the company were from the first interested in promoting religion among the colonists as well as in the conversion of the Indians. Undoubtedly the example of Spain was ever before the early promoters of English colonization. Spain, the chief Roman Catholic nation of the whole world, had established her great colonial empire in the New World, and hand in hand with the Spanish conquerors had gone the Spanish Catholic missionaries, and tens of thousands of the natives of New Spain and Peru had been won to, at least, a nominal acceptance of Catholic Christianity. Should not England, the leading Protestant nation in the whole world, do as much? And thus, by planting colonies in the New World, England herself would not only be benefited but the cause of Protestantism would likewise be advanced, and the power of Spain might also be held in check.

Among the 105 colonists who landed on the low-lying shores of the James in Virginia, on May 13, 1607, was Robert Hunt the chaplain, a "clergyman of persevering fortitude and modest worth," in whose appointment Archbishop Bancroft had been consulted. Hunt seems to have exercised a wholesome influence over the notoriously quarreling members of the council and on more than one occasion, by his "good doctrine and exhortation" allayed the envy and jealousy so that, to quote Captain John Smith, "our factions were oft qualified, our wants and greatest extremities so comforted that they seemed easy in comparison of what we endured after his memorable death." It was on June 21 of that first year that Chaplain Hunt administered the first sacrament to Englishmen in America, under an old sail hung between three or four trees, to keep off the hot sun of that first Virginia summer, while the worshipers were seated on unhewed logs, the chaplain's pulpit being a "bar of wood nailed to two neighboring trees." After this, we are told, there were daily prayers, morning and evening, while on Sunday there were two sermons and every three months the sacrament.

Just how long Chaplain Hunt lived is not known, but there is evidence that he continued his faithful ministrations at least through part of the year 1608, and then probably died, a victim to the famine and pestilence which swept away so many hundreds of the early Virginia colonists. During the first year a rude, barnlike church was erected, which within a few months was destroyed by fire, together with most of the other buildings in the fort, and in the general destruction went the chaplain's meager library. But in the midst of all these distresses, the chaplain was never heard to repine.

In 1609 a new charter was granted to the Virginia Company, independent of the Plymouth Company. The stockholders in this new company numbered 765, among them numerous clergymen, including the bishops of London and Lincoln, as well as 21 peers and other individuals representing every "rank, profession or trade in England and included the merchant guilds of London." The old charter had placed the government in the hands of two councils, one in London, the other in America; the new charter abolished the council in Virginia and in its place was a governor. Lord De La Warr, or Delaware, was the first Virginia governor under the new charter, but not being able to come out immediately Sir Thomas Gates was sent as his deputy, and with Gates came the second clergyman to Virginia, Master Richard Bucke, successor to the lamented Robert Hunt. Bucke was an Oxford graduate and was recommended for the place by the Bishop of London who termed him "an able and painful preacher."

The increased number of shareholders in the Virginia Company bears testimony to a growing interest in colonization in England. As a result larger expeditions were soon in preparation, and for the first time sermons were preached in the churches of London to those about to leave for the New World. One such sermon was that by William Crawshaw, preacher at the Temple in London, before Lord Delaware and the council, which has been termed the first missionary sermon ever addressed by a priest of the Church of England to members of that church. Toward the close of his sermon he gives this sound advice:

> A Christian may take nothing from a Heathen against his will, but in fair and lawful bargain. Abraham wanted a place to burie in, and liked a piece of land; and being a great man, and therefore feared, a just and meek man and therefore loved of the heathen, they bad him chuse where hee would, and take it. No, saith Abraham, but I will buy it, and so he paid the price of it; so must all the children of Abraham doe.

Further on, he says, referring to profits to be obtained by the members of the Company:

> If there be any that come in, only or principally for profit, or any that would so come in, I wish the latter may never bee in, and the former out again. If the planting of an English Church in a heathen country; if the conversion of the Heathen, of the propagating of the Gospell, and the inlarging of the kingdome of Jesus Christ, be not inducements strong enough to bring them into this businesse, it is a pity they be in at all. . . . Let us therefore cast aside all cogitation of profit, let us looke at better things; and then I dare say unto you as Christ hath taught us, that if in this action wee seeke first the kingdome of God, all other things shall be added unto us.

Wise advice indeed, but the most casual reading of the story of the founding of Virginia will show how poorly that advice was followed.

At the arrival of Deputy Governor Gates conditions in the colony were discouraging in the extreme. In 1609 there had been more than 500 colonists, but by May, 1610, no more than 60 were alive. On landing, the new governor and the colonists who came with him proceeded at once to the church, now rebuilt after the fire, where the bell was rung and "the dispirited and starving people dragged" themselves to the house of God where Chaplain Bucke offered up a "zealous and sorrowful prayer," and at the close of service the governor's commission was read and the deputy assumed office. But conditions were too bad to be long endured, and very soon the governor, after consulting with Captain Newport and others, decided to abandon the colony. But before the ships with the colonists on board could leave the James, they were met by Lord Delaware coming up the river, who ordered the departing colonists to return. So affected was Lord Delaware by the terrible conditions in which he found the colony, that when the emaciated remainder were drawn up to receive him, he fell on his knees and prayed in the presence of all the people.

As long as Lord Delaware's personal administration lasted especial attention was given to the religious condition of the colony. There is evidence that there were several preachers in Virginia during his brief stay. The secretary and recorder of the colony under Delaware states that:

The Captaine Generall hath given order for the repairing of (the Church), and at this instant hands are about it. It is in length threescore foote, in breadth twenty-foure, and shall have a Chancell in it of Cedar, and a Communion Table of Black Walnut, and all the pews of Cedar, with faire broad windowes, to shut and open, as the weather shall occasion, of the same wood, a Pulpet of the same, with a Font hewen hollow, like a Canoa, with two Bels in the West end. It is so cast as to be very light within, and the Lord Governour and Captain Generall doth cause it to be kept sweete, and trimmed up with divers flowers, with a Sexton belonging to it; and in it every Sunday wee have Sermons twice a day, and every Thursday a Sermon, having true preachers, which take their weekly turnes, each man addresseth himself to prayers, and so at Foure of the clocke before Supper. Every Sunday, when the Lord Governour and Captaine Generall goeth to Church, hee is accompanied with all the Counsailers, Captaines, other officers and all the Gentlemen, with a guard of Holberdiers, in his Lordship's Liverey, faire red cloakes, to the number of fifty both on each side, and behind him: and being in the Church, his Lordship hath his seat in the Quier, in a greene velvet chaire, with a cloath, with a velvet cushion spread on a table before him, on which he kneeleth, and on each side sit the Counsell, Captaines, and Officers, each in his place, and when he returneth home againe, he is waited on to his house in the same manner.

But while the governor, with his regal show and guard in red coats were worshiping in the little church at Jamestown, conditions in the colony remained desperate and sickness and disease continued to take its toll from among the settlers. Lord Delaware was nominal head of the colony until his death in 1618, but the affairs of Virginia after 1611 were administered by a series of deputy governors. Sir Thomas Dale, whose title was High Marshal of Virginia, during the absence of Deputy Governor Gates, was in charge much of the time from 1611 to 1616, and this period marks the end of "the starving time" and the beginning of happier conditions. With Dale came the Rev. Alexander Whitaker, whose zeal in the cause of Christianity won him the title "Apostle to Virginia." About this time the Virginia Council issued a pamphlet containing a declaration of the purpose and end of the colony, in which they state that religion is the "maine and cheefe purpose" of the plantation. They call upon their countrymen for help, asking them to "remember that what was at first but of conveniency, and for honor, is now become a case of necessity and piety." In conclusion they declare that only those of blameless lives and character should go out to the infant colony. But in spite of the expressed desire of the council, numerous "idle and wicked persons" continued to find their way to Virginia and were to prove "to bee poyson to one so tender, feeble and yet unformed" as was the infant colony.

Sir Thomas Dale has left a reputation for cruelty which he does not fully deserve. He ruled with a strong arm, enforcing a code of laws characterized as "lawes, divine, morall and martiall" in which twenty crimes were punishable by death. But he brought order out of chaos, though the severity of the laws regulating the church tended to make it odious in the eyes of the settlers. In estimating Sir Thomas Dale it is but fair to remember that his punishments were no more cruel than were those practiced in Europe at the same time and as a whole he administered these savage laws with moderation. Through his energy new settlements were formed seventy miles up the James; one was given the name Henrico in honor of Prince Henry of Wales, while the other was called New Bermuda. Here churches were formed; Alexander Whitaker was in charge of the New Bermuda church while Henrico seems to have been in charge of a curate, Mr. Wickham, under Whitaker.

Of all the early ministers in Virginia we know most concerning Alexander Whitaker. He was the son of Dr. William Whitaker, Regius Professor of Divinity at Cambridge and one of the best known of the Puritan clergy of his day. Alexander Whitaker left a pleasant parish in the north of England, "without any persuasion (but God's and his own heart)" and "to the wonder of his own kindred, and amazement of all that knew him, undertook this hard but, . . . heroicall resolution to go to Virginia and helpe bear the name of God unto the Gentiles." Seventy miles up the James from Jamestown in the midst of a group of new settlements he built his parsonage, "a faire framed house," and a hundred acres was impaled for a glebe. Thus Whitaker became the first country parson and missionary in Virginia.

In 1613 there was published in London a pamphlet entitled "Good Newes from Virginia, sent to the Counsell and Company of Virginia, resident in England, From Alexander Whitaker, Minister in Henrico in Virginia," which was a part of a sermon which he had preached from the text "Cast thy bread upon the waters: for after many days thou shalt finde it." To this is added a description of the country and the Virginia Indians, and a plea is made for men and money "who may venture their persons hither, and heere not only serve God but helpe these poore Indians." Young men, he states, are "fittest for this country, and we have no need either of ceremonies or bad livers." Some years later in writing to a friend in London Whitaker says: "I much more muse, that so few of our English ministers that were so hot against the Surplis and subscription, come hither where neither are spoken of," a clear indication that Puritan notions prevailed in Virginia. This good man, imbued with an unselfish and tireless zeal for religion, worked faithfully until his death in 1617, which came by drowning in the James.

Through the influence and labors of Whitaker the first Indian convert was won to Christianity in the person of Pocahontas. All are familiar with the story of her rescue of Captain John Smith from death, to which he had been condemned after his capture by the tribes over which her father, Powhatan, was the ruler. Largely through her influence a treaty was made between the Indians and the English, and the princess became a familiar figure about Jamestown. After Smith's departure the Indians again became hostile, but Pocahontas retained her affection for her white friends, although she now was no longer permitted to visit them. In the spring of 1613 she was taken captive by Captain Argall and held as hostage for the release of some English captives which the Indians had taken in the course of the war. The princess was turned over to High Marshal Dale for safe-keeping, who evidently took her to his plantation on the upper James, where she was near Alexander Whitaker and from whom she received religious instruction. Within a few weeks she was willing to renounce her Indian superstitions and accepted Christian baptism, receiving the name Rebecca.

But Whitaker and Dale were not the only Englishmen who were interested in the Indian princess and in her progress in Christianity. John Rolfe, one of the most progressive of the young planters, and the first to produce tobacco for export, and withal a widower, was soon in love with the enchanting maiden and he confesses, that in her "my

hartie and best thoughts are so entangled, and enthralled in so intricate a laborinth, that I was even awearied to unwinde myself thereout."
Nor did he ever succeed in unwinding himself, for on the first of April,
1614, he and the princess Pocahontas were married at Jamestown, the
old chief Powhatan giving his reluctant consent and sending a brother
and two sons to witness the ceremony. Two years later, accompanied by
her husband, her young son Thomas Rolfe and Sir Thomas Dale, Pocahontas sailed for England, together with some ten or twelve Indian
youths who were to be educated in England. Here she was met by her
old friend Captain John Smith; was introduced at court to the king and
queen where we are told she, "carried herself as a daughter of a King"
and was received everywhere with respect by "divers persons of honor."
In the early part of 1617 she was about to return to Virginia with her
husband who had been appointed secretary and recorder general of
Virginia, when, in the language of the chronicler: "At her return
towards Virginia she came at Gravesend to her end and grave, having
given great demonstration of her Christian sinceritie, as the first fruits
of Virginia conversion, leaving here a good memory and the hopes of
her resurrection. . . ."

The year following the death of Lord Delaware (1619), Sir George
Yeardley became the governor of Virginia and with him a new era began for the colony. The moving spirit in the company was now Sir Edwin Sandys, who was a man of liberal and progressive ideas, whose ambition was to make of Virginia a "free and popular state." He was a
friend of the Puritans and an opponent of the arbitrary government of
James I, and naturally his election to the treasurership of the company
was opposed by the king, who advised the company to "chose the devil
if you will, but not Sir Edwin Sandys." It was under the guidance of this
liberal man, seconded by the wise Yeardley, that the first representative
assembly in America was constituted. The old cruel laws were abrogated
and provision was made that a General Assembly was to be held once a
year, made up of "the Governor and Counsell, with two Burgesses from
each Plantation freely to be elected by the inhabitants thereof." At this
time there were four boroughs in the colony and a total population
of about 1,000. The first assembly met in the "Quire of the Churche" at
Jamestown on July 30, and sat for six days. Twenty burgesses were
present. In their order of business, first came the prayer by Master Bucke
when the assembly proceeded to business, and in the course of the first

session passed thirty-four laws, and of this number twelve had to do directly or indirectly with religion.

The enactment of laws regulating activities of the Virginia clergy and prescribing specifically the religious duties of the colonists indicates that the English canon law as well as the civil law was in force. Early acts of the House of Burgesses (1620-1621) provided that the clergymen were to be paid in tobacco and corn, each receiving fifteen hundred pounds of the former and sixteen barrels of the latter, though accompanied with the statement that if the full amount could not be raised, "the minister was to be content with less." The religious enactments were extremely puritanical in character, prescribing church attendance twice each Sunday, while the other acts condemned "gaming, drunkenness and excess in apparel."

The visit of the princess Pocahontas to England, together with the coming of the Indian youths to be educated, evidently aroused a larger interest in the education and Christianization of the Virginia Indians. Even King James displayed interest and at about the time of the death of Pocahontas, sent a letter to the archbishops asking their assistance in raising funds for the erection "of some Churches and Schooles for ye children of those Barbarians wch cannot but be to them [the colonists] a very great charge." As a result of this appeal some £1,500 was subscribed through the several English bishoprics for a college in Virginia and the company instructed the governor to undertake the planting of a university at Henrico, at the same time setting aside ten thousand acres for its endowment. Judged from the number and generosity of other subscriptions, interest in the enterprise was widespread. A London merchant gave £300 for the university besides £24 which was to be distributed to three godly men who would "bring up three of the Infidal's children in the Christian Religion and some good course to live by." The Bishop of London, Dr. John King, manifested a great interest in the affairs of the colony at this time; was chosen a member of the Council for Virginia and the spiritual jurisdiction of the Bishop of London over the church in America seems to date from this period.[1] He collected £1,000 for the Henrico university; Sir Edwin Sandys, the company's treasurer, sent £500 for the education of Indian youth, while

[1] The question of the origin of the Bishop of London's colonial authority is an obscure question, which has never been solved satisfactorily. For a discussion of this point see Arthur Cross, *The Anglican Episcopate and the American Colonies* (New York, 1902), especially Chap. I.

gifts of books, Bibles, Prayer Books, communion plate and linen were contributed for the godly work.

This was a period of great activity in Virginia. During the years 1620 and 1621 seven ministers came to the colony, while new colonists and servants were coming over in increasing numbers. Plans were made for increasing the number of tenants on the lands belonging to the company and "young single women of blameless reputation" were brought over to be the wives of the bachelor planters and tenants. At the same time the practice of sending convicts to Virginia was begun, a policy which was evidently distasteful to the company officials, and for which the king was responsible. About the same time some Virginia planters purchased twenty negro slaves from some Dutch traders and thus were introduced two most unfortunate elements in the population of the colony.

Meanwhile money was pouring in for the establishment of schools which were to be feeders for the new university at Henrico. One was to be established at Smythe's Hundred with funds sent to Sir Edwin Sandys by an unknown donor. Another was to be founded at Charles City with money raised by the chaplain of an East Indiaman, the Rev. Mr. Copeland, to which the company gave a thousand acres as an endowment, while books were promised and even a builder and apprentices were secured to erect the building and an usher was appointed. Prosperity at last seemed to have come to Virginia after the many dreary years of failure and suffering. During the year 1621 some twenty vessels had arrived with more than a thousand new colonists and experiments in manufacturing iron, glass, silk and wines were under way with a fair prospect of success. So pleased was the company at the prospects of their colony that they arranged for a thanksgiving service, which was held April 18, 1622, at which the Rev. Mr. Copeland preached the sermon which was later published under the title "Virginia's God be Thanked."

Little did the Company or the preacher realize what havoc had been wrought in Virginia by a terrible massacre of the planters and their families nearly a month before. On the morning of March 22, 1622, the Indians, no longer held in check by Powhatan, fell upon the settlements on the upper James and within a few hours 347 persons had been killed in cold blood, without respect for age or sex. In this remote region the settlements were almost completely wiped out, among the slain being John Rolfe. The destruction was not so general, however, in the older settlements, because of the fact that here the Indians were more friendly and also because here the settlers had been warned by a young Christian Indian. The plantations on the upper James were now abandoned for the time being, while expeditions were organized to punish the Indians, but while many were driven into the deep forest, few were actually killed. The progress of the colony was only temporarily checked, but the most unfortunate consequence of the massacre was that it completely changed the attitude of the colonists toward the Indians as a whole. The opinion, previously held by only one of the Virginia ministers, that "till their priests and Ancients have their throats cut there is no hope to bring them to conversion," now, according to Captain John Smith, became general. As a result the elaborate plans for the education of Indian youth, which had been so nearly worked out, were now abandoned and it was to be many years before any further attempts were made to revive that interest.

In 1624, on June 16, the Virginia Company came to an end, and the control of the colony passed directly into the hands of the king. The alleged reason for this action was the misconduct of the company in its failure properly to propagate the Christian religion, increase trade and enlarge the Empire. The real reasons, however, were undoubtedly the refusal of the company to appoint the king's nominees to office; the king's dislike of the leaders; and his desire to please the King of Spain, whose daughter Prince Charles was at the time courting. For the next six years there was a rapid succession of royal governors until the arrival of John Harvey in 1630. Under the rule of this tyrant the church suffered greatly and was left largely to care for itself. Up to this time the ministers who had come out to Virginia were generally men of character and sincerely devoted to the advancement of true religion, but from this period forward the type of ministers in the colony changed for the worse.

The fact that the church in Virginia was completely under secular control accounts largely for its weaknesses. The laws for its regulation were passed by the General Assembly: the appointment of ministers in each parish was in the hands of the vestry, while the removal of ministers was obtained on complaint of the vestry to the governor and his council. The vestries, after 1661, were closed corporations, empowered to fill their own vacancies, and the tendency was for the church to be controlled by a local aristocracy. These men as a whole, while thinking of the church as a necessary institution, were devoid of deep religious feeling. Each parish was responsible for the payment of its own minister, and after 1662 the ministers were to receive a uniform salary—16,000 pounds of tobacco. This worked a hardship on many of the Virginia clergymen, since the price of tobacco was tending downward through the eighteenth century. Another factor causing discontent was the fact that the varieties of tobacco differed in value. In certain counties where the best grade, the sweet-scented tobacco, was raised, the ministers received in actual value twice the amount received by ministers serving in districts where only the poorer grade, Aranoka tobacco, could be grown. The glebes provided by law for the clergy proved disappointing; in many instances the minister's tenure was so uncertain he was reluctant to spend time or money in keeping up his little plantation; in other cases the land was so poor it was not worth cultivation or placing buildings upon it.

Until the loss of the charter (1624) the Virginia Church was largely under Puritan control, but with the coming of the royal governors Puritan influence came to an end and acts were passed forbidding all non-Episcopal ministers from officiating in the colony. At the beginning of Sir William Berkeley's first administration (1641) seventy-one Virginia colonists signed an appeal asking the General Court of Massachusetts "to send ministers of the gospel into that region, that its inhabitants might be privileged with the preaching and ordinances of Jesus Christ." In response to this appeal three Puritan ministers were sent to Virginia, carrying letters of commendation from Governor Winthrop, but they were soon silenced, though one of them removed to Maryland where he ministered to some of the Virginia Puritans who had migrated to that colony.

During the period of the Civil Wars (1642-1649) and the Commonwealth (1649-1660), Virginia was greatly disturbed. Religion was at a low ebb and at the time of the restoration few of the parishes had ministers. When Governor Berkeley was restored to power in 1660, among the first acts passed by the Virginia Assembly was one providing "for the building and due furnishing of churches, for the canonical performance of the liturgy, for the ministration of God's Word, for a due observance of the Sunday, for the baptism and christian education of the young." It was in 1671 that Governor Berkeley included in his report to the Commissioners of Foreign Plantations the following account of the religious situation in the colony: "There are forty-eight parishes, and the ministers well paid. The clergy by my consent would be better if they would pray oftener and preach less. But of all commodities, so of this, the worst are sent us. But I thank God there are no free schools, nor printing, and I hope we shall not have these hundred years."

The picture of the Virginia clergy generally given is perhaps darker than they deserve. A recent historian of the Colonial Church of Virginia states that in a list of some one hundred and twenty Virginia clergy before 1700 hardly more than a dozen had anything recorded derogatory to their moral or religious character. On the other hand, there is much evidence to show that there were entirely too many incompetents and second-rate men in charge of the Virginia churches. In 1696 one of the Virginia rectors wrote to the Bishop of London that "Several ministers have caused such scandals of late and have raised such prejudices amongst the people against the clergy, that hardly can they be persuaded to take a clergyman into their parish." One of the principal causes for the prevalence of inefficient clergymen was the practice, which prevailed throughout the entire colonial period, of vestries employing lay readers from year to year, instead of having their ministers inducted into office by the governor. A minister inducted into office held his place for life, a condition which would not find favor among the vestrymen. The Rev. Morgan Godwyn, a clergyman who had spent some time in Virginia, wrote to Sir William Berkeley in 1681 a brief description of religion there.

The Ministers [he says] are most miserably handled by their Plebeian Juntos, the Vestries: to whom the hiring . . . and admission of Ministers is solely left. And there being no law obliging them to any more than procure a layreader (to be obtained at a moderate rate) they either resolve to have none at all, or reduce them to their own terms; that is, to use them how they please, pay them what they list, and to discard them whensoever they have a mind to it.

And again he states:

Two-thirds of the Preachers are made up of leaden Lay-Priests of the Vestries Ordination: and are both the shame and grief of the rightly ordained Clergie there.

Blame for the laxity of religion in Virginia during the colonial period must not be laid solely at the door of the colonial clergy. The great size of the parishes and the scattered population made regular attendance upon religious worship impossible for a great majority of the people. Some of the parishes were from fifty to a hundred miles in length. One is reported as "120 miles long and ten miles broad upon the River," while parishes twenty-five and thirty miles in length are but average. Says a contemporary writer (1661):

The families of such parishes being . . . at such distances from each other, many of them are remote from the house of God, though placed in the midst of them . . . and divers of the more remote Families being discouraged by the length or tediousness of the way, through extremities of heat in Summer, frost and snow in Winter, and tempestuous weather in both, do very seldom repair thither.

The minister on the Upper Parish reports in 1724 that:

This excessive length of my parish [60 miles long and 20 wide] I have found by long experience to be so incommodious that I could never perform my pastoral office as I ought altho' I have spared neither cost nor labor on the attempts and endeavours thereof.

An estimate of the church membership among Virginians at the close of the seventeenth century places the number at one in twenty. It is quite evident that the church did not reach the lower classes and a vast majority of the population had little interest in religion. But it must be borne in mind that during the same period religion was at a low ebb in England, as well as in the colonies, and the Established Church had settled down into a deathlike stupor, from which no power seemed to be able to arouse it. A fatal weakness of the Virginia Colonial Church was the lack of spiritual supervision, which was not entirely overcome until independence had been won and bishops were ordained for America.

Two events of great importance to the Virginia Church took place toward the end of the seventeenth century; one was the appointment of the Rev. James Blair as commissary of the Bishop of London for Virginia; the other was the establishment of William and Mary College, "that the church in Virginia may be furnished with a seminary of ministers of the Gospel, and that the youth may be piously educated in good manners and that the Christian faith may be propagated amongst the western Indians to the glory of almighty God."

James Blair was the leading Virginia clergyman of his day. A Scotchman, educated at Edinburgh, he came out to Virginia in 1685 under the appointment of the Bishop of London and became the minister at Henrico. He seems to have been a careful observer and a man of sterling character admirably suited to take the task of supervision which was soon assigned him. The bad condition of the Virginia Church had been brought to the attention of the Bishop of London by a pamphlet entitled "Virginia's Cure" prepared by one who had fled to Virginia during the period of the Commonwealth and "for the space of ten years" had been an eyewitness of the things he describes. Among the remedies proposed by this writer was the sending of a bishop to the colony, and there seems to have been an attempt to carry out this suggestion and a bishop was nominated for Virginia. When this attempt failed, James Blair was appointed commissary and was the first such official in any of the English colonies. His duty was to inspect churches, deliver charges, and to a limited extent administer discipline, though he could not confirm or ordain. Although greatly limited in authority, Blair performed an invaluable service to the church in Virginia.

The great massacre of 1622 had completely ended the early attempts at founding colleges in Virginia. But in 1661 at the first meeting of the Virginia Assembly after the restoration, an act was passed providing for a "colledge" "for the advance of learning, education of youth, supply of the Ministry, and promotion of piety." But it was more than thirty years before a college was finally established and this was accomplished through the energy and zeal of James Blair. At first he was unable to obtain the assistance of the legislature, but after he had obtained gifts from private givers, amounting to more than 2,000 pounds, he at last secured authority by legislative enactment to proceed to England to seek a charter for a college. King William and Queen Mary were not only cordial to the petition, but the king granted 2,000 pounds due the crown from Virginia quitrents to the project. But all the royal officials were not so cordial, for when Commissary Blair urged the attorney general, Seymour, to prepare the charter, with the admonition that the Virginians had souls to save as well as Englishmen, the haughty official answered: "Souls! Damn your souls! Make tobacco." But in spite of this contemptuous official the charter was soon forthcoming and was signed, February 8, 1693, and the same year the Virginia Assembly passed an act providing for the erection of a building at the place afterward selected as the site of Williamsburg.

The college was endowed with twenty thousand acres of choice land and was to receive the income from a tobacco tax as well as an export duty on furs and skins. But from the beginning the college encountered difficulties, one being the destruction of the building by fire in 1705 when it was but half completed. At first few students were in attendance and therefore it could not at once supply the demand for clergymen. Blair was the president of the college from its foundation until his death forty-nine years later. He died at the age of eighty-eight, having been commissary for Virginia fifty-three years.

In 1720 Virginia contained twenty-nine counties and forty-four parishes, large and small. In each parish there was a church either of stone, brick or wood, while in the larger parishes there were one or more chapels in addition. At first the churches were made of logs, to be followed in a few years with larger and more pretentious frame buildings accommodating from 150 to 300 worshipers. In most instances, in the more populous parishes, the frame buildings in the course of time gave place to brick churches, following in some instances the cruciform design, though the larger number were plain rectangular buildings, seating from 300 to 500 worshipers. The chancel was uniformly in the east end, the pulpit against the north wall, while the body of the church was filled with square pews, seating from twelve to twenty-five, each pew surrounded by high sides so that the worshipers could not see from one pew into another. The church stood in a yard of never less than two acres, in which there was always a good spring of water, and frequently there was a graveyard attached. Near the church was the vestry house, which was frequently used for the meetings of county officials.

The service of the church was according to the liturgy, though the clerk, being the only person in the congregation supplied with a Prayer Book, made all the responses alone. The clerk also lined out and led the "Psalms of David in Metre," generally with the aid of a tuning fork. The congregation was seated in order of social rank; the gentry in their own pews in front and others according to their social position. Considerable time was given to the sermon, which was apt to be dry and repetitious. On certain Sundays children and servants were catechized by the minister, as this was a part of the clergyman's duty.

Turning now from Virginia, brief attention will be given to the beginnings of the Established Church in Maryland. The early religious history of Maryland, however, belongs to another part of this story;

that which relates to the first experiments in religious liberty in America.

It was not until near the end of the seventeenth century that the Established Church began to emerge in the colony of Maryland. The first official notice of it in that province was due to a letter written in 1676 by the Rev. Mr. Yoe, who seems to have been one of three Episcopal clergymen in Maryland at the time, addressed to the Archbishop of Canterbury. The letter draws a picture of the deplorable religious conditions in the colony and implores the archbishop to provide some means for the better support of the Protestant religion in the province. The archbishop laid the letter before the Bishop of London. From this time forward official attention, to a limited degree, was given to Maryland and the number of Established Church ministers increased, though the quality of those sent out left much to be desired. The great majority of the people were undoubtedly Protestant and an increasing concern for a church and a settled ministry was manifest among the better settlers. The overturn of James II in 1689 in what is known as the Protestant Revolution furnished the Maryland Protestants with the opportunity to rid themselves of Roman Catholic rule, and in 1692 Maryland became a royal colony. One of the first acts of the assembly after this change was "An Act for the Service of Almighty God and the Establishment of the Protestant Religion."

The act divided the ten Maryland counties into thirty-one parishes and a poll tax of forty pounds of tobacco was levied for the building and repairing of churches and the support of the ministry. Two years following the Act of Establishment, Sir Francis Nicholson became lieutenant governor, a most important event for the Established Church in Maryland. Nicholson was a devoted friend of the church, incongruous as that may seem, for he was profane, arbitrary, conceited and lacking in self-restraint, and yet his interest and liberality were a prime factor in firmly establishing the church in the colony. It is stated on good authority that he did more for "the erection of Episcopal churches than all the other colonial governors combined," and thirty churches in various parts of the colony owed their existence to his efforts. The capital was now moved from St. Mary's to Annapolis where a new brick church was begun. All this activity on the part of the Establishment met with strong opposition from the Roman Catholics and Quakers, who opposed the poll tax for the support of the church and the other measures. This opposition, together with a large immigration of Irish Catholics which now set in, aroused fear on the part of the Protestants, of the reëstablishment of Catholicism and the reinstatement of the old proprietors. The latter was actually accomplished in 1715, only, however, after the fourth Lord Baltimore had become a Protestant. It was during this period of great activity on the part of the Established Church, that agitation began for the appointment of a commissary for Maryland, a movement which was supported both by the governor and the assembly, and resulted in the fortunate selection of Dr. Thomas Bray who received the appointment from the Bishop of London in April, 1696.

Dr. Bray was a successful rector of a parish in Warwickshire, and is described as one of the first of the "working clergy." Four years elapsed after his appointment before he sailed for America, but these were years filled with plans and work for the American Church. He knew well the difficulty of securing suitable ministers for America, and also the handicaps under which they worked after reaching their distant parishes. Accordingly he exerted himself in securing missionaries and before he sailed for Maryland the number of clergymen in that province had been increased to sixteen. He likewise began the work of collecting libraries for the missionaries, and succeeded in establishing thirty-nine of these, the funds for which he collected, heartily assisted by many of the English bishops and others. This activity eventually resulted in the formation of the "Society for the Promotion of Christian Knowledge" (1698) which took form before he left England for America.

Commissary Bray reached Maryland March 12, 1700, and was warmly welcomed by Governor Nicholson. His first concern was to secure the passage of a law requiring every minister within the colony to use the Book of Common Prayer, which proved a most unwise measure as it aroused the bitter enmity of Catholics and the dissenting groups who now became a unit in opposing the Establishment. His next concern was to reform the clergy within the colony and bring to bear upon them effective discipline. At his own expense he visited all the parishes within the colony to observe the work and manner of life of the clergy. Two of the most flagrant clerical offenders against morals and decency were disciplined, though the Commissary's energetic attempts to better conditions frightened and offended the clergy and people as most of them would have preferred to have been let alone. The hot-tempered governor was likewise offended for he was jealous of his authority in appointing the incumbents.

At this juncture Dr. Bray returned to England, having heard that there was active opposition to the Act of Establishment in the English Parliament. The act was disapproved by the attorney general, though Bray succeeded in having another act presented, and passed which established the church in Maryland, but at the same time extended to the dissenters and Quakers the English Act of Toleration of 1689, though denying it to the Roman Catholics. This has been termed one of the sarcasms of history. Maryland, which had been founded for the sake of religious freedom by the toil and treasure of Roman Catholics, was now open to all who call themselves Christians save Roman Catholics.

During the agitation over this measure Dr. Bray published a "Memorial upon the State of Religion in America," which aroused great public interest. He declared there was need at once for forty missionaries in America and that the "refuse of the clergy in England would not do for American missionaries," and he submitted a scheme whereby young, learned, strong and able clergymen were to be obtained for America. The plan itself failed, but it soon resulted in the foundation of the "Society for the Propagation of the Gospel in Foreign Parts." Dr. Bray never returned to America. For a while he continued to hold the office of commissary, but soon resigned in order that another might be sent, but his zeal for and interest in America never lagged and until his death in 1734 he continued to labor for the good of the Colonial Church.

The founding of the Society for the Propagation of the Gospel in Foreign Parts in 1701 was an event of prime importance for the future of the Established Church not alone in the American colonies, but throughout the world. At the time of its organization the Established Church had hardly made a beginning in the colonies outside Virginia and Maryland. King's Chapel in Boston, begun in 1688 through the influence of the royal governor of Massachusetts, was the only Episcopal church in the Puritan colonies; in North Carolina there were two church settlements but no minister; South Carolina had several congregations, but here also there was a dearth of clergymen; Pennsylvania had one Church of England minister; the Jerseys none; New York one only; while Rhode Island had a church but no minister. The work of planting and fostering the Established Church in these colonies was to be the great task of the venerable society in America during the first half of the eighteenth century.

CHAPTER IV

✤ ✤ ✤

THE PURITAN COLONIES: THE BEGINNINGS
OF AMERICAN CONGREGATIONALISM

FOR about ten years the Pilgrims, as the Plymouth colonists came to be called, lived in Holland. Here they had failed to prosper economically as they had hoped, and there seemed to be no prospect of bettering their condition. Renewal of war was also threatening between Spain and Holland, but the chief reason which determined them to leave Leyden and to seek a new place of refuge was the painful realization that their children were being "drawne awaye by evill examples into extravagante & dangerous courses, getting ye raines off their neks, & departing from their parents . . . so that they saw their posterietie would be in danger to degenerate & be corrupted."

By the end of Queen Elizabeth's reign all of the Separatists or radical Puritans in England had either been driven underground or had gone into exile. It was the Scrooby congregation under the leadership of John Robinson, their pastor, that fled to Leyden, attracted by the liberal government of the Dutch. These radicals were no more acceptable to the great Puritan party within the Church of England than to the conservative Anglicans, for the great body of English Puritans were firm believers in the national church and looked upon the Separatists as schismatics, self-righteous and exclusive. But it was this little band of radicals, despised by all parties among their own countrymen, which was destined to lay the foundations of New England, and to furnish the model of church government which was afterward to be accepted and developed by the far more numerous and influential Puritans, the founders of Massachusetts Bay.

After considerable negotiation with the Virginia Company, they having been invited to the Virginia colony by Sir Edwin Sandys, the Puritan treasurer, an agreement was finally reached, granting the Leyden congregation land in what was termed the "northern parts of Virginia." The hired *Mayflower,* upon which the one hundred and two Pilgrims embarked for their new home, instead of bringing them to the territory for which they had negotiated, brought them, on November 11, 1620, to the barren shores of Cape Cod, a region belonging to the Plymouth Company. Here they were compelled to land without charter or grant of any kind, from any government, and the settlement which they were about to establish would therefore have no legal basis. It was once thought that the coming of the Pilgrims to Cape Cod was due to an act of treachery on the part of the captain of the *Mayflower,* who was supposed to have had a secret agreement with the Council of New England to land the colonists within their grant. This, however, has now been completely discredited and the good character of the *Mayflower's* captain, Christopher Jones, has been fully established. Contrary winds and inaccurate navigation charts were most probably the reasons for the miscalculation of the captain which brought the Pilgrim fathers to New England rather than to Virginia. Because of this, certain of their party began to talk of doing as they pleased, when they had landed, and it was to ward off this threatened rupture in their ranks that they gathered in the cabin of the *Mayflower* and there drew up the famous *Mayflower Compact.* This instrument, modeled after the agreement by which they had constituted the church at Scrooby, sixteen years before, was to serve as a model for other groups of New England colonists in the years to come. The *Compact* remained the basis of the Plymouth government until 1691, when the colony was united with Massachusetts.

For nine years the Pilgrims at Plymouth were without a pastor, for John Robinson had died before he could join them, but during these years they were led in their worship by William Brewster, the ruling elder. Brewster had been advised by Robinson not to administer the sacraments, but twice every Sabbath he "taught to ye great contentment of ye hearers, and their comfortable edification" and we are told that he had a "singular gift in prayer, both public and private . . . and he always thought it were better for ministers to pray oftener, and divide their prayers, than to be long and tedious in the same." It was not, indeed, until 1629 that the Plymouth church secured a satisfactory minister, in the person of Ralph Smith, who had come first to Salem. It is true that their partners in England had sent over John Lyford to be their minister in 1624, but he proved entirely unworthy and was expelled from the colony. Though Lyford professed an interest in Puritan principles he was actually antagonistic to Puritanism and all it stood for. Adams calls him a "canting hypocrite, a sort of lascivious Uriah Heep," and his going was good riddance.

The Plymouth colonists had been too poor to pay for their transportation to America, nor were they able to meet the expense of maintaining themselves while building the colony. They were, therefore, forced to form a partnership with some London merchants, who advanced them £7,000. The merchants, of course, were primarily interested in profits, and wished to send over active young men who would make good fishermen and fur gatherers, while the colonists were anxious to bring over the remainder of the Leyden Pilgrims, and above everything else, desired to maintain their congregational institutions. The returns to the London merchants on their investment, were very small, and after the colony had rejected Lyford as their minister, the merchants became distrustful of the enterprise and after some negotiations the colony bought itself free from their unsympathetic partners, agreeing to pay £1,800 in nine annual installments. Soon after this the remainder of the Leyden colonists were brought out, and by skillful trading and hard work they were able within a few years to pay off their debt.

The colony, however, grew very slowly, no doubt, partly because of the poorness of the soil, but especially because the Separatists were few in number, while their strictness and exclusiveness was not attractive to outsiders. By 1630, however, the permanence of the colony seemed assured. In that year there were 300 inhabitants at Plymouth while in the years following new settlements were established, so that by 1643 there were 10 towns and about 2,500 people.

The heart and center of the Pilgrim colony at Plymouth was their church. A Dutch merchant of New Amsterdam, who visited Plymouth in 1627, thus describes the meetinghouse, with the order in which the people gathered for worship:

Upon the hill they have a large square meeting house, with a flat roof, made of thick sawn planks, stayed with oak beams, upon the top of which they have six cannons, which shoot iron balls of four and five pounds, and command the surrounding country. The lower part they use for their church, where they preach on Sundays and the usual holidays. They assemble by beat of drum, each with his musket or firelock, in front of the captain's [Myles Standish's] door; they have their cloaks on, and place themselves in order, three abreast, and are led by a sergeant without beat of drum. Behind comes the Governor [William Bradford] in a long robe; beside him, on the right hand, comes the preacher [Elder Brewster], with his cloak on, and on the left hand the captain, with his side arms and cloak on, and with a small cane in his hand; and so they march in good order, and each sets his arms down near him.

Here they were free to carry out the type of church government in which they believed, and to worship according as their consciences dictated. To gain this was to them sufficient reward for all the untold sufferings through which they had come, and the "windswept graveyard" on the hill and the "rude street of hewn-plank houses bore mute witness" as to how much it had cost.

Of far greater importance historically than the Pilgrim colony at Plymouth were the settlements about Massachusetts Bay. A sober historian has stated that: "Probably no colony in the history of European emigration was superior to that of Massachusetts in wealth, station or capacity." In this respect it was in great contrast with the humble and poor people who settled Plymouth.

The first step in the great migration of English Puritans was undertaken through the influence of the Rev. John White, a Puritan minister at Dorchester, England. It was his idea to form a fishing company and found a settlement on the Massachusetts coast, part of whose purpose was to care for the moral and religious welfare of the many transient English fishermen who came to that region year by year during the fishing season. This enterprise proved a failure, but it served to arouse White's interest in the founding of a Puritan colony. Securing help from a group of Puritan capitalists, a company was formed and a grant of land obtained from the Council for New England. In September, 1628, the vanguard of the great Puritan migration arrived at what is now Salem. Here they found a few remnants of White's fishing colony, and it was after some differences between the two groups had been peacefully settled that they named the place Salem (peace). John Endicott, a rigid Puritan and a member of the company, was named governor and by the next year some three hundred people were living under his authority. This was the beginning of Massachusetts.

The next year (1629) twenty-six Englishmen secured a charter for the *Massachusetts Bay Company*. Although the original purpose of this corporation was primarily commercial, control soon passed from the hands of those chiefly interested in business to those whose interests were primarily religious. Just why King Charles I was willing to grant a charter to such a group has never been found out, but it is quite probable that he was not unwilling to have some of the more pestiferous Puritans leave England for his own peace of mind. In August, 1629, still another change took place in the corporation, when all those withdrew who did not intend to go to America. Thus the governing body of the company was removed to American soil, while at the same time they rid themselves of the absentee stockholder, thus minimizing the possibility of governmental interference from England. Such was the business arrangement of the great Massachusetts Bay colony.

At once the full tide of Puritan migration to America set in. In 1629 about 900 colonists arrived; in 1630, 2,000 and by 1640, it has been estimated that 20,000 had found their way across the Atlantic to take up their abode in New England. But we must not suppose that all the colonists were Puritans, nor were they all "gentlemen." It has been found that hardly a fifth of the Massachusetts Bay colonists were even professed Christians, though all the ministers were Puritans, as were the leading laymen. The majority were middle class people, small tradesmen, farmers or artisans.

The Puritans of the Massachusetts Bay colony had, at the beginning, no intention of separating from the Church of England. One of the first two ministers to set foot on Massachusetts soil, Francis Higginson, is reported to have said, as the ship was bearing him out of sight of the shores of England:

> We will not say as the separatists were wont to say at their leaving England, "Farewel, Babylon! Farewel, Rome!" but we will say "Farewel, dear England, Farewel the Church of God in England and all the Christian friends there!" We do not go to New England as Separatists from the Church of England, though we cannot but separate from the corruptions in it; but we go to practice the positive part of church reformation, and propagate the gospel in America.

And doubtless many, if not most, of the Puritans leaders on leaving England felt as did Winthrop and others who esteemed it an "honour to call the Church of England, from whom wee rise, our dear Mother. . . ."

How then did the churches of the powerful Massachusetts Bay colony come to be Congregational? This is one of the most important developments in the history of New England and marks a turning point of vast significance. One of the influences which led in the direction of Congregationalism was exerted by Dr. Samuel Fuller, a deacon in the church at Plymouth. During the first winter, Endicott's colony at Salem was soon in great distress because so many settlers fell ill and there was no doctor among them to care for the sick. The only physician then on the whole coast of New England was the deacon-doctor at Plymouth, Samuel Fuller. In desperation Endicott wrote to Plymouth asking that the doctor come to their aid. Fuller gladly responded and in spite of the lack of proper medicines did what he could to stay the ravages of disease. As Governor Endicott, who formerly had regarded the Separatists at Plymouth with suspicion, conversed with Dr. Fuller and saw him so faithfully laboring among the sick, his prejudices melted away and he is soon writing to Governor Bradford at Plymouth—in May, 1629—as follows:

Right Worthy Sir: It is a thing not usual that servants to one Master and of the same household should be strangers. I assure you I desire it not; nay to speak more plainly I cannot be so to you. God's people are marked with one and the same mark, and sealed with one and the same seal, and have for the main, one and the same heart, guided by one and the same spirit of truth: and where this is there can be no discord—nay here must needs be sweet harmony. The same request with you I make unto the Lord, that we may as Christian brethren be united by a heavenly and unfeigned love, bending all our hearts and forces to furthering a work beyond our strength, with reverence and fear fastening our eyes always on him that only is able to direct and prosper all our ways.

I acknowledge myself much bound to you for your kind love and care in sending Mr. Fuller among us, and I rejoice much that I am by him satisfied touching your judgments of the outward form of God's worship. It is as far as I can yet gather, no other than is warranted by the evidence of truth, and the same which I have professed and maintained ever since the Lord in mercy revealed himself to me, being very far different from the common report that hath been spread of you touching that particular. But God's children must not look for less here below, and it is the great mercy of God that he strengthens them to go through with it.

I shall not need at this time to be tedious unto you, for, God willing, I purpose to see your face shortly. In the meantime I humbly take leave of you, committing you to the Lord's blessed protection, and rest

Your assured loving friend and servant,

John Endicott.

The basic reason, however, for the adoption by the Salem Church of Congregational polity, which was to become the model for all the New England churches to be built about the Bay, was not so much the Plymouth example as the fact that the Massachusetts Bay leaders had already become convinced that the Congregational form of church government was the only true Scriptural form, and it would have been adopted had there been no previous Plymouth example. The principal difference between the Plymouth and Massachusetts Bay churches lay in their differing attitudes toward the Church of England.[1] The Plymouth Pilgrims repudiated the Church of England in all its parts and would have nothing to do with it; the Puritans of the Massachusetts Bay colony, following the lead of William Bradshaw and William Ames, the leading Puritan casuists, while accepting the Congregational form of church government as Scriptural, at the same time avowed their loyalty to the Church of England.

Meanwhile several ordained clergymen of the Church of England arrived in Massachusetts, and July 20, 1629, was set aside as the day for choosing a pastor and teacher for the Salem congregation. A church had already been formed at Salem; at least its first members had united into a covenant in the early spring. After prayer and preaching the two ministers under consideration, Francis Higginson and Samuel Skelton, were asked as to their views concerning a proper call to the ministry, and both stated that an inward sense of fitness and election by male members of "a company of believers . . . joined together in covenant" constituted such a call. Then they proceeded to take a vote by ballot, which resulted in the choice of Skelton as pastor and Higginson as teacher. Then "accepting ye choyce, Mr. Higginson, with 3. or 4. of ye gravest members of ye church, laid their hands on Mr. Skelton, using prayer therewith. This being done, there was imposission of hands on Mr. Higginson also." Thus was the Congregational principle, that every Christian congregation has the right to choose and ordain its own officers, inaugurated in Massachusetts Bay colony. At this time also a ruling elder and deacons were elected, though they were not ordained until later.

In June of the next year (1630) John Winthrop arrived with 840

---

[1]For a clear presentation of the two types of Puritanism see Perry Miller, *Orthodoxy in Massachusetts* (Cambridge, 1933). For a brief summary see W. W. Sweet, *Religion in Colonial America* (New York, 1942), pp. 73-76.

colonists and a large number of cattle and horses, and new settlements were forming at Charlestown, Boston and Newtowne. By the end of the year there were eight settlements, each marking the beginning of towns. In July two churches were formed, one at Watertown, the other at Charlestown. Both drew up covenants and later elected their pastors and teachers and ordained them "by imposition of hands." In May the next year (1631) by the action of the Massachusetts General Court the franchise was limited to church members, and thus Congregationalism became the state church and the government of Massachusetts semi-theocratic. But the notion, often expressed, that the ministers in early New England were practically in control of the government is without basis in fact. It is true that they were highly respected and were usually consulted by the civil authorities, but public sentiment kept them from holding public office, and even the ultimate control of the churches was in the hands of the civil officials. The great political importance of the ministers in Massachusetts and New Haven was largely due to the fact that no one was likely to be admitted to church membership without their consent and as the suffrage was limited to church members they thus had indirect control over the voting members.

Massachusetts was far from being a democracy. The General Court was made up of Governor Winthrop and twelve freemen, with full legal authority. Governor Winthrop could find no basis in Scripture for democracy, stating that "Among nations it has always been accounted the meanest and worst of all forms of government," and in this opinion he was supported by leaders in both church and state. Nor was there religious toleration. It must be remembered that the Massachusetts leaders were Church of England men, nor were they opposed to a state church. They never thought of establishing religious toleration, nor did they think of it as in the least desirable. "Tis Satan's policy, to plead for an indefinite and boundless toleration," declared one of their preachers in an election sermon, while another stated, "All familists, Antinomians, Anabaptists, and other Enthusiasts shall have free liberty to keepe away from us." It is true that others besides Puritans were welcomed into the colony, but with the full understanding that they were to accept what they found, and refrain from disturbance. It was not toleration which the Puritan sought, but rather the freedom to carry out his own religious notions, undisturbed.

Year by year, as the stream of immigration continued, new towns were established and new churches formed, following the Congregational practice established by Salem, Watertown and Charlestown. Thus in the course of about ten years the churches in New England had grown to thirty-three in number, all having adopted Congregational polity, though one or two of the pastors were somewhat inclined toward Presbyterianism.

The disturbers who arose among them were expelled. This practice was begun in 1629 at Salem, when two brothers, John and Samuel Browne, who had objected to the Congregationalizing of the Salem church, began to hold service, using the Prayer Book of the Established Church. This led to their expulsion from the colony. The most famous of those who were exiled from the Massachusetts Bay colony because they did not harmonize with the ruling element were, of course, Roger Williams and Anne Hutchinson, whose story belongs to the establishment of Rhode Island and will be related in the following chapter.

Hardly had the first Puritan colonies been established before the restless spirit and land hunger, which were to prove so largely responsible for the ultimate conquest of the American continent, began to appear. The leader of the first movement westward was the Rev. Thomas Hooker. He had come to Boston in 1633 and soon became the minister at Newtowne. Almost at once he was irked by the autocracy of the government and protested against the limitation of the suffrage, but it was to no avail. In his controversy with Governor Winthrop he states that "in matters that concern the common good, a general council, chosen by all, to transact business which concerns all, I conceive most suitable to rule and most safe for the relief of the whole people." But autocracy was too firmly intrenched to be shaken, and very soon we find a petition before the magistrates, presented by Hooker's congregation, asking permission to migrate to the valley of the Connecticut. At first refused, permission was finally granted, providing they agree to continue under the government of Massachusetts. By 1636 three towns had been founded on the Connecticut River, Weathersfield, Hartford and Windsor, by colonists chiefly from Newtowne, Dorchester and Watertown. The Newtowne church, under the leadership of Hooker the pastor and Stone the teacher, made up the nucleus of the settlement at Hartford, while the minister at Dorchester, John Warham, with his congregation migrated to Windsor. Thus it was that two of the Massachusetts churches were practically transplanted to the Connecticut.

For a few years these Connecticut towns continued under the Massachusetts government, but in 1638 a constitution was adopted, called the "Fundamental Orders," which was based upon the popular consent. The government was somewhat less theocratic than was that of Massachusetts, as only the governor was required to be a church member, while the suffrage was granted to all who had taken the oath, and had been admitted to citizenship by the township. It seems quite probable, however, that in the elections to citizenship care was taken that only church members or those directly in sympathy with the religious aims of the constitution became "freemen."

At the very time the Connecticut settlements were taking shape, a new Puritan colony was being established directly from England. The chief instigators in this enterprise were the Rev. John Davenport, who had been vicar of a London church until Archbishop Laud's regulations had driven him to Holland, and one of his London parishioners, Theophilus Eaton, a wealthy and influential merchant. Their plan included both religion and trade, and attracted several other English Puritan ministers and their congregations. Accordingly a considerable group sailed for Massachusetts in the spring of 1637. The Massachusetts authorities would have been glad to have had them remain under their jurisdiction, but Davenport and Eaton had an independent colony in mind, and after some exploring they decided to locate in what is now the southern part of Connecticut, to which they gave the name New Haven. They had neither charter nor patent for the land, but after obtaining lands by treaty from the Quinnipiack Indians, whom they protected from the Mohawks, they proceeded during the years 1638 to 1640 to the founding of several towns In June, 1639, a government was framed, based on the Bible, and it was voted that "Scriptures doe holde forth a perfect rule for the direction and government of all men in all duet[ies]. . . ."

In this Bible commonwealth the suffrage was restricted, as in Massa· chusetts, to church members. Annual elections were ordered and the first governor chosen was Theophilus Eaton, and year by year, for nearly twenty years, until his death, he was reëlected to that office. The other towns founded in the vicinity, Milford, Guilford and Stamford, were at first independent of New Haven, but in 1643, at the formation of the New England Confederation, a central government was organized and the four towns were united. Twenty years later (1664) Connecticut and

New Haven were united, and with this union the chief characteristics of New Haven disappeared, such as the limitation of the suffrage to church members and the Scriptural constitution.

With the large number of educated clergymen in the Puritan colonies, most of them graduates of Cambridge, it was but natural that there should be early agitation looking toward the founding of a college. Indeed, before 1647 one hundred and thirty ministers had arrived in New England and it is stated on good authority that "such a concentration of educated men in a new settlement, in proportion to the population, has never occurred before or since." Accordingly, on September 8, 1636, the General Court of Massachusetts advanced "four hundred pounds by way of essay towards the building of something to begin a Colledge." But, to quote the opinion of Cotton Mather, "that which laid the most significant stone in the foundation, was the last will of Mr. John Harvard, a reverend, and most excellent minister of the gospel, who dying at Charlestown, of a consumption, quickly after his arrival, bequeathed the sum of seven hundred, seventy nine pounds, seventeen shillings and two pence, toward the pious work of building a Colledge, which was now set on foot." Soon a society of scholars was lodged in the "New Nests," under the direction of Mr. Nathaniel Eaton, who proved such a tyrant, however, beating a young gentleman unmercifully with a cudgel, that he was fined by the court, and was dismissed. Under Eaton's direction Harvard was little more than a school, so that Henry Dunster who became the president in 1640, soon after his arrival in America, was really the first president of the college. In *New England's First Fruits* (1643) Dunster is described as "a learned, considerable and industrious man, who had so trained up his pupils in the tongues and arts, and so seasoned them with the principles of Divinity and Christianity, that we have, to our great comfort, and in truth beyond our hopes, beheld their progress in learning and godliness also." Dunster remained the president until his adoption of Baptist views caused his resignation in 1654.

In 1642 the first class had graduated, and by the end of the century a large majority of the ministers in both Massachusetts and Connecticut were her graduates; seventy-six of the eighty-seven in Massachusetts; and thirty-one of the thirty-five in Connecticut. Thus Harvard most admirably served its primary purpose, that of training young men for the ministry.

By the middle of the seventeenth century four Puritan colonies were firmly rooted in New England soil, in each of which the Congregational Church was the dominating influence. During these years of the rapid development of American Congregationalism, the Puritan party in England began to express concern as to their dangerous tendencies in the direction of separatism. This concern led to questioning, and in the answering of these questions the leading New England ministers formulated the Congregational system of church polity. The ministers particularly responsible for the exposition of the New England Congregational system were John Cotton of Boston, Richard Mather of Dorchester, John Davenport of New Haven and Thomas Hooker of Connecticut. This activity in defending the Congregational system against its English critics led finally to the calling of the "Cambridge Synod" (September 1, 1646) by the General Court of Massachusetts, at which the churches of Massachusetts, Plymouth, New Haven and Connecticut were invited to send their ministers and their representatives, "there to discuss, dispute, & cleare up, by the word of God, such questions of church government & discipline . . . as they shall thinke needfull & meete." This synod adopted the Westminster Confession as an expression of the Congregational belief, and drew up what came to be known as the *Cambridge Platform*, which constitutes the Congregational constitution.

The *Cambridge Platform* is simply the gathering up of the administrative experience of the New England Congregational fathers. Each church was considered as autonomous, though dependent upon other churches for council and fellowship. A church was constituted by a group of Christians uniting into a voluntary agreement, known as a convenant. At first the forming of a church was more or less of a private matter, but later, in Massachusetts and Connecticut, the consent of the government and the neighboring churches was required. The early covenants were simply promises to worship together, following the divine commandments and promising faithfulness to each other, and were largely free of doctrinal statements. This absence of doctrinal matter in the covenants was largely due to the creedal uniformity prevailing, rather than to any lack of concern in the matter of doctrine. The officials of a Congregational church were pastor, teacher, elders and deacons, but by the end of the seventeenth century, in most instances, the teacher and elders had disappeared, leaving the pastor and deacons as the sole officers. At first the officers were selected by the adult male members, and this continued to be the practice in choosing deacons, but later, all the voters in the township, since they were taxed to support the minister, obtained the right to a voice in his selection, whether they were members of the church or not.

At first the minister was ordained by the officers of the congregation, but as fellowship between the churches developed, it became the custom to call in neighboring ministers to perform this service. According to the *Cambridge Platform* Congregationalists do not attach as much significance to ordination as do other Protestant churches, considering it simply "the solemn putting of a man into his place & office . . . wherunto he had right before by election, being like the installing of a magistrat in the common wealth." Nor did a minister without a church continue to hold his ministerial character. At first the ministers were supported by voluntary contributions, but within a few years laws were passed compelling all who had not given voluntarily to be assessed by the constables, and later in Massachusetts the county courts were directed to fix ministers' salaries and collect them. During the early eighteenth century, after other religious groups began to gain a foothold in New England, laws were passed allowing members of other churches to pay their assessments to their own clergymen, in towns where there were such ministers. Otherwise their assessments went to the Congregational minister.

Throughout the whole period of the colonies the meetinghouse was not only the place of worship, but it was likewise the social center for every New England community, as well as a meeting place for political discussion. The typical New England meetinghouse was a plain, rectangular, frame structure, sometimes with a tower and a bell if the congregration could afford it, with a pulpit at one end opposite the main door. In the early churches there were two pews, somewhat raised above the others, facing the congregation, for elders and deacons. The sexes were divided in the seating, men on one side, women and the smaller children on the other, while the boys and young men occupied the gallery or the back seats where they were under the watchful eye of the tithing man. This functionary was a township official who assisted the constable in watching over the morals of the community. There was one such official for every ten families, who besides keeping order at the services, was on the lookout for Sabbath breaking, tippling, gaming and idleness. Frequently the worshipers were seated according to their social rank, which remained true of a number of New England churches until well on in the nineteenth century. Except for little foot stoves, which were used for women and children, the churches were without means for heating.

The main service of worship of a New England congregation began at nine o'clock on a Sabbath morning. The people were summoned in the larger communities by the church bell, or in the smaller and poorer towns by a drum or conch shell. Services were opened by a long prayer in which the minister brought the immediate needs of the members and of the community to the Divine attention, and no matter how long the prayer, the congregation stood. Next came the Bible reading, the pastor expounding as he read, for "dumb reading," as reading without comment was called, seemed to smack of the ritualistic service of the Church of England. The sermon was the main element in Puritan worship, but contrary to the usually accepted notion, the sermons were generally not more than an hour in length, though there are instances of sermons two and three hours long. The sermon completed, a shorter prayer closed the service.

The musical part of New England worship consisted of Psalm singing, in which the Psalm was lined out by the ruling elder, or by one designated by the minister. The people knew few tunes and as late as the beginning of the eighteenth century New England congregations were rarely able to sing more than three or four. Even the few melodies commonly known became so corrupted that no two individuals sang them alike, so that a congregation singing sounded "like five hundred different tunes roared out at the same time" often one or two words apart. An eighteenth century New England minister states: "I myself have twice in one note paused to take breath." The story is told of a New England deacon who, because of failing eyesight, found difficulty in reading the first line of the Psalm and he apologized by observing:
"My eyes, indeed, are very blind."
The choir thinking this the first line of a common-meter hymn immediately sang it; whereupon the deacon exclaimed:
"I cannot see at all."
This the choir also sang. Astonished, the deacon cried out:
"I really believe you are bewitched"
and the choir responded, "I really believe you are bewitched," where-

upon the deacon added, "The mischief's in you all," and after the choir had sung that, the deacon sat down in disgust.

The Plymouth colonists brought with them a Psalm book which had been prepared for their use in Holland by Henry Ainsworth in 1612. This the churches of the Plymouth colony used until they were merged with Massachusetts Bay in 1692. The more famous Bay Psalm Book, a new American book, was first published at Cambridge in 1640 and was many times reprinted.

A question of great importance, which arose in the last third of the seventeenth century, and which continued to agitate the New England churches for more than a decade, was that known as the "Half-Way Covenant." It was a question which had to do with church membership. The early New England Congregationalists maintained that only adult persons of Christian experience should be admitted to full membership in the church, but they also held that children shared in the covenant taken by their parents and were therefore members of the church on that ground. Because of this latter provision, there came gradually to be numerous people, belonging to the second generation, who were members of the church but who made no profession of an experience, but were living good lives, and of course desired that their children receive baptism. The stricter element among the ministers held that only the immediate offspring of believing parents could be admitted to baptism, while there arose a more liberal group contending that children of nonregenerate members, who owned the covenant, might receive baptism, but that they might not receive the Lord's Supper, nor were they to be allowed to vote in church affairs.

As the question became more and more agitated, the General Court of Connecticut proposed to settle the matter through a convention of ministers, representing the four Congregational colonies. Such a convention was called to meet in 1657, but only Massachusetts and Connecticut sent delegates. It went on record, however, as supporting the Half-Way Covenant. Their decision had little effect in allaying the discussion, and finally the Massachusetts General Court decided to try its hand in settling the matter, by calling a General Synod of all the Massachusetts churches, to meet in Boston in March, 1662. Here, after warm discussion, the Half-Way Covenant again won the day. Still the strife continued and pamphlets for and against were multiplied, while churches were split over the issue, as was the case of the churches in

Hartford, Stratford and Windsor in Connecticut, while even the First Church, Boston, was torn asunder, and a congregation from the old New Haven colony migrated to northern New Jersey where they founded New Ark, in order that they might be free from such abomination as that established by this innovation, and where the old strictness might be maintained.

The adoption of the Half-Way Covenant marks the passing of the founders of New England and the beginning of the domination of the second generation. Among the ministers of the first generation John Cotton is the outstanding figure. Coming to Massachusetts in 1633, after twenty years as vicar of the church in Boston, England, he at once took first rank among the leaders of Massachusetts, and was chosen teacher of the First Church in Boston. His grandson, Cotton Mather, characterized him as "a most universal scholar, and a living system of liberal arts, and a walking library," and such confidence was reposed in him that many "believed that God would not suffer Mr. Cotton to err." While hating heresy, and an avowed enemy of democracy, he was likewise suspicious of all hereditary power, and, contradictory as it may seem, he at the same time "was verging toward progress in truth and in religious freedom." Cotton's ambition was to found a theocratic state modeled after that of the Hebrews, "in which political rights should be sub-ordinated to religious conformity," with magistrates to be chosen from a narrow group, whose authority was to be beyond the reach of the popular will, and "with the ministers serving as a court of last resort to interpret the divine law to the subject-citizens of Jehovah." In his philosophy there is no trace of the doctrine of natural rights; but freedom and righteousness were to go hand in hand, while the sinner was to "remain subject to the saint."

Standing out almost, if not quite, as prominently in the second generation, as did John Cotton in the first, is Increase Mather. Born in the Dorchester parsonage, the son of Richard Mather, he graduated from Harvard at seventeen in 1656, and at once sailed for Ireland, where he matriculated at Trinity College, then under Puritan control, for the master's degree. He undoubtedly intended to remain a pastor in England, but the ending of the Commonwealth drove him back to New England, where he became the teacher in the Second Church of Boston, remaining there until his death in 1723. After the division of the First Church, which we have noted, this was the most influential pulpit in

Massachusetts, as well as perhaps in the whole of New England. At this influential post, Increase Mather became the stanch defender of the old order of things, both in state and in church. The last thirty years of his life his influence was foremost as an ecclesiastical leader, and well-nigh as great in politics and in education. From 1685 to 1701 he was the acting president of Harvard College, driving back and forth from his Boston parsonage to Cambridge every day in his carriage. In 1688, after the loss of the charter, he was sent to England, as the best-prepared man in Massachusetts, to plead the cause of the colony against Governor Andros. And so successful was he in this important mission that the new charter of 1691 was secured and Mather was granted the right to nominate those who should first bear office under it.

Increase Mather was the prime mover in securing the calling by the General Court of Massachusetts of the Reforming Synod of 1679. A series of disasters, such as the two fires in Boston, in 1676 and 1679, a smallpox scourge, King Philip's War, together with the threats against self-government, which finally resulted in the loss of the charter in 1684, seemed to indicate clearly to Mather that God's wrath was turned against New England for their sins. The purpose of the synod was to consider the condition of the New England churches and to adopt such measures as would remedy conditions which were considered the cause of the divine anger. Under Increase Mather's presidency the synod adopted a series of recommendations looking toward a more faithful administration of church discipline and calling for a strict execution of the laws. It also adopted a confession of faith, modeled after the Savoy Confession of the English Congregationalists, which had been formulated in 1658 and which remains the fullest and clearest state-ment of the faith of seventeenth century Congregationalists.

The disaster which came to Massachusetts in October, 1684, when she was deprived of her liberal charter has already been noted. It was the plan of King James II to unite the American colonies into one royal jurisdiction, and in December, 1686, Sir Edmund Andros came to Bos-ton, first as governor of Massachusetts, Maine, New Hampshire and Plymouth, while later his jurisdiction covered Connecticut, Rhode Island, New Jersey and New York in addition. All popular rights were lost, and with them the freedom of the press and the power of taxation. Not the least of the accusations lodged against Andros was that he had introduced the Established Church among them. The governor had asked for the use of one of the meetinghouses at such a time when it would not interfere with the services of the owners. When this was refused Old South Meetinghouse was taken by force and Anglican services were held on Good Friday and Easter, 1687. The next year King's Chapel was begun, the first Anglican church in Massachusetts. The danger from Anglicanism soon passed, for when the news arrived in New England that James II had vacated the throne, the beating of drums on Boston Common summoned the militia; a town meeting was held, and Governor Andros and two other royal officials were soon in prison. A provisional government was at once formed which was to carry on until the new charter was obtained. The new charter, though distasteful to Increase Mather because of its limitations on the old privileges, nevertheless retained much that was dear to the New England Puritan. It put an end, however, to Puritan theocracy, by sweeping away all religious qualifications for the suffrage, substituting in its stead property qualifications. Local government was left unchanged, though the governor hereafter was to be an appointee of the crown, while only the lower house of the legislature was to be chosen by the direct vote of the people.

That the hanging of twenty witches at Salem and the execution of ten others at different places, in 1692, was the direct effect of the political and religious disturbances through which New England was passing at this time is perhaps an unwarranted conclusion. There is no doubt, however, but that the public mind was in a most feverish and disturbed state. It is quite the mode in these days to heap wholesale condemnation upon New England Puritanism, and such condemnation usually begins or ends with a description of the Salem witchcraft delusion. As a matter of fact and fairness, it needs to be said that witchcraft delusions were common all over Europe from the fourteenth to the eighteenth century, and during these years the European witch fires were responsible for the death of at least five hundred thousand victims. Between 1645 and 1647 in England one notorious witch-finder alone was responsible for sending three hundred condemned witches to the gallows. This, however, is not a justification for the happenings at Salem, but rather an explanation of them.

The theory concerning witches, usually accepted, was that the witch had sold herself to the devil, to be used as his special instrument and agent, to carry out his evil purposes. Concern over strange apparitions and witches had been expressed previously by the New England ministers and in 1684 Increase Mather had written a book entitled *An Essay for the Recording of Illustrious Providences,* in which he describes several cases of witchcraft. The craze at Salem began in March, 1692, when several children through their strange actions, were thought to be bewitched, and finally they named three old women who they said had bewitched them. These miserable old women were brought to trial in a court held in the Salem church, with the children as the chief witnesses, and all were convicted and condemned. The jails were now filled with accused witches. The royal governor, himself of New England birth, appointed a special court to try the cases, and by January, 1693, twenty-two persons had been condemned, two of whom died in prison and the remainder were hanged. Among the judges who sat in the special court was the high-minded Samuel Sewall.

The delusion passed almost as quickly as it had come, though belief in witches by no means disappeared. Soon critics of the proceedings began to make themselves heard, among them Increase Mather, who contended that other evidence should be required, since "a Daemon may, by God's permission, appear even to ill purposes, in the Shape of an innocent, yea, and a virtuous Man." The trials were stopped by Governor Phipps in October, 1692, and five years later the Massachusetts Court publicly repented and set apart a special day of fasting and prayer, that prayers might be offered asking for forgiveness for "the late Tragedy raised amongst us by Satan," while the twelve jurors published a declaration of sorrow for accepting insufficient evidence against the accused, and Judge Sewall rose in his pew in the South Church and made public confession of his sense of guilt.

Toward the close of the seventeenth century liberal tendencies began to make their appearance in some of the New England churches. Especially was liberalism noticeable at Harvard and in Cambridge where the tutors, William Brattle and William Leverett, began to advocate certain changes in the church. They contended that all baptized persons should have a part in selecting the minister; that no longer should admission to church membership depend upon the relation of a religious experience before the congregation; while they also wished to bring about certain changes in the conduct of the public services. This agitation finally led to the formation of Brattle Church, which was organized without the consent of the other churches, where these innovations were put into practice. This particular incident, which marked the waning influence of Increase Mather at Harvard, was also largely responsible for an attempt on the part of the conservatives, led by the Mathers, Increase and his son Cotton, to create new ecclesiastical machinery which would hold in check this growing radicalism. This led to what is known as the *Massachusetts Proposals* of 1705.

Ministerial associations had gradually come into existence toward the end of the sixteen hundreds, the first having been formed in 1690, made up of the ministers of Boston and the surrounding towns. It met regularly in the college buildings at Cambridge. It was purely a voluntary affair, but it seemed to meet a real need, for it was not long until there were five such associations in Massachusetts. The next step was the "Ministerial Convention," made up of delegates from the several associations, which met once a year during the spring meeting of the General Court. In 1705, the convention, through a circular letter to the churches, began to advocate reforms in church administration. This led to the gathering of nine ministers, representing the associations of Massachusetts, at which a series of recommendations were formulated, the most important being that ministerial associations were to be formed where they did not now exist, and that these associations have the power to examine and license ministerial candidates, while churches without ministers were to apply to the associations for candidates. The second proposal was that there should be a "standing Council" in each association whose decisions were to be final. The first part of the recommendations were put into operation, but the second proposal, due to the strong opposition which arose, was never carried out.

Out of the welter of discussion which arose over the proposed changes in church government, there appeared an able defender of Congregational polity in the person of John Wise, the pastor at Ipswich, who "possessed the keenest mind and the most trenchant pen of his generation." In two brilliant little books, *The Churches Quarrel Espoused* (1710) and *A Vindication of the Government of the New England Churches* (1717), Wise defended the democracy of the old system, in which the democratic element was emphasized, not alone by an appeal to the Scripture, but also on the ground of natural rights. His books stirred the mind of New England profoundly, and so convincing was his argument that it was accepted as authoritative. He asserted that "Democracy is Christ's government in Church and State"; that "Power is originally in the people";

and further that "by natural right all men are born free." This philosophy of democracy was not alone to influence the affairs of the church, but fifty years later (1772) Wise's books appeared in a new edition, and played their part in the political discussion of the time.

Though partially defeated in Massachusetts, the Massachusetts Proposals were three years later (1708) embodied in the *Saybrook Platform* of the Connecticut churches, and were by them accepted. Thus, the Congregationalism of Connecticut and Massachusetts entered upon divergent courses, the Connecticut churches becoming more and more Presbyterian in their system of church polity. This made fellowship and coöperation with the growing Presbyterianism of the middle colonies natural, a fact which later was to have far-reaching influences in the adoption of the Plan of Union of 1801. The Massachusetts churches, on the other hand, continued to follow the old plan of independent Congregationalism.

The tendency of Connecticut Congregationalism to go its own way, more or less independently of the Massachusetts churches, is further evidenced by the founding of Yale College in 1701. The reason given for the establishment of Yale was that the Connecticut churches desired "a nearer and less expensive seat of learning," though undoubtedly the enterprise met the hearty approval of the more conservative ministers, who hoped that the new seat of learning might offset the more liberal and less orthodox tendencies which were developing at Harvard. At first the new college was located at Saybrook, but in 1716 it was permanently removed to New Haven, and two years later it received the name Yale in recognition of the gifts of Elihu Yale, who, though a son of one of the founders of New Haven, had amassed wealth in India where for a number of years he was governor of Madras under the East India Company. His interest in the college had been aroused by the London agent of the New Haven colony, and through a letter written him by Cotton Mather.

New England Congregationalism has now been traced through its first one hundred years and the changes which had gradually come about with the second and third generations have been noted. During the last years of the seventeenth century the question of church polity had occupied the chief attention of the New England ministers, an indication in itself that vital religion was at a low ebb. The religion of the Puritans had become unemotional, with a type of preaching unconducive to revivals and conversion. Out of this general situation had come the necessity for the Half-Way Covenant. The Puritan fathers had held that conversion was solely the work of God, but with the second and third generations, as the number of conversions decreased, gradually the idea began to emerge that there were certain "means" which might be used in putting the soul in a position to receive the regenerating influence of the Spirit of God. Such "means" were owning the covenant, attending divine worship, leading a moral life, reading the Scriptures and prayer. Thus there came to be more and more reliance upon the use of "means" and less and less upon the miraculous power of God, which led to a cold and unemotional religion. Such was the general religious situation in New England when through the preaching and personality of Jonathan Edwards a new and highly emotional reaction set in which we know as the Great Awakening.

CHAPTER V

✣ ✣ ✣

THE FIRST EXPERIMENTS IN RELIGIOUS LIBERTY: RHODE ISLAND AND MARYLAND: BAPTIST AND ROMAN CATHOLIC BEGINNINGS

IT MAY appear to students of American history as unsound to bring together in one chapter two such divergent themes as Rhode Island and Maryland; one a New England and the other a southern colony; one founded by liberal Puritans and the other by Roman Catholics. But the thing which brings them together and makes it appropriate to discuss them in relation to each other is the fact that in each of these colonies, at about the same period, the principle of religious liberty was put into practice. The beginning of each colony centers about the name of an individual, each of great historic interest and importance, Roger Williams and the first Lord Baltimore, and to understand how the first experiments in religious liberty began in America it will be necessary to tell the story of each of these men.

To a large degree religious liberty, or at least a wide toleration, had come to prevail in America by the end of the colonial period. This achievement had come about mostly as a result of circumstance rather than because of any widely accepted principle propounded and urged by colonial leaders. Wide diversity of religious belief, due to the fact that the colonies had attracted numerous settlers fleeing from persecution in the Old World; the necessity of attracting settlers to the great proprietary grants to assure their success, resulting in the letting down of religious bars; and the fact that by the close of the colonial era the great majority of the people were unchurched, due to their long remove from Old World controls, were among the principal causes for this achievement. There were few colonials contending for religious liberty on the basis of principle, and Roger Williams was one of the few. His colony of Rhode Island was the only one to be established squarely on the principle of the separation of church and state, and was the first civil government in the world to achieve complete religious liberty.

1

Roger Williams and his wife embarked in the ship *Lyon* from the port of Bristol in the year 1630 bound for New England and on the fifth of February, 1631, after a tempestuous voyage landed at Boston. At this time Williams was about thirty years of age and is described as "a young minister, godly and zealous, having precious gifts." He was London born, of substantial middle-class parents. Early in his youth he manifested a tendency toward Puritanism, much to the displeasure of his parents, who were loyal Anglicans, members of St. Sepulchre's parish church. An early interest in legal matters led him to visit the Court of the Star Chamber in Wesminster Hall, where he practiced shorthand by taking down the speeches in the court. This brought him to the attention of Sir Edward Coke, destined to become the leading figure in the defense of Parliamentary powers against the claims of the royalists. Sir Edward became young William's patron, secured for him an appointment to Charterhouse School (1621), of which Sir Edward was one of the governors, and two years later young Williams entered Pembroke College, Cambridge, which was Sir Edward's college, where he received his bachelor's degree in 1627. After leaving Cambridge he became the chaplain in the home of a Puritan member of Parliament, Sir Edward Masham, and here he found Mary Barnard, the maid of one of Mrs. Masham's daughters, who became Mrs. Roger Williams in 1629. Thus Williams in his youth had established friendships with influential Puritans, which were to stand him in good stead when he came seeking a charter for his colony of Rhode Island. Before coming to America he had already adopted liberal views in regard to both civil government and the Church and was an avowed Separatist, and possessed that type of mind which would not allow him to keep his views to himself. Indeed, he had hardly landed in the New World before he was in trouble with the authorities for advancing views out of harmony with the principles upon which the Massachusetts colony was established. He refused to join the congregation of the Boston church, for he considered that it had not yet completely separated itself from the corruptions of the English Church, a church which bore on its skirts the blood of saints and martyrs. Accordingly, when a few weeks later he received an invitation to become the pastor of the more liberal church at Salem, he accepted, but on the very day he was to begin his ministry there, the General Court of the colony interfered—a flagrant violation of the Congregational principle of the independence of each congregation—and this interference on the part of the General Court led Williams to depart for Plymouth. Here for two years he resided, earning his living by farming and trading with the Indians. At the same time he served as an assistant to Ralph Smith, the minister, and, says Governor Bradford, "he was freely entertained, according to our poor ability, and exercised his gifts among us; and after some time was admitted a member of the church among us and his teaching well approved."

During his residence in Plymouth Williams became interested in the Indians living in the vicinity, and began a study of Indian languages, and gained an acquaintance with the Narragansett chiefs which was to prove so useful to him when finally he was banished from Massachusetts.

Again in September, 1634, the church in Salem invited Williams to be their pastor, their first minister, Mr. Skelton, having died the previous month. Here, it seems, he preached for two years and during this time won a number of adherents to his views, especially in reference to separation of civil and religious authority. It is difficult for us in this day to understand the controversy which now ensued between Roger Williams and the authorities of Massachusetts. Williams' chief opponent was John Cotton. Though a recent arrival in Boston, Cotton's advice was at once given great weight in arranging the civil and religious affairs of the colony. The charges against Williams were thus summed up by John Cotton, and acknowledged as correct by Roger Williams. He held:

First, That we have not our land by patent from the king, but that the natives are the true owners of it, and that we ought to repent of such a receiving it by patent.

Secondly, That it is not lawful to call a wicked person to swear, (or) pray, as being actions of God's worship.

Thirdly, That it is not lawful to hear any of the ministers of the Parish assemblies in England.

Fourthly, That the civil magistrate's power extends only to the bodies, and goods, and outward state of men.

Williams' position seemed particularly dangerous to the Massachusetts officials, for if the state had nothing to do with religion then, of course, the whole Massachusetts government was founded on a false basis. It is, therefore, clear why the Massachusetts authorities now proceeded against Williams and drove him into exile.

Called before the General Court in July, 1635, to answer to the charge against him, his opinions were declared to be "erroneous and dangerous," and the calling of him to Salem "was judged a great contempt of authority." Williams and the Salem church were given until the next session of the court to consider the matter. In the October session Roger Williams was sentenced to "depart out of our jurisdiction within six weeks." Meanwhile, Williams' health was declining, evidently because of his troubles, and it seems that on this account the court relented to the extent of granting him until spring to leave the colony. Williams withdrew at once from the Salem church, but his friends and followers gathered at his house, where he preached "even of such points as he had been censured for." This was too much for the magistrates, who took steps to have him sent out of the colony at once on a ship then at anchor in Boston bay. A pinnace was sent to Salem to bring him to Boston, "but when they came to his house, they found he had been gone three days before; but whither they could not learn." His wife and two children were left behind, while a mortgage had been placed on his property to raise money for his exile. He then plunged into the forest; being "denied the common air to breathe in, and a civil cohabitation upon the same common earth; yea and also without mercy and human compassion, exposed to winter miseries in a howling wilderness."

After fourteen weeks of wandering, during which he says he did not know "what bread or bed did mean," Williams found hospitality among the Indians and in the late summer of 1636 purchased from them a plot of ground at the mouth of the Mohassuck River where he founded the town of Providence. Shortly afterward these lands were reconveyed to his companions, for it was not long until a considerable number of his followers had found their way thither. In a deed of 1661 Williams thus states his purpose in establishing his colony: "I desired it might be for a shelter for persons distressed for conscience. I then considering the condition of divers of my distressed countrymen, I communicated my said purchase unto my loving friends . . . who then desired to take shelter here with me." Williams and his associates adopted a "plantation covenant" in which they agreed to abide by the will of the majority but "only in civil things." The new colony, however, was without legal standing, for they had as yet no charter from any English authority.

One of the accusations which had been lodged against Roger Williams at Salem was that he was inclined toward Anabaptist views, but there is no evidence that he was a Baptist at this time. In 1638, however, a church was formed at Providence, made up of rebaptized members. A Mr. Holliman who had been a member of the Salem church was selected to rebaptize Williams, and then Williams rebaptized Holliman and ten others. Thus was formed the first Baptist church in America.[1] Williams became pastor of the newly formed church, though only for a few months. He soon became disturbed as to his right to administer the ordinances of the church, conceiving that a true ministry must derive its authority from apostolic succession and, therefore, he could not assume the office of pastor. He, however, continued to hold Baptist views, though he finally came to the conclusion that the church was so corrupt that there could "be no recovery out of that apostacy till Christ shall send forth new apostles to plant churches anew."

A recent interpreter of New England thought has stated that "Roger Williams was the most provocative figure thrown upon the Massachusetts shores by the upheaval in England, the one original thinker among a number of capable social architects." His great contribution, however, was made in the realm of political philosophy rather than as a theologian and his was the first great blow struck at the theory of divine right, for which he substituted the "compact" theory of government. Government to Roger Williams was man-made and rested upon common consent of equal subjects. His idea of the position of religion in the state is thus clearly stated in the preface of his *The Bloudy Tenent of Persecution*.[2]

(1) *God* requireth not an *uniformity* of *Religion* to be *inacted* and *inforced* in any *civill state;* which inforced *uniformity* (sooner or later) is the greatest occasion of *civill Warre, ravishing of conscience, persecution* of *Jesus Christ* in

---

[1] The usual contention that the members of the first Baptist church were baptized by immersion in 1638 is challenged by Professor R. E. E. Harkness in an article in the *Crozer Quarterly* (Vol. V, 1928, pp. 440-460) entitled "Principles of the Early Baptists of England and America," in which he contends that the rebaptizing which took place in 1638 was not by immersion and that Williams opposed the new manner of dipping when it was first introduced some years later.

[2] Vol. III, p. 76.

his servants, and of the *hypocrisie* and destruction of millions of souls. (2) It is the will and command of *God,* that . . . a *permission* of the most *Paganish, Jewish, Turkish,* or *Anti-christian consciences* and *worships,* bee granted to *all* men in all *Nations and Countries*: and they are only to be fought against with the *Sword* which is onely (in *Soule matters*) *able* to *conquer,* to wit, the *Sword of Gods Spirit,* the *Word of God.* (3) True *civility* and *Christianity* may both *flourish* in a *state* or *Kingdome,* notwithstanding the *permission* of divers and contrary consciences, either of Jew or *Gentile.*

How different is our opinion of Roger Williams today from that of Cotton Mather who compared him to a certain windmill in the Low Countries, which

whirling with such extraordinary violence, by reason of a violent storm then blowing; the stone at length by its rapid motion became so intensely hot, as to fire the mill, from whence the flames, being dispersed by the high winds, did set the whole town on fire. But I can tell my reader, about twenty-five years before this, there was a whole country in America like to be set on fire by the rapid motion of a windmill, in the head of one particular man. Know then that about the year 1630, arrived here one Roger Williams, who being a preacher that had less *light* than *fire* in him, hath by his own sad example, preached unto us the danger of that evil which the apostle mentions in *Rom.* 10-2. *They have a zeal, but not according to knowledge.*

The colony of Rhode Island was eventually made up of three elements, the first being Roger Williams' Providence plantation. A second element was made up of another group of religious exiles from Massachusetts—Anne Hutchinson, with her husband, her brother-in-law Mr. Wheelwright, and their followers—who settled what is now Portsmouth and Newport; while a third group, led by a well-educated but combative individual, Samuel Gorton, founded a colony on the west shore of Narragansett Bay to which was given the name Warwick. In 1644 Roger Williams was sent to England to secure authorization from the Puritan authorities for the Narragansett settlers to form a government. Three years later (1647) it was organized—embodying the principles advocated by Roger Williams—separation of church and state—no church membership qualification required for voters, while every man was to be protected in the "peaceful and quiet enjoyment of lawful right and liberty," . . . not withstanding our different consciences touching the truth as it is in Jesus."

Mrs. Anne Hutchinson, like Williams, was born out of due time. In England she and her husband had been parishioners of John Cotton, and according to Winthrop was "a woman of ready wit and a bold spirit," who "brought over with her two dangerous errors." Some time after her arrival in Boston she began the practice of holding meetings at her house where the sermons preached the Sunday previous were discussed and the ministers criticized, and finally she seemed to have evolved a doctrine of her own in which she professed a direct divine inspiration. All the ministers in Boston, she contended, were preaching a covenant of works, except John Cotton and her brother-in-law, Mr. Wheelwright, who was at the time preaching as a supply minister in a branch of one of the Boston churches. Over against the covenant of works she set the covenant of grace, by which she meant that every man had direct communication between himself and his Maker, while the covenant of works meant conformity to a prescribed order as laid down by the minister.

At first Mrs. Hutchinson found powerful supporters in John Cotton and Sir Henry Vane, the governor, and the majority of the Boston church members were on her side. As long as Vane was governor Mrs. Hutchinson was safe, but in the midst of the excitement of the controversy an election resulted in victory for the conservatives and Winthrop once more became governor, though the three representatives from Boston to the General Court were favorable to Mrs. Hutchinson. Wheelwright was first brought before the court in March, but his case was deferred until November when he was declared guilty of sedition and contempt and was banished from the colony. Mrs. Hutchinson was next tried, and her conviction was a foregone conclusion. She too was banished from the colony and excommunicated from the church. The words of excommunication pronounced upon Mrs. Hutchinson by the Rev. John Wilson reveal the enormity of her offense in the eyes of the Massachusetts theocrats:

Forasmuch as you, Mrs. Hutchinson, have highly transgressed and offended and forasmuch as you have so many ways troubled the church with your errors and have drawn away many a poor soul, and have upheld your revelations; and forasmuch as you have made a lie, etc. Therefore in the name of our Lord Jesus Christ and in the name of the Church I do not only pronounce you worthy to be cast out, but I do cast you out and in the name of Christ I do deliver you up to Satan, that you may learn no more to blaspheme, to seduce and to lie, and I do account you from this time forth to be a Heathen and a Publican and so to be held of all the brethern and sisters of this congregation and of all others; therefore I command you in the name of Christ Jesus and of his Church as a Leper to withdraw yourself out of the Congregation; that as formerly you have despised and contemned the Holy Ordinances of God, and turned back on them, so may you now have no part in them nor benefit from them.

With Mrs. Hutchinson into exile went numerous of her followers and others who were out of sympathy with the intolerance of the Massachusetts authorities. Most important of those who now went to Rhode Island and established Portsmouth and Newport was Dr. John Clarke. We know very little about the early history of this talented and interesting man, who had an intellectual outlook and a breadth of view unusual for his day, but he arrived in Boston in 1637 just at the time the excitement was at its height over Mrs. Anne Hutchinson. He immediately identified himself with the defeated supporters of the Covenant of grace and was at once recognized as their natural leader. The year Newport was founded (1638) a church was established with Clarke as teaching elder. Whether this was a Baptist church from the first cannot be determined, though by 1648 it is known that there was a Baptist church at Newport with fifteen members. In 1651 Clarke was sent to England by the colonists to secure a new charter, and there for twelve years he remained, finding it impossible to gain the charter under the Protectorate. Finally in 1663, under Charles II, a new charter was obtained which declared that no person should be "anywise molested, punished, disquieted or called in question for any differences of opinion in matters of religion" provided he did not disturb the "civil peace." Roger Williams was still living when the new charter was secured, embodying his great principle of "soul liberty." On Clarke's return to Rhode Island he served two terms as deputy governor, retiring to private life in 1676. During his long residence in England he wrote *Ill News from New England* in which he advocated liberty of conscience, a book which deserves to take rank with Roger Williams' *The Bloudy Tenent of Persecution.* His services to the colony and to the cause of religious liberty were quite as great, though less known, as were those of Roger Williams.

With the establishment of the first Baptist churches in Rhode Island, Baptist views began to make their appearance in the older Puritan colonies, and among the members of the Congregational churches. Cases of parents withholding their children from infant baptism became increasingly common so that in 1644 the General Court of Massachusetts enacted a statute providing that whosoever "shall either openly condemn or oppose the baptizing of infants, or go about secretly to seduce others from the approbation or use thereof, or shall purposely depart the congregation at the ministration of the ordinances, etc. . . . shall be sentenced to banishment." The most conspicuous case of this kind was that of Henry Dunster, the president of Harvard College from 1641 to 1654.

About 1650 Dunster had become convinced that infant baptism was wrong, and in 1653 when his fourth child was born he failed to present it at the proper time for baptism. His new views he now set forth in several sermons, which naturally caused much excitement. Dunster had been so successful in conducting the affairs of the college that the assistants were reluctant to proceed against him. In 1654 nine of the leading ministers held a conference with Dunster and a few months later the General Court issued an order commanding the overseers of the college not to permit any to teach "that have manifested themselves unsound in the faith." In June Dunster offered his resignation, but expressed his willingness to continue the work "for some weeks or months" until his successor could be secured. His resignation was not accepted at this time, but in the autumn he interrupted the service in the Cambridge church to make a statement as to his position on infant baptism, which he gathered under five points. This was the last straw. His resignation was now accepted and he was indicted for disturbing worship, was tried and condemned to receive an admonition from the General Court. Dunster spent the last five years of his life as pastor of the church at Scituate in the Plymouth colony and was succeeded at Harvard by Charles Chauncy who had been the minister at Scituate.

The most notable case of persecution of Baptists by Massachusetts authorities occurred in 1651 near Lynn, where John Clarke and Obadiah Holmes had gone to minister to an aged Baptist, William Witter, and also perhaps to encourage others who where inclined toward Baptist principles. Here on a Sabbath they were holding services in Witter's home when two constables broke into the house, arrested Holmes and Clarke, who were haled before the court, where they were fined, and in default of which they were to be whipped. A friend of Clarke's paid his fine and he was set free against his protest. Holmes, however, was "whipped unmercifully" in the streets of Boston. There were numerous other cases of persecution, though it must be said in some justification of the Massachusetts authorities that much of what both Baptists and

Quakers did would, if done today, have brought them before the police court. Thus Witter had been before the court in 1643 for saying that infant baptism was a "badge of the whore," and three years later he was again in trouble for saying that "they who stayed while a child is baptized doe worshipp the Dyvell."

The first Baptist church in Massachusetts was formed at Rehobeth in 1663, by John Myles, a Welsh Baptist minister who had been driven to America by the Act of Uniformity of 1662. No attention was given to this church by the authorities until 1667 when Myles and James Brown were haled before the court "for setting up a public meeting without the knowledge and approbation of the Court, to the disturbance of the peace of the place." They were assessed a fine of £5 and required to remove their church to a distance from the church of the standing order, so as not to disturb the peace of the church and town. The same year a place was set aside for them by the court near the Rhode Island border, which was called Swansea after their Welsh home. Here the church prospered and has maintained an uninterrupted existence to this day. A Baptist church was formed in Boston in 1665 under the leadership of Thomas Gould, who like his friend President Dunster had refused to present his child for baptism. In the above year a church was formed in his house which almost immediately fell under the wrath of the officials. Three of its members, Gould, Turner and Forman were tried and convicted and sentenced to leave the colony, and if they were found in the colony after a certain time they were to be imprisoned without bail. The church was forbidden to assemble again on pain of imprisonment and banishment. In spite of such harsh measures the number of Baptists increased and in 1678 a Baptist meetinghouse was begun in Boston. In answer to this bold step the General Court ordered the marshal to nail up the doors, which he proceeded to do. This proved to be the last serious persecution of Baptists in Boston, and the doors remained closed but one Sunday.

The controversy over the Half-Way Covenant served to further the development of Baptist sentiment in New England, since the question under discussion was the matter of allowing children of unconverted parents to be baptized. Many began to ask what is the use of infant baptism since it confers no special privilege? Why not, therefore, postpone baptism until after a personal confession is possible?

As the seventeenth century neared its close persecution of Baptists gradually died out. The English Congregational ministers protested against the intolerance of Massachusetts, stating that dissenting interests in England were greatly injured by it, and even Charles II rebuked the Massachusetts authorities for their cruel persecutions. By the end of the century the Puritan theocracy had proven to be an impossible form of government and the new charter of 1691, uniting Plymouth and Massachusetts Bay, granted "Liberty of conscience to all Christians, except Papists," but "liberty of conscience was so interpreted as to allow the taxation of dissenters for the support of Congregational ministers." It was not until 1728 that an act was passed exempting Anabaptists and Quakers "from being taxed for and toward the support of" ministers, but in order to secure exemption Baptists were required to obtain certificates signed by "two principal members of that persuasion" which must be presented to the town officials.

The most important Baptist center during the colonial period was not in New England, however, but in the middle colonies and especially in Pennsylvania and New Jersey where a large degree of religious freedom was allowed from the first. Philadelphia was the center of this group of churches, and in 1707 the first Baptist Association in America met at Philadelphia with five churches represented. In 1742 this body adopted a strong Calvinistic confession of faith which is considered a turning point in the history of the American Baptists. Up to this time the Arminian Baptists had been more numerous, especially in New England, but from this time forward the majority of American Baptists have been Calvinistic in their theology, and the Philadelphia Association became and remained the strongest and most influential Baptist body. In the southern colonies Baptist churches were barely getting started by the middle of the eighteenth century; the rapid extension of the Baptists into the southern colonies, therefore, belongs to a later period in this story.

In 1740 there were but eight Baptist churches in Massachusetts, four in Connecticut and eleven in Rhode Island. In the Philadelphia Association in 1762 were twenty-nine churches, embracing Pennsylvania, New York, Virginia and Maryland; while a Baptist church had been formed in Charleston, South Carolina, in 1684. Most of these churches owed their origin to small groups of men and women who had been Baptists before coming to America, most of whom were either English or Welsh. To term Roger Williams the founder of the Baptist Church in

America, and the church he founded "the venerable mother of American Baptist churches," as is often done, is historically incorrect, for after all the part played by Williams in American Baptist history is extremely small, and the church he founded bore no living children. The relation of Roger Williams and the American Baptists to the beginnings of the fight for religious liberty in America, however, has a deep significance, for standing first among the five principles of all American Baptists is "Complete separation of Church and State," and the part they played in the triumph of that great principle is of greatest importance.

II

It is a strange anomaly that the first colony in America to be established embodying the principle of religious toleration should have been founded by a Roman Catholic. It must be understood, however, that the founding of Maryland was not due in any way whatever to the Roman Catholic Church, but was solely the result of the plan and intention of one Roman Catholic nobleman—a recent convert—George Calvert, the first Lord Baltimore.

Lord Baltimore's purpose in establishing a colony embodying the principle of religious liberty was vastly different from that of Roger Williams in the establishment of Rhode Island. Roger Williams was a political philosopher, and based his position on great fundamental truths. To him a great principle was at stake, and for that principle he was willing to and did undergo every danger and hardship. Roger Williams was a prophet of the coming of the new day of religious liberty and the separation of church and state; Lord Baltimore was neither a political philosopher nor a prophet. He was rather a practical and hard-headed investor in a great land venture, in which his whole fortune was at stake. He founded Maryland upon the principle of religious toleration in spite of his religion rather than because of it. He knew well enough that ruin would come speedily to his vast enterprise in Maryland if his colony were planted in the interests solely of his church and his coreligionists. It has already been noted that Catholics in England of his day did not belong to the migrating class, and if Baltimore were to sell his land he must depend upon the non-Catholics, and he evidently did not propose to allow his "religious predilections to interfere with business."

George Calvert, first Lord Baltimore, was a man of importance in the government of England in the reigns of James I and Charles I, and was greatly interested in all colonization and trading enterprises. He was a member of both the London and Plymouth companies as well as the East India Company; was a member of Parliament and one of the Secretaries of State. His political career, however, was closed when be became a Catholic, since the oath taken by officeholders required renunciation of the authority of the Pope. He succeeded, however, in spite of his conversion to Catholicism, in retaining the good will and friendship of Charles I who made him an Irish peer as Lord Baltimore.

His first attempt at colonization was in Newfoundland in 1620, which after nine years of hardship and the loss of £30,000 he abandoned with the thought of trying again in Virginia. Here his conversion to Catholicism blocked his way, for in answer to the announcement of his intention to "plant and dwell" among them, the authorities of Virginia welcomed him on the same terms with themselves, that is, they presented for his acceptance the oath of supremacy, to which as a true Catholic he could not subscribe. He now sailed back to England, where his influence at court finally was successful in securing from the king a separate province, granted as a hereditary possession, and thus this Catholic nobleman became the founder of the first proprietary English colony, a type of grant which was to become most common by the end of the century. The territory given Baltimore was claimed by Virginia, but the loss of its charter in 1624 left it no legal grounds for procedure.

Death ended the first Lord Baltimore's colonization venture, but his eldest son, Cecil Calvert, inherited his father's title and proceeded with the enterprise. The second Lord Baltimore was even more hard-headed and practical than his father and with a high degree of tact carried out the colonization scheme, and for forty years ruled the colony at long range with skill and economic success. By far the largest part of the settlers from the very first (1634) were Protestants, and in the instructions to his brother Leonard who came out as the first governor his religious plans are made clear. Care was to be taken by the officials "to preserve unity & peace among all the passangers" while "no scandall nor offence" was "to be given to any of the Protestants." They were to be careful not to parade the Roman Catholic religion before the non-Catholics and as far as practicable their peculiar practices were to be conducted "as privately as possible." From the above instructions it is easy to infer that the Lord Proprietor knew well enough the difficulties he faced and desired to run no unnecessary risk of losing his charter.

Maryland prospered moderately from the first, for Leonard Calvert went about the work in hand in a very orderly way; and he was wise enough also to profit by the mistakes of Virginia. The first year corn and tobacco were planted in some Indian fields which they had purchased, and other land was cleared. The location of the settlement was healthy and well drained and at the end of the first summer they were able to send a shipload of corn to New England in exchange for fish.

The colony was thrown open to all religious groups—Anglicans, Puritans and Catholics—the charter stating that "all liege subjects of the king" might freely transport themselves and their families to Maryland, though the government was largely under Catholic control, since most of the large manors were owned by the Catholic friends of the proprietor. On the first expedition two earnest Jesuit priests were quietly added "as it passed the Isle of Wight," and for some time were the only representatives of religion in the colony. These priests ministered faithfully to the settlers and among the neighboring Indians, and soon most of the Protestants in the colony were Roman Catholic, and even converts were won from among the Indians. This surprising success on the part of the Jesuits was soon reported to the English Protestant authorities, which brought a rebuke from the proprietor, who now proceeded to limit the authority of the priests, annulled the grants of land made to the missionaries by the Indian chiefs, and finally had the Jesuits replaced by secular priests, and a few years later (1643) even made overtures to secure Puritan immigration from Massachusetts.

The oath prescribed by Lord Baltimore in 1636, to be taken by the Maryland governors, shows plainly his insistence upon maintaining religious toleration in the colony:

I will not myself or any other, directly or indirectly, trouble, molest, or discountenance any person professing to believe in Jesus Christ, for or in respect to religion: I will make no difference of persons in conferring offices, favors, or rewards, for or in respect of religion: but merely as they shall be found faithful and well deserving, and endued with moral virtues and abilities: my aim shall be public unity, and if any person or officer shall molest any person professing to believe in Jesus Christ, on account of his religion, I will protect the person molested, and punish the offender.[3]

[3] Tiffany, p. 58.

While the religious toleration authorized in Maryland by Cecil Calvert was quite evidently primarily based upon practical and business reasons, yet undoubtedly "it was also the outcome of his convictions and kindly nature."

As the number of Protestants in the colony increased, they naturally tended to become more aggressive, which was especially true of that group of Puritans who had been given refuge in Maryland when they were driven from Virginia. Soon they had become bitter antagonists of the proprietor and all his Catholic subjects. The religious troubles brewing in Maryland were brought to the point of explosion by the breaking out of the Civil Wars in England. With the triumph of the Parliamentary party and the establishment of the protectorate, the Maryland situation was bound to be profoundly affected. At this juncture, in order to avoid criticism and allay suspicion of his colony, Lord Baltimore appointed a Protestant governor (1649), William Stone, with instructions to continue the policy of religious toleration, and urged upon the Maryland Assembly the passage of an Act of Tolera-tion. The assembly passing the measure was composed of both Catholics and Protestants, though the proprietor's wish in the matter was quite probably the deciding factor.

Since the passage of this act marks an important epoch in the history of religious liberty, it is well to consider it in some detail. The act does not go far enough to be accounted ideal, since it provides toleration only for Christians, while those who deny "the Holy Trinity or the Godhead of any of the Three Persons etc. was to be punished with death, and confiscation of lands and goods." The great variety of re-ligious groups in Maryland at the time may be inferred by the third provision of the act, which promises punishment by fine or whipping and imprisonment for any person who "in a reproachful manner" calls any person within the Province a "Heretic, Schismatic, Idolater, Inde-pendent, Presbyterian, Popish Priest, Jesuit, Jesuited Papist, Lutheran, Calvinist, Anabaptist, Brownist, Antinomian, Barrowist, Roundhead, Separatist, or any other Name or term, in a reproachful manner." The fifth is the most important provision of the act, which reads:

And whereas the enforcing of the conscience in matter of religion, hath frequently fallen out to be of dangerous consequence in those common wealths where it has been practiced, and for the more quiet and peaceable government of this Province, and the better to preserve mutual love and unity among the inhabitants, etc. No person or persons whatsoever, within this Province, or the Islands, Ports, Harbours, Creeks, or Havens, thereunto belonging, professing to believe in Jesus Christ, shall from henceforth be in any ways troubled, molested, or discountenanced, for in respect of his or her Religion, nor in the free exercise thereof, within this Province, or the Islands thereunto belonging, nor any way compelled to the belief or exercise of any other religion, against his or her consent, so as they be not unfaithful to the Lord Proprietor, or molest or conspire against the civil government established, or to be established, in this Province, under him or his heirs.

The punishment for the violation of this act was treble damages to the wronged party and fine for each offense, to be divided between the proprietor and the damaged person, and in default of payment, whipping and imprisonment.

But unfortunately the passage of this act did not satisfy the aggressive Puritans, and their dissatisfaction was the more intensified when, in the absence of the Protestant governor "his Catholic deputy" issued a proclamation declaring allegiance to King Charles II, then in exile. This untactful move brought things to an immediate crisis and a Parliamentary Commission took over the management of Maryland affairs, and when Governor Stone refused to recognize the Parliamentary title to the province, he was removed and the government placed in the hands of a committee. The Protestant party were now in complete control in Maryland and proceeded at once to change the Act of Toleration "excluding from its benefits practically everybody except the Puritans." In this, however, the Maryland Puritans failed to receive the support of the Lord Protector Cromwell, now in power in England, and in 1657, when the proprietor once more regained control, the Toleration Act was again put in effect. Thus the Protestants again became the aggrieved party, claiming that although the Act of Toleration was in effect they failed to receive their share of the offices.

The overthrow of James II in the revolution of 1688 brought Maryland affairs to a new crisis. Though the new king and queen, William and Mary, were proclaimed in Maryland by the proprietor's government, yet the whole general situation was favorable to the Protestants, and the trend of events played into their hands. A Protestant Association was now formed under the leadership of a cheap agitator, John Coode, and soon an insurrection was under way which succeeded in seizing the government. Justification for the insurrection was placed on the ground that a Protestant government was needed in view of an impending war with a Catholic nation. A convention made up of members of the insurgent group was held in 1690 in which a committee was appointed to carry on the government until a royal governor could be sent over. For two years Sir Lionel Copley, a member of the Established Church, was governor and two years later (1692) Maryland was declared a royal colony and the same year the Maryland Assembly passed an act establishing the Church of England in the colony. This act was not approved by the Board of Trade and Plantations, and it was not until 1702 that the establishment act became a law.

At the time of the establishment of the Anglican Church in Maryland the Protestant element made up more than three-fourths of the population. In 1669 there were but two Catholic priests in the colony to minister to perhaps two thousand communicants. In 1673 two Franciscans founded a mission in Maryland and four years later three other Franciscans and three Jesuits arrived. This increase in the Catholic forces soon led to the establishment of a Jesuit school in the colony, while Catholic work expanded somewhat into Pennsylvania and in the seaboard settlements north of Maryland. These feeble Roman Catholic beginnings give little indication of the vast expansion of Roman Catholicism in America, which was to proceed largely from Maryland, in the two centuries to follow.

CHAPTER VI

✤   ✤   ✤

RELIGIOUS DIVERSITY IN THE MIDDLE COLONIES: DUTCH REFORMED, AND ENGLISH QUAKERS

THE middle colonies, from the very first, contained a great mixture of people. At the time of the colonization of America, Holland was the most liberal country in the world and became a refuge for persecuted sects. Representatives from almost every country in Europe had taken up their residence in this little free country, as had the English Pilgrims in 1607, and when Holland began to obtain colonies of her own it was but natural that the population of her colonies should resemble that of the mother country. When the English captured New Netherlands in 1664 it was reported that fourteen languages were spoken on Long Island, and ten years later eighteen nationalities were to be found in the colony of New York. William Penn's colony of Pennsylvania and the other Quaker colonies, New Jersey and Delaware, dominated as they were by the liberal ideas of Penn and his associates, likewise attracted a great variety of peoples. The Dutch, the Swedes, the Welsh, English Quakers, and the several German groups, and last of all the Scotch-Irish, were attracted to the middle colonies. Out of this great variety of people came a corresponding variety of religious bodies. The most important of these religious groups was the Dutch Reformed, which was the state church of the Netherlands; the English Quakers, the Swedish Lutherans, the German Reformed, Mennonites, Dunkers, Schwenkfelders, Welsh Baptists, German Lutherans, Moravians and Scotch-Irish Presbyterians. It is the purpose of this and the following chapters to tell of the beginnings in America of these several religious bodies.

The Dutch colony of New Netherlands, like several of the early English colonies, was established by a trading company known as the

Dutch West India Company. This company received its charter in 1621, giving it the privilege of trading and founding colonies in America. Two years later, in spite of the protests of the English against the Dutch invasion of territory which they claimed, thirty families of Dutch and Walloon Protestants came out to America and two posts were established. One near the present site of Camden, New Jersey, was called Fort Nassau and the other, where Albany now stands, received the name Fort Orange. By 1625 there were two hundred people in the colony and in 1626 Peter Minuit, the first and the best of the Dutch governors, was sent out as director general. Soon after his arrival he made the famous purchase of Manhattan Island from the Indians, and a third fort was built on the southern tip of the island which was named New Amsterdam.

The Dutch came primarily as traders and the fur trade with the Indians was their chief interest. For the carrying on of such trade peace had to be maintained with the Indians and the Dutch were necessarily scattered over a large area. Nor did the Dutch come out to America in great numbers, largely for the reason that the long wars with the Spaniards had depleted the population of the Netherlands and the great East Indian trading and colonizing interests of the Dutch left comparatively few people for their American enterprise. When the Dutch colonies passed into English hands they contained not more than seven thousand inhabitants. Throughout the entire period of Dutch control of New Netherlands trade and commercial interests dominated the colony, to the neglect of education and religion.

It was not until 1628, five years after the coming of the first colonists, that a minister was brought out, though two years before (1626) two comforters of the sick came in response to the plea of a few anxious souls. These two lay workers not only visited among the people, but also held informal services in a large room above the horse mill which had been fitted up by its owner to serve as a place of worship. This building even boasted a tower in which were placed bells captured by the company's fleet in the Spanish colony of Porto Rico.

The Dutch West India Company declared the Reformed religion established in their colonies, and ministers, schoolmasters and sick visitors were maintained at their expense. The ministers sent out from time to time were approved by the Classis, or Presbytery, of Amsterdam and the Classis continued to exercise ecclesiastical authority over the Reformed Church in America throughout most of the period of the colonies.

The first Reformed minister to arrive in New Amsterdam was the Rev. Jonas Michaelius (1628), who has left us an interesting account of religious conditions in the colony at the time of his coming. He says:

> Our coming here was agreeable to all, and I hope, by the grace of the Lord, that my services will not be unfruitful. The people for the most part, are free, somewhat rough, and loose; but I find in almost all of them both love and respect toward me. . . .

Michaelius organized a church the year of his arrival, with the director of the company, Minuit, and the storekeeper as elders. The minister thus describes the first communion service:

> We have had at the first administration of the Lord's Supper full fifty communicants—not without great joy and comfort for so many—Walloons and Dutch; of whom a portion made their first confession of faith before us and others exhibited their church certificates. Others had forgotten to bring their certificates with them, not thinking that a church would be formed and established here; and some who brought them had lost them, unfortunately, in a general conflagration; but they were admitted upon the satisfactory testimony of others to whom they were known, and also upon their daily good deportment, since we cannot observe strictly all the usual formalities in making a beginning under such circumstances.

Michaelius found that the French-speaking Walloons understood very little of the service in Dutch and he accordingly arranged to administer the Lord's Supper to them in the French language using the French mode. He tells us that the discourse preceding the sacrament he had before him in writing for, he says, "I could not trust myself extemporaneously."

Just how long Michaelius remained in New Amsterdam is not known. In 1637 he was in Holland, as the Classis was then discussing sending him back to America. It is probable that he had left New Netherlands previous to the coming out of Everardus Bogardus in 1633, who was the second minister to arrive in the colony, coming in the same ship with the second governor, Van Twiller.

Bogardus remained in the colony under the incompetent and corrupt administrations of the next two governors—Van Twiller (1633-1638) and Kieft (1638-1647)—and it is to his lasting credit that throughout the whole time he was in constant conflict with them both, because of his outspoken denunciation of their corruption and mismanagement. During these years of discord, however, two meetinghouses were built, the first a barnlike structure of wood, while under Kieft (1642) a stone church was erected within the fort. This building was seventy-two feet long by fifty wide and its cost was two thousand five hundred guilders. A contemporary has left us the following account of how the director took subscriptions for this church:

> The Director then resolved to build a church, and at the place where it suited him; but he was in want of money and was at a loss how to obtain it. It happened about this time that the minister, Everardus Bogardus gave his stepdaughter in marriage; and the occasion of the wedding the Director considered a good opportunity for his purpose. So after the fourth or fifth round of drinking, he set about the business, and he himself showing a liberal example let the wedding guests subscribe what they were willing to give towards the church. All then with light heads subscribed largely, competing with one another; and although some well repented it when they recovered their senses, they were nevertheless compelled to pay—nothing could avail to prevent it.

A few years after the establishment of New Amsterdam the West India Company, in order to stimulate Dutch settlement of America, issued what was known as the "Charter of Freedoms and Exemptions." This provided that anyone bringing over fifty adult colonists within a space of four years was to become a "patroon" or lord of the manor, and would receive a great landed estate on one of the two great rivers of the colony. Each "patroon" was to support a minister, and several ministers were brought out under this arrangement. The best known of all the patroons was Killian Van Rensselaer, a wealthy Amsterdam jeweler whose patroonship was a vast estate near the present city of Albany. And of all the ministers brought over by the patroons John Van Mekelenburg, better known as Megapolensis, the minister at Rensselaerwyck, is the best and most favorably known. Van Rensselaer agreed to provide the minister with a residence and guaranteed him a salary of one thousand guilders a year for six years and two hundred guilders additional for the three following years, if his services were satisfactory. Megapolensis worked faithfully among the Indians as well as with the settlers. The second year after his arrival a church was built. He learned the Mohawk tongue and was able to preach to the Indians, some of whom joined his church, and the claim is made that he was the first Protestant missionary to the Indians.

During Megapolensis' stay as the minister at Rensselaerwyck he was largely instrumental in saving the life of Father Jogues, a French Jesuit missionary, who had been captured by the Mohawks and brought to Fort Orange. Here the Dutch commander and Megapolensis befriended him and kept him concealed until they could send him to New Amsterdam. We are indebted to Father Jogues' stay at Fort Orange and New Amsterdam for a particularly interesting description of New Netherlands. Concerning the religious situation at New Amsterdam, he says: "No religion is publicly exercised but the Calvinist, and orders are to admit none but Calvinists. But this is not observed, for there are, besides Calvinists, in the colony, Catholics, English Puritans, Lutherans, Anabaptists,—here called Mennonists." Of the colony at Fort Orange Father Jogues says: There is "a colony sent here by this Rensselaer, who is the patroon. This colony is composed of about a hundred persons, who reside in some twenty-five or thirty houses, built along the river. In the principal house resides the patroon's agent; the minister has his part, in which service is performed. . . ."

Under the incompetent administrations of Van Twiller and Kieft the affairs of the West India Company had gone from bad to worse and the company was on the verge of bankruptcy with assets of five millions of florens less than its liabilities. The last governor, Peter Stuyvesant, was of different stripe from his two predecessors, for he was an earnest and capable man and an elder in the Reformed Church, though inclined to be arbitrary in his administration. It was during his administration that the people rose and demanded a share in the government, and the governor was compelled to yield, though much against his will. Under Stuyvesant the affairs of the company began to revive; trade increased and people began to come in from surrounding colonies, some of them driven from New England by the exclusive religious policy there. These new settlers were promised "liberty of conscience according to the custom and manner of Holland," with the result that the religious groups became even more numerous than the racial elements in the colony.

During the latter part of Stuyvesant's administration, probably without the knowledge of the directors of the company, a policy of religious exclusiveness was adopted and there was some persecution, especially of the Dutch Lutherans and the Quakers. In this policy Stuyvesant was supported by the ministers of the Dutch Church, who in 1656 made a formal complaint to the governor against the great increase of sects, which led to the passage of an ordinance forbidding preaching by un-qualified persons and the holding of conventicles. The law was en-forced by fines and imprisonment, which led to complaints directly to the West India Company and to the States-General. The net result of the whole matter was that the company finally disapproved Stuyvesant's action, though their reason for so doing was based on their desire not to hamper the economic welfare of the colony nor discourage settlers.

The company's rebuke to Stuyvesant was brought about through his attempt to put a stop to Quaker worship at Flushing, Long Island. John Bowne, a Friend, had built a new house at Flushing and he and his wife called in their fellow members of the Society of Friends to wor-ship. Bowne was arrested and finally banished. He went to Holland and appeared before the directors of the company who were, by Bowne, so fully convinced that Stuyvesant's policy was wrong that they wrote a letter to him stating, among other things:

Wherefore it is our opinion that some connivance would be useful; and that the consciences of men, at least ought to remain free and unshackled. Let every one be unmolested as long as he is modest, moderate, his political conduct irreproachable, and as long as he does not offend others or oppose the government. The maxim of moderation has always been the guide of our magistrates in this city, and the consequence has been that people have flocked from every land to this asylum. Tread thus in their steps, and we doubt not you will be blessed.

This put an end to Stuyvesant's policy of persecution, and when two years later (1665) Bowne returned to America and met Stuyvesant as a private citizen, the old ex-governor seemed heartily ashamed of what he had done, as well any self-respecting Dutchman might, in the face of the two hundred year record of religious toleration in the Netherlands.

While the Dutch were busy with their American colony on the Hud-son, a rival colony appeared on the Delaware, or South, River. These rivals were the Swedes. Like the Dutch, the Swedes proceeded in their colonizing project through the medium of a commercial company, which had been chartered in 1626, but because of the participation of the great Swedish king, Gustavus Adolphus, in the Thirty Years' War, and finally his tragic death, they were not able to send out colonists until 1638. Peter Minuit, the first governor of the Dutch colony, offered his services to the Swedes and it was under his leadership that the first expedition of fifty colonists set out. Land was purchased of the Indians, though it was already claimed by the Dutch, and a fort was built near the present site of Wilmington, Delaware, and called Fort Christina. Altogether the Swedes sent out twelve expeditions, but New Sweden never became a numerous or prosperous colony. With the first group of Swedish settlers came the Rev. Reorus Torkillus, who has the distinction of being the first Lutheran minister in North America. Torkillus died in Christina in 1643 of a sickness that swept away great numbers of the settlers.

The Rev. John Campanius came out the year Torkillus died, and he not only ministered faithfully to the settlers, but also undertook the work of Christianizing the Indians in the vicinity. His work among the Indians was probably induced by a regulation of the great Swedish chancellor, Oxenstiern, which stated:

The wild nations, bordering upon all other sides, the Governor shall understand how to treat with all humanity and respect, that no violence or wrong be done to them by Her Royal Majesty or her subjects aforesaid; but he shall rather, at every opportunity, exert himself that the same wild people may gradually be instructed in the truths and worship of the Christian religion, and in other ways brought to civilization and good government, and in this manner, properly guided.

Campanius learned the Delaware tongue and translated Luther's Small Catechism, though it was not printed until 1696 and then at the personal expense of King Charles XI. On Campanius' return to Sweden other ministers came out, and at the time of the Dutch capture of New Sweden in 1655, at least two Lutheran churches had been established. Nearly thirty years later when William Penn founded his colony of Pennsylvania he found from five to seven hundred Swedes living on the Delaware. They were an honest, industrious and religious people, and today two of their churches still stand as monuments to the honorable part they played in the early religious history of America, old Gloria Dei Church in South Philadelphia and Old Swedes Church in Wilmington, Delaware, at the southern end of which lie the remains of the first Lutheran pastor, Torkillus.

The Dutch capture of the Swedish colony was followed a few years later (1664) by the English capture of New Amsterdam, and the complete overthrow of Dutch authority. In March, 1664, King Charles II had granted all the territory which the Dutch claimed in America to his brother, the Duke of York, and during the summer the new proprietor sent a fleet to seize the territory from the Dutch. Governor Stuyvesant was completely unprepared to defend the colony, though he vowed he would never surrender, but he finally was persuaded to listen to the advice of the ministers and others, and the colony was turned over to the English without striking a blow. Article VIII of the terms of surrender reads:

The Dutch here shall enjoy the liberty of their consciences in divine worship and in church discipline.

The Dutch minister at New Amsterdam informed the Classis of Amsterdam of the surrender in a letter dated September 15, 1664. Toward the end of his letter he states:

It is stipulated in the articles [of surrender] that the religion and doctrine shall continue as heretofore, and the ministers shall remain. We could not abandon our congregations and hearers. We judged that we must continue with them, for a time at least, and perform our offices, lest they should become entirely scattered and grow wild.

Nor did he forget to add·

The West India Company owes me quite a sum, which I hope and desire will be paid.

At the time of the surrender of the colony there were six Dutch ministers in America and thirteen churches. Altogether thirteen ministers had come out from 1628 to 1664. For many years the Dutch Reformed Church remained the strongest religious group in the colony, though, of course, it no longer received special recognition from the government and could not be classed as a dissenting body. From the time of the surrender until 1696 the status of the Dutch Reformed Church was uncertain. The early English governors seemed to consider the Dutch ministers as entitled to receive support from taxation. In 1670 the governor guaranteed a salary to any Dutch minister who would come over to assist the Dutch minister, Drisius, at New York, and in response to this promise the first recruit after the surrender arrived from Holland.

The best of all the early English governors of New York was the Irish Roman Catholic, Governor Dongan (1682-1688). He was an honest and broad-minded man and on his arrival announced to the Dutch minister at New York, upon whom he called, that the Duke intended to allow liberty of conscience. During this administration numerous

French settlers arrived, driven to America by the revocation of the Edict of Nantes. Several of the Dutch pastors who could preach in French occasionally ministered to the Huguenots, though the French were soon numerous enough to form their own congregations and have their own ministers. It has been stated, with justice, that religious toleration was almost perfect during the administration of Dongan, though instructions were sent out to the governor by James II, who we will remember was himself a Catholic, establishing the Church of England in the colony. The list of instructions contains the following:

> You shall permit all persons of what Religion soever quietly to inhabit within your Government without giving them any disturbance or disquiet whatsoever for or by reason of their differing Opinions in matters of Religion, Provided they give no disturbance to ye public peace, nor do molest   or disquiet others in ye free Exercise of their Religion.

This liberality of King James was, of course, due to the fact that he was anxious to gain toleration for Catholics.

In 1687 Governor Dongan made a report of conditions in the colony which include a summary of the general religious situation:

> Every town ought to have a minister. New York has first a Chaplain belonging to the Fort of the Church of England; secondly a Dutch Calvinist; thirdly a French Calvinist; fourthly a Dutch Lutheran. Here bee not many of the Church of England; few Roman Catholocks, aboundance of Quaker; preachers, men and Women especially; Singling Quakers; Ranting Quakers; Sabbatarians; Anti-Sabbatarians; some Anabaptists; some Jews; in short, of all sorts of opinions there are some, and the most part of none at all. The Great Church which serves both the English and the Dutch within the Fort, which is found to be very inconvenient. Therefore I desire that there may bee an order for their building another; ground being already layd out for that purpose, and they not wanting money in store wherewithall to build it. The most prevailing opinion is that of Dutch Calvinists. It is the endeavor of all persons here to bring up their children and servants in that opinion which themselves profess; but this I observe, that they take no care of the conversion of their slaves.

A notion was prevalent at this period that baptism of slaves would *ipso facto* free them, and to the credit of King James he insisted that they be baptized, and instructions to governors frequently contained such admonitions. In the Dutch churches this seems to have been the practice, as the records of the churches show.

At the overthrow of James II the people of New York rose in revolt and Lieutenant Governor Nicholson fled. A Committee of Safety was chosen to take over the government until the new Dutch king, William III, could appoint a new governor. At the head of the revolutionary government was Colonel Jacob Leisler, who was generally considered as the representative of William and Mary and Protestantism. But, strange to say, the Dutch ministers in New York refused to recognize him or his authority. As a result the people refused to hear the ministers preach, nor would they pay their salaries. Undoubtedly the ministers were wrongly advised in this whole affair, although they no doubt thought Leisler unfit for the position he held, and were also very probably influenced by social reasons.

When the new governor, Sloughter, arrived in the colony, he brought instructions from King William, "to permit a liberty of conscience to all Persons (except Papists), so they be contented with a quiet and Peaceable enjoyment of it, not giving offence or scandall to the Government." The new governor was also instructed to require of the officeholders in the province the oaths and tests required in the Test Act of 1673, which required, besides the oaths of allegiance and supremacy to the king, the taking of the sacrament according to the form of the Church of England, as well as the signing of a declaration against the Roman Catholic doctrine of transubstantiation. These instructions seemed to favor the establishment of the English Church, and the next step on the part of the governor was to suggest the passage of the "Ministry Act," providing for the "proper maintenance of a minister in every town where there were forty families or more." Proposed first in 1691, similar bills were introduced in 1692 and again in 1693, though when finally adopted the application of the measure was limited to the City of New York, and the counties of Richmond, Westchester and Queens.

This measure by no sense established the English Church, though Governor Fletcher, who urged it, attempted so to interpret it. The act provides that "there shall be called, inducted, and established, a good sufficient Protestant minister" in the counties indicated. The several dissenting groups claimed equal benefit from the act, and in every place outside New York City the dissenters were able to maintain their own ministers under the act. When called upon to interpret the meaning of the act in 1695, the New York Assembly stated, "Vestrymen and church-wardens have power to call a dissenting Protestant minister, and that he is to be paid and maintained as the law directs." The governor, on the other hand, refused to accept this interpretation, stating that "there is no Protestant Church admits of such officers as Church wardens and Vestrymen but the Church of England." It seems to have been assumed in later legal documents adopted from time to time that the Church of England had been established in New York, and many came to believe it. To hold to this legal fiction may have given satisfaction to the royal governors, but it had little effect upon the stubborn Dutchmen, who made up the majority in the assembly.

The Anglican chaplain of the English troops in New York wrote a description of conditions in the colony in 1695 for the information of the Bishop of London. He speaks of the lack of churches and ministers, though, he says, there are many pretended ministers, Presbyterians and Independents. He urges the necessity of a bishop for America, who he suggests might be a suffragan of the Bishop of London. He adds a table of churches, ministers and families. In New York City there are 6 churches including the chapel at the fort where the chaplain presided. The Dutch Calvinists had 475 families, the French 200, the Dutch Lutherans 30, the Jews—already beginning to appear in some numbers in New York—20, while the families to whom he ministered numbered but 90. Summarizing the figures for the whole province, the Dutch had 1,754 families; the English dissenters, 1,365; the French, 261; the Lutherans, 45; the Anglicans, 90; and the Jews, 20.

The passage of the Ministry Act as described above greatly disturbed the Dutch minister at New York concerning the legal status of his church, for he felt that the privileges which they then enjoyed might very easily be taken away. This led to a petition for a charter. At first unsuccessful, a charter was finally granted May 11, 1696, which was the first church charter granted in New York. After conceding to the church the right to hold property, the charter explains the reasons for granting the same, and then declares:

That our royal will and pleasure is, that no person in communion with the said Reformed Protestant Dutch Church within our city of New York, at any time, hereafter, shall be in any ways molested, punished, disquieted, or called in question for differences of opinion in matter of the Protestant religion, who do not disturb the civil peace of our said province; etc.

With the securing of the charter the Dutch minister in New York City, Domine Selyns, now felt that their position was secure, and in reporting to the Classis of Amsterdam he says referring to the charter:

"This is a circumstance which promises much advantage to God's Church, and quiets the formerly existing uneasiness." Other Dutch churches from time to time sought and received charters. The only other churches in New York, however, to receive charters were the Anglican churches, and the first of these was granted to Trinity Church in 1697. This charter made Trinity Church the established church in New York City, while the churchwardens and vestrymen instead of being chosen by the freeholders of the city, according to the act of 1694, were now to be chosen by those in communion with the Church of England alone. The explanation of this fact seems to be that the Dutch members of the assembly were so elated over receiving their own charter that they were willing to allow Trinity Church to claim all its charter allowed. For the next century and more the Dutch and the English churches and their ministers lived together in peace and harmony, though the Dutch Church was more or less static until aroused through the activities of Theodore J. Frelinghuysen, and the Great Awakening.

THE QUAKERS

Within ten years after George Fox had begun his new reformation in England (1647) his disciples made their appearance in America, and by the end of the century they were to be found in every colony under British rule. They were imbued with a dauntless missionary spirit, for as one of them wrote "the Lord's word was as a fire and a hammer in me."

The first Quakers to appear in America were two women, Mary Fisher and Ann Austin, who landed in Boston in 1656. From the beginning, women had been active as Quaker missionaries and these women were but doing what numerous others were attempting in other parts of the world. Already they had conducted a successful mission to Barbados, where influential converts had been won. In Boston, however, they were to have no opportunity to preach the new gospel. Before they could land, orders were received from the lieutenant governor that they should be kept on shipboard, and their effects searched. Later they were imprisoned for five weeks, the windows of the jail boarded up so they could not see or be seen, and among the indignities heaped upon them, they were stripped and subjected to an examination for "tokens" of witchcraft on their bodies while their books were burned by the common hangman in the market place. The captain of the vessel which had brought them to Boston was now compelled to return them to Barbados, evidently at his own expense, while the Boston jailer had to content himself with their bedding and their Bibles in lieu of fees. But Boston was not done with the Quakers so easily, for hardly was the vessel bearing Mary Fisher and Ann Austin out of sight before another ship landed eight more Quaker missionaries. After eleven weeks' imprisonment they were also sent out of the colony, so fearful were the Puritan fathers that the new heresy would contaminate their people.

Nor is it at all strange that the New England Puritans should have looked upon the coming of the Quakers as a real peril. The ideals and practices of the Quakers were flatly antagonistic to those of the religious leaders of Massachusetts. "The Quaker aimed at a complete separation between Church and State"; while "the government of Massachusetts was patterned after the ancient Jewish theocracy in which State and church were identified. The Quaker was tolerant of differences in doctrine; the Calvinist regarded such tolerance as a deadly sin." Laws were now passed in Massachusetts against the Quakers—for Ann Austin and Mary Fisher had been imprisoned before there were laws providing for their punishment—the first passed in 1656 fixing penalties for bringing Quakers into the colony; the second in 1657 increasing the penalties; the third in 1658 forbidding Quakers from holding meetings under penalty of heavy fines, while the same year a law was passed imposing the death penalty upon Quakers who should return after having been banished. These laws were vigorously enforced, and by 1661 had brought to the gallows four victims, one of whom was Mary Dyer. But in spite of this cruel array of legislation against them the Quakers continued to come, and gradually their treatment became less and less severe, especially after Charles II had sent a letter (1661) to Governor Endicott forbidding further proceedings against the Quakers and directing that in the future they be sent to England for trial. Twenty years later the laws against Quakers were suspended, though numerous Friends were imprisoned thereafter for their refusal to pay tithes. The Connecticut and New Haven colonies passed laws similar to those of Massachusetts, and even in liberal Rhode Island the aged Roger Williams entered the lists against them, and challenged Fox to debate and later produced a pamphlet called "George Fox digged out of his Burrows" which was characterized by Fox as "a very envious and wicked book." It needs to be said, however, that there was no persecution of Quakers in Rhode Island, even though Roger Williams was opposed to their teaching and practice. When in 1657 the Commissioners of the New England Confederation—which had refused membership to Rhode Island—protested that the Quaker pests were finding a refuge in Rhode Island the governor, Benedict Arnold, replied: "As to the dammage that may in likely-hood accrue to the neighbor collonys by their being here entertained, we conceive it will not prove so dangerous as the course taken by you to send them away out of the country as they come among you.

Quakers appeared in New York about the same time as in New England and at first were well treated by the Dutch, but as we have already noticed, during the administration of Governor Stuyvesant, there was a period of persecution, and Quaker missionaries were imprisoned and sent out of the colony. This period of persecution, however, lasted but a short time, and was brought to an end (1663) by the appeal of John Bowne to the directors of the Dutch West India Company against the policy of Governor Stuyvesant. In the southern colonies Quaker missionaries early made their appearance; in Virginia as early as 1656, in Maryland in 1657, and in the Carolinas at least as early as 1672. Everywhere they were persecuted, outside the so-called Quaker colonies, except in Rhode Island and the Carolinas.

The first Monthly meetings formed in America were those of Sandwich and Scituate in Massachusetts, both founded before 1660, while the New England Yearly Meeting, established in 1661, is likewise the oldest organization of its kind in America.

Of great importance in the early history of the Quakers in America was the visit of George Fox. Fox landed in Maryland in the spring of 1672, whence after a short period he went to Rhode Island where he was entertained by the governor, Nicholas Easton, who was himself a Quaker, and who traveled with Fox through the colony. Later Fox visited Long Island, where he held a number of meetings, thence into New Jersey, where new meetings were established. In November he visited Virginia and under his preaching the number of Friends in that colony was doubled. Of his trip into the Carolinas he has left us a graphic account in his Journal, where on one occasion he says:

Wee passed all day, & saw neither house nor man through ye woods & swamps, & many cruel boggs & watery places, yt wee was wet to the knees most of us, & at night wee tooke up our Lodginge in ye woods, & made a fire.

He traveled more than a thousand miles southward from Boston, "all of which wee have traveiled by land & downe bayes & over Rivers and Creeks & boggs & wilderness."

The center of Quaker activity in America, however, was in New Jersey, Delaware and Pennsylvania, which are sometimes called the Quaker colonies.

The great Quaker experiment in America had its beginnings in New Jersey. The early political history of this colony is in great confusion. It was included in the grant made to the Duke of York in 1664, who soon gave it to two of his friends, Sir John Berkeley and Sir George Carteret. The governors of New York, however, claimed jurisdiction over the territory, which claim was resisted by the proprietors, who in the end were upheld by the king. The proprietors were anxious for settlers, and made liberal concessions to induce colonists to come to their province. In response to their invitation a considerable number of Puritans came from New England. Some Quakers settled early along the Raritan River, and by 1670 a meeting was formed at Shrewsbury and a meeting-house built. In 1674 Berkeley sold out his rights to two Quakers, Fenwick and Byllingy, who made an agreement with Carteret to divide the province into East and West Jersey, and it was accordingly in West Jersey, in the region bordering on the Delaware River that the first important Quaker experiment in government began. Later the two Quaker proprietors sold out their rights in West Jersey to a number of Quaker gentlemen, among them being William Penn, which marks the beginning of Penn's personal interest in America. The Quaker proprietors now drew up a liberal constitution and towns and settlements sprang up along the Delaware.

The spirit of the charter of West New Jersey, which was drawn up in 1676 and called "Concessions and Agreements," is characterized by this statement of the Quaker proprietors:

Thus we lay a foundation for after ages to understand their liberty as men and Christians, that they may not be brought into bondage but by their own consent; for we put the power in the people. No person to be called in question or molested for his conscience or for worshipping according to his conscience.

By 1681 more than a thousand immigrants had come to West Jersey, most of them Quakers. Burlington, founded in 1677, became the most important Quaker center. At first, worship was conducted under a tent made of sailcloth, and here in July, 1678, a Monthly Meeting was set up. In May, 1680, the Burlington Quarterly Meeting was established and the next year it was determined to establish a Yearly Meeting. The next turn in the affairs of the Quakers in the Jerseys was brought about by the death of Sir George Carteret, the proprietor of East Jersey, whose heirs sold out their rights to another group of twelve Quakers, among whom also was William Penn. Soon after, the number of proprietors was increased to twenty-four, among them being several Scotchmen. Under the influence of the Scottish partners numerous Scottish immigrants came out to East New Jersey, many of whom were Presbyterians. Thus was the Presbyterian element introduced into New Jersey. Other immigrants came from New England, as well as numerous Scotch-Irish from North Ireland, and later these Calvinistic elements combined to make Presbyterianism the outstanding religious force in the colony.

It was in 1681 that William Penn was granted Pennsylvania in consideration of a debt of £16,000 which was due him from the crown. The beginnings of William Penn's interest in American colonization has already been noticed. The next year the Duke of York gave to Penn what is now Delaware, which was called "the territories." This was governed as a part of Pennsylvania until 1702 when it secured its own assembly and eventually became a separate colony. The long-drawn-out boundary dispute, especially between Maryland and Pennsylvania, is hardly a part of this story, though it kept Penn in England when he might have been with his people in America.

No single Englishman engaged in colonization made such a success of his enterprise as did William Penn. He termed it "an Holy Experiment" and thus explains his intention in planting the colony:

My God that has given it me through many difficulties, will, I believe, bless and make it the seed of a nation. . . . I have so obtained it and desire to keep it, that I may not be unworthy of His love; but do that which may answer His kind providence and serve His Truth and people; that an example may be set up to the nations. There may be room there, though not here, for such an experiment.

In April, 1682, he issued his *Frame of Government,* which soon proved too complicated to be used, but which clearly shows Penn's desire to establish the principles of English liberty. In October of the same year Penn arrived in his colony and by 1701 the government had been greatly simplified and popular freedom increased.

The outstanding reason for the success of Pennsylvania was the religious freedom which the proprietor not only guaranteed but also widely advertised. His guarantee of religious freedom included all law-abiding citizens who "acknowledged one Almighty and Eternal God to be the Creator, Upholder and Ruler of the world," which would include Protestants, Catholics and Jews. Later Catholics were excluded from officeholding through pressure from the home government and officeholding was limited to Christians, which, of course, is a limitation which would not be made today in a country where there is complete religious liberty. In spite of these limitations Pennsylvania proved an attractive haven for numerous religious sects and no colony gave them a larger opportunity of working out their own theories.

The majority of the early colonists were English and Welsh Quakers. By 1683 the population was reported as 4,000 and six years later Delaware and Pennsylvania contained not less than 12,000 people. But this was just the beginning of the great inflow, not only from the British Isles, but from Germany, France and Holland. In 1685 Penn estimated that only about half of the people in the colony were English.

At first the Pennsylvania Quakers held their meetings in the homes of the people, but it was not long until meeting-houses began to be built. The first Monthly Meeting was held in January, 1682, and "within three months nine meetings for worship and three monthly meetings had been set up." In 1683 the Pennsylvania Friends attended the Yearly Meeting at Burlington and the same year a Yearly Meeting was held in Philadelphia. The absurdity of holding two separate Yearly Meetings so close together led in 1685 to an agreement that Yearly Meetings should be held alternately in Burlington and Philadelphia. The number of Friends continued to increase and by 1700 there were forty meetings or congregations in Pennsylvania. By 1760 the number of Quakers, or Friends, in America was near 30,000. The size of some of the Pennsylvania meetings particularly was very large, several numbering as many as 1,500 members each.

But as numbers increased spiritual life seemed to decline. This condition was inevitable with the establishment of what is known as birthright membership. This meant that increasing numbers of Friends became members of the Society through birth rather than through any conviction of their own. The increase of wealth among the Quakers was undoubtedly another reason for their spiritual decline, as is pointed out by an aged Friend in 1760, looking back over a period of about sixty years. In the early days, he says:

Friends were a plain lowly-minded people, and that there was much tenderness and contrition in their meetings. That at 20 years from that date, the

Society increasing in wealth and in some degree conforming to the fashions of the world, true humility was less apparent, and their meetings in general not so lively and edifying. That at the end of 40 years many of them were grown very rich; and many made a specious appearance in the world, that marks of outward wealth and greatness appeared on some in our meetings of ministers and elders, and as such things became more prevalent so the powerful overshadowings of the Holy Ghost were less manifest in the Society. That there had been a continual increase of such ways of life even until the present time, and that the weakness that had now overspread the Society and the barrenness manifest among us is a matter of much sorrow.

Traveling Friends in the eighteenth century speak of "a dry lifeless state" in many of the meetings; "excessive drinking" on the part of some of the members; some who are living "in open profaneness and are riotous in conversation"; while some of the young Friends take part in shooting matches, games of "hustlecap" and are prone to do much drinking, carousing and fighting. The question of drink caused much concern among the Friends of the eighteenth century. Among the first rules adopted by the Friends was one prohibiting the selling or giving away of strong drink to the Indians. The custom of serving liquor at burials became common which led the Yearly Meeting in 1729 to recommend that "When wine or other strong liquors are served (which many soberminded people think needless) that it be but once."

The Quakers from the beginning were a loosely organized body, and what little organization there was among them in America was brought over from England. George Fox was responsible for the establishment of the Monthly and Quarterly Meetings "for better ordering the affairs of the Church; in taking care of the poor; and exercising a true gospel discipline for a due dealing with any that might walk disorderly under our name; and to see that such as should marry among us did act fairly and clearly in that respect." At the First Yearly Meeting held in London in 1668 there was drawn up what is known as the *Canons and Institutions,* of which Fox was the probable author. Here are listed under nineteen heads, advices and regulations concerning all matters which might arise in the church, and these served as the model for the regulations of the early meetings in America. The first regular Books of Discipline did not appear in America until 1759, and then only in manuscript, but with the appearance of these rules of conduct Quakerism tended more and more to become a matter of observing the outward regulations and less and less that of establishing that vital relationship with God, which characterized the earlier years. It was during these years that the "Birth-right membership" arose. This came from the legislation of the London Yearly Meeting in 1737 which stated that "All Friends shall be deemed members of the Quarterly, Monthly and Two-Weekly Meeting within the compass of which they inhabited or dwelt the first day of the Fourth Month, 1737"; and "the wife and children to be deemed members of the Monthly Meeting of which the husband or father is a member, not only during his life but after his decease." This act, in the words of a Quaker historian, "changed the Society of Friends from a church of believers, at least in theory, to a corporation or association of persons some of whom would be among the unconverted."

CHAPTER VII

✥ ✥ ✥

RELIGIOUS DIVERSITY IN THE MIDDLE COLONIES: THE GERMAN BODIES

I

THE first German settlement in America was Germantown, ten miles north of Philadelphia, and the first German settlers were Mennonites. After Penn's first visit to Germany (1671) a Frankfort Land Company was formed, which eventually purchased 25,000 acres of land in Pennsylvania. A young lawyer, Francis Daniel Pastorius, became the agent of the company, and under his direction, on October 6, 1683, the ship *Concord* arrived in Philadelphia bringing thirteen Mennonite families, which marks the beginning of German migration to America. These first arrivals were from Crefeld on the lower Rhine and were a thrifty and industrious people, mostly weavers. Eventually many of them became members of the Society of Friends, though in 1688 a Mennonite congregration was formed, and in 1708 the first Mennonite church erected. Later immigrations brought Mennonite settlers into Bucks, Berks and Northampton Counties and by 1712 there were 200 Mennonites in Pennsylvania and a church membership of at least 100. Perhaps the largest Mennonite community in America before the Revolution was in what is now Lancaster County, which was made up largely of Swiss immigrants. Some of these were Amish Mennonites, which represented the most conservative branch of that body. By the end of the colonial period it has been estimated that there were 2,000 Mennonite families in America, most of them in Pennsylvania.

The Mennonites were the direct descendants of the Anabaptists of the Reformation. They receive their name from Menno Simons, a Dutch Catholic priest, who at forty years of age renounced the Catholic faith and cast in his lot with the humble Anabaptists, and it seems that his followers adopted the name "Mennonites" to escape persecution which was everywhere meted out to Anabaptists. The outstanding features of the Mennonite faith correspond to the Baptists as to accepting the Bible as the only rule of faith, and the rejection of infant baptism. They did not, however, always insist upon immersion. They taught that the office of magistrate cannot be held by a Christian, though a Christian must be obedient to his rulers and pray for them and pay taxes to support the government. They also held that a Christian cannot take up the sword; that Christians must live secluded from the world; and that it is wrong to take an oath. In many respects the Mennonites were similar to the Quakers and were well treated as long as the Quakers were the ruling element in the colony. They took up good agricultural lands and their settlements soon became prosperous and even wealthy communities.

Another small German religious sect which made its appearance in Pennsylvania in the early eighteenth century was the Taufers, or Dunkers (German Baptists) as they came to be known in the colonies. The first Dunker immigration to America came from the same locality from which had come the first Mennonite settlers, Crefeld on the lower Rhine, and in response to the same set of influences, namely, the advertisement of Penn's agent and the Frankfort Land Company. Peter Becker, one of the ministers of the Crefeld congregation, led out the first settlers in 1719, numbering about 120 persons. They came to Germantown, but soon scattered into several settlements in the vicinity. It was not, however, until 1723 that their first congregation was formed, though worship was held from the beginning in the homes of some of the leaders. In 1729 a second group from West Friesland, numbering 126 people and under the leadership of Alexander Mack, came to Pennsylvania, while four years later a third company, but smaller than the first two, arrived under the leadership of John Naas. Within a few years these settlers were scattered widely, some migrating into Maryland and Virginia, and by the end of the colonial period some 19 congregations had been formed, 12 of them numbering 200 members or more.

Among the early Dunker ministers in America is Conrad Beissel who holds particular interest because he became the founder of the Ephrata community in Lancaster County, Pennsylvania. This was a schismatic movement and was not the main Dunker interest in the colonies, as is frequently inferred. Beissel from the beginning of his ministry was an advocate of "strange doctrines," such as the denunciation of the marriage state and the advocacy of the seventh day as the Sabbath. Eventually Beissel and his followers withdrew from the Dunkers and a community was established known as Ephrata, where by 1745 a large group of buildings had been erected and prosperous industries had been established. Here the "brothers" and "sisters" lived in separate houses and practiced a kind of monasticism. Several of the early Dunker congregations went over completely to Ephrata, but it was never entirely Dunker, since it drew Germans from other groups particularly the Reformed.

Like the Mennonites and Quakers, the Dunkers were fundamentally opposed to war and advocated nonresistance. It is probable that at first they did not wear a distinctive dress as later became the practice, but the influence of the Quaker hat and bonnet made plainness of dress the symbol of the nonresisting people. The Dunkers held strictly to trine immersion, face forward, and for adults only. They were strictly Congregational in their form of church government and it was not until 1742 that their "Great Meeting" was formed, which soon became a vital factor in the expansion of the "Church of the Brethren."

The most important Dunker leader in the colonial period was Christopher Saur, who was the first German printer in America and the first to edit and print a German newspaper. It is true that Benjamin Franklin had done some printing for the Germans, previous to the establishment of the Saur press, but he used roman type and his attempt to publish a German weekly paper proved a failure. Saur began his publications in 1738 and on his death his son, Christopher Saur, Jr., carried on the work. Of great significance to the religious life of early German settlers in America of all creeds was the Saur German Bible, the first edition of which appeared in 1743, with other editions in subsequent years. This was the first Bible to be printed in America in a European language. The Saurs were undoubtedly the most influential Germans in the colonies, and Germantown, through their activities, was the cultural center for the colonial Germans.

Another small German sect, which also, about this time found refuge in Pennsylvania, were the Schwenkfelders. Their founder, Kasper Von Schwenkfeld, a German nobleman, was a contemporary of Luther, though he was anti-Lutheran as well as anti-Catholic in his theology, and his followers were persecuted by both Lutherans and Catholics. It was in Silesia that they had their greatest success and here they became, after the death of their founder, a distinct sect. In 1720 a movement to convert them to Catholicism by force was begun, which caused most of them to flee into Saxony, Holland, England and America. Their migration to America took place largely in 1733-1734. Previously a group of them had been received on the Saxony estate of Count Zinzendorf where they remained eight years, but the Saxon government would not allow them to stay longer and from thence they migrated to Pennsylvania, some by way of Denmark and others from Holland. The two groups arrived in Philadelphia in September and October, 1734, and settled mainly in the Pennsylvania German counties of Montgomery, Bucks, Berks and Lehigh. Like the Mennonites and Dunkers, they were a simple and industrious people and made a worthy contribution to colonial Pennsylvania.

Among those connected with the German settlement of Pennsylvania, none are more interesting than Nicholaus Ludwig Zinzendorf, a Saxon nobleman and a religious and social reformer, who was chiefly responsible for the Moravian migration to America. Zinzendorf had been raised amidst Pietistic influences, his parents being followers of Philipp Jakob Spener, and accordingly he was sent to the University at Halle. His parents planned that he would prepare himself for a diplomatic career, but his great interest in religion caused him to abandon this plan and led him to settle down on his great estate at Berthelsdorf in Saxony, as a Christian landlord, and attempt to carry into practice the Pietistic ideas of his godfather Spener. In 1722 he offered an asylum to a number of persecuted wanderers from Bohemia and Moravia known as the "Moravians" and built for them on a corner of his estate, a village which was called Herrnhut.

The Moravians trace their origin back to the Hussite movement in Bohemia. At first they were an organization within the Bohemian Church, but later they broke away entirely from the papacy and formed a Church of their own which they called "Unitas Fratrum." The Unitas Fratrum became an episcopal church, consecration of their first bishop being received from the bishop of the Austrian Waldenses, who traced his ordination back to the Roman Catholic bishops at the Council of Basel. Throughout the sixteenth century they grew rapidly and were particularly active in printing and distributing books, among them a translation of the Bible into Bohemian. During the Thirty Years' War the Unity of the Brethren were driven from their homes and for almost a hundred years were nearly extinct, but during much of this period their bishop, John Amos Comenius (1592-1672), held a remnant together. The revival of the Brethren in the eighteenth century was largely due to a humble carpenter, Christian David, and it was under this new leader, when persecution broke out afresh, that they came as refugees to the estate of Count Zinzendorf in Saxony. Zinzendorf and his wife devoted themselves to these refugees and finally brought order and unity out of confusion and differences. Zinzendorf, who was a Pietistic Lutheran, at first tried to lead the Moravian refugees to accept the Pietistic principles and for a time they attended the parish church at Berthelsdorf and considered themselves as Lutherans. Gradually, however, the Moravian Church began to emerge, and with the approbation of the Count, a bishop was consecrated for the Herrnhut group in 1735 and two years later Zinzendorf himself was consecrated a bishop. The formation of the Herrnhut Moravians into a separate church now brought persecution upon them, which accounts for the beginning of their migration to America.

With the beginning of the Georgia enterprise under the leadership of General Oglethorpe, Count Zinzendorf took steps to obtain a refuge for some of the persecuted people who were living upon his Saxon estate. In 1733 he received a promise from the Georgia trustees of land and a free passage for the Schwenkfelders. After the Schwenkfelders left Saxony, however, they changed their plans and proceeded to Pennsylvania instead. Zinzendorf now proceeded to secure the Georgia tract for the Moravians, and in April, 1735, a company of nine, under the leadership of Spangenberg who had recently joined the Moravians, arrived in Georgia. The next year twenty additional colonists arrived. On shipboard with this latter group was John Wesley, coming out as chaplain to General Oglethorpe, who has left us in his *Journal* a memorable account of his impressions of the Moravian Brethren. The Moravian colony in Georgia failed to prosper, because of sickness and death of the settlers and also because of misunderstanding with the authorities when they refused to bear arms in the war with Spain. Accordingly, when in 1740, George Whitefield offered them free passage on his sloop to Philadelphia, they accepted, and thus the first American Moravian colony was transplanted to Pennsylvania.

At this time Whitefield had a plan to erect a colony for destitute

Englishmen at the forks of the Delaware, which he called Nazareth, and had negotiated for the purchase of 5,000 acres of land. He now proposed to the Moravians that they come into his employ to erect the buildings for his enterprise. This they agreed to do. All went well until doctrinal disputes arose between Whitefield and Böhler, the Moravian leader, and the Moravians were dismissed and ordered to quit the land at once. The next spring, however, Whitefield found himself unable to pay for the land he had purchased, because of the death of the man who had agreed to loan him the money, and Whitefield was now more than willing to sell out his interest to the Moravians whom he had so recently expelled. Thus the Moravians acquired the region which was to become their chief center in America.

The chief interest of the Moravians in coming to America was to carry on missionary work, both among the German settlers and also among the Indians. By this time Herrnhut had become a great foreign missionary center, and Moravian missionaries from 1732 on were going to various parts of the world. The destitute religious situation of the various German settlers of Pennsylvania was well known. Thousands who had flocked to the New World were living without schools and churches, and their children were growing up in ignorance and without spiritual instruction. It was the knowledge of this condition of affairs that led to the sending out of the first Moravian missionaries to Pennsylvania. In December, 1741, Zinzendorf himself arrived in Philadelphia on a great missionary enterprise. Just before Christmas he reached the Moravian settlement at the forks of the Delaware, and on Christmas eve he named the place Bethlehem, "in token of his fervent desire and ardent hope that here the true bread of life might be broken for all who hungered."

The thirteen months of Zinzendorf's stay in America were filled with activity. His first great project was an attempt to bring about unity among numerous German groups in Pennsylvania. Altogether seven synods were held within six months, to advance this worthy project, and in the first four every German religious body in Pennsylvania was represented. But after the fourth synod all withdrew except the Lutherans, the Reformed and the Moravians, and Zinzendorf's dream of union soon came to naught. Later the Lutherans of Philadelphia requested him to become their pastor, and he accepted for a time, but the coming of Henry M. Muhlenberg put a stop to that arrangement, and

Zinzendorf, at his own expense, built a stone church for those who were willing to continue under his leadership, and this became the first Moravian church of that city.

With the failure of his project to unite the German denominations in America Zinzendorf turned to the work of promoting missions among the Indians, and during the latter half of his stay in America made three missionary tours into the Indian country. In the first of his visits he obtained permission, from the chiefs of the Six Nations, for the Moravian Brethren to pass through their country and to live as friends within their domains. In his second journey Zinzendorf visited the Mohican town of Shekomeko, between the Housatonic and the Hudson, where a Moravian missionary had been at work since 1740, and here he formed the Christian Indians into a congregation. His third journey, from September 24 to November 9th, was to Shamokin the most important Indian village in the Susquehanna valley. Two months after his return from this latter journey Zinzendorf departed for Europe. The following is a summary of his accomplishments while in America: "He inaugurated the first form of government for the Moravian Church in America," giving to Bishop David Nitschmann the oversight of the Indian missions, while to Peter Böhler was given the oversight of the "itineracy"; seven congregations had been either established or aided in Pennsylvania, and two in New York, while four schools had been founded.

Bethlehem and Nazareth became semicommunistic communities; there was community of labor but the holding of personal property was allowed. Their common labor was for the support of the great missionary activities of the church, and the two communities bcame veritable hives of industry. By 1747 thirty-two different industries were in operation, besides several farms, and they were supporting about fifty missionaries and itinerants, besides furnishing the necessities for the workers and their children.

Zinzendorf, who during his last years lived in London, was in virtual control of the Moravian activities in both Europe and America until his death, which occurred in 1760. Just before his death, however, a board of directors had been formed, which now took over the control. In 1764 the Zinzendorf heirs were paid $90,000 and the church became the owner of the Zinzendorf estates, assuming all debts which had been contracted for the church by the count, which amounted to $773,162.

Meanwhile the Moravians continued to extend their Indian missions. Under David Zeisberger, their best-known missionary leader, a Christian village was established on the north branch of the Susquehanna in 1765 which was called *Friedenshütten*—"tents of peace." Two years later another mission was begun in western Pennsylvania on the left bank of the Alleghany. Persecution drove Zeisberger and his associates farther westward, and in 1770 he accepted a tract on the Tuscarawas River in Ohio and *Schönbrunn* and *Gnadenhütten* were established and later *Salem*. Here for a time all was peaceful and prosperous. Numerous converts were made; hundreds of acres were brought under cultivation and cattle multiplied into great herds. Tents gave place to log cabins, while the churches were unable to accommodate the great number of Indian worshipers. Such was the situation in the great Moravian Mission when the American Revolution began.

II

So far only the smaller German religious groups in the colonies have been noted. These groups have attracted much more attention than their actual numbers warrant, because of the fact that they are more picturesque than were the more numerous German Reformed and Lutheran bodies.

In most instances the large number of German immigrants who swarmed into Pennsylvania, especially from 1727 to 1745, came without ministers or schoolmasters, and several of the earliest German Reformed congregations were formed without pastors. The first German Reformed church was that at Germantown, built in 1719, but there was evidently no settled pastor at the time, for the cornerstone was laid by a Swedish minister. By 1725 three German Reformed congregations had been established, at Falkner's Swamp, Skippack and White Marsh; and in that year they asked John Philip Boehm, who had been a schoolmaster at Worms and had come to America in 1720, to act as their minister. After some hesitation he consented, though he warned the people that it was a violation of the order of the Reformed Church. Boehm, in spite of his lack of ordination, performed a useful service to the scattered German communities, baptizing hundreds of children and preaching in outlying districts. In 1729 Boehm was ordained. After asking the advice of the Dutch Reformed ministers of New York, he and his friends communicated with the Classis of Amsterdam, explaining the situation which had led him to undertake the work of a minister before he had received proper ordination. The Classis in its reply wisely stated that "under the circumstances all the transactions of the said Boehm—his teachings, even his administration of the Lord's Supper—must be deemed lawful," but that now he must receive ordination. This was the beginning of the close relationship between the German Reformed churches in America and the Dutch Church, which lasted for many years.

From 1725 to the middle of the century several German Reformed ministers came out to the colonies, though the great majority of the Reformed people in the colonies were still without ministers and conditions generally were deplorable. Among the most useful of these early ministers was George Michael Weiss who arrived in America in September, 1727, having been sent by the Classis of the Palatinate. Weiss organized a church in Philadelphia, but also preached in the surrounding territory, where he came into contact and conflict with Boehm. Later when Boehm was ordained, Weiss was present and from this time on the two worked in perfect harmony. Between 1730 and 1736 there was a large Swiss immigration, which came largely to the region between the Delaware and Schuylkill rivers. Two young Swiss pastors, John Henry Goetschius and Conrad Wirtz, labored among these people and formed several congregations.

A special interest is attached to the arrival in 1730 of John Peter Miller, who at twenty years of age was sent to America by the Classis of Heidelberg, with special authority to administer the sacraments. Soon after his arrival he was ordained by the Presbyterian Synod of Philadelphia, upon whom he made a most notable impression. Becoming the pastor of the church at Tulpehocken (Reading), he labored among his people with great success. But at the end of four years he came under the influence of Conrad Beissel, who visited Tulpehocken, with the result that Miller and his elders with several of the members of his church joined Beissel and removed to the community at Ephrata. On the death of Beissel, Miller became the head of the community, where he died in 1796. Miller was a linguist of note, and during the Revolution was engaged by the Continental Congress to translate the Declaration of Independence into several European languages.

The most important name in the formative period of the German

Reformed Church in America is Michael Schlatter. Schlatter was a native of the town of St. Gall in Switzerland and came out to America in 1746 under the Synods of Holland. The poor German emigrants passing through the Dutch ports on their way to America had aroused the sympathy of the leaders of the Dutch Church, and when an appeal was made to them to take over the care of the German Reformed congregations in America they finally consented. Hearing of this, young Schlatter went to Holland and presented himself as a candidate for the proposed mission. He was accepted, and set sail for Boston in June, 1746. Schlatter's chief mission was to organize the American congregations into a synod. He was a young man of great energy and zeal and by October he had visited all the more important German Reformed centers, and had made plans for the formation of a synod, or Coetus, which held its first meeting in Philadelphia in September, 1747. In 1751, at the request of the Coetus, Schlatter went to Europe, and in a short time had raised £12,000 to be invested for the benefit of the churches in America, under the condition that the Coetus was to remain under the Classis of Amsterdam. The next year he returned to America bringing with him six young ministers and seven hundred Bibles for free distribution.

A rather curious result of Schlatter's success in Europe was a kindred movement begun in England to raise money to establish schools for the Germans of Pennsylvania. "A Society for the Promotion of the Knowledge of God among the Germans" was formed in England and a large sum of money raised. Charity schools were now established in the German communities with this fund, but the management of the enterprise was so untactful that it aroused the resentment of many of the leading Germans, among them Christopher Saur. Schlatter unfortunately consented to become the superintendent of these charity schools which resulted in bringing to him great unpopularity, and he became the main object of attack. Finally, saddened by the attacks he resigned and went into retirement.

The German Reformed Church was, of course, Presbyterian in its form of organization, though there developed a number of independent Reformed churches in the colonies. In most respects the Lutheran and German Reformed people were much alike in doctrine and worship and lived and worked harmoniously together. Schlatter and Muhlenberg were close friends, and were engaged in similar tasks in America, and in many places the two congregations, Lutheran and Reformed, worshiped in the same church.

III

Most important, at least from the standpoint of numbers, of all the German religious bodies in the American colonies, were the Lutherans. Lutheranism, however, had its beginning in America in the Dutch colony of New Amsterdam, and among the Swedes along the Delaware. The Lutheran congregation formed at New York, as has already been noted, was greatly retarded by the intolerant policy of Governor Stuyvesant and it was not until near the end of Dutch rule that they secured a regular pastor. From the beginning this congregation was extremely cosmopolitan in its make-up, for the majority of the members were Danes, Swedes, Norwegians or Germans, although the language used was Dutch. The story of the early Swedish Lutheran churches has already been related. While the Dutch and Swedish Lutheran beginnings have considerable interest, yet historically they are more or less unimportant, as compared to the German Lutherans who began to swarm across the Atlantic from 1720 onward.

Like the German Reformed settlers the early German Lutherans generally came without pastors or schoolmasters and they were desperately poor. The story of the exploitation of the poor German immigrants during the eighteenth century by the *Neulanders,* or immigrant agents, and the ship captains has been well told by Faust in his *German Element in the United States.*[1] Many of them were too poor to pay their passage and when they arrived in America were sold for a period of years to the person who agreed to pay the shipmaster. Thus many of them became indentured servants for their passage money, and not alone was this true of artisans and tillers of the soil, but students and schoolmasters were not infrequently sold in this labor market. The following is a description of what took place when a ship laden with German immigrants arrived in Philadelphia:

Before the ship is allowed to cast anchor in the harbor, the immigrants are all examined, as to whether any contagious disease be among them. The next step is to bring all the new arrivals in a procession before the city hall and there compel them to take the oath of allegiance to the king of Great Britain. After that they are brought back to the ship. Those that have paid their passage

[1] Chap. IV and V.

are released, and the others are advertised in the newspapers for sale. The ship becomes the market. The buyers make their choice and bargain with the immigrants for a certain number of years and days, depending upon the price demanded by the ship captain or other "merchant" who made the outlay for transportation, etc. Colonial governments recognize the written contract, which is then made binding for the redemptioner. The young unmarried people of both sexes are very quickly sold, and their fortunes are either good or bad, according to the character of the buyer. Old married people, widows, and the feeble, are a drug on the market, but if they have sound children, then their transportation charges are added to those of the children, and the latter must serve the longer. This does not save families from being separated in the various towns or even provinces. Again, the healthiest are taken first, and the sick are frequently detained beyond the period of recovery, when release would frequently have saved them.

This description of the conditions of German immigration will help explain why the German Lutherans, as well as the German Reformed, were slow in organizing churches. Their spiritual destitution was acute, in spite of the fact that a few devoted pastors were active among them. Among the earliest of these ministers were Daniel Falkner, Anthony Jacob Henkel, the Stoevers, father and son, and John Christian Schulz. Falkner was the "first regular pastor of the first German Lutheran congregation in America." Henkel was active in visiting the German settlements and was probably the founder of the congregations in Philadelphia and Germantown. The Stoevers were earnest missionaries; the elder Stoever worked among the Germans in Virginia while the younger stayed in Pennsylvania, preaching in all the German settlements, but especially in Lancaster and Montgomery counties. The last important name among these earliest German Lutheran pastors is John Christian Schulz, whose chief importance lies in the fact that he ordained the Stoevers and after a brief stay in America, as pastor of the congregations in Philadelphia, the Trappe and New Hanover, of less than a year, returned to Germany with two laymen from his congregations to collect funds and to secure ministers and teachers for America.

At this time (1733) a German king (George II) was on the English throne, and the court chaplain was Dr. Ziegenhagen, a Lutheran pastor. Naturally appeals from the American Germans were made to him, as well as to Lutheran leaders in Germany, especially to Professor Francke at the University of Halle. Both were sympathetic and were anxious to to do something for the destitute colonists, and efforts were made to secure funds and pastors. Ten years were to elapse, however, before the proper man was secured in Henry Melchior Muhlenberg. The delay was caused largely by a dispute over the matter of a fixed salary for the pastor. Ziegenhagen and Francke insisted that a definite arrangement be made as to the support of a minister, while the Pennsylvania Lutherans steadily refused to bind themselves. The Germans were of course, accustomed to a state church in the Old World, where the salary of the ministers was paid by the state authorities.

While this dispute over the matter of a fixed salary was going on between these Pennsylvania Lutherans and their European friends, another group of Lutherans were finding their way to America, and were settling in the new colony of Georgia. These were the Salzburgers, who a few years before had been driven from their homes in Austria by the Roman Catholic Archbishop of Salzburg, who had stated in 1728 that "he would drive the heretics out of the country, even though thorns and thistles should grow upon the fields." In 1731 all Protestants were commanded to leave Salzburg and in the midst of winter thousands set out toward Prussia whose king, Frederick William I, had offered them a refuge on his estates. Fourteen thousand passed through Berlin alone, and their sufferings and simple faith aroused the sympathy of every Protestant nation in Europe. The new societies but recently organized in England for "Promoting Christian Knowledge" and for "Propagating the Gospel in Foreign Parts" became interested, and provision was soon made to send some of the Salzburgers to Georgia. Free passage and provision in Georgia for a full year were provided, and land for themselves and children, free of all quitrent for ten years was promised, as well as freedom of worship and the privileges of native Englishmen.

The first of the Salzburgers arrived in Georgia in March, 1734; the next year others came; in 1736, 150 arrived and with them John and Charles Wesley and a group of Moravians. And so year by year others arrived until their new settlement of Ebenezer, 25 miles up the Savannah River, contained some 1200 colonists. Almost at once the colony prospered, for piety and industry generally go hand in hand.

The Salzburgers were provided with religious leaders from the beginning, for Francke had sent over two young Halle instructors as pastors, John Martin Boltzius and Israel Christian Gronau. Both labored faithfully and harmoniously among the colonists, and Boltzius was not alone the spiritual leader but became the business head of the colony as well.

The colony continued to prosper until the outbreak of the Revolution, when the British destroyed the place and the people were scattered to the surrounding settlements, where they joined Lutheran congregations in the other southern states.

The coming of Henry Melchior Muhlenberg in 1742 marks the beginning of a new epoch in the history of American Lutheranism. The Germans were more numerous than any other non-English element in the colonies, but they were widely scattered and disorganized, and were divided into numerous religious groups, though undoubtedly the Lutherans were the most numerous. The coming of Zinzendorf to America in 1741 and his attempt to unite the several German religious bodies into one church stirred the Halle authorities to immediate action, and Muhlenberg was sent to America to save American Lutheranism.

When Muhlenberg came to America he was a young man of thirty-one, educated at Göttingen with fifteen months' teaching experience gained at the Halle Orphanage. Urged by Francke to accept the call to America, he consented and in the fall of 1742 landed at Charleston, South Carolina. After spending some time among the Salzburgers in Georgia he sailed for Philadelphia, where he arrived November 25. He had come as the pastor of the three congregations of Philadelphia, New Hanover and the Trappe, but he had come unannounced and affairs were in confusion. Zinzendorf was busy with his scheme of union, and the majority of the Philadelphia congregation was favorable to that plan, while the other congregations were presided over by unworthy preachers. It took the energetic Muhlenberg but one month to "gain full possession of his field" and before the year ended was installed as pastor of the three congregations by the Swedish pastor at Wilmington.

Muhlenberg, however, conceived of his task as much larger than merely the care of the three congregations of which he was the pastor. The year of his arrival he took over the care of the Germantown church and later Lancaster, Tulpehocken and then York. Soon calls for help began to reach him from many places, to which he responded whenever possible. During these years Muhlenberg sent regular reports of his activities to the authorities at Halle. These were published from time to time, and served to keep the needs of the American brethren before the people of Germany. As a result men and money were soon forthcoming to aid in the work. In 1745 three helpers arrived from Halle, with funds to help build new churches. Schools were established in each of the churches, and the new helpers enabled Muhlenberg to give more attention to the general field.

By the year 1748 Muhlenberg was ready to form a synod. There were now several strong congregations and able ministers in America; new churches had been erected, and candidates for the ministry were seeking ordination. In response to this necessity six ministers and twenty-four laymen representing ten congregations met in the new St. Michael's Church in Philadelphia and there formed the first Lutheran synod in America, which came to be known as the Ministerium of Pennsylvania. At the time of the formation of the synod there were perhaps seventy Lutheran congregations in America. The synod exerted a strong influence over American Lutherans in general and greatly aided in the growth of the church. At the outbreak of the Revolution it is estimated that there were seventy-five thousand Lutherans in Pennsylvania alone, though no doubt a great majority of these were outside churches. By the end of the colonial period there were seventy Lutheran congregations in Pennsylvania and Maryland and some thirty in Virginia, the Carolinas and Georgia. Many German communities in the colonies were without religious leadership of any kind, and it is probable that there were more unchurched among the Germans than were to be found among any other racial group in the colonies.

The most pressing problem which faced the German churches in America was to find suitable pastors. Muhlenberg was soon convinced that it was futile to depend upon an Old World supply. Too frequently, disreputable pastors running away from bad reputations in the Old World secured congregations in America where they consistently wrought havoc. Muhlenberg encouraged the raising up of a native ministry and several candidates were trained in his own home. The Swedish pastor, Charles Mangus Von Wrangle, the Provost of the Swedish Lutheran churches on the Delaware, gave private instruction to three young German candidates, among them one of Muhlenberg's sons. The most able Lutheran pastors in colonial America were Pietists, as were both Muhlenberg and Von Wrangle, and a mild type of Pietism was a continuing influence among the colonial Lutherans.

CHAPTER VIII

✣ ✣ ✣

THE COLONIAL PRESBYTERIANS

I

COLONIAL Presbyterianism stemmed from two main sources; first, from the Presbyterian phase of English Puritanism, transplanted to the colonies by way of New England in the great Puritan migration of the seventeenth century; second, from Scottish Presbyterianism, coming to America mostly by way of North Ireland, in the great Scotch-Irish immigration of the eighteenth century, although a few came directly from Scotland. Presbyterianism of Scotch-Irish origin accounts for the major proportion of the rank and file of the colonial Presbyterian membership, but the principal Presbyterian colonial leadership came from the second and third generation New England Puritanism. English Puritanism finally broke into two distinct bodies, the Presbyterians and the Congregationalists, but this break did not come until after the great Puritan migration to New England from 1628 to 1640, so that there were some among them who had Presbyterian leanings from the beginning. Even after the division had taken place, the Presbyterians and Congregationalists were in agreement on most doctrinal matters, but differed in their conception as to what constituted the Church and also in regard to church polity.[1]

Political, economic and religious factors all played their part in bringing Scotch-Irish colonists to America. The people who had colon-

---

[1]For a concise statement as to the differences between the Presbyterians and Congregationalists on these matters see L. J. Trinterud, *The Forming of an American Tradition—A Re-examination of Colonial Presbyterianism* (Philadelphia, 1949), pp. 16-21.

ized North Ireland had come largely from the Lowlands of Scotland and had brought to Ireland with them "the strenuous Protestant spirit of Scotch Presbyterianism." Since their coming there had been little intermarriage with the native Irish, and therefore their religious and social beliefs and practices had undergone little change and the Presbyterian Church was there well organized with an able and aggressive ministry, largely educated in Scottish universities.

This emigration from North Ireland to the American colonies began in the early eighteenth century, and continued until well past the middle of the century. Between 1714 and 1720 it came largely through the port of Boston, and during these years fifty-four ships landed immigrants at the principal New England ports. New England attracted them, at first, because of their common Calvinism with the New England Puritans. Settlements were established in central Massachusetts, in southern New Hampshire and what is now Vermont and in Maine. The two villages of Londonderry in both the present states of New Hampshire and Vermont are living testimonies of that early immigration. The Scotch-Irish soon found, however, that they did not mix well with the New England Puritans, and after 1720 they began to find their way into New York, where they gave the names "Orange" and "Ulster" to two of the counties on the west side of the Hudson. But by far the largest part of this immigration landed at the several Delaware river ports and found its way into central Pennsylvania, then the farthest frontier, where they took up land in the valleys of the parallel mountain ranges of the Alleghanies, and gradually moved southward into western Maryland, Virginia, the Carolinas and Georgia.

By the opening of the American Revolution the Scotch-Irish were to be found in every colony in sufficient numbers to make their influence felt. Of all the races which had colonized the American colonies, they were the only one with a uniform religion. In contrast to this uniformity, note the great diversity of the German immigrants. Scotch-Irish distribution through the several colonies at the opening of the Revolution was as follows: in New England there were 70 communities; in New York from 30 to 40; in New Jersey from 50 to 60; in Delaware and Pennsylvania 130; in Virginia and Maryland and over the mountains into what is now east Kentucky and Tennessee more than 100; in North Carolina 50; in South Carolina and Georgia near 70.

To a large degree American Presbyterianism owes its rapid growth to the coming of the Scotch-Irish, though, as has been noted, there were feeble beginnings previous to this immigration. Several of the Puritan leaders of the Massachusetts Bay colony were Presbyterian in theory, and Presbyterian ideas of church polity were put into operation in several of the New England churches. John Eliot, the apostle to the Indians, was a supporter of Presbyterianism, and as has already been seen, Increase and Cotton Mather were advocates of what was really the Presbyterian system, when at the Ministerial Convention of 1705 they urged the adoption of the Massachusetts Proposals. In this contest Congregationalism won the day in Massachusetts, but in Connecticut the movement was strongly in the direction of Presbyterianism. With the adoption of the Saybrook Platform (1708) a modified Presbyterian system came into operation in Connecticut and the names Presbyterian and Congregational came to be used there interchangeably.

With the movement of New England Puritans into the middle colonies, especially into New York, where they came into an atmosphere strongly charged with Presbyterian ideas, their transformation into Presbyterians was but natural. Thus there came to be several Presbyterian congregations of New England origin on Long Island, by the middle of the seventeenth century. The beginning of Scottish migration to East New Jersey in the latter sixteen hundreds has already been mentioned, so that here also was a nucleus for Presbyterian organization. Indeed, in practically all the colonies, by the end of the seventeenth century, there were small bodies of Scottish or Scotch-Irish settlers, and in such localities Presbyterianism would naturally have the right of way.

II

The father of the Presbyterian Church in America, the one who, more than any other, deserves the honor for laying the foundations of organized American Presbyterianism, is Francis Makemie. Makemie was an Ulsterman, a licentiate of the Presbytery of Laggan who had come to the Island of Barbados in 1683 and from there had proceeded to Maryland where he established preaching stations among the several Scottish and Scotch-Irish communities on the eastern shore. In 1684 he formed a church at Snow Hill, and for the next several years he journeyed from place to place, preaching in the scattered settlements in Maryland, Virginia and the Carolinas. Impressed by the great need in America for ministers, he crossed the Atlantic and made his appeal to the Independent and Presbyterian Ministers' Union of London, and in 1703-1704 John Hampton and George McNish came with him to Maryland with promise of support from the London Union. By this time the Anglican Church had been established in Maryland, and in the very year Hampton and McNish arrived, South Carolina likewise had adopted the Anglican as the state church, and the progress of Presbyterianism in these colonies as well as in Virginia was hampered by persecution and intolerance. By 1706, however, a number of congregations had been gathered, under the direction of Makemie and his helpers, and in that year six ministers met in Philadelphia and there formed the first American presbytery, with Makemie as moderator. The men who made up the membership of this first presbytery well illustrate the several elements which went into the making of colonial Presbyterianism. Francis Makemie, the moderator, was a Scotch-Irishman; Samuel Davis, the minister at Lewes, Delaware, was also, probably, from North Ireland; Jedediah Andrews of the Philadelphia church was a native New Englander and a graduate of Harvard College; likewise also was John Watson a New Englander, as well as a protege of Increase and Cotton Mather. A third New England man was Nathaniel Taylor, pastor of a church in Maryland. Of the two men sent over by the Presbyterian and Congregational Union of London, George McNish and John Hampton, the first was a Scotchman, the second a Scotch-Irishman, and both were educated at the University of Glasgow. The congregations over which these several ministers presided were made up of members as diverse in their backgrounds as were their ministers, while the principal encouragement and assistance came from Boston and London rather than from North Ireland or Scotland.

An example of the kind of persecution which the Presbyterian ministers met at this period is that experienced by Makemie in New York in 1707. After a called meeting of the presbytery in Freehold, New Jersey, in December, 1706, Makemie and Hampton set out for New York, where Makemie was invited to preach in a private house. From thence they proceeded to Newtown, Long Island, intending to preach there. The next day they were both arrested on a warrant of the governor, Lord Cornbury, on the ground that they had preached without a license. The charges against Hampton were dropped, but Makemie was brought to trial the following June. He was defended by three able lawyers and was acquitted on the ground that he had complied with the English

Toleration Act in that he had secured a license under that act while in Barbados which was recognized as valid throughout the queen's dominions. Though he had won his case, Makemie was compelled to pay the cost of his prosecution, which amounted to more than £83. This travesty on English justice caused reverberations which soon brought about the recall of Lord Cornbury. It also brought the Presbyterians to the favorable attention of the growing number of Dissenters throughout the colonies. The long imprisonment and the harrowing experiences connected with the trial doubtless hastened Makemie's death which came the following year.

From year to year the number of preaching places increased, and by 1716, the year in which the first synod was formed, the number of ministers had grown to seventeen, recruited from Scotland, Ireland and New England. In the minutes of 1707 is found this item:

[let] every minister of the Presbytery supply neighbouring desolate places where a minister is wanting, and opportunity of doing good offers.

At each meeting of the presbytery petitions were presented by communities asking that ministers be sent them. Thus in 1708 the minutes record that

a letter sent by the people of and about White Clay Creek, in New Castle County, importing their desire and petition to the Presbytery, to have the ordinances of the gospel administered with more convenience and nearness to the place of their abode, for the greater advantage and ease to their several families, promising withall due encouragement to the minister that shall be appointed thus to supply them.

Although such petitions were numerous and the need for ministers great, yet there was a serious attempt to maintain educational standards for ministers. In 1710 information came to the presbytery that a certain David Evan, "a lay person," was preaching and teaching among the Welsh settlers in the Great Valley, and they consider that Evan "had done very ill." But evidently recognizing the need of just such men as David Evan they suggested that "he lay aside all other business for a twelve month, and apply himself closely to learning and study" under the direction of two members of the presbytery. Year by year Evan was examined by the presbytery as to his progress and it was not until 1715 that he was finally ordained.

The presbytery corresponded with the Dublin Presbytery; with Sir

Edwin Harrison, an eminent dissenter of London; with the Synod of Glasgow; with Cotton Mather, and with others from whom they hoped to obtain assistance. In a letter addressed to the Presbytery of Dublin in 1710 is this description of American Presbyterianism within the bounds of the Philadelphia Presbytery:

> In all Virginia there is but one small congregation at Elizabeth River, and some few families favouring our way in Rappahanock and York. In Maryland only four, in Pennsylvania five, and in the Jerseys two, which bounds with some places of New York makes all the bounds we have any members from, and at present some of these be vacant.

Much of the business of the Philadelphia Presbytery and later of the synod had to do with quarrels between congregations and their ministers and moral offenses of both ministers and people. Van Vleck, a minister of Dutch extraction, was accused and found guilty of bigamy; there were "unhappy jarrings among the people of Woodbridge" and with their minister, Mr. Wade. In 1720 a minister is brought before the synod for fornication which he confessed "with great seriousness, humility, and signs of true repentence" and his attitude was so satisfactory to the synod that after a suspension of four Sabbaths he was permitted "again to preach the gospel." Another minister "had been diverse times overtaken with drink" and was accused of using "abusive language, and quarreling and stabbing a man." Still another is charged "with a lie relating to a bargain of a horse," and also with "folly and levity unbecoming a gospel minister," while a Mr. Laing is rebuked and suspended "for violating the Lord's day, by washing himself in a creek." All of which seems to bear out the characterization of the Scotch-Irish settlers made by James Logan, the secretary of William Penn, who termed them "bold and indigent strangers" from Ireland, and who occupied land without legal title on the ground that it was "against the laws of God and Nature, that so much land should be idle while so many Christians wanted it to labour on."

It was the great migration of Scotch-Irish settlers into the middle colonies which so increased the number of Presbyterians that it became necessary in 1716 to divide the Presbytery of Philadelphia into four presbyteries and organize a synod. The presbyteries now organized were the Long Island, which included the churches in New York and eastern New Jersey; the Philadelphia, which embraced the churches in eastern Pennsylvania and western New Jersey; the New Castle which at its

formation had six ministers and was made up of churches in Delaware,
and the Snow Hill Presbytery in Maryland and Virginia. The territory
covered was from eastern Long Island to Virginia, and the number of
ministers at the formation of the synod was nineteen.

The Presbyterian Church naturally grew in proportion to the migration from North Ireland, and this was particularly large from 1720 onward. By 1730 the number of ministers had increased to thirty, the
largest share coming from New England, though Ireland, Scotland,
England and Wales contributed a considerable number. Jonathan Dickinson, a graduate of Yale College, destined to play a prominent part in
the affairs of the church for forty years, came from Massachusetts;
Thomas Craighead, the first of a long list of Craigheads, was the son of
an Irish minister, who worked first in New England, where Cotton
Mather became his loyal friend. But perhaps the most significant name
to be added to the list of ministers in these early years was that of William Tennent. Tennent had been a priest of the Church of Ireland,
though born in Scotland and educated at Edinburgh, and had previously
been licensed by a Scottish presbytery. On his arrival in Pennsylvania,
he was admitted to membership in the Presbyterian synod in 1718, after
he had given six reasons why he dissented from the Established Church
in Ireland. Perhaps no single minister in the synod at that time was to
have so large an influence upon the Presbyterian church in America.

During these years of rapid growth in the middle colonies, the few
Scotch-Irish who had remained in New England were engaged in forming congregations and in 1729 organized a presbytery, known as the
Presbytery of Londonderry, or as it was called by their neighbors, "the
Irish Presbytery." In communities where this new migration mingled
with the native New Englanders they encountered strong prejudice, and
in most cases were compelled to support the Congregational minister.
Persecution was particularly severe in Boston and Worcester. In the
latter town a small body of Presbyterians attempted to erect a meetinghouse, and the building was in process of construction when a mob, some
of whom were persons of "consideration and respectability," gathered at
night and demolished the structure. In a few places, however, such as
Londonderry, New Hampshire, the new Irish settlers were in the great
majority and conducted the affairs of their town to suit themselves. In
a few instances also an older community was dominated by the new arrivals from Ireland, with the result that the Congregational Church

became Presbyterian. But as a whole Presbyterianism remained weak in New England throughout the whole colonial period and has since remained so.

III

Of great importance to American Presbyterianism was the passage by the synod of the Adopting Act[2] of 1729. This provided that all ministers and licentiates must subscribe to the Westminster Confession. The New Castle Presbytery was the first to require subscription. The issue arose out of the unwillingness of the Presbyterians to discipline ministers guilty of scandalous immoralities. The movement for subscription to the Confession was led by the New Castle Presbytery, where a particularly notorious case of ministerial moral laxity had been glossed over, and the guilty minister permitted to continue after a short suspension, the inference seemingly being that doctrinal orthodoxy would automatically correct moral laxity—a dubious inference to say the least. The purpose of the act was to protect the American Presbyterians against the "many pernicious and dangerous corruptions in doctrine" which have "grown so much in vogue and fashion," such as "Arminianism, Socinianism, Deism, Freethinking, etc." Such a proposal had already split the Presbyterian Church in Ireland and its adoption was much opposed in America, particularly by the New England and Welsh ministers. Jonathan Dickinson stated that it would neither "detect hypocrites, nor keep concealed heretics out of the church," and occurrences which soon followed proved this to be true. Eventually, however, the Adopting Act was passed, though not until a concession had been made allowing ministers and licentiates to express any scruples they felt as to any article in the Confession while the presbytery, or synod, were to judge whether such scruples were "essential and necessary articles of faith." With the great increase in the number of Scottish and Irish ministers, however, the tendency was to override the scruples any minister might have, and to demand strict adherence to the Confession "without the least variation or alteration." Thus the early attempts to introduce liberality into the Presbyterian Church in America on the part of the New England group met with prompt and decisive defeat at the hands of the Scotch-Irish. But the provision permitting a candidate to

2For an understanding of the agitation which led to the passage of the Adopting Act see W. W. Sweet, *Religion in Colonial America* (New York, 1942), pp. 263-265; also Trinterud, *op. cit.*, Chap. II, pp. 38-52.

express scruples to any article in the Confession provided a way for liberalizing influences to gain a hearing.

The feeble attempts to gather Presbyterian churches in Virginia by Makemie and his helpers resulted in no permanent organization. In fact by Makemie's death in 1708 the Presbyterian Church ceased to exist in Virginia. But within a few years from that time Scotch-Irish immigrants were moving into the region west of the Blue Ridge in considerable numbers. Governor Gooch, himself a Scotchman, began his administration in 1727. He knew the Scotch-Irish and welcomed their coming. Indeed, he instituted the policy of granting patents to all applicants without reference to their religious belief, but only with the provision that within the required time a sufficient number of settlers should be found upon the grants. This generous policy attracted not only the Scotch-Irish but the Germans and English as well, and there soon came to be representatives of numerous religious bodies in the Great Valley of Virginia. In 1738 two new counties were formed west of the Ridge, Augusta and Frederick, the former being almost exclusively settled by Scotch-Irish people. At the same time the new counties were formed into parishes of the Established Church and provision made to elect vestries. In Augusta the vestry was composed largely of dissenters and when an Established Church minister was sent them, he preached without a surplice, while the congregation received the sacrament standing according to Presbyterian usage, and eventually the congregation dwindled away.

As early as 1719 occasional preachers visited the Valley from the Synod of Philadelphia and several of these visiting ministers organized congregations. Indeed, by 1738 there had come to be four or five congregations in western Virginia, and in that year application was made to the Synod of Philadelphia for aid, with the result that John Craig was sent as the minister over two congregations, Tinkling Spring and Augusta. The same year the synod sent a representative to Governor Gooch of Virginia in the interest of certain Presbyterians who were considering settling on the Virginia frontier. The synod's representative brought with him an address to the governor asking that the settlers be allowed "liberty of consciences and of worshipping God in a way agreeable to the principles of their education." In his reply the governor stated:

And as I have always been inclined to favor the people who have lately removed from the provinces to settle on the western side of our great mountains: so you may be assured that no interruption shall be given to any ministers of your profession who shall come among them, so as they conform themselves to the rules prescribed by the Act of Toleration in England, by taking the oaths enjoined thereby, and registering the place of their meeting, and behave themselves peaceably toward the government.[3]

From this time forward Presbyterianism made rapid progress in western Virginia, though the greatest impetus to southern Presbyterianism was to come from Hanover County in central Virginia. This, however, is a part of the story of the Great Awakening, and will be told in that connection.

[3]With the coming to the throne of William and Mary, English dissenters for the first time obtained legal recognition and toleration, with the passage of the Toleration Act of 1689. The act suspended the penal laws against those who attended other places of worship besides the Established Church, provided they took the oath of allegiance and supremacy and subscribed to a declaration against transubstantiation. Dissenting ministers, however, had to subscribe to thirty-five of the Thirty-nine Articles and a greater part of two more. Papists and those who did not believe in the Trinity were excluded from the benefits of the act.

CHAPTER IX

✢ ✢ ✢

THE GREAT AWAKENING IN NEW ENGLAND

THE latter seventeenth and early eighteenth centuries were crowded with disturbing influences for the New Englander. First of all it was a time of almost continuous warfare. The hundred years' struggle between France and England for the Mississippi Valley began in 1689 with the War of the Palatinate, known in America as King William's War. Within four years after the treaty was signed closing this war, the War of the Spanish Succession, or Queen Anne's War, began (1701), which did not end until 1713 with the signing of the famous Treaty of Utrecht. Then after a considerable period of peace there followed in rapid succession the War of the Austrian Succession (1739-1748) and the Seven Years' War (1756-1763). In all of these intercolonial wars New England bore the brunt of the struggle, and since the Indians played a conspicuous part in them, the New England frontier was never out of danger from Indian forays. Thus the whole atmosphere of the New England frontier, for years together, was filled with alarm. It was also a period of political unrest. From 1660 on to the end of the century the political status of the New England colonies was uncertain, and this served to occupy the attention of the Puritan leaders at the expense of moral and religious affairs.

The intensity of New England religion had considerably cooled by the end of the seventeenth century. The second and third generation Puritan was much less "religious" than had been his father and grandfather. It has been noted that by the adoption of the Half-Way Covenant unawakened persons were permitted to become "half-way" church members, and thus there came to be large numbers of people in every church whose relation to the church was merely formal. It is true that the Calvinistic doctrine of conversion was still theoretically held by the majority of the ministers—that is that conversion was the work of God alone—but it was now recognized by many ministers that there were certain "means" which might be used to put the soul in position to receive the regenerating touch of God's spirit. In other words, a new doctrine of conversion was evolving which laid increasing emphasis upon human responsibility. It was the combination of these two influences—the presence among the people of a "tremendous amount of latent fear" and the doctrine of human responsibility in conversion—that largely accounts for the Great Revival which began in central Massachusetts in the fourth decade of the eighteenth century.

I

At the very center of this great religious movement stands Jonathan Edwards, the minister of the church of the standing order at Northampton, at that time the most important inland town in the colony. In many respects Jonathan Edwards is the outstanding intellectual figure of colonial America and has been generally recognized as one of the greatest minds America has produced. "In Edwards there was a rare combination of fervor of feeling, of almost oriental fertility of imagination, and intellectual acumen."

Jonathan Edwards was born in East Windsor, Connecticut, where his father, Timothy Edwards, was the minister. He graduated from Yale in 1720 at seventeen years of age and after several years of further study and some preaching, and teaching at Yale, became the minister at Northampton, where for sixty years his maternal grandfather, Solomon Stoddard, had been the pastor. Soon after coming to Northampton he married Sarah Pierpont, the daughter of the Rev. James Pierpont of New Haven, and throughout her husband's great career her name was intimately associated with his. Indeed, she has been termed the ideal New England minister's wife. Hers was a joyous piety, while she saved her husband from all the troubles of household affairs, training and disciplining the numerous children, maintaining a genial and attractive hospitality until her home became like a sanctuary to multitudes. To understand Jonathan Edwards, Sarah Pierpont must not be left out of the picture. The town of Northampton at the opening of the great revival contained about two hundred families and generally speaking the people were intelligent and religious. During Solomon Stoddard's long ministry there had been five periods of religious awakening, an unusual condition for those years. This better spiritual condition at Northampton was due to the wise, common-sense position of Stoddard, in regard to the birthright members. It was his practice to admit them to the sacrament, as a means of leading them to conversion. The standard of regenerate membership was well enough for an age of deep religious emotions, "but it was too exacting in a period when such deep emotions were lacking."

Young Edwards came to Northampton in 1727, at a time "of extraordinary dullness in religion." He thus describes certain conditions in the town just before the revival began:

Licentiousness for some years greatly prevailed among the youth of the town; there were many of them very much addicted to night walking and frequenting the tavern, and lewd practices wherein some by their example exceedingly corrupted others. It was their manner to get together in assemblies of both sexes, for mirth and jollity, which they called frolics; and they would often spend the greater part of the night in them, without regard to order in the families they belonged to: indeed family government did too much fail in the town.

It was not long, however, until a change in the general religious atmosphere began to be manifest under the preaching of this tall, slender, grave young man. Edwards was by no means what might be called a popular preacher. He lived the life of a student, spending thirteen hours daily in his study, writing two sermons each week, one to be preached on Sunday, the other at the weekly lecture. To him sermon preparation and study were far more important than pastoral ministration, for he seldom visited among his people. In the pulpit he was quiet, speaking without gesture, and in a voice not loud, but distinct and penetrating. It was the content of his sermons, filled as they were with fire and life, combined with the remarkable personality and presence of the preacher, which accounts for the results which now began to be manifest among his hearers.

The revival began in December, 1734, while Jonathan Edwards was preaching a series of sermons on justification by faith alone. The sermons were intended to meet the growing tendency toward Arminianism which was considered by Calvinists as a matter for alarm. They felt that when men once began to trust in human measures for salvation they would cease to depend on Christ. Indeed, they were sure that Arminianism was a long step in the direction toward popery, and could only end in complete acceptance of a salvation won by good works, such as penance and offerings prescribed by priests. So sure were the Calvinists that Arminianism led to popery that even John Wesley, the great advocate of Arminian principles in the eighteenth century, was accused of being a Jesuit in disguise. In his sermons Edwards denied that any action "however good in itself, done by an unconverted man" could avail in procuring salvation. Salvation was the gift of God alone. With terrible vividness and earnestness Edwards depicted the wrath of God from which his hearers were exhorted to flee. Although Edwards' sermons were doctrinal, his way of presenting the old themes caused the members of his congregation to feel singled out. To use Miss Winslow's phrase, it was as though he were walking up and down the village street, pointing his accusing finger "at one house after another, unearthing secret sins and holding them up for all to see."[1] Soon religion became the chief topic of conversation throughout the town among people of all ages.

Again, Jonathan Edwards relates the happenings attendant upon the beginning of the revival:

Presently upon this a great and earnest concern about the great things of religion and eternal world became universal in all parts of the town, and among persons of all degrees and all ages; the noise among the dry bones waxed louder and louder; all other talk but about spiritual and eternal things was soon thrown by; all the conversation in all companies, and upon all occasions, was upon these things only, unless so much as was necessary for people carrying on their ordinary secular business. Other discourse than of the things of religion would scarcely be tolerated in any company.

"Soon," he tells us, "a glorious alteration" was to be noted in the town, "so that in the spring and summer following, anno 1735, the town seemed to be full of the presence of God: it was never so full of love, nor so full of joy, and yet so full of distress as it was then." "There was scarcely a single person in the town, either old or young, that was left unconcerned about the great things of the eternal world."

During the first year of the revival in Northhampton more than three hundred professed conversion, among both the aged and the young, though by May, 1735, the excitement began to die down, probably be-

---

[1]Ola Elizabeth Winslow, *Jonathan Edwards, 1703-1758* (New York, 1940), Chap. VIII and IX.

cause the "physical power to endure excitement was exhausted." Through the next several years revivals, independent of each other, began to appear in various parts of New England, especially in the Connecticut valley, until by 1740 the movement could be described as general throughout New England. Meanwhile a similar revival was in progress in New Jersey, especially among the Presbyterians, produced by the fervid preaching of the Tennents, particularly Gilbert Tennent. This revival seems to have begun entirely independent of the New England awakening, though the movements were in a sense brought together through the influence of George Whitefield, who began his first extensive evangelistic tour of America in 1740.

II

In 1737-1738 Jonathan Edwards wrote his *Narrative of the Surprizing Work of God,* which was soon being read on both sides of the Atlantic. At the same time the Methodist revival was just beginning in England, under the preaching of the Wesleys and Whitefield.

The Wesleyan revival may be said to have begun in 1737, when a little group of Oxford students, who had formed at that ancient university a Holy Club, whose members had been nicknamed "Methodists," removed to London and began the work of carrying religion and morality to the masses. "Their voice was soon heard in the wildest and most barbarous corners of the land, among the bleak moors of Northampton, or in the dens of London, or on the long galleries, where in the pauses of their labor the Cornish miners listened to the sobbing of the sea." Never had England heard such preaching; never had England witnessed such results. It was from this little group that the greatest preacher of the century sprang in the person of George Whitefield.

Whitefield was the son of a tavern keeper in Gloucester, and spent his childhood amidst the scenes common in the English public houses of that degraded time. Fortunately in Gloucester there was an endowed school, and here Whitefield was admitted as a pupil. Here he was prepared for Oxford, and in 1732 entered Pembroke College as a "Servitor," where he earned his way waiting on the tables of Fellows and Gentlemen Commoners. When he entered Oxford the "Holy Club" had been organized for three years, and the next year he became identified with this one spiritual oasis in the university. His conversion he dated from Easter Week, 1735. Graduating in 1736 he was ordained to the

priesthood of the Church of England by the Bishop of Gloucester and
began to supply churches in Oxford and London, at the same time offer-
ing himself to go to Georgia to take up the work there at which the
Wesleys had failed.

Within a year after his graduation, and while he was waiting to set
out for Georgia, Whitefield leaped into fame as the greatest preacher
of his day. From Gloucester to Bristol, thence to Bath, England's most
fashionable resort, thence to London, everywhere pulpits were opened
to him and the people flocked to hear him. He could not begin to meet
the calls which poured in upon him, though he preached nine times
each week. "On Sunday morning," he tells us, "long before day, you
might see streets filled with people going to church, with their lanterns
in their hands, and hear them conversing about the things of God." So
dense were the crowds which filled the churches, that "one might, as it
were, walk upon the people's heads," and thousands were turned away,
unable to enter even the largest churches.

In 1738 Whitefield made a brief visit to Georgia to look over the
ground preparatory to the beginning of his work there and the founding
of his orphanage. The next year, in August, he again landed in America
at Lewes, Delaware, and this marks the real beginning of his American
evangelistic tours. He visited the Tennents, in whose work he took
great delight; he was in Philadelphia in November, where throngs came
to hear him every day in Christ Church. From Philadelphia he went to
New York, where he heard Gilbert Tennent preach the most searching
sermon he had ever heard; thence back to Philadelphia and then southward to Georgia, passing through Maryland, Virginia and the Carolinas. Returning in April in his own sloop, he again visited Philadelphia
and New Jersey, thence back to Georgia. On September 14, 1740, he
landed in Rhode Island and the next month was given to a tour of
New England, already filled with religious excitement by the events
of the last several years. Everywhere he was received with enthusiasm.
Newport and Boston gave him an immense hearing. The students at
Harvard heard him and under the spell of his matchless oratory men
wept, women fainted and hundreds professed conversion.

Leaving Boston in October, Whitefield journeyed toward Northampton, preaching as he went, drawn by the fame of the great revival
that had begun there six years before. Whitefield's four sermons at

Northampton greatly moved both Edwards and his congregation, and a new revival broke which was to continue for two years. Whitefield in turn was so favorably impressed with Edwards and especially with Sarah Pierpont that he wrote in his diary "she caused me to renew those prayers which for some months I have put up to God, that He would send me a daughter of Abraham to be my wife."

Whitefield's short visit to New England caused a renewal of evangelistic activity. From December, 1740, to March, 1741, the New England revival reached high tide. A number of the more successful revivalist preachers, among them Jonathan Edwards, Eleazer Wheelock and Joseph Bellamy, became for the time being itinerant evangelists, and under their preaching physical demonstrations were common in many communities; strong men fell as though shot, and women became hysterical. When Jonathan Edwards preached at Enfield, Connecticut, in July, 1741, taking as his theme "Sinners in the Hands of an Angry God," "there was such a breathing of distress, and weeping, that the preacher was obliged to speak to the people and desire silence, that he might be heard." These bodily exercises were defended, even by such men as Edwards, and it is not strange that some among the ministers went to even greater extremes in their appeal to the emotions, and adopted extravagant methods to arouse the people. Such a minister was James Davenport of Long Island, who "more than any other man . . . embodied in himself and promoted in others, all the unsafe extravagances into which the revival was running," and who declared "that most of the ministers of the town of Boston and of the country are unconverted, and are leading their people blindfold to hell."

During the years from 1740 to 1742 there was a wonderful ingathering of members into the New England churches. Out of a population of 300,000, from 25,000 to 50,000 were added. The general moral effect of the revival upon New England communities was clearly manifest. Speaking of Northampton in 1743, Jonathan Edwards states: "I suppose the town has never been in no measure so free from vice—for any long time together—for these sixty years, as it has this nine years past." Similar testimonies of moral changes in other communities are numerous and there is no doubt but that the whole moral and religious life of New England was raised to a higher plane, and the revival amply deserves the name generally given it—the "Great Awakening."

III

Out of the New England awakening came several influences of great significance. In the first place, the revival definitely divided the New England ministers into two groups. One heartily supported the revival and its methods; the other condemned it and looked upon its results as but temporary. At the head of the first group stood Jonathan Edwards; the leader of the latter was Charles Chauncy, the liberal pastor of First Church, Boston, who in 1743 published an attack upon the revival called "Seasonable Thoughts on the State of Religion in New England." Those favoring the revival were soon known as "New Lights," those opposing it were designated "Old Lights," and it was not long until these two opposing parties were filling New England with controversy. In Connecticut a General Consociation of ministers condemned itinerant ministers and later the legislature passed an act forbidding the practice. Congregations split over the question, the revivalists withdrawing and forming themselves into separate churches and becoming known as "Separatists." For attending a Separatist meeting two students were expelled from Yale College in 1744. The Ministerial Convention of Massachusetts likewise condemned the revival, especially "its errors in doctrine, and disorders in practice," though a strong minority gathered in Boston to affirm "that there has been a happy and remarkable revival of Religion in many parts of the land."

Under these conditions it is not strange that the revival interest passed away almost as quickly as it had arisen. According to Jonathan Edwards' own statement, the church at Northampton from 1744 to 1748 was utterly dead, not a single application for membership being made during those years. When in the fall of 1744 Whitefield began his second tour of New England he met with opposition on every hand. Many pulpits were now closed to him; associations took action against him, while both Harvard and Yale colleges issued declarations opposing his conduct and methods. But thousands flocked to hear him and he still had stanch friends among the ministers who supported him to the last. Altogether he made five tours of New England, the last three in 1754, 1764 and 1770, dying in Newburyport in the latter year, where he lies buried under the pulpit of the Old South Presbyterian Church. Whatever limitations Whitefield may have had, he was undoubtedly one of the chief "human factors in the greatest religious overturning that New England has ever experienced."

It will now be necessary to consider the doctrinal discussion which arose in New England following the Great Awakening, and which resulted in the forming of two distinct doctrinal schools. These ultimately led to the division of Congregationalism into two wings, orthodox and liberal, or Unitarian, though the actual severance did not take place until the opening years of the nineteenth century.

The liberal doctrinal school had its roots in the tendency, already noticed, to emphasize the use of human "means" in salvation. At the same time, there was a rising tide of Arminian views among certain English writers whose works began to be read in America. Two of these writers were the Rev. Daniel Whitby, an Anglican clergyman, and the Rev. John Taylor, a Presbyterian. Both Whitby and Taylor made attacks upon Calvinism, Whitby's discourse upon the five points of Calvinism being considered an unanswerable argument by the Arminians. Taylor inveighed chiefly against the imputation of Adamic sin upon the race and advanced a new theory of the atonement in opposition to the limited atonement held by Calvinists. These views were soon adopted by a few New England ministers who in turn began to write in defense of what was termed the Liberal Theology. Thus Experience Mayhew, in 1744, published a treatise entitled "Grace Defended" in which he advocated the use of means of grace in obtaining pardoning grace, though he affirmed himself essentially a Calvinist. This publication aroused little interest compared to the furor caused by a published sermon of a young minister, Lemuel Briant, in 1749 on "The Absurdity and Blasphemy of Depreciating Moral Virtue." Sermons were preached in reply and tracts were issued attempting "to put a stop to the prevailing contagion of Arminian errors and other loose opinions . . . which threaten to banish vital piety out of the land." Eastern Massachusetts especially was now in the midst of a "general doctrinal ferment" which was to continue with little let-up until the split in the church was consummated two generations later. The churches and ministers holding the liberal views were generally those which had opposed the revival, and this opposition was confined largely to Boston and its immediate vicinity.

At the opposite pole from this liberal school stood Jonathan Edwards and those associated with him, who were responsible for what has come to be known as the New England Theology. In 1750 Edwards was dismissed from Northampton amidst bitterness and slander, after he had

announced his change in view regarding the admission of the unconverted to participation in the sacrament. Turned out of his pastorate at
the age of forty-seven, with ten living children, it was at once necessary
that he find a new field of labor. Finally in December, 1750, he received
a call to the frontier village of Stockbridge, in western Massachusetts,
where he was to be the missionary to the Housatonic Indians. Here he
came in the summer of 1751 and here he remained until January, 1758,
when he was called to the presidency of the college at Princeton. He
took up that office, however, only to lay it down, for in March of the
same year he died of inoculation for smallpox at the age of fifty-five.

The period which Edwards spent at Stockbridge "was the harvest time
of his intellectual activity." Altogether twenty-seven publications of
Edwards' appeared during his lifetime and nine were published after
his death. The most important of his publications, the one on which
his fame as an original thinker principally rests, is his treatise on "The
Freedom of the Will," which was written during his Stockbridge residence and made its appearance in 1754. Edwards maintained that man
had the power to act in accordance with the choice of his mind, but with
the origin of the inclination man has nothing to do. This left some
room for moral responsibility and for human choice. Four years later
he published a book defending the doctrine of Original Sin against
attacks by Charles Chauncy and the Rev. Samuel Webster and the English liberals. Edwards departed somewhat from historic Calvinism,
though his chief aim was to defend it against the Arminian school. He
always held stanchly to the sovereignty of God, but was at the same
time convinced that larger recognition must be given to man's responsibility. He thus became chiefly responsible for the establishment of
what came to be known as the "New Divinity," or the Edwardian school.

Edwards was a man of warm friendships and soon loyal disciples
were defending his views from the attacks of the liberals on the one hand
and the Old Calvinists on the other. Among the most influential of
these Edwardian leaders were Joseph Bellamy and Samuel Hopkins
who were companions of Edwards' later life, while in the next generation the chief supporters of the New Divinity were Stephen West, John
Smalley, Jonathan Edwards the younger, Nathaniel Emmons and
Timothy Dwight. Bellamy and Hopkins were controversialists of great
power, and were responsible for adding certain important features to
the New Divinity. Among these new features was their assertion of a

general atonement, though Edwards himself was inclined to a limited theory of the atonement. Hopkins, especially, developed Edwards' teachings beyond Edwards and put his own stamp upon them so fully that he often is considered as the founder of a new school of thought called Hopkinsianism.

The development of this ultra-Edwardian school headed by Hopkins and others led to a heated pamphlet warfare between the Old Calvinists and the advocates of the New Divinity, while both Old Calvinists and the supporters of the New Divinity united in their attacks upon the liberals in and about Boston, who were inclining more and more toward Universalism and Unitarianism. Thus Charles Chauncy in 1782 came out boldly on the side of Universalism in a tract published anonymously called "Salvation for all Men Illustrated and Vindicated as a Scripture Doctrine" which was ably answered by Edwards the younger. This, however, was a development which came largely after the Revolution.

It is an interesting fact, and one of considerable importance for an understanding of later developments, that the Edwardian school came to be the dominant party in Connecticut and western Massachusetts. The struggle between Old Calvinism and the Edwardian party long continued in these sections, but by the end of the century the New Divinity had won the victory. These views of modified Calvinism also spread among the Presbyterians of the north middle region, a fact which was to have large significance in the Presbyterian Church in the nineteenth century. Though Calvinism in its modified form triumphed in western Massachusets and Connecticut, the liberal theology won the day in eastern Massachusets, especially in and about Boston. The cleavage between the two parties was destined to grow deeper and deeper until a complete separation was to be the result. The account of this separation, however, belongs to a later period in our story.

The fifty years following the Great Awakening may be characterized as one of spiritual deadness, a period of religious and moral indifference throughout New England. The bitter doctrinal controversy was undoubtedly one of the causes, but there were other causes, among them two wars including the American Revolution, and a long period of great political unrest.

CHAPTER X

✢ ✢ ✢

THE GREAT AWAKENING IN THE MIDDLE AND SOUTHERN COLONIES

THE MIDDLE COLONY REVIVAL

THE series of great religious awakenings which swept over the American colonies in the middle of the eighteenth century were in many respects the most far-reaching social movements of the whole colonial period. They influenced all the churches, either directly or indirectly. In New England, of course, the Congregationalists were the ones primarily affected, though the indirect influence upon the Baptists was large. In the middle colonies it was a movement largely among Presbyterians, though it began among the German sectarians and the Dutch Reformed churches of central New Jersey. In the southern colonies the revival manifested itself first among the Presbyterians, especially in Virginia; in its second phase it was largely a Baptist movement, while it continued in a third phase as a Methodist movement.

The great variety of racial and religious groups to be found in colonial Pennsylvania, New Jersey and New York have been noticed. Many of the German colonists, though representing several religious sects, were Pietists. The founder of the Pietists was Philip Jacob Spener who advocated the establishment of devotional groups within the Lutheran churches of Germany for the purposes of Bible study and of promoting true piety. The new university at Halle became the center of the Pietists and it was to Francke, the successor of Spener at Halle, that the Lutherans in America looked for aid, and the great Lutheran leader Muhlenberg came out to America from this Pietistic center. There were Pietists also among the German Reformed leaders in the colonies, but the Pietistic, or evangelical, influence was particularly strong among the smaller German groups, such as the Mennonites, the Dunkers and the Moravians. This Pietistic emphasis among the Pennsylvania Germans was one of the sources of the great revival movement in the middle colonies, though it was an indirect rather than a direct influence.

I

Of much greater importance was the revival among the Dutch Reformed churches begun under the influence of Theodore J. Frelinghuysen,[1] a German born near the Dutch border and ordained in the Dutch Church, who came out to America in 1720 to be the pastor of some Dutch churches on the New Jersey frontier. From the moment of his landing in America Frelinghuysen began to fight against formality and dead orthodoxy which he found completely permeating the Dutch churches in America. In his first sermon, preached in New York soon after landing, Frelinghuysen struck such an evangelical note that he at once aroused the opposition of some of the Dutch ministers. He became the pastor of four churches in the Raritan valley in New Jersey, and his earnest preaching, in which he laid emphasis upon the necessity of conversion, so astonished his Dutch congregations that many were outraged, and soon parties began to develop, one opposing, the other accepting the new doctrines. At the end of three years his new gospel had disrupted his churches. The disaffected published their *Complaint* against him in a book of 246 pages, and an answer was soon forthcoming prepared by two of Frelinghuysen's friends, and thus the Dutch ministers were divided into hostile camps.

Meanwhile Frelinghuysen's fervid evangelical preaching was bearing fruit and numerous conversions were taking place. In 1726 the ingathering of new members was particularly large, and invitations to visit other churches began to pour in upon him. Some of these he accepted and soon the revival was spreading beyond the Raritan valley. Of particular importance is the fact that the revival spirit began to manifest itself among some English-speaking Presbyterians scattered through the region, who in 1726 called a young Presbyterian licentiate, Gilbert Tennent, to be their pastor. Frelinghuysen gave every as-

[1] Trinterud states that there is no clear evidence connecting Frelinghuysen with German Pietism; there is every evidence, however, that his emphasis upon religion as an inner experience was of a piece with the German Pietists. (See Trinterud, *op. cit.*, pp. 54-56.)

sistance to this young Presbyterian minister, encouraged his own members to subscribe toward his salary, permitted him to use the Dutch meetinghouses, and sometimes held joint services with him. All this was abundantly helpful to the cause of Christianity in central New Jersey, but it brought down increased maledictions upon the head of Domine Frelinghuysen, whose enemies objected to the use of English in Dutch churches.

II

Gilbert Tennent, the young Presbyterian minister welcomed so heartily by Domine Frelinghuysen, was destined to be the heart and center of a revival movement among the Presbyterians of much greater significance than that among the Dutch Reformed. Gilbert Tennent was the son of William Tennent, whose admission to the synod in 1718 has already been noted. In 1726 the elder Tennent became the Presbyterian minister at Neshaminy, Bucks County, Pennsylvania, and here he established what came to be known as the "Log College."

William Tennant had four sons, Gilbert the eldest having already been trained for the ministry under his father's care. To better facilitate the education of his younger sons a log cabin was built in his yard to serve as a school and here three of his own sons and fifteen other young men received their training for the ministry. The elder Tennent not only drilled his students in the languages, logic and theology, but he imbued them with an evangelical passion which sent them out flaming evangelists. The sons of William Tennent—Gilbert, William Jr., John and Charles—all became ministers of Presbyterian churches in central New Jersey, while Samuel Blair, also a graduate of the Log College, became the pastor of several small churches centering at Shrewsbury. Thus there came to be a group of ministers, evangelical in sentiment, settled near New Brunswick, and in 1738 the New Brunswick Presbytery was formed of these five evangelical ministers. At their first meeting the presbytery licensed John Rowland, another graduate of the Log College, and later ordained him. The conservative ministers, most of whom were of Scottish and Scotch-Irish background, educated in Scottish universities, objected to this action, as they were fearful lest the Presbyterian ministry would be deluged with half-educated enthusiasts. This fear led the synod to pass a regulation permitting presbyteries to examine and ordain only those candidates who were graduates of New England or European colleges. This action, of course, was intended to check the activities of the Log College and the admission of its graduates.

The real motive back of this action was bitter opposition of the conservative ministers to the revival. Thus the Presbyterian ministers in New Jersey were soon divided into two parties. Meanwhile a great revival was getting under way induced by the fervid preaching of the Log College evangelicals. Especially was John Rowland's preaching effective in stirring his people, and religion became the single topic of conversation in the little rural communities where he ministered. The revival spirit was now manifest in many centers. At Newark, where Aaron Burr was the minister, the revival attained its height in 1739 and 1740; in the highlands of New York and on Long Island the revival flame burst forth, while a group of Yale graduates, among them Jonathan Dickinson, now came over to the evangelical party and took their part in the revival. Even some of the conservative Scotch-Irish congregations in Pennsylvania responded to the revival preaching of Samuel Blair and a revival broke out at Fagg's Manor, where he had become the pastor in 1739, which soon spread to other places in Pennsylvania. Here was the very center of the opposition to the revival, but so strong was the movement among the people that even unfriendly ministers were constrained to invite the evangelists to visit their communities.

III

Such was the general situation among the Presbyterians in the middle colonies when George Whitefield arrived in America on his first evangelistic tour. Whitefield was one of the most catholic-spirited ministers of his time, and could coöperate with Quakers, Baptists, Lutherans, Moravians, Presbyterians, Congregationalists, Dutch Reformed and all others so long as they, like himself, advocated vital religion and preached conversion. On one occasion, preaching from the balcony of the courthouse in Philadelphia, Whitefield cried out: " 'Father Abraham, whom have you in Heaven? Any Episcopalians?' 'No.' 'Any Presbyterians?' 'No.' 'Have you any Independents or Seceders?' 'No.' 'Have you any Methodists?' 'No, no, no!!' 'Whom have you there?' 'We don't know those names here. All who are here are Christians—believers in Christ—men who have overcome by the blood of the Lamb and the word of his testimony.' 'Oh, is this the case? Then God help us, God help us all, to forget party names, and to become Christians in deed and in truth.' " On this first tour Whitefield spent several days in Philadelphia and then passed through central New Jersey toward New York. He met the aged elder Tennent in Philadelphia; at New Brunswick he preached in Gilbert Tennent's meetinghouse, and from thence to New York Gilbert Tennent accompanied him. In New York he preached in the Presbyterian church, as well as in the fields where great throngs assembled. Journeying back to Philadelphia, Whitefield was invited by Jonathan Dickinson to preach at Elizabethtown, and coming again to New Brunswick he met Domine Frelinghuysen and several of the evangelical leaders.

The year 1740-1741 marks the high tide of the revival in the middle colonies. Whitefield's preaching had stirred all classes and all the churches. Even the deistic Franklin became his admirer and lifelong friend, and the revival became exceedingly popular with the common people. But from the beginning the revival had aroused criticism, and unfortunately the revivalists themselves were partly responsible for it in that they tended to become censorious and critical of those who did not agree with them. Gilbert Tennent preached his famous sermon on "Danger of an Unconverted Ministry" in March, 1740, which did not help allay opposition, while others of the evangelical preachers were ready to indict all ministers who did not support the revival movement.

IV

Opposition to the revival among the Presbyterians came to a head at the meeting of the synod in 1741. At this meeting a protest was presented against the action of the evangelical ministers in intruding uninvited into the bounds of other ministers; for their censorious judgments of those who did not walk with them; for violating the act of the synod in regard to the examination of candidates; for preaching the terrors of the law "in such a manner and dialect as has no precedent in the Word of God"; and for claiming that truly gracious persons are able to judge with certainty both of their own state and that of others. These were the grounds on which the New Side party, or the evangelicals, were now excluded by the Old Side, or conservatives, from membership in the synod. The ministers and elders of the New Brunswick Presbytery and others who were in sympathy with them now withdrew. The evange-lical, or the New Side party however, did not form a new synod until efforts had been made to undo the action taken in 1741. This was in vain, however, and in September, 1745, the New Side party formed the New York Synod at Elizabethtown, New Jersey.

From 1745 to 1758 the Presbyterians in the colonies were divided into two main bodies. The New Side body embraced a large proportion of the able and fervent men of the church and grew rapidly in numbers and influence. On the other hand, the Philadelphia, or the Old Side, Synod made no progress during the years of separation. At the time of the schism the Old Side numbered twenty-five ministers, while the New Side numbered twenty-two. In 1758 at the time of the reunion the Old Side had decreased and numbered but twenty-two, while the New Side had grown by leaps and bounds and numbered seventy-two. "The New Side churches were active, growing and full of young people," while the heroism of their enthusiastic leaders, such as Rowland, Blair and Brainerd, all of whom burned themselves out while still young men, attracted other young and enthusiastic men to take their places. The members of the conservative group, on the other hand, were old men; while their opposition to the popular revival movement rendered them and their churches unpopular with the young people. These years of separation mark the unmistakable triumph of the revival party with-in the Presbyterian Church.

Fortunately for American Presbyterianism the schism caused by the Great Revival was soon healed. The first step in the direction of re-union was taken by the New York Synod in 1749. In that year Gilbert Tennent published his *Irenicum* in which he attempted to allay the bitterness caused by his earlier attacks upon those who opposed the revival. At first the Philadelphia Synod spurned these friendly gestures, but the New Side Synod persisted and refused to allow their own temper to be ruffled, while their reunion committee headed by Gilbert Tennent continued its negotiations. Finally in 1758 an agreement was reached. The question of the examination of candidates as to their learning and religious experience was left to the presbyteries, and nothing was said about synodical examination or college degrees. It was provided that ministers should not intrude into the parishes of other ministers unin-vited, while the act of 1741 expelling the New Brunswick Presbytery was declared irregular. The reunited church now entered upon a period of great activity and rapid growth which was to continue up to the outbreak of the American Revolution.

It was during the period of the Great Awakening that two other branches of Presbyterianism found their way into the colonies: these were the Reformed and the Associate Reformed, representing the most conservative Scottish and Irish groups known as the "Covenanters." Naturally, representatives of these groups found their way to America in the great migration from North Ireland in the eighteenth century. At first they united with the larger body, but when the schism between the New and Old Side occurred the Covenanter ministers adhered to the New Side, upon whom they urged the necessity of renewing the Covenants. When this was refused an appeal was sent to the Reformed Presbytery of Scotland and eventually helpers were sent to minister to the scattered Covenanters of Pennsylvania. In 1644 a split had occurred among the Covenanters of Scotland, and the Associate Reformed Presbytery was formed, while this latter group divided (1746-1747) over the question of the lawfulness of the oath exacted of burgesses, into Burghers and Anti-Burghers.

V

The educational influence of the great revival in the middle colonies was particularly significant. William Tennent's school, called in derision the Log College, was the seed of a whole group of similar institutions, some of which have lived to this day. All of its sixteen or eighteen graduates were men of earnestness and zeal, more than half of whom became preachers of extraordinary power, and several became eminent as educators as well. Many of these Log College graduates established log colleges, or private schools, modeled after that of William Tennent at Neshaminy and out of these classical and theological schools came graduates destined to take a notable place in the leadership of American Presbyterianism. One such school founded on the model of the Log College was that established by Samuel Blair at Fagg's Manor in Chester County, Pennsylvania. The first graduate of this school was Samuel Davies, who was to become the leader of the Presbyterian Church in Virginia and finally president of the College of New Jersey. Other students at the Fagg's Manor school were John Rodgers, of New York, James Finley and Robert Smith, all of whom became leaders of distinction. Another such school was that established at Nottingham, Pennsylvania, by Samuel Finley. From this school came other noted leaders in both church and state, among them Dr. Benjamin Rush, while Finley himself succeeded Davies as president of Princeton. Pequea, in Lancaster County, Pennsylvania, was another such school, established by Robert Smith, a graduate of the Fagg's Manor school. From the Pequea school came John McMillan, one of the founders of Jefferson College who in turn conducted a Log College in connection with his work in the Redstone country of western Pennsylvania.

Of greater importance than these academies was the establishment by the New York Synod of the College of New Jersey. Tennent's Log College ceased with his death in 1746, and the same year a charter was obtained, largely through the efforts of Jonathan Dickinson, for a new college. The trustees selected Dickinson as the president and in May, 1747, the college opened in Dickinson's house at Elizabethtown, New Jersey. Dickinson's death occurred in the fall of the same year, and the trustees turned to Aaron Burr, the minister at Newark, to take up the work of education. The college was now removed to Newark. In 1755 the college was permanently established at Princeton, and on the death of Burr in 1757 his father-in-law, Jonathan Edwards, succeeded to the presidency. The revival leaders in New England had grown suspicious of the New England colleges, especially after their condemnation of the revival, which accounts for Edwards' willingness to accept the presidency, though he hardly lived to enter upon his office. The College of New Jersey, as Princeton was called in its early years, admirably served the purpose of its founding and poured a stream of zealous young men into the ministry of the Presbyterian Church.

The founding of the University of Pennsylvania came indirectly out of the Great Awakening. During Whitefield's several visits to Philadelphia, Benjamin Franklin became his admirer and finally his stanch friend. Franklin states in his biography, "Our friendship was sincere on both sides and lasted to his death." At first the evangelist was permitted to preach in the Established Church in that city, but on his later visits this was denied him, and it became necessary for him to preach in the fields or from the courthouse steps. Finally Whitefield's Philadelphia friends conceived the idea of erecting a building to accommodate the great crowds who wished to hear him. Thus Franklin describes the erection of the building: "Sufficient sums were soon received to procure the ground and erect the building, which was a hundred feet long, and seventy broad. Both house and ground were vested in trustees," of whom Franklin was one, "expressly for the use of any preacher of any religious persuasion, who might desire to say something to the people of Philadelphia." Here Whitefield preached when he visited the city and here his friends, the Tennents, Blair, Rowland and others, occasionally ministered, and here for nine years the Second Presbyterian Church of Philadelphia, of which Gilbert Tennent was pastor, worshiped. In 1751, largely through the efforts of Franklin, the building was used for an academy, and two years later it was chartered as the "College, Academy and Charitable School of Philadelphia," which finally (1791) grew into the University of Pennsylvania. There now stands, appropriately, in one of the quadrangles of the university a life-size statue of George Whitefield, erected by the Methodist students and graduates of the University of Pennsylvania.

Shortly after the establishment of the Academy in Philadelphia steps were taken to found a college in New York. This was accomplished by royal charter in 1754, after Trinity Church had agreed to convey to the institution a part of the queen's farm which Queen Anne had given to Trinity parish. This was done with the express provision that the president of the college should forever be a member of the Established Church and that the liturgy of the church should always be used at the morning and evening service of the college. There was much opposition to these restrictions on the part of the Dutch Reformed, Presbyterian and Lutheran groups, who would have preferred that the college be established by an Act of the Assembly. The new King's college opened in a building belonging to Trinity Church, with President Samuel Johnson the entire faculty. The first advertisement of the college disclaims any intention of imposing "on the scholars the peculiar Tenets of any particular Sect of Christians; but to inculcate upon their tender Minds, the great Principles of Christianity and Morality, in which true Christians of each Denomination are generally agreed."

Since the beginning, the Reformed Church in the colonies had been completely dependent upon the Classis of Amsterdam, but the elder Frelinghuysen began to realize the necessity of training up young men in America for the ministry and was the first to favor some degree of independence for the American churches. This agitation finally culminated in the formation of an American Coetus, or presbytery (1747),

subject, however, to the Classis at Amsterdam. Soon after the establishment of King's College certain Dutch Reformed leaders began to
advocate the establishment of a Professorship of Theology for the
Dutch Church, in the New York College, but this eventually failed. The
Dutch Church was now divided into two parties, the one desiring to
remain under the complete control of the Holland Classis, and to
continue to depend upon Holland for its ministry; the other stood for
an American trained ministry and a degree of independence for
the American churches. The latter party was made up of the friends of
the Great Revival, who were anxious to establish a college where the
young men who had been stirred by the evangelical passion might
receive training for the ministry. Eventually the opposers of the revival
and of an American trained ministry withdrew from the Coetus and
formed a body called the "Conferentie," and thus a schism similar to
that in the Presbyterian Church was precipitated in the Dutch Church.
The conservatives also insisted upon the use of the Dutch language in
the churches while the evangelicals were more and more introducing
English, and English preaching became very popular, especially among
the young people in New York City. Eventually (1772) the disputes in
the Dutch Church came to a happy end through the wisdom and tact
of a young minister, John H. Livingston, a native of New York but
educated for the ministry at the University of Utrecht, who now was
called to a pastorate in New York. He brought with him a plan of
union approved by the Classis of Amsterdam, which fully upheld every
contention of the Coetus, and led to the establishment of Queen's College at New Brunswick in 1770, of which Livingston eventually became
the president. The triumph of the evangelical party and the policies
it advocated undoubtedly saved the Dutch Church from final extinction.

Dartmouth College and what is now Brown University grew out of
the general educational interest created by the Great Awakening, as
did also Liberty Hall, later known as Washington College, and Hampden-Sidney College in Virginia. The story of the beginnings of these
institutions, however, will be related in another connection.

THE REVIVAL IN THE SOUTHERN COLONIES

The coming of the Scotch-Irish settlers into the western valleys of
Virginia and the suspension of the intolerant ecclesiastical laws in
their favor soon led to the formation of several Presbyterian congrega-

tions in these new settlements. Itinerant missionaries and then pastors were sent them by the Synod of Philadelphia, so that by 1738 there came to be four or five congregations west of the Blue Ridge. But the greatest expansion of Presbyterianism into the South was to come from another source, namely, Hanover county in central Virginia. The churches and ministers in the Great Valley were generally opposed to the revival, and Hanover county became the revival center of southern Presbyterianism. The revival in Hanover county began as a spontaneous movement among a small group of laymen of whom Samuel Morris was the leader. He and several others became interested in some religious books which fell into their hands, such as Whitefield's sermons and some of Luther's writings, and they met together in one another's houses where these books were read. Finally, the meetings attracted such crowds that their houses became too small to accommodate them, and special houses were built, the first such building being called Morris's Reading House.

In 1742-1743 William Robinson, a graduate of the Log College, was sent out by the New Brunswick Presbytery to visit Presbyterian settlements in western Virginia and North Carolina, and on this tour visited Hanover County. Other revival missionaries followed Robinson, and in 1748 Samuel Davies was sent to Hanover County as the first settled Presbyterian minister in the region. Here Davies, perhaps the most brilliant Presbyterian preacher of the colonial period, was so successful that within a few years the work was greatly extended and a presbytery was formed (1755), called the Hanover Presbytery, destined to become the "Mother" Presbytery of the South and Southwest.

Davies succeeded in winning the good will of Governor Gooch by his eloquent support of the cause of the colonies in the French and Indian War and his fame spread far and wide. He obtained concessions from the Virginia government in favor of increasing the number of Presbyterian chapels, winning his cause against the opposition of the attorney general of Virginia. Soon he was itinerating over seven counties, under a license issued by the colonial authorities, while all of his chapels were legally registered. Davies never proceeded on any new enterprise until he had won the legal right to proceed, and thus he gave Presbyterianism a stable legal status in Virginia, such as no other dissenting body had succeeded in gaining.[2] The growing unpopularity of

2For this phase of Samuel Davies' influence in Virginia see George H. Bost, *Samuel Davies: Colonial Revivalist and Champion of Religious Toleration* (Typed Ph. D. Thesis, University of Chicago, 1942).

the Established Church, due to the Twopenny Acts (1755, 1758) and the Parson's Cause, aided the growth of Presbyterianism and numerous defections from the Establishment of Presbyterianism took place. Once the status of Virginia Presbyterianism was legally defined their churches entered upon a period of rapid growth and expansion. Revivals were of frequent occurrence and by the year 1758, in which the schism between the Old and New Side was healed, Presbyterianism was firmly established in central Virginia, and from then until the outbreak of the Revolution expanded rapidly both southward and westward.

Samuel Davies left Virginia in 1759 to accept the presidency of the College of New Jersey. He, with Gilbert Tennent, had previously visited England and Scotland to raise money for the support of the college, and their mission had proved most successful. After three times refusing the presidency on the death of Edwards, Davies finally was persuaded to accept, though his term of office lasted less than two years, he dying of a fever in February, 1761.

The Presbyterian revival in Virginia has more than a religious significance. Indeed, it was the "first mass movement that was to bring about a social and political upheaval in Virginia—the first breach in the ranks of privilege." But this movement received even greater impetus from the next two phases of the revival, in which Baptists and Methodists were to play the principal role.

VI

To understand the Baptist revival and expansion into the South it is necessary first to glance at the influence the Great Awakening in the New England and middle colonies exerted upon them. At first the Baptists took little part in the New England revival, probably because of the fact that they had been so harshly treated by the Congregationalists that they felt little inclination to join them in this movement. But the Baptists reaped great indirect benefit from the revival through the controversies and divisions which soon appeared in many New England Congregational churches. In numerous instances those favoring the revival separated from those who opposed it and formed "Separate" congregations. Many of the Separate congregations became Baptist, though some of them returned to the older congregations, while others because of internal dissensions, were soon disintegrated. Thus the number of Baptist churches in Massachusetts grew from six to thirty; in Connecticut from four to twelve; in Rhode Island from eleven to thirty-six, while Baptist churches were established in New Hampshire, Vermont and Maine.

While the growth of the Baptists in New England during the period of the Great Awakening was proportionately rapid, in the middle colonies there seems to have been but normal growth. This is accounted for by a Baptist historian with the statement that ground once pre-occupied by Presbyterians is relatively irresponsive to Baptist effort. Though there were many schisms in Presbyterian churches in the middle colonies as a result of the revival, yet there seems to have been no Baptist church formed as a result.

The rapid increase of Baptists in New England and especially in Rhode Island, from about 1740 onward, and the appearance of a better educated leadership, led naturally to the establishment of educational institutions, first and chief of which was Rhode Island College. The idea of founding an institution to be controlled by Baptists originated with Morgan Edwards of the Philadelphia Association, though he soon obtained the coöperation of a brilliant young graduate of the College of New Jersey, James Manning. The idea once suggested was immediately taken up by the leading Baptists of Rhode Island and in 1764 a liberal charter was obtained. Baptists were to control the institution, but Quakers, Congregationalists and Episcopalians were to share in its government, while no religious tests were ever to be required and places on the faculty were to be open to all denominations of Protestants. The founding of the college of Rhode Island, however, had little to do with the expansion of Baptists southward.

While there were Baptist congregations in Virginia as early as 1714, yet they remained unnoticed and unmolested and had little part in Baptist expansion. Those responsible for the Baptist revival in Virginia and North Carolina came directly from New England and were the products of the great New England awakening. The leaders were Shubal Stearns and his brother-in-law, Daniel Marshall, who were Separate Baptists from Connecticut. Stearns was a convert of the Great Revival and was one of those who withdrew to form a Separate congregation. Becoming a Baptist, he began to preach and was ordained in 1751. Three years later he left New England and settled on Opekon Creek, Virginia, where there was already a Baptist church. Here he was joined by his brother-in-law, Daniel Marshall, who had gone through much the same experience as had Stearns, though he had come from Presbyterian ancestry. At first Stearns and Marshall preached as evangelists in Virginia, but here they met opposition from the Baptists as well as others, and they determined to remove to North Carolina, where they located in Guilford County, on Sandy Creek, in 1755.

Soon after their arrival in North Carolina a church was organized called the Sandy Creek Church and Stearns became the pastor. Soon Stearns, Marshall and other Baptist evangelists were traveling throughout a wide territory and Sandy Creek Church grew from 16 to 606 members. Other churches were formed, preachers were "raised up," among them James Reed, Dutton Lane and, most important of all, Samuell Harriss, a man of influence and education, who had held several offices, among them burgess of the county and colonel of militia Five years after the formation of the Sandy Creek Church (1760) the Sandy Creek Association was organized, which is called the Mother Association, as Sandy Creek Church became the "mother, and grandmother and great-grandmother of forty-two churches."

For the next ten years the progress of the Separate Baptists is almost unparalleled in Baptist history. Whole communities were stirred and strong Baptist churches established. The following is a description of the type of work performed by Harriss and Reed in Virginia:

> In one of their visits, they baptized seventy-five at one time, and in the course of one of their journeys, which generally lasted several weeks, they baptized upwards of two hundred. It was not uncommon at one of their great meetings, for many hundreds to camp on the ground, in order to be present the next day. . . . There were instances of persons travelling more than one hundred miles to one of these meetings; to go forty or fifty was not uncommon.

In these meeting there were many excesses and the preaching of the Baptist evangelists undoubtedly encouraged extravagances. An eyewitness at one of their meetings saw

> multitudes, some roaring on the ground, some wringing their hands, some in extacies, some praying, some weeping; and others so outrageously cursing and swearing that it was thought they were really possessed of the devil.

Unlike the Presbyterians in Virginia, the Baptists were little inclined to conform to the letter of the law in securing licenses for their meetinghouses. They were also more open and extreme in their attacks upon the Established Church; and these facts, added to the fear aroused that their rapid increase constituted a menace to society, brought down upon them bitter persecution. The years from 1768 to 1770 are known as the Period of the Great Persecution. Baptist ministers were arrested as disturbers of the peace, and more than thirty, to use the phrase of one of their number, "were honored with the dungeon."

As is usually the case, persecution, instead of retarding, served to promote their cause, and when it became generally known that the Baptists held as one of their principles the separation of church and state many leading men came to favor them. The patient manner in which they bore persecution gave them a reputation for piety and goodness and "every month," to quote their chief historian, "new places were found by the preachers whereon to plant the Redeemer's standard." Although but few, perhaps, became Baptists in each place, yet the majority would be favorable. Such was the Baptist situation in Virginia and in the other southern colonies when the Revolution opened. Though still relatively a small body, the Baptists were strong enough to make it important for either side to gain their influence and support, an advantageous position which the Baptists were not slow in perceiving. More and more the religious issue became associated in men's minds with the political issue, and many came to see that Baptist notions were in harmony with the political philosophy of the American Revolutionary leaders, for was not the paying of taxes to support the Established Church taxation without representation?

Just as the Baptists were becoming well established in Virginia and North Carolina a third phase of the revival began under Devereux Jarratt, an evangelical Anglican minister, who was associated with the early Methodist preachers. Jarratt had been converted under Presbyterian influence and was thoroughly imbued with evangelical ideas. He became rector of the parish of Bath in Dinwiddie county in 1763 and his warm evangelical preaching soon filled his church to overflowing. He got very little sympathy or assistance from his fellow clergymen, however, in his attempt to evangelize the Establishment. Speaking of his isolation he says in his autobiography:

> At that time I stood alone not knowing of one clergyman in Virginia like minded with myself; yea I was opposed and reproached by the clergy—called an enthusiast, fanatic, visionary, dissenter, Presbyterian, madman, and whatnot;—yet was I so well convinced of the utility and importance of the truths I declared and the doctrines I preached, that no clamor, opposition, or reproach could daunt my spirit, or move me from my purpose and manner of preaching. . . .

VII

Organized Methodism first appeared in the American colonies in 1766 when Philip Embury began to hold meetings in his house in New York and soon afterward formed a society. Probably two years earlier Robert Strawbridge began to preach in Maryland and likewise formed a society near Sam's Creek where a log meetinghouse was erected. Three years later (1769) Mr. Wesley sent out two of his preachers from England, Mr. Boardman and Mr. Pilmoor, to the American colonies. A little later Robert Williams, a local preacher, arrived, having come of his own accord, though Wesley gave him a permit to work under the direction of the missionaries. Boardman and Pilmoor worked in Pennsylvania, New Jersey and New York, while Williams went to Maryland and Virginia. Jarratt states that Williams was the first Methodist preacher he conversed with, and in 1772-1773 Williams was welcomed in Jarratt's parish, where he preached several sermons. Williams assured Jarratt that the Methodists were true members of the Church of England, and its preachers did not assume to administer baptism or the Lord's Supper but looked to the parish ministers to perform that service. With this assurance Jarratt welcomed the Methodist itinerants, seeing in them a means of reviving the Established Church in Virginia and the Carolinas.

Because of Jarratt's coöperation with the Methodist lay preachers Methodism grew more rapidly in Virginia than anywhere else in America. In 1775 Thomas Rankin, Wesley's assistant in America, visited Virginia and with Jarratt made a preaching tour of the southern counties and into North Carolina. They preached to great assemblies under the trees as well as in "preaching houses." So great was the demand for preaching that Rankin speaks of preaching almost to the point of exhaustion. Jesse Lee, the first American Methodist historian, was a Virginian and was a witness to many of the revival scenes. He states:

In almost every assembly might be seen signal instances of divine power; more especially in the meeting of the classes. . . . Many who had long neglected the means of grace now flocked to hear. . . . This outpouring of the spirit extended itself more or less, through most of the circuits, which takes in a circumference of between four and five hundred miles. . . .

At a Quarterly Conference in May 1776 the power of the Lord came down upon the assembly, and it seemed as though the whole house was filled with the presence of God. A flame kindled and ran from heart to heart. Many were deeply convinced of sin; many mourners were filled with consolation, and many believers were so overwhelmed with love, that they could not doub* but God had enabled them to love him with all their heart. . . .

Such a work of God as that was. I had never seen, or heard of before. It continued to spread through the south parts of Virginia, and the adjacent parts of North-Carolina all that summer and autumn.[3]

Devereux Jarratt's account of the revival is the most complete of all the contemporary descriptions, and was reproduced by Asbury in his *Journal*. The results of the revival are reflected in the statistics of the Virginia and North Carolina circuits. In 1774 there were but two circuits in the region, with a combined membership of 291; the following year there were 3 circuits with a membership of 935; in 1776 the number of circuits had increased, the Brunswich circuit alone reporting 1,611 members. The following year there were 6 circuits with a combined membership of 4,379. In this year the number of Methodists in America totaled 6,968, which meant that two-thirds of all the Methodists in the colonies were found in the vicinity of Devereux Jarratt's parish, a fact which would seem to indicate that this region was the cradle of American Methodism. Since none of Wesley's lay preachers were ordained, the Methodists in the great area were entirely dependent upon Jarratt for the sacraments. To meet this increasing demand Jarratt traveled continually, visiting in all 29 counties in the two colonies, for the purpose of ministering to the new Methodist converts.

The rise of these three large bodies of dissenters in Virginia in the years just preceding the Revolution helps to explain the part played by Virginia in that struggle. Their presence also explains why the struggle for the separation of church and state was won in Virginia.

The Presbyterians, with their emphasis upon an educated ministry, established educational institutions in Virginia as soon as they became strong enough to support them. Thus in 1776 Hampden-Sidney College was established in Prince Edward County, while west of the Ridge, Liberty Hall Academy was planted the same year. The Baptists, on the other hand, standing as they did for an unpaid and uneducated ministry, were naturally slow in establishing schools. The Methodists were too few before the Revolution to think of schools, though soon after the war steps were taken to establish a college.

[3] Jesse Lee, *A Short History of the Methodists, in the United States of America, etc.* (Baltimore, 1810), pp. 55-59.

CHAPTER XI

✣   ✣   ✣

MISSIONS AND BENEVOLENT ENTERPRISES IN THE AMERICAN COLONIES

WHEN the Spaniard began the colonization of America he came with a strong and sincere desire to spread the Catholic faith and in the midst of his many and various activities he never lost sight of his religious purpose. With hardly an exception priests accompanied every colonizing or conquering expedition and no opportunity was ever lost for establishing Christian worship among the natives of America. At the end of the colonial period the religious establishments in the English colonies could not compare with those of Roman Catholicism in the Spanish colonies. When England began colonization the Spanish colonial empire in America had been in existence more than a hundred years, and through the efforts of Spanish missionaries thousands of natives had been brought to at least a nominal acceptance of Christianity.

Of all this the English were well aware, and one of the frequent arguments used to advance the cause of English colonization was that it would bring the Christian religion to the savages. Thus Sir George Peckham glowingly describes the great benefits which English colonization would bring to the natives of America; of these benefits

First and chiefly [he says, are those] in respect of the most gladsome and happy tidings of the most glorious gospel of our Saviour Jesus Christ, whereby they may be brought from falsehood to trueth, from darkness to light, from the hie way of death to the path of life, from superstitious idolatrie to sincere Christianity, from the devil to Christ, from hell to heaven. And if in respect of all the commodities they can yeelde us (were they many more) that they should receive this onely benefit of Christianity, they were more than fully recompenced.

It is undoubtedly true that religion was frequently used as a disguise and a decoy to attract the religious-minded to the support of colonization, and much of what we read about the desire to convert the natives was but pious fraud, but at the same time there was undoubtedly a real missionary interest on the part of many of the leaders in the colonizing enterprise.

I

The early interest in the Christianization and education of the Indians in the Virginia colony was destroyed by the great Indian massacre of 1622. The New England Puritans seem to have been genuinely concerned about the conversion of the Indians from the beginning. The charter of the Plymouth colony called for "the conversion of such savages as yet remain wandering in desolation and distress to civil society and the Christian religion." Likewise the Massachusetts Bay charter called upon the colonists to win the savages "to the knowledge and obedience of the only true God and Saviour of mankind," while the seal of the colony was the figure of an Indian with a label at his mouth representing him as saying "Come over and help us." In the Plymouth colony, even during the hard early years, the Indians in the neighborhood were not neglected by the ministers, and in 1636 laws were passed providing for the preaching of the gospel among them.

The work of Indian Christianization in early New England is generally gathered about the name of John Eliot, though the Mayhew family on Martha's Vineyard began their work among the island Indians, off the Massachusetts coast, at about the same time and with much the same degree of success. John Eliot, a graduate of Cambridge, came to Boston in 1631 and the next year became the teacher at the Roxbury Church, where he remained until his death in 1690. From the beginning of his ministry at Roxbury, Eliot began to prepare himself to work among the Indians. Through several years he studied the Indian language, aided by an Indian captured in the Pequot War, who lived with him and accompanied him on his visits to the Indians in the neighborhood.

Finally in 1646 he preached his first sermon in the Indian tongue five miles from Roxbury. These early efforts aroused the general interest of the Massachusetts ministers and a few weeks later, probably incited by what Eliot had already done, the Massachusetts Assembly passed an act ordering the ministers to elect every year two of their number to act as missionaries to the Indians. The work was now carried on with great success, and villages of Christian Indians were erected in the vicinity of Boston, which adopted simple regulations, on Eliot's advice, for their civil and religious regulation. Eventually there came to be a number of such Indian towns, all under the care of Eliot and his helpers. One of the most successful of these Indian towns was Natick. It was located on both sides of the Charles River and consisted of three streets of Indian wigwams and a meetinghouse fifty by twenty-five feet, which was used also for a school. Thus is its founding described by Cotton Mather:

> Here it was that in the year 1651 those that had heretofore lived like wild beasts in the wilderness now compacted themselves into a town; and they first applied themselves to the forming of their civil government. . . . Mr. Eliot on a solemn fast, made a public vow; that seeing these Indians were not prepossessed with any forms of government, he would instruct them into such a form, as we had written in the word of God, that so they might be a people in all things ruled by the Lord. Accordingly he expounded unto them the eighteenth chapter of Exodus; and then they chose rulers of hundreds, of fifties, of tens. . . .
>
> The little towns of these Indians being pitched upon this foundation, they utterly abandoned that polgamy which had heretofore been common among them; they made severe laws against fornication, drunkenness, and sabbath-breaking, and other immoralities. . . .
>
> At length was a church-state settled among them; they entered as our churches do, into an holy covenant, wherein they gave themselves, first unto the Lord, and then unto one another, to attend the rules, and helps, and expect the blessing of the everlasting gospel. . . .

England learned of these early successes among the Indians through several pamphlets describing the Indian work. One such tract was that written by Eliot in 1647 entitled "The Day-Breaking if not the Sun Rising of the Gospel with the Indians in New England," while the next year "The Clear Sun-shine of the Gospel Breaking Forth Upon the Indians in New England," by the Rev. Thomas Shepard of Cambridge, appeared. So stirred was Cromwell's Parliament with this cheering information that a corporation was created by their act called "The President and Society for the Propagation of the Gospell in New England," which was given power to hold lands, goods and money. Collections were now ordered to be taken throughout England and by 1661 a sum producing £600 a year had been collected. The administrators of this fund were the commissioners of Massachusetts, Plymouth, Connecticut and New Haven. With the assistance provided by this society the work of Christianizing the Indians went forward more rapidly, while the money furnished by the society was used not only for the salaries of missionaries but also for printing books and furnishing tools and clothing for the Indians.

When Charles II came to the throne, the Society for Propagation of the Gospel in New England went out of existence, since all the acts of the Long Parliament were now declared illegal. Fortunately, however, those in charge of the interests of the society were successful in catching the king when he was anxious to please all parties and succeeded in securing a royal charter. The society was now reorganized under this charter, with the name "The Company of Propagacion of the Gospell in New England, and the parts adjacent in America." The incorporators numbered forty-five and included both Anglicans and Nonconformists, among them some of the high officials of state.

One of the outstanding achievements of John Eliot was his translation of the Bible into the tongue of the Massachusetts Indians. Cotton Mather points out some of the difficulties in learning the Indian tongue; the strange harshness of pronunciation, the enormous length of many of the words, and its unlikeness to any of the languages of Europe, all of which rendered the task peculiarly difficult. In 1661 the society published at Cambridge Eliot's translation of the New Testament and two years later the whole Bible was issued from the same press. Other translations followed, including treatises by the Mathers and Baxter as well as the Cambridge Platform.

The very year Eliot began his work among the Indians of Massachusetts a similar work was begun among the Indians on the island of Martha's Vineyard by Thomas Mayhew, the minister on the island. Mayhew's father had been given these islands as a grant, they originally not being included in any of the New England governments. On this and the surrounding islands there was a native population of several thousands, and Mayhew, like Eliot, soon after his settlement as minister on the island began the study of the Indian tongue. In 1646 he began to preach to them, and four years later two of the principal *powwows* or medicine men professed conversion. This circumstance so amazed the natives that they began to flock to Mayhew by whole families, and soon two congregations of natives had been formed.

In 1657 Thomas Mayhew, Jr., lost his life while on a voyage to England to procure greater assistance for his Indian work. After this tragic loss, the elder Mayhew, though governor of the island and nearly seventy years of age, took up the work of preaching to the Indians. Two natives were now ordained to work with the elder Mayhew while he continued as an evangelist until his death. Shortly before his death one of his grandsons, John Mayhew, became the settled pastor on the island and he likewise took up the work among the Indians. A few years following his early death, his son, Experience Mayhew, continued the Indian work until his death in 1758. Experience Mayhew was considered especially skillful in the Indian language since he had been familiar with it from childhood, and published translations of the Psalms and the Gospel of John, and much of what we know of the Indian work is due to his account of thirty Indian converts.

The Society for the Propagation of the Gospel in New England also gave some assistance to the Indian work on the islands. By 1674 there were four Indian congregations on the island of Martha's Vineyard made up of some eighteen hundred Indians. In eastern Massachusetts there were at the same time four congregations with more than two thousand Indians. The praying Indians, however, were mostly from the weaker tribes, located between the powerful and warlike rivals, the Narragansetts and the Mohegans. Eventually these Indian churches disappeared because of the almost complete dying off of these weaker tribes or their intermarriage with the Negroes, which caused the absorption of the Indians into the Negro population of New England.

King Philip's War (1675-1676) was a great blow to the New England Indian missions. Much to the distress of the missionaries a few of the praying Indians went back to their savage kinsmen during this terrible struggle, though most of the converts proved faithful to their Christian profession. When the war ended, work among the Indians was again vigorously carried on, though it was now a crippled enterprise. With the death of Eliot in 1690 the first period of New England Indian missions comes to a close, though there continued to be some interest manifested, even though the whole religious life of New England was at low ebb. It was the Great Awakening which aroused new interest in Indian Christianization, as well as in other humanitarian movements.

This reawakened interest in Indian missions is well illustrated by the work among the Housatonic Indians, a small tribe in western

Massachusetts, begun in 1734 by the Rev. John Sargent, a former tutor at Yale. Here Sargent labored with success until his death in 1749. The Indians were gathered into a new settlement called Stockbridge where a plan was devised for the education and training of the Indian children. To help carry forward this plan for an Indian Charity School a subscription was begun in England, headed by the Prince of Wales, but the sum raised was not sufficient to put the plan into operation. A Baptist minister, however, the Rev. Mr. Hollis, established a small charity school in coöperation with Sargent. The work of Sargent resulted in the baptism, of 182 Indians, most of whom were living in houses built in the English style at Stockbridge instead of in bark wigwams, while a school was conducted with fifty or more children in attendance. On the death of Sargent (1749) Jonathan Edwards became the minister at Stockbridge, where we are told he labored "with no remarkable success," though his work was satisfactory to both the English and the Indians as well as to the commissioners of the New England Society who had the direction of the mission. Edwards was succeeded at Stockbridge by a Mr. West and he in turn by John Sargent, the son of the founder of the mission. Following the Revolution the Stockbridge Indians, as they came to be called, were removed to the Oneida country, where New Stockbridge was built.

Upon the great seal of Dartmouth College are the words *Vox Clamantis in Deserto,* "the voice of one crying in the wilderness." To explain this motto it is necessary to recount the story of Moor's Indian Charity School conducted at Lebanon, Connecticut, by the Congregational minister, Eleazer Wheelock, who was one of the most active of the revival preachers during the course of the Great Awakening. The first graduate of this school was a Mohegan Indian, Samson Occom. To this school also came several Mohawk youths, among them Thayendanegea, known to history as Joseph Brant. This school also welcomed the sons of the colonists, and thus Samuel Kirkland, the son of the minister at Norwich, Connecticut, became a scholar there, where he was prepared for the College of New Jersey. In November, 1761, Wheelock sent young Brant and Kirkland into the Mohawk Valley to seek other Indian pupils, and in 1767 Samson Occom, who had become a minister after his conversion in the Great Awakening, was sent to England with Nathaniel Whitaker to raise money for the school at Lebanon. Occom caught the popular fancy in England, where he preached over three hundred sermons and raised more than £10,000. Previous to this Wheelock had received allowances from the Commissioners of the New England Society, as well as private gifts from both England and America, while the Scotch Society for Propagating Christian Knowledge also helped his school with appropriations for the support of Indian scholars.

As the school developed Wheelock conceived the plan of making it into a college, the primary purpose of which would be to train young white men for missionary work among the Indians. Accordingly, after having investigated several possible locations, it was finally decided to locate the institution in the province of New Hampshire where Governor Wentworth had made a generous offer of land and endowments. This was thought a proper location because it was near the Indian country, and its selection was recommended by Lord Dartmouth who had been made chairman of the trustees of the funds which had been collected in England and Scotland by Occom and Whitaker. It was George Whitefield who was responsible for Lord Dartmouth's interest in the new college, for it was he who had arranged for Occom and Whitaker to meet and dine with him. The college began at Hanover, New Hampshire, in the autumn of 1770. Wheelock had arrived in August to push forward the building operations, but before they were completed his family and twenty or thirty students arrived. His wife and the "females" of his family were placed in one hut, while his sons and students made booths and beds of hemlock boughs, "and in this situation," he says, "we continued about a month, till the 29th day of October, when I removed with my family to my house." The house for the students, eighty by thirty-two feet and two stories high, was finally completed and Dartmouth College thus was started upon its honorable and useful career.

Perhaps the best known of all the Indian missionaries, in the period following the Great Awakening, is David Brainerd. Brainerd was a convert of the Great Revival and, like many others, soon after his conversion (1739) felt the call to preach and entered Yale College to prepare for the ministry. Here he won distinction for his scholarship and was the leader of his class. His sympathy for the revival, to which the college had become opposed, caused him to make a disparaging remark concerning one of the tutors, which was overheard by several students. This, together with the accusation that he had attended a

Separatist meeting, caused his expulsion. This act on the part of the college was strongly opposed by some of the ministers, who were led on this account to become greatly interested in Brainerd. In 1742 he was licensed to preach in the Congregational Church, and the same year was sent as a missionary to the Indians under the auspices of the Society in Scotland for Propagating Christian Knowledge. His first mission station was about halfway between Stockbridge and Albany, but here the Indians were few in number and he soon persuaded them to join the settlement at Stockbridge where they could be under the instruction of Sargent. After receiving ordination by the New Side Presbytery of New York in 1744, he took up his Indian work in New Jersey, where remarkable success attended his efforts. Since his student days Brainerd had suffered from tuberculosis and the terrible exposure which his work entailed soon brought the disease to a crisis. Several times he made long journeys to the Indians on the Susquehanna, which further drained his strength. Early in the year 1747 his health would no longer permit the continuation of his work and he died at the home of Jonathan Edwards at Northampton, to whose daughter Jerusha he was engaged to be married.

Brainerd's saintly character and his absolute obedience to duty in spite of bodily weakness and pain made a profound impression upon his generation. Soon after his death Jonathan Edwards published an account of his life together with his diary, which proved a tremendous stimulus in promoting the cause of missions. For many this little book was a manual of religious guidance and few books have had a larger religious influence. Indeed, David Brainerd dead was a more potent influence for Indian missions and the missionary cause in general than was David Brainerd alive.

In the years following the Great Awakening the Presbyterians began to take great interest in missions to the Six Nations, and succeeded in securing the coöperation of the Society in Scotland for Propagating Christian Knowledge. In 1764 Samuel Kirkland, the former companion of Joseph Brant at Wheelock's school, on his graduation from the College of New Jersey began his work as a missionary, first to the Senecas and later to the Oneidas. Kirkland continued his work with considerable success to the outbreak of the Revolution, and even during the war made frequent visits to the Indian country and when the war was over returned to them. The Presbyterians also worked among the Indians on Long Island where the revivalist, James Davenport, began a remarkable work which was carried on by Simon Horton.

The most successful Protestant missions of the whole colonial period were undoubtedly those conducted by the Moravians. To the Moravian, missionary work was the most important thing in life, and Moravian industries at Nazareth and Bethlehem, Pennsylvania, were carried on in order to give support to their missionaries.

The first Moravian missionary in America was Christian Henry Rauch who began work among the New York Indians in 1740. He took up his residence at the Mohegan town of Shekomeko and here he was visited by Count Zinzendorf in 1742 when the first Indians were baptized and admitted into the church. The number of missionaries was now increased and the work progressed rapidly. Settlers in the region, however, stirred up by false reports that the Moravians were allies of the French, finally secured the passage of an act prohibiting the missionaries from giving instructions to the Indians. This caused the withdrawal of the missionaries from Shekomeko and finally the Christian Indians were invited to remove from New York and settle in the vicinity of Bethlehem. Land was purchased about thirty miles distant from Bethlehem and here a town was built called "Gnadenhütten," or Tents of Grace. Here within a few years the Indian congregation grew to about five hundred.

The outbreak of the French and Indian War brought terrible suffering to the Moravian missionaries and their Indian converts. The Indian town of Gnadenhütten was attacked on November 24, 1755, and completely destroyed. Nitschmann was shot, other missionaries were burned to death, and but four out of fifteen remained to tell of the fate of their brethren. The Indians, however, escaped and fled to Bethlehem, and throughout that anxious winter were cared for by the Brethren. Later another town called "Nain" was built about a mile from Bethlehem, while some of the Indian converts were removed beyond the Blue Ridge where a second town was erected, called "Wechquetank." This isolated settlement was later destroyed by the infuriated Scotch-Irish settlers, though not until its Indian inhabitants had been removed to Philadelphia, where they were under the care of the English government.

On the return of peace it was determined to remove the Christian Indians to the Indian country since they could not live in the neighborhood of the whites without being continually molested by them. Accordingly in 1765, after a journey of five weeks, they came to the banks of the Susquehanna where "Friedenshütten" or Tents of Peace, was built, which soon became a prosperous community attracting visitors from many of the Indian tribes, all of whom were given generous hospitality. Under the leadership of David Zeisberger the Indian work now went forward rapidly. Other towns were founded on the Alleghany, but because of persecution of the Christian Indians by the non-Christian members of their tribe they again moved on. Finally in 1770 they accepted an offer of a tract of land in what is now Ohio on the Tuscarawas River, and here a group of villages was founded, the principal one being Schönbrunn. Here prosperity reigned and all was happiness and peace when the American Revolution began.

The Roman Catholics were active in the propagation of their form of Christianity throughout this whole period. The Spanish missionaries conducted missions in Florida, Texas, New Mexico, Arizona and California; the French in New York, around the Great Lakes and along the rivers flowing into the Gulf of Mexico. These missions were carried on by the several orders, by the Franciscans and Jesuits chiefly. Seventy years after the founding of St. Augustine the Christian Indians in Florida numbered from 25,000 to 30,000, distributed among 44 mission stations. The conquest and Christianization of New Mexico began in 1595 under Don Juan Oñate, and after many hardships the Franciscan missionaries carried forward the work at a marvelous rate. In 1609 Santa Fé was founded and by the end of ten years 8,000 baptisms were reported and 60 friars were at work. Eighty years after (1680) the founding of this prosperous mission, however, an Indian uprising swept away, at one blow, all the Spaniards had accomplished and the cause of Catholic Christianity never completely recovered. Father Kino, a Jesuit from the Mexican province of Sonora, established the first mission work in what is now Arizona in 1687, while a Franciscan, Padre Hidalgo, planted the first mission in Texas at San Antonio in 1718. Mission work in California was not begun until 1769 when another Franciscan, Junipero Serra, founded the mission at San Diego; in 1776 the mission at San Francisco was established, and later Padre Serra founded nine other missions on the Pacific coast of what is now the United States.

It is generally agreed that the French exercised a greater influence among the Indians of America than did the English. Their first settlements were primarily based on the fur trade with the Indians, which led to the establishment of trading posts in widely separated regions. They also intermarried more readily with the natives, which gave them some advantages, but at the same time brought them into conflict with other tribes, such as the Iroquois, who served as an effectual check upon French expansion. At the opening of the French and Indian War (1756) the French had established posts down the St. Lawrence, around the Great Lakes, and along the Mississippi and its tributaries. When this vast region became English at the end of the French and Indian War (1763) there was little left of the mission work which had been carried on by the French Jesuits at various places. Successful work had been begun among the Iroquois, first by Father Jogues, and later (1667) by three other Jesuits. In ten years, more than two thousand baptisms had taken place, all among the Iroquois in New York, but by the end of the century this work had practically disappeared, because of the expulsion of the French missionaries. It is interesting to note that the expulsion of the French Jesuits came during the administration of the Catholic Governor Dongan who feared that the French priests were influencing the Iroquois against the English. He was, however, willing that English Jesuits should replace the French.

The Catholic missions about the Great Lakes were more successful than were those among the Iroquois, and their work has lasted until this day. The French Jesuits were intrepid explorers as well as devoted missionaries, and America is in their debt for making known to the world for the first time much of the region which now is included in the states of Michigan, Wisconsin and Minnesota. By 1690 missions had been established at Mackinaw, Green Bay, Sault Ste. Marie, besides new missions on the St. Joseph and St. Croix rivers. In 1701 the mission at Detroit was established which twenty years later included three villages of Christian Indians. During the early eighteenth century French missionaries entered the region of the lower Ohio and Mississippi, following the French traders as they pushed southward, and missions were founded at Kaskaskia and even as far southward as the Tennessee.

The work performed by the great Anglican society, "The Society for the Propagation of the Gospel in Foreign Parts," remains to be noted. The Anglican Church in the American colonies has been judged very largely by the church and ministry of Maryland and Virginia. It is true the Establishment was stronger there than anywhere else in the colonies, but it is hardly just to judge the more than three hundred un-selfish S.P.G. missionaries, who labored in the colonies from 1701 to 1785, by the worst class among the clergy to be found in America.

The society met popular approval from the start and received numerous subscriptions. Its incorporators included the noblest names in England, headed by the Archbishop of Canterbury, while its first action was characterized by good sense. The instructions issued to applicants for appointment state that before embarking they shall call upon the Archbishop of Canterbury for instructions; on shipboard they shall conduct themselves so as to be examples of piety and virtue to the ship's company; that they shall try to prevail upon the captain to have morning and evening prayer and special services on Sunday; on arrival in the country where they are sent they shall "be circumspect; not board or lodge in public-houses; game not at all; converse not with lewd persons, save to admonish them; be frugal; keep out of debt; not meddle with politics; keep away from quarrels, say the service every day, when practicable, and always with seriousness and decency; avoid high-flown sermons; preach against such vices as they see to prevail; impress the nature and need of the Sacraments; distribute the Society's tracts; and visit their people." Their salary was to be £50 a year besides £10 for outfit.

The first representatives of the society to visit America were the Rev. George Keith and his friend, the Rev. Patrick Gordon, who were sent on a tour of inspection in 1702. Keith had previously been in America, where as a Quaker he had quarreled with that society and had separated from them, and was well endowed with energy and was now an enthusiastic churchman. Gordon died soon after landing, but Keith was joined by the ship's chaplain, John Talbot, who became his companion in his journey through the colonies. The tour lasted two years, and covered the territory from Boston to Charleston. "From this time until the War of Independence the History of the Church in America is to be looked for in the records of the Venerable Society."

The following is a summary of the work of the society in the American colonies from its origin to the opening of the War for Independence:

It had maintained 310 ordained missionaries, had assisted 202 central stations, and had expended £227,454 or nearly a million and a quarter of dollars. It had stimulated and supported missions to the negroes and the

Indians, as well as to the white colonists. Its labors were chiefly in those colonies where the church was not established.

The society's most successful mission to the Indians was that conducted by the Rev. Henry Barclay, who was appointed catechist to the Mohawks at Fort Hunter on his graduation from Yale College in 1734. Three years later he became rector of the church at Albany, but continued also his work among the Indians. In 1741 he reported to the S.P.G. that he had, besides his Albany congregation, five hundred Indians under his pastoral care, settled in two towns about thirty miles from Albany, and that only two or three out of the whole tribe remained unbaptized. When Barclay became the rector of Trinity Church, New York City, he continued his interest in the Indians, while at this period the society employed sixteen missionaries to work among the Indians and negroes in New York.

II

Considerable attention was given by the society to Negroes and its missionaries received instruction to work for their conversion. In 1741 the society made a special appeal for funds to promote this work and received a considerable sum for that purpose. These efforts met strong opposition at first among the slave owners, but the policy of the society was very definitely in favor of such work. Other societies closely allied to the S.P.G., such as the "Society for Promoting Christian Knowledge," the "Associates of Dr. Bray" and the "Society for Promoting Christian Learning," were likewise interested in Negro work. Negro schools were established by the Associates of Dr. Bray in New York, Newport, Rhode Island, and Williamsburg, Virginia, while the other two societies maintained missionaries for work among the Negroes and sent books and tracts to be distributed to the slaves.

Among the dissenting churches in the American colonies the Quaker was the only one to question the right of church members to hold slaves. But many Quakers, especially in the South, held slaves, though the Yearly Meetings generally manifested an interest in their religious welfare. In the New England Yearly Meeting (1769) slave owners were advised to take the slaves to their places of worship and give them instruction; as did also the Yearly Meetings in Virginia and North Carolina. This, however, was not the universal practice even among Quakers, and some ignored or completely neglected the Negro's religious welfare.

Among the other churches there was no uniformity of practice in regard to their treatment of the slaves. The clergy were frequently slave owners and in some instances slaves were accepted as a form of endowment. Here and there a minister is found who because of his personal opposition to slavery manumitted his slaves, which was true of Freeborn Garrettson. Samuel Davies during his ministry in Virginia gave particular attention to the Negroes and frequently preached to them and admitted them as communicants. Samuel Hopkins, the Congregational minister at Newport, was active in his opposition to slavery and the slave trade and fearlessly denounced both on every possible occasion in this most active center of the American slave trade. During the Baptist revival in Virginia and North Carolina many Negroes were converted and were frequently admitted with their masters to church membership, and there are instances of Negroes speaking in their meetings. As a whole the moral and religious condition among Negroes in America at the end of the colonial period left much to be desired. Writing of conditions toward the close of the Revolution, a contemporary states "One thing is very certain, that the Negroes of that country, a few only excepted, are to this day as great strangers to Christianity, and as much under the influence of Pagan darkness, idolatry and superstition, as they were at their first arrival from Africa."

III

Throughout the eighteenth century, especially after the Great Awakening, there were many educational and charitable projects begun in the American colonies, and their agents were frequently sent to England or the continent to solicit funds. Samuel Davies and Gilbert Tennent (1754) collected considerable funds in Scotland, Ireland and England for the College of New Jersey. In London alone they received more than £1,200, while collections were ordered in all the churches in Scotland and Ireland by the General Assembly of the Church of Scotland and by the Synod of Ireland. When some twelve years later Morgan Edwards (1767) went to England to solicit funds for the College of Rhode Island, he was dismayed by the amount of begging going on, and despaired of raising any large sum. He secured only about £900, though Samson Occom, the Mohegan Indian, and Nathaniel Whitaker, the agents of Eleazer Wheelock's Indian School, who were in England at the same time, were successful in securing ten times that amount.

Michael Schlatter, the German Reformed minister, was active in raising funds on the continent for churches and schools among the destitute Germans of America. His appeal to the Synod of North Holland and to the German churches in the Palatinate (1751-1752) soon brought the sum of £12,000. His appeal was translated into English by the English preacher in Amsterdam who was a member of the Classis and was circulated widely in Scotland and England. So profound was the impression made that eventually £20,000 was raised and an English Society formed to manage this fund, known as the "Society for the Promotion of the Knowledge of God among the Germans." A scheme was then drawn up for the forming of Charity Schools which were to be open to Protestant youth of all denominations. Schlatter became the superintendent of these schools, which soon, however, became extremely unpopular among the Germans. Part of the German opposition was due to their injured pride in being represented as ignorant and "proper subjects to be civilized by a foreign charity." In 1760 there were eight of these schools maintained in several of the Pennsylvania German counties with an attendance of some six hundred students.

Perhaps the most widely known of all the American colonial benevolent enterprises and certainly the most widely advertised was George Whitefield's Orphan House in Georgia. While Charles Wesley was serving as secretary to General Oglethorpe, the governor of the colony, he had drawn up a plan for an orphanage at the request of the trustees. Both Charles and John Wesley had written Whitefield about joining the work in Georgia, and when he offered himself to the trustees he was accepted. In preparing for his first visit to the colony (1738), then but six years old, Whitefield collected from his friends more than £300 to be used for the poor of Georgia, which he used for the purchase of everything which he thought might be needed by the colonists from prayer books and spelling books to clothing, provisions of all kinds of hardware, including gunpowder. This first visit was brief, as it was necessary for him to return to England to obtain priest's orders, but during his stay of four months he had satisfied himself as to the need of an orphanage, and throughout the remainder of his life, it occupied chief place in his thoughts.

Returning to England, Whitefield spent the next nine months in raising funds and making other necessary provisions for the establishment of the Orphan House. The trustees granted him five hundred acres, for its location and support, and by the time he was ready to leave England he had collected about £1,000 besides large sums for English charities. Whitefield named the place where the orphanage was located —ten miles from Savannah—Bethesda, "a house of mercy," and here were begun in March, 1740, several brick buildings, which were completed early the next year. By the time the main building was completed forty-nine children had been collected, only twenty-two of them, however, orphans. So indefatigable was Whitefield in gathering children for his orphanage that he brought them from other colonies and in one voyage brought some from England.

The school maintained at the orphanage was at first vocational rather than classical, but within a few years, probably influenced by the founding of the College of Philadelphia and the College of New Jersey in which he had had a part, Whitefield conceived the idea of changing his Orphan House into a college. This plan, although it met the hearty approval of the governor and council, failed because of the insistence of the Archbishop of Canterbury that its charter require that the head of the college be a member of the Established Church and that the liturgy of the church be used in its services. Whitefield insisted that "it should be on a broad bottom and no other." The archbishop and the Earl of Dartmouth, President of the Privy Council, held to their position and the plan was ultimately frustrated.

Whitefield objected to the policy of the trustees in prohibiting the use of slaves in the colony for the first fifteen years, and asserted that "Georgia never can or will be a flourishing province without negroes are allowed." He purchased a plantation and slaves in South Carolina in an attempt to reduce the costs of maintaining the orphanage and justified himself on the ground that the enslavement of Negroes made possible their conversion. Later when slavery was permitted in Georgia (1750), the South Carolina property was sold and a plantation near Bethesda was purchased for a similar purpose.

During the thirty years from 1740 to the death of the founder in 1770, there was a total expenditure of £15,000 for the maintenance of the orphanage, a large part of which had been raised by Whitefield—£3,300 had been contributed at various times by Whitefield from his own funds, to meet the debts. The classic example of the great evangelist's success as a money raiser is that related by Benjamin Franklin in his *Autobiography*:

I did not disapprove of the design, [of the orphanage] but as Georgia was then destitute of materials and workmen and it was proposed to send them from Philadelphia at a great expense, I thought it would have been better to have built the house here and brought the children to it. This I advis'd; but he was resolute in his first project, rejected my counsel and I therefore refus'd to contribute. I happened soon after to attend one of his sermons in the course of which I perceived he intended to finish with a collection, and I silently resolved he should get nothing from me. I had in my pocket a handful of copper money, three or four silver dollars, and five pistoles in gold. As he proceeded I began to soften and concluded to give the coppers. Another stroke of his oratory made me asham'd of that and determin'd me to give the silver; and he finish'd so admirably that I empty'd my pocket wholly into the collector's dish, gold and all.

One of the immediate by-products of the great colonial awakenings was the rise of a new social consciousness and a broad humanitarianism, which manifested itself in a greater concern for the poor and the alleviation of distress and suffering. The central emphasis in the revivalistic theology of Samuel Hopkins was *disinterested benevolence,* or complete unselfishness in the interest of others. The theology gained a great vogue throughout New England Congregationalism. A part of Samuel Hopkins' theological system was a general atonement—that is, that Christ died for all, negroes, Indians and the underprivileged, as well for the privileged few. Samuel Hopkins may well be called the father of the antislavery movement in America. There was also a new attitude toward children manifest in the advertisements of toys for children in the almanacs throughout the colonies and the increasing number of portraits of children found in the homes of the people.

CHAPTER XII

✤ ✤ ✤

THE WAR OF INDEPENDENCE AND THE
AMERICAN CHURCHES

THE political historian has failed to take adequate account of the influences which came both directly and indirectly from the Great
Awakenings. For the first time the American people found, in the revival, a common intellectual and emotional interest; for the first time
intercolonial leaders emerged, which broke over political as well as
sectarian lines; "Whitefield, Edwards and Tennent preceded Franklin
and Washington as rallying names for Americans irrespective of local
distinctions." The leaders in the revival were the advocates of coöperation and union; the whole movement was the foe of denominational
and racial prejudice. It was the direct and indirect cause of the movement of people from one colony to another which helped create a common American spirit. One of the ties binding the colonies to the mother
country was the Anglican Church; the revival weakened that tie by
winning over to the evangelical churches a considerable share of its
nominal membership, while the Calvinistic churches—Congregational
and Presbyterian—were drawn together in a combination against the
Anglican body. In these respects the Great Awakening may be considered one of the important contributing factors in preparing the way
for the Revolution.

The most recent attempt to enumerate the religious organizations in
the American colonies at the close of the colonial period gives the total
at 3,105, with about 1,000 each for New England, the middle colonies
and the South. Of this total the Congregationalists had 658, most of
which were in New England. Ranking next came the Presbyterians
with 543, located largely in the middle colonies; then came the Baptists

with 498, the Anglicans with 480, Quakers, 295, German and Dutch
Reformed, 251, Lutherans, 151, Catholics, 50, and the Methodists with
37 circuits, mainly in Maryland and Virginia. In 9 of the colonies there
were established churches. In Massachusetts, Connecticut and New
Hampshire it was the Congregational that was supported by taxation
and established by law, though since the beginning of the century other
churches had been tolerated. In 6 of the colonies the established church
was the Anglican, which included all the colonies south from Pennsylvania and New York, though in the latter it was only established in
New York City and in 3 counties surrounding. In none of these colonies
was the English Church in the majority, and in none of them did it include even half of the population, with the possible exception of
Virginia.

A recent writer on the period of the American Revolution has stated
that "the religious temper of America was one of the prime causes of the
Revolution," which is borne out by the statement made by Edmund
Burke before Parliament in his famous speech on *"Conciliation."* In
America, he said, religious beliefs and practices were in advance of those
of all other Protestants in the world. In America the people were accustomed to free and subtle debate on all religious questions, and there
was among them little regard for priests, councils or creeds. Their
church organizations were simple and democratic, as were those of the
Congregationalists and Baptists, or republican as the Presbyterians,
and they were accustomed to elect and dismiss their own religious leaders. In short, in America at the end of the colonial era there was a larger
degree of religious liberty than was to be found among most of the
people of the world, and possession of religious liberty naturally leads
to a demand for political liberty.

I

One of the questions which came up for frequent discussion in the
colonies in the two decades previous to the opening of the Revolution
was that concerning the establishment in America of an Anglican
bishop. John Adams states that this agitation contributed "as much as
any other cause, to arouse the attention, not only of the inquiring mind,
but of the common people, and urge them to close thinking on the
constitutional authority of parliament over the colonies." In his discussion of this whole question, Professor Cross, in his *Anglican Episco-*

pate and the American Colonies, concludes that if the agitation of this question "did not contribute a lion's share in causing" American hostility to England, it was at least strongly involved and must "be regarded as an important part of it."

The Established Church in the colonies was undoubtedly greatly handicapped because of its complete dependence upon the Bishop of London and the Society for the Propagation of the Gospel in Foreign Parts. The earnest missionaries of the S.P.G. were particularly concerned for an American bishop and at intervals throughout the first three-quarters of the eighteenth century were largely responsible for agitating this question. During Queen Anne's reign, in the early years of the century, the project came near succeeding, but George I and Robert Walpole were not interested in the project, though Thomas Secker, Bishop of Oxford, and Sherlock, Bishop of London, later revived the issue in the middle of the century.

Beginning in 1763 a bitter attack was begun on the S.P.G. by Jonathan Mayhew, the minister at the West Church, Boston. He declared that the purpose of the S.P.G. was to "root out Presbyterianism," and he warned his countrymen that: "People have no security against being unmercifully priest-ridden but by keeping all imperious bishops, and other clergymen who loved to lord it over God's heritage, from getting their feet into the stirrup at all." A newspaper and pamphlet warfare now ensued which involved both sides of the Atlantic. Bishops were denounced as "Apostolical monarchs," or "right reverend and holy monarchs," who, once established in America, would introduce "canon law—a poison, a pollution." So real did this danger seem to the New England Congregationalists and the Presbyterians of the middle colonies that from 1766 to the opening of the Revolution they united in a series of annual conventions, the primary purpose of which was "to prevent the establishment of an Episcopacy in America." The conversion of President Timothy Cutler and Samuel Whittlesey—the whole teaching staff of Yale College—in 1722 to Anglicanism, together with five respected Congregational ministers, and the later conversion of others in Connecticut, including Samuel Seabury, Sr., "shook Congregationalism throughout New England like an earthquake, and filled all its friends with terror and apprehension."

Opposition to the S.P.G. and the establishment of an American episcopate was much stronger in those colonies where the S.P.G. missionaries were the most active. Thus opposition was largely confined to the New England and the middle colonies. But in Virginia and Maryland even among churchmen themselves there was no great desire for an American bishop. The Established Church in Virginia was under colonial control and the Virginia laity did not relish interference from the British government. Even some of the clergymen were fearful that agitation would "infuse jealousies and Fears into the Minds of the Protestant Dissenters," while Arthur Lee regarded the whole idea of an American bishop "as threatening the subversion of both our civil and religious liberties." The question of an American episcopate sharply divided the members of the Established Church in the colonies, and when the Revolution came those who had favored an American bishop went largely into the Loyalist party while those who had opposed it generally identified themselves with the patriots.[1]

In the autumn of 1776 the rector of Trinity Church, New York City, reported to the secretary of the S.P.G.:

All the Society's Missionaries, without excepting one, in New Jersey, New York, Connecticut, and, as far as I can learn, in the other New England Colonies, have proved themselves faithful, loyal subjects in these trying times; and have to the utmost of their power, opposed the spirit of disaffection and rebellion which has involved this continent in the greatest calamities.

He further states that the missionaries went about their duties in the midst of the tumult and disorder, preaching the gospel without touching on politics, but everywhere they were threatened and reviled and some of them were seized and confined for several weeks. After the Declaration of Independence the difficulties of the loyal clergy were increased and in many places they were compelled to close their churches. The Rev. Samuel Seabury, Jr., the Anglican minister at Westchester (New York) and later to become the first American bishop, whose father had been one of the Congregational ministers in Connecticut to enter the Established Church, was suspected of unpatriotic acts and of the authorship of the *Westchester Farmer*, was seized by a party of armed men and taken to New Haven where he was committed to prison. Later he was released, but after the battle of Long Island, Seabury fled to the British lines where he became a chaplain in the British army.

---

[1] Richard J. Hooker, *The Anglican Church and the American Revolution* (Typed Ph. D. Thesis, University of Chicago, 1942) is a most competent treatment of the later phases of the Episcopal controversy.

Other prominent loyalist ministers in the Established Church were President Myles Cooper of King's College and Jonathan Boucher of Virginia. The Rev. Jacob Duché, the rector at Christ Church, Philadelphia, at first identified himself with the American cause, as also did Jonathan Boucher, and preached some notable sermons in its defense, but after the Declaration of Independence he left America because of his loyalty to the crown. He was succeeded by the Rev. William White, the assistant rector, who took the oath of allegiance to the United States, became a chaplain of Congress, and later was to take the leading part in organizing the Protestant Episcopal Church in the United States. Bishop Perry states that two-thirds of the signers of the Declaration of Independence were members of the Established Church and that six of them were either sons or grandsons of Anglican clergymen, while such leaders as George Washington, James Madison, John Marshall, Patrick Henry and Alexander Hamilton were counted among its members. It is incorrect to identify the Established Church in the American Revolution solely with either one side or the other, for it was much divided; in New England both clergy and laity were largely loyalist; in the southern colonies, especially Virginia and Maryland, it was strongly American, while in the middle colonies it was about equally divided. With these facts in mind it will not be surprising to learn that at the end of the War for Independence no American church was in so deplorable a condition as was the Anglican.

II

No church in the American colonies had so large an influence in the War for Independence as had the Congregational. Its ministry had been most influential in public affairs from the beginning, and although the political influence of the New England ministers in the eighteenth century was not so great as in the century previous, yet their opinions on all public matters were still of great weight. As a whole the New England clergy at the time of the Revolution were American trained and were graduates of Harvard or Yale. As early as 1633 in Massachusetts and 1674 in Connecticut the practice of preaching election sermons arose. These were delivered before the governor and assembly year by year. Frequently these sermons were printed at government expense and distributed among the towns, and the themes there discussed were rediscussed in the pulpits throughout New England. The first adequate study of these election sermons in their bearing upon the American Revolution has been made by Miss Alice M. Baldwin in a volume entitled *The New England Clergy and the American Revolution.* In these sermons she discovers the whole political philosophy of the American Revolution set forth many years before the opening of the war. They preached the doctrines of civil liberty as taught by Sidney, Locke and Milton. Civil government, they claimed, was of divine origin; rulers were God's delegates and derived their power from Him, not directly but through the people. They emphasized fundamental law and its binding quality. God and Christ, they claimed, always governed by fixed rules, by a divine constitution. There are certain great rights given us by nature and nature's God and no ruler may violate these rights, and rulers as well as people are strictly limited by law. Thus the Congregational ministers "gave to the cause of the colonies all that they could give of the sanction of religion."

At each crisis in the ten years from 1765, the passage of the Stamp Act, to 1775, the beginning of the war, the New England pulpits "thundered" and dwelt more and more on the right of resistance. When the news came in 1766 that the hated Stamp Act was repealed Charles Chauncy at First Church, Boston, preached from the text, "As cold waters to a thirsty soul, so is good news from a far country." The ministers piously magnified the Boston Massacre and John Lathrop preached in Boston on the subject "Innocent Blood Crying to God from the Streets of Boston," while in the same year the Rev. Samuel Cooke in a sermon before Governor Hutchinson and the Massachusetts House of Representatives preached from the text, "He that ruleth over men must be just, ruling in the fear of God," etc. The New England ministers, to quote Miss Baldwin, "With a vocabulary enriched by the Bible . . . made resistance and at last independence and war a holy cause," and through their influence, perhaps more than any other, New England, and the Congregationalists particularly, gave to the Revolution overwhelming support.

When actual fighting began many New England ministers became "fighting parsons." Ministers exerted their influence to raise volunteers and sometimes marched away with them, as did Joseph Willard of Beverly, where two companies were raised largely through his influence. At Windsor, Vermont, David Avery, on hearing the news of Lexington, preached a farewell sermon, then called the people to arms and marched away with twenty men, recruiting others as they went. Many New England ministers became officers of troops raised among their parishioners. The fiery and sharp-tongued John Cleaveland of Ipswich "is said to have preached his whole parish into the army and then to have gone himself." Besides acting as recruiting agents, chaplains, officers and fighters, the New England ministers supported the war with their pens, and gave of their meager salaries to support the cause.

III

As noted earlier, the Presbyterians in the colonies at the opening of the Revolution were largely Scotch-Irish and represented the most recent immigration, that from North Ireland, and were still burning with hostility to England for the wrongs which had caused their migration. Scotch-Irish settlements everywhere throughout the colonies were strong supporters of the cause of liberty. The famous Mecklenburg Resolves of May 31, 1775, came from the Scotch-Irish of western North Carolina, while the battle of King's Mountain was won on October 7, 1780, by bands of Scotch-Irish frontiersmen. Joseph Galloway, a leading loyalist of Pennsylvania, stated before a committee of Parliament in 1779 that about one-half of the American army was made up of Irish, while five years before he had stated that the chief opponents of the British government were "Congregationalists, Presbyterians and Smugglers." A report (1776) to the S.P.G. by the rector of Trinity Church, New York, already referred to, states:

I have it from good authority that the Presbyterian ministers, at a Synod where most of them in the middle colonies were collected, passed a resolve to support the Continental Congress in all their measures. This and this only, can account for the uniformity of their conduct; for I do not know one of them, nor have I been able, after strict inquiry, to hear of any, who did not, by preaching and every effort in their power, promote all the measures of the Congress, however extravagant.

The Presbyterian leader of greatest influence during the Revolution was John Witherspoon, who in 1768 came from Scotland to accept the presidency of the College of New Jersey. Without delay he entered into the spirit of the new country, and soon won recognition as an educational and religious leader. In 1776 he was chosen a member of the New Jersey provincial congress to frame a constitution, and from then until the close of the Revolution, Witherspoon "was busy applying the

Presbyterian theories of republicanism to the constitution of the new civil governments." He was chosen one of five delegates to represent New Jersey in the Continental Congress and was the only minister to sign the Declaration of Independence. He also signed the Articles of Confederation, and was particularly active and effective in his work on the finance committee of the Congress, in which he was associated with Robert and Gouverneur Morris, Elbridge Gerry and Richard Henry Lee.

A Tory Anglican minister, Jonathan Odell, who fled from his parish at Burlington, New Jersey, to the British lines in 1777, where he wrote numerous characterizations of leading patriot Americans, thus pays his respects to Witherspoon:

> Known in the pulpit by sedicious toils,
> Grown into consequence by civil broils,
> Three times he tried, and miserably failed,
> To overset the laws—the fourth prevailed.
> Whether as tool he acted, or as guide,
> Is yet a doubt—his conscience must decide.
> Meanwhile unhappy Jersey mourns her thrall,
> Ordained by the vilest of the vile to fall;
> To fáll by Witherspoon!—O name, the curse
> Of sound religion, and disgrace of verse.
> Member of Congress, we must hail him next:
> "Come out of babylon," was now his text.
> Fierce as the fiercest, foremost of the first,
> He'd rail at kings, with venom well-nigh burst,
> Not uniformly grand—for some bye-end,
> To dirtiest acts of treason he'd decend;
> I've known him seek the dungeon dark as night,
> Imprisoned Tories to convert, or fright;
> Whilst to myself I've hummed, in dismal tune,
> I'd rather be a dog than Witherspoon.
> Be patient, reader—for the issue trust;
> His day will come—remember, Heaven is just.

While John Adams was attending the Continental Congress in Philadelphia in the spring of 1775 he was frequently present at the services of the Third Presbyterian Church of that city, where George Duffield was the minister. In his letters to his wife Adams sometimes speaks of the minister's sermons, whom he describes as "a preacher in this city, whose principles and prayers, and sermons more nearly resemble those of our New England clergy than any that I have heard." During the summer of 1776 Duffield joined the patriot army as a chaplain and remained with it throughout the disastrous campaign in which Washington was defeated on Long Island and during his retreat across New Jersey. Returning to his pulpit in the fall, Duffield rebuked his congregation because there were so many men in the house and stated "there would be one less tomorrow, and no lecture on Wednesday evening." Another Presbyterian minister whose name has lived because of his sturdy support of the cause of independence is that of James Caldwell, pastor of the church at Elizabethtown and chaplain of a New Jersey regiment. During a skirmish at Springfield (New Jersey), when wadding for the muskets of the patriots was running low, Caldwell ran to the Presbyterian Church and returned with an armful of Watts' Psalm Books exclaiming "Now, boys, give them Watts!" an incident which Bret Harte thus describes:

> Think of him as you stand
> By the old church today; think of him and that band
> Of militant ploughboys. See the smoke and the heat
> Of that reckless advance, of that straggling retreat!
> .... They were left in the lurch
> For the want of more wadding. He ran to the church,
> Broke the door, stripped the pews, and dashed out in the road
> With his arms full of hymn-books, and threw down his load
> At their feet. Then above all the shouting and shots
> Rang his voice; "Put Watts into 'em! Boys, give 'em Watts."

Later both Caldwell and his wife were killed by the British and his church was burned.

At the meeting of the Presbyterian Synod in 1783 the "Pastoral Letter" prepared by a committee of which Witherspoon was a member stated:

We cannot help congratulating you on the general and almost universal attachment of the Presbyterian body to the cause of liberty and the rights of mankind. This has been visible in their conduct, and has been confessed by the complaints and resentment of the common enemy. . . . Our burnt and wasted churches, and our plundered dwellings, in such places as fell under the power of our adversaries, are but an earnest of what we must have suffered, had they finally prevailed. The Synod, therefore, request you to render thanks to Almighty God, for all his mercies, spiritual and temporal, and in particular manner for establishing the Independence of the United States of America.

IV

The Dutch Church supported the Revolution with almost as great unanimity as did the Presbyterian, although their chief churches were located in that region where the British were most active during the war, in the Hudson valley and in New York. As a result many Dutch congregations were driven from their churches, pastors and flocks were separated and much of their property was destroyed. One of their churches in New York was used by the British as a riding school while another served as a hospital. John H. Livingston in a sermon reopening one of these churches in 1790, that on Nassau Street, said:

> I dare not speak of the wanton cruelty of those who destroyed this temple, nor repeat the various indignities which have been perpetrated. It would be easy to mention facts which would chill your blood! A recollection of the groans of dying prisoners, which pierced this ceiling; or the sacrilegious sports and rough feats of horsemanship exhibited within these walls might raise sentiments in your minds, perhaps, not harmonizing with those religious affections, which I wish, at present, to promote, and always to cherish.

The two largest German churches, the German Reformed and the Lutheran, were on the whole decidedly patriotic. There was some pro-British sentiment among the German Reformed body, as represented by one of the ministers in New York City, the Rev. John Michael Kern, who on the close of the war migrated to Nova Scotia. The most prominent loyalist among the Germans was Dr. John Joachim Zubly, of Savannah, Georgia. Like several of the Anglican ministers, he at first supported the cause of the colonies and wrote and preached in its behalf. He was one of five representatives sent by Georgia to the Continental Congress and no man in that colony had greater influence. But the idea of separation from the mother country completely cooled his ardor for the cause and he was finally banished from Savannah. On the other hand, there was a large number of stanch patriots among the German Reformed ministers and people. At the opening of the war one of their ministers got into trouble for preaching on the text, "Better is a poor and wise child, than an old and foolish king, who will no more be admonished," while the Rev. C. D. Weyberg of Philadelphia suffered imprisonment because of his too great activity for the patriot cause. The Reformed minister at Lancaster preached to the Hessian prisoners there, taking for his text, "Ye have sold yourselves for naught; and ye shall be redeemed without money."

Although the Lutheran patriarch, Henry M. Muhlenberg, found it impossible to give outright support to the Revolutionary cause, because of conscientious scruples against violating his oaths of allegiance to George III both as Elector of Hanover and King of England, his sons were active in the cause, and few Lutherans were out-and-out Tories. The elder Muhlenberg at the opening of hostilities moved from Philadelphia to the country, where he maintained a cautious neutrality. To him war was an unspeakable sin and to sing the *Te Deum* after a military victory was like doing so after a man had committed adultery without being caught.[2] Of the sons of the elder Muhlenberg, John Peter Gabriel Muhlenberg became a brigadier general in the Continental army, and at the close of the war was breveted major general. When the war began he was minister of a German Lutheran church at Woodstock, Virginia. Having accepted a commission as colonel of a Virginia regiment, he preached his farewell sermon to his congregation in January, 1776. In his sermon, after describing the situation in the colonies, he concluded by saying, "In the language of Holy Writ, there is a time for all things. There is a time to preach and a time to fight; and now is the time to fight." After the benediction he stripped from his shoulders his pulpit robe and stood before his congregation in a colonel's uniform, and then with roll of drums stood at the church door and enlisted his frontier parishioners. His brother, Frederick Augustus Conrad Muhlenberg, was a minister of Christ Lutheran Church in New York, but fled on the approach of the British. He later became a member of the Continental Congress and of the Pennsylvania Assembly; was a member of the state constitutional convention; president of the convention of Pennsylvania which ratified the Federal Constitution, and from 1789 to 1797 was a member of the lower house of the National Congress and had the distinction of being chosen the first speaker of that house. In New York City one of the Lutheran ministers was a stanch loyalist and when the city was evacuated by the British fled with a large part of his flock to Nova Scotia, while in Georgia there was also some pro-British sentiment among the Lutherans.

Isaac Backus, the leader among the New England Baptists in the latter eighteenth and early nineteenth centuries, has left us a detailed

2Theodore G. Tappert, "Henry M. Muhlenberg and the American Revolution," *Church History*, Vol. XI (1942), pp. 284-301. See also numerous references in the *Journals of Henry M. Muhlenberg*, Vol. II, 1765-1766 (Philadelphia, 1945).

account of Baptist activities in the Revolution and in the period immediately following, in his *History of New England Baptists*. He tells us that the Baptists joined the Revolutionary cause because Baptists had suffered most from Episcopalians; because the "worst treatment received by Baptists comes from the same principles and persons that the American war did"; because the Baptists hold to the compact theory of government; because the British claims are unjust, and finally because the deliverance of America might regain for the Baptists their invaded rights. During the whole period of the war the Baptists kept up a continual fight for religious liberty. The Warren Association, made up of Baptist churches in New England, furnished the machinery for the assault while Isaac Backus, President Manning of Rhode Island College, John Gano and Morgan Edwards were the leaders in the movement. On every occasion the grievances of the Baptists were presented: first to the Continental Congress; then to the provincial congress of Massachusetts. But at this period their work was in vain, for as John Adams is reported to have said, "The Baptists might as well expect a change in the solar system as to expect that the Massachusetts authorities would give up their establishment." The Baptists, however, could not be completely ignored, for their support of the patriot cause was too whole-hearted and too valuable to lose. Accordingly in 1779 the Baptist minister at Boston was invited to preach the election sermon of that year, and in other ways the Baptists were given to understand that their support of the patriot cause was at least appreciated by the "Standing Order," even though they were not yet willing to give them all that they demanded.

Likewise in Virginia the Baptists used the principles of the Revolution to advance the cause of religious liberty and the separation of church and state. In Virginia they were an even more important factor, because of their support of the war, than they were in New England. In 1775 a concession was made in allowing them to hold services for their adherents in the army, while the next year the philosophy of religious liberty was incorporated in the organic law of the state.

Unfortunately for the Methodists in America during the Revolution, John Wesley, their great founder, was a stanch Tory and a loyal supporter of the policies of George III and his ministers. At the opening of the war Wesley was inclined to be critical of the government measures in regard to America, but the reading of Samuel Johnson's famous

tract, "Taxation no Tyranny," completely converted Wesley to the
king's side and from that time forward he was most active in his support
of the king. Almost immediately Wesley printed under his own name
an abridged edition of Johnson's pamphlet under the title, "A Calm
Address to the American Colonies," which the English historian
Trevelyan estimates as much more influential in shaping British public
opinion than was Johnson's original tract. Later Wesley wrote other
pamphlets bearing on the American war, and frequently preached on
the question, which brought him the gratitude of the English governmental officials, but also brought down upon the heads of his followers
in America the accusation of Toryism and persecution. Wesley advised
his American preachers, when the war began, to remain free of all party,
"and say not one word against one or the other side."

Soon all of Wesley's English preachers who were in America returned
to England, except Francis Asbury, who determined to identify himself with the Americans. Some of the Methodist preachers were non-
combatants from principle, as was Jesse Lee, and others refused to take
the oath required in some of the states. This was true of Asbury, who
on being required to take the oath in Maryland, refused, and on that
account was forced to leave the state and seek refuge in Delaware, where
the oath was not required of clergymen. Here he was practically in
exile for two years, but finally, having become a citizen of Delaware, he
was permitted to travel in other states under the protection of his
adopted state. In Maryland the Methodists suffered great hardships
because of their supposed Toryism. Here "some of the preachers were
mulcted and fined, and others imprisoned" for preaching, while others
"were bound over in bonds and heavy penalties, and surities not to
preach in this or that county." Some were thrown into jail; some were
beaten, while others were tarred and feathered. All the native ministers
among the Methodists were loyal to the cause of liberty, as were Philip
Gatch, Freeborn Garrettson and William Watters. In spite of handicaps, the Methodist revival reached its high point in Virginia at the
opening of the Revolution, continued through the war, and by 1780
Methodist membership numbered more than 13,000 in the United
States as compared to less than 4,000 in 1775.

The influence of the wealthy Carroll family of Maryland was largely
responsible for determining the course of the small body of American

Roman Catholics during the Revolution.[3] Catholics, in recent years, have laid claim to a larger share in winning the Revolution than they deserve, as instanced by a recent book by Michael J. O'Brien entitled *A Hidden Phase of American History: Ireland's Part in America's Struggle for Liberty*, but there is no doubt but that the Catholics of Maryland and Pennsylvania did give practically unanimous support to the cause. Archbishop Carroll, himself an ardent patriot, wrote some years following the war,

They [Catholics] concurred with perhaps greater unanimity than any other body of men in recommending and promoting that government from whose influence America anticipated all the blessings of justice, peace, plenty, good order, and civil and religious liberty. The Catholic regiment, "Congress Own," the Catholic Indians from St. John, Maine, under the chief Ambrose Var, the Catholic Penobscots, under the chief Orono, fought side by side with their Protestant fellow colonists. Catholic officers from Catholic lands—Ireland, France, and Poland—came to offer their services to the cause of liberty.

Among the signers of the Declaration of Independence was Charles Carroll of Carrollton, a Catholic who at the time of signing pledged his fortune to the cause.

The first diplomatic representative sent to the United States was from France, and on July 4, 1779, the French minister plenipotentiary invited the American officials in Philadelphia to attend a *Te Deum* in the new Catholic Chapel in celebration of the independence of the United States of America. The presence of many French Catholic soldiers in America, with their Catholic chaplains, brought Roman Catholicism for the first time into many localities and introduced to the American people the solemn Catholic service of worship.

The American Revolution brought a radical change in the attitude toward Roman Catholics throughout the country. It probably had little effect in changing attitudes toward Catholicism as a religion, but it wrought a transformation toward Catholics as persons. The American people learned that Catholic people could be good citizens and good Catholics at the same time; and they could be good neighbors and and good friends in spite of their Catholicism.[4]

The effect of the Revolution upon the "Conscientious Objectors,"

[3] For the part played by Charles Carroll of Carrollton in the American War for Independence see Ellen Hart Smith, *Charles Carroll of Carrollton* (Cambridge, 1942).

[4] See Sr. Mary Augustana (Ray), *American Opinion of Roman Catholicism in the Eighteenth Century* (New York, 1936), pp. 318-323.

located largely in Pennsylvania—the Quakers, the Mennonites and the Moravians particularly—makes a tragic chapter in the history of the War for Independence. Already a large number of Quakers, especially in Philadelphia, had adopted the principles of James Logan, the Penn family agent, who considered a defensive war Christian and justifiable. Many wealthy Quaker merchants in Philadelphia supported the preliminary nonimportation measures, for such methods of passive resistance suited their principles. Two Quaker firms were the consignees of the tea sent to Philadelphia in 1773, both of whom agreed to the citizens's decree that the tea should not be landed. The Friends were not only opposed to war, but were also against revolution, the latter position based probably on the advice of George Fox that, "Whatsoever bustlings or troubles or tumults or outrages should rise in the world keep out of them." This seemed to put the Friends in opposition not only to the war but also to the new government, set up for the purpose of independence. Their opposition was not active, however, and many of them undoubtedly sympathized with the American cause, but likewise there were doubtless many who were loyalists at heart.

During the early years of the war many were expelled from the Monthly Meetings for paying war taxes, or placing guns for protection on their vessels; for paying fines in lieu of military service or in any way aiding in the war on either side. Thomas Mifflin, who later became a general and governor of Pennsylvania, was one of the first to be disowned. Altogether there were four or five hundred Quakers who came out for the American side, and probably not more than a half dozen who joined the British army. Some of the "disowned" Friends formed a society known as the Free Quakers, which followed the old Quaker customs as to worship and business but encouraged its members in the performance of their military duties. They built a meetinghouse on Arch Street in Philadelphia to which both Washington and Franklin subscribed. Among the original members of this society was Betsy Ross, but eventually their numbers dwindled and worship was discontinued (1836).

When the war came to Philadelphia in 1777 and 1778 the Quakers suffered from both sides. A number of leading Quakers accused of being friendly to the British were arrested on the approach of General Howe and sent to Winchester, Virginia, where they were confined during the winter. Nothing was ever proved against them, however, though some of them may have desired the success of the British. When the Americans reëntered the city, extreme revolutionists gained control and the Quaker residents were made to suffer. Rufus M. Jones estimates the property loss to Quakers at not less than £50,000, from fines and distraits and foraging parties. Quaker school teachers were imprisoned for refusal to take a test of allegiance; others were arrested and confined to prison for months without trial; Friends were elected to offices which it was known they would not accept and were then fined for noncompliance. As is always the case in time of war, the position of the conscientious objector was misunderstood, though the courage required to maintain such a position is far greater and finer than that which sweeps men along with the popular current.

The Mennonites scattered through the Pennsylvania German counties held principles similar to that of the Quakers regarding war. Most of them, no doubt, sympathized with the American side, though there were a few out-and-out Tories among them who at the close of the war migrated to Canada. In 1776 the first split among American Mennonites occurred over the question whether Mennonites should pay the war tax. One group led by Christian Funk contended that the tax should be paid, stating that "Were Christ here, He would say, give to Congress that which belongs to Congress and to God that which belongs to God." The opposition party, however, were in the majority and Funk and his followers were expelled and formed their own congregations. As a whole, the Mennonites were treated leniently by the state authorities, since it was known that most of them were at heart patriots, though some of the horses and wagons of the rich Mennonite farmers were pressed into service by the quartermaster during the Pennsylvania campaigns.

Of all the nonresistant groups the Moravians suffered most in the American Revolution, though directly and indirectly they rendered great service to the American cause. Their buildings at Bethlehem were used as a general hospital for the American army during several years of the war while they cheerfully responded to numerous requisitions for supplies. It was through their Indian missions, however, that they rendered their greatest service. Zeiberger was responsible for keeping the Delawares from taking up the hatchet in the early years of the war, a service that later won generous recognition. Twice during the war Zeisberger and the other Moravian missionaries were taken to Detroit accused of being American spies, but in both instances he and his associates were successful in establishing their innocence. The war bore particularly hard upon the Moravian Indians. Frequently they persuaded Indian war parties to turn back, and on several occasions warned settlements of projected raids. This they did not do because of a preference for one side or the other in the contest, but because of their humanitarian principles. This, of course, was misunderstood by the British as well as the Americans and they were forced into the British lines, where they spent a dreadful winter, almost without food. Later they were allowed to return to their villages on the Tuscarawas in Ohio. Here after hospitably receiving a company of American militiamen, who the Indians thought had come to assist them, they were herded into two buildings and butchered in cold blood, only two boys of the whole number escaping to tell the sad tale. Thus were they rewarded for their loyalty to what they had been tar ght was the teaching and will of Christ.

CHAPTER XIII

THE NATIONALIZATION OF THE AMERICAN CHURCHES

IN NINE of the American colonies at the opening of the War for Independence there were established churches. Congregationalism was established in three of the New England colonies, Anglicanism in five of the southern colonies and New York. In every case the political connections of these churches were with the colonial governments rather than with the mother country, so that when the colonies became independent states that change did not affect the relationship of the churches to the governments. Nor did the war in itself make any change in the religious situation in any of the colonies, but it was inevitable that "the shock of revolution would necesarily loosen the bonds which bound unwilling multitudes to any church establishment with which they had no sympathy."

I

Increased agitation for the separation of church and state began with the opening of the war, especially in New England and Virginia. In New England the forces for separation were led by Isaac Backus, the agent of the Baptist churches in Massachusetts and Rhode Island assisted by several of the other leading Baptists, among them President Manning of Rhode Island College. The agitation was continued throughout the war, the Baptists bombarding the Massachusetts assemblies particularly with memorials and petitions, but Congregationalism was too firmly intrenched with the majority of the people to be endangered at this time. The New England Congregational ministers and church members generally were on the American side, while in

most instances the New England political leaders were likewise affiliated
with the state church. In the Massachusetts constitution, adopted in
the very midst of the Revolution (1779), article three asserts "the right
and duty of the legislature to authorize and require the several towns,
parishes, precincts, and other bodies politic, or religious societies to
make suitable provision at their own expense, for the instruction of the
public worship of God." The Baptists protested against this article, but
to no immediate avail, and it was not until 1833 that Massachusetts
provided for disestablishment. In New Hampshire disestablishment
came in 1817 and in Connecticut in 1818.

In most of the colonies where the Episcopal Church was established
by law, disestablishment came with more or less ease. In the southern-
most colonies, in Maryland and in New York disestablishment came
early in the war, but in Virginia the struggle was prolonged and bitter.
The rapidity with which the Presbyterians, Baptists and Methodists
increased in the southern colonies and especially in Virginia, in the
two decades previous to the Revolution, was a determining factor in the
struggle. Before the Declaration of Independence, however, the Baptists
were alone in demanding the separation of church and state. The Presbyterians were simply demanding their rights under the act of Toleration and nothing more, while the Methodists were still nominally a
part of the Anglican establishment, and seemed at first to favor its
continuance. With the close of the Revolution these three dissenting
bodies, and especially the Baptists and Presbyterians, united in the
fight for complete religious liberty.

In Virginia the dissenting bodies were greatly aided in their struggle
by such statesmen as George Mason, James Madison, Patrick Henry
and Thomas Jefferson, all of whom had become thoroughly convinced
of the desirability of religious liberty. In 1776 the Virginia Convention incorporated the philosophy of religious liberty into its organic
law as article sixteen, introduced by Mason and amended by Madison,
which declared:

That religion, or the duty which we owe our creator, and the manner of
discharging it, can be directed only by reason, and conviction, not by force
or violence; and therefore, all men are equally entitled to the free exercise
of religion according to the dictates of conscience; and that it is the duty of all
to practice Christian forbearance, love, and charity towards each other.

But it is one thing to endorse a philosophy and quite another to put that philosophy into practical operation, and the Baptists, especially, were not satisfied to let matters rest with simply a declaration; they were soon asking how this philosophy of religious equality was to be applied. Accordingly when the first Virginia legislature met under the new constitution petitions were numerously presented from Baptist associations and churches and also from Presbyterians and Lutherans asking for the disestablishment of the state church. A bill was soon introduced and passed repealing all laws forcing dissenters to contribute to the support of the state church, but this was not enough to satisfy the dissenters; they were now demanding complete religious equality and nothing else would suffice.

For the next three years (1776-1779) petitions flooded the Virginia Assembly, from churches, associations, presbyteries, and conferences, urging complete disestablishment, while the Anglicans, now thoroughly aroused to the danger confronting them, were equally active in behalf of their cause. The next step in the process of disestablishment was the passage on December 13, 1779, of an act repealing portions of the "Act for the support of the Clergy and for the regular collecting and paying the Parish Levies," and all and every other act or acts providing salaries for the ministers, and authorizing the vestries to lay the same. Thus were the purse strings of the establishment cut. But even yet there was not equality, for there were certain grievances still existing in the civil laws and these were now subject to the attack of the dissenters led by the Baptists. Laws were still in existence prohibiting dissenting ministers from performing marriage ceremonies, while the Episcopalian vestries in the several Virginia counties were in charge of certain public duties, and these vestries were closed corporations.

The final struggle over the issue came between the years 1779 and 1785. In the former year several bills were offered, among them one prepared by Thomas Jefferson which was finally to be written into the laws of Virginia, as the "Bill for Establishing Religious Freedom." But the road to the passage of this famous measure was long and painful, and for six years it was discussed pro and con both in and out of legislative halls. In 1784 the cause was almost lost through the introduction of a bill providing for a general assessment for the teaching of religion. According to this measure, persons might declare the denomination to which they wished their assessment to go, but if no declaration was made the money would be used to encourage schools in their respective counties. Washington could see nothing wrong with this measure and it was likewise supported by Marshall, Patrick Henry and Richard Henry Lee, but Madison and Jefferson were against it. At first certain of the Presbyterian clergy favored it, but as usual the Baptists saw the flaw in the measure and stood stanchly in opposition. Madison, writing to Monroe concerning the situation, states: "The Episcopal people are generally for it though I think the zeal of some of them has cooled. The laity of the other sects are generally unanimous on the other side. So are all the clergy except the Presbyterians, who seem as ready to set up an establishment which is to take them in as they were to pull down that which shut them out." The Baptists, however, standing firmly by their avowed principle of the complete separation of church and state, declared it "to be repugnant to the spirit of the Gospel for the Legislature thus to proceed in matters of religion, that no human laws ought to be established for this purpose." The Hanover Presbytery now passed strong resolutions opposing the bill which were later approved by the Virginia Presbyterian Convention. This combined opposition finally succeeded in defeating the measure though by a majority of only three votes.

The way was now open for the final victory, and on December 17, 1785, Jefferson's measure was passed, and on January 19, 1786, was signed by the Speaker and became law. Section II reads thus:

We the General Assembly of Virginia, do enact that no man shall be compelled to frequent or support any religious worship, place or ministry whatsoever, nor shall be enforced, restrained, molested or burdened in his body or goods, nor shall otherwise suffer on account of his religious opinions or belief; but that all men shall be free to profess, and by argument to maintain, their opinions in matters of religion, and that the same shall in no wise diminish, enlarge or effect their civil capacities.

Religious freedom had triumphed in Virginia and was soon to spread throughout the nation, and a few years later in the form of the first amendment to the Federal Constitution was to become a part of the fundamental law of the land. At the time of the passage of the measure Jefferson, its author, was in France, but so proud was he of his part in the memorable struggle that he asked that it be recorded on his gravestone: "Thomas Jefferson, Author of the Declaration of Independence, of the Statute of Virginia for Religious Freedom, and Father of the University of Virginia." But justice compels the admission that Jefferson's part in this accomplishment was not so great as was that of James Madison, nor were the contributions of either or both as important as was that of the humble people called Baptists.

The years immediately following the close of the War for Independence was a period of general constitution making, both within the states and in the ecclesiastical bodies. Several of the American churches had, previous to independence, Old World connections. Thus the Episcopalians had been subject to the Bishop of London; the Roman Catholics to the Vicar Apostolic of London; the Methodists were under the control of John Wesley; the Reformed churches, both Dutch and German, had connections with the Classis of Amsterdam, while the Presbyterians, Quakers, and Lutherans were not so specifically tied to Old World organizations. The Congregationalists and Baptists were, of course, indigenous American churches with each congregation theoretically independent.

II

The Methodists were the first American religious body to form a national organization and their priority in this respect is due to the fact that their national organization was largely worked out for them by Mr. Wesley. At the close of the Revolution the Methodists in America, as well as those in Great Britain, were still a part of the Anglican Church. Francis Asbury and the other American preachers were unordained men and their societies were dependent upon Anglican clergymen for the administration of the sacraments. But during the war the Anglican Church was so disrupted and so many of the clergymen fled that the growing body of Methodists had no way of securing the ordinances of the church. This situation became so serious that a movement was begun in the South under the leadership of Philip Gatch to declare complete independence of Wesley and the English Church and to ordain ministers to administer the sacraments. In 1779 Asbury, in semiexile in Delaware, called a small body of preachers together in a conference, who chose him General Assistant for America, and on this basis Asbury claimed authority over the whole body of American Methodists. A much larger group of preachers met in Fluvanna, Virginia, a little later in the same year, took no notice of the northern conference or the selection of Asbury as assistant and proceeded to take steps looking toward ordination of ministers. Schism was threatened, but in the end a peaceful settlement of differences was reached and the southern preachers agreed to delay their action regarding ordination and to recognize Asbury as Wesley's assistant. Such was the situation when the war closed.

On the close of the war, Wesley immediately turned his attention to the American problem. He again assumed control of his American followers and advised that none be received who made any "difficulty of receiving Francis Asbury as the General Assistant." He then proceeded to provide an organization for the American Methodists suitable to their independence. After thorough consideration he decided that under the situation he as a presbyter of the Church of England had the right to ordain ministers for America. This right he based on the precedent of the Alexandrian Church where bishops had been ordained by presbyters. Accordingly he called together two ordained clergymen of the Church of England who were associated with him, Thomas Coke and James Creighton, and they assisted him in the ordination of Richard Whatcoat and Thomas Vasey as deacons, and the next day as elders. Two days later Creighton and Whatcoat assisted in ordaining Coke as superintendent of the Methodist Societies in America. Wesley's next step was to remodel the Thirty-nine Articles of the Church of England, reducing them to twenty-four, leaving out all reference to Calvinistic teaching. He also prepared a "Sunday Service" which was an abridged form of the English liturgy, and compiled a hymnbook "full-freighted with Methodist theology," and these he sent with Coke, Whatcoat and Vasey to America. With them also he sent a letter to "Dr. Coke, Mr. Asbury, and our brethren in North America" in which he explains his action:

I have [he says] appointed Dr. Coke and Mr. Francis Asbury to be joint suprintendents over our brethren in North America; as also Richard Whatcoat and Thomas Vasey to act as elders among them by baptizing and administering the Lord's Supper. I have prepared a liturgy, little differing from that of the Church of England (I think the best constituted national church in the world), which I advise all the travelling preachers to use on Lord's Day in all congregations.

Dr. Coke and his two companions landed in New York, November 3, 1784. A week later they met Asbury in Barrett's Chapel in Delaware where Coke unfolded Wesley's plan for the American Church. It was decided that before the plan could be put into operation it must be accepted by the preachers, and we are told that Freeborn Garrettson was sent out "like an arrow" to summon the preachers to meet in Baltimore, December 24, 1784. On the day assigned the "Christmas" Conference opened; Coke read Wesley's letter, which made a profound impression on the fifty-odd preachers present. It was agreed to follow Mr. Wesley's advice and form an Episcopal Church, the name Methodist Episcopal being suggested by John Dickins. Asbury refused to accept Wesley's appointment as superintendent and the conference then proceeded to elect both Coke and Asbury to that office. Asbury was now ordained deacon, elder and superintendent, on succeeding days, while twelve other preachers were elected and ordained elders and three to the order of deacons. A form of discipline was drawn up and adopted; the twenty-four articles of religion drawn by Wesley with one additional, making twenty-five, were accepted, together with the Sunday Service and hymns After enacting some other regulations the Christmas Conference adjourned, having been in session ten days. Jesse Lee the first historian of American Methodism states that "The Methodists were pretty generally pleased at our becoming a Church, and heartily united together in the plan which the Conference had adopted, and from that time religion greatly revived." Though Wesley remained in nominal control of the American Methodists until his death, yet as a matter of fact the work of the Christmas Conference practically severed the connection of the American Methodists with their founder. They accepted most of Wesley's suggestions, it is true, but they did so as free agents, and three years later we find them annulling the agreement to obey Wesley in matters of church government.

III

Of all the American churches the Episcopalian suffered most as a result of the Revolution. The S.P.G. missionaries left the country almost to a man at the opening of the war, leaving deserted the country parishes, outside Virginia and Maryland. At the opening of the war, in Virginia there were 95 parishes, 164 churches and chapels and 91 clergymen. When the war closed 23 of the 95 parishes were either forsaken or extinct and of the remainder only 34 had ministers. Everywhere also the church had suffered in its prestige. It had been the church of the royal officials and this fact alone was a severe blow to its popularity. It is interesting to observe that in the reorganization of the Episcopal Church the strongest leadership came from the states in which there had been no establishment.

The outstanding Anglican leader in America at the close of the Revolution was Dr. William White, the rector of Christ Church in Philadelphia. He was born and educated in America, and began his ministry in 1772 as assistant minister at Christ Church, where he became the rector on the retirement of Mr. Duché to England after the Declaration of Independence. Toward the close of the war (1782) White wrote a pamphlet, published anonymously, called "The Case of the Episcopal Church Considered." This pamphlet outlined an organization for the American Episcopal Church and proposed that since there was no immediate prospect of obtaining an American bishop that, as a temporary expedient, the church be organized without. This pamphlet has particular significance since the form of organization it proposed was that later followed, though it was not necessary to proceed without a bishop. Later White explained that the nonepiscopal ordination he proposed was simply to be considered as conditional, though he never gave up his liberal views on the subject, and stated that "a temporary departure from Episcopacy would have been warranted by the Church of England's doctrines and practices." His proposal of lay representation in the annual assemblies and in the national convention indicates the influence of the new American spirit in government.

At about the same time, Dr. William Smith, formerly the provost of the College of Philadelphia but now in Maryland, called a conference of clergymen and laymen of that state (November 9, 1780) to petition the General Assembly for an act empowering the vestries and wardens to raise money to keep in repair the churches which were rapidly falling into ruin. It was in this petition that the name "Protestant Episcopal Church" was first used, probably at the suggestion of Dr. Smith. In August, 1783, a second convention of Maryland clergymen met in Annapolis and adopted a "Declaration of Certain Fundamental Rights and Liberties," in which they declare their independence of the church in any other state, and here also Dr. William Smith was chosen bishop elect for Maryland.

A third movement looking toward the reorganization of the Episcopal Church took place in Connecticut just as the war closed. The Connecticut churches had been largely manned by native clergymen, working under the S.P.G. and ten of these earnest men, several of whom had been loyalists in the war, met at the home of one of their number in December, 1783, and there selected two men, either of whom was to go to England to secure episcopal consecration. One of the two selected, the Rev. Jeremiah Leaming, declined because of his age, but the other, Samuel Seabury, Jr., accepted the charge and the next spring sailed for England. He bore with him letters from the clergy of Connecticut and New York to the Archbishop of Canterbury. Though he was politely received by the English ecclesiastical authorities, they hesitated and then finally refused his request for consecration, on the ground, first, that the oaths of allegiance to the king, in the ordination office, placed there by Parliamentary act could not be omitted, and second, they felt that before they could consecrate a bishop for Connecticut that state should indicate its consent. Seabury now turned to the nonjuring bishops of Scotland, the descendants of the Scotch bishops, who in 1688 had refused to disown James II or to take the oath of allegiance to William of Orange. The church had been disestablished in Scotland because of its participation in the uprisings of 1715 and 1745, but there was no doubt as to the validity of their orders. Seabury's consecration took place on November 14, 1784, in the house of John Skinner, Coadjutor Bishop of Aberdeen, with Bishops Skinner and Kilgour as consecrators. Bishop Seabury returned home at once and on August 3, 1785, held the first convocation of his clergy with no laymen present. Seabury's consecration was not at all pleasing to several of the other church leaders in America, who felt that his course during the Revolution would still further discredit the church in the eyes of the people.

The first step in the formation of a national organization was the calling of a convention to be held in New York in October, 1784, to which eight states sent representatives, there being twenty-six delegates in all, eleven of them laymen. The basis for the discussion of the delegates was a series of resolutions which had been adopted by a Pennsylvania meeting under the leadership of Dr. White and sent to the several states. The Seabury movement could not have resulted in a national church, for reasons already indicated. The New York Convention adopted a general plan for a national organization which called for a general Episcopal Church for the United States, to be governed by clerical and lay representatives from each state; while the liturgy and doctrines of the Church of England were adopted so far as they were consistent with the changed political situation in the United States. This plan was now sent to the several states to be ratified and if adopted they were to elect delegates to a general convention to convene September 27, 1785, at Philadelphia.

The Philadelphia Convention opened on the appointed day with seven states represented by sixteen clergymen and twenty-four laymen, and William White was chosen to preside. Bishop Seabury's consecration was a serious complication, and although he had been invited to the Philadelphia convention, neither he nor any representative from the New England states was present. The great work of the convention was the preparation of the "Ecclesiastical Constitution of the Protestant Episcopal Church in the United States of America," which provided for equal clerical and lay representation in the governing body. The Prayer Book submitted was never adopted, though it was published, but never widely used. The second session of the constitutional convention met in Philadelphia in June, 1786, and in October at Wilmington, Delaware, when some slight alterations were made in the constitution. Meanwhile other bishops had been elected by the state assemblies, in addition to William Smith of Maryland. These were William White for Pennsylvania, Samuel Provoost for New York and Dr. Griffith for Virginia. Griffith because of ill health and poverty never went to England for consecration, while Smith, as bishop-elect for Maryland, was refused certification on grounds of conduct, but White and Provoost sailed for England in November, 1786, and through the help of John Adams, then minister to the Court of St. James, their consecration took place in Lambeth Palace, February 4, 1787. On their return the two new bishops received a letter from Bishop Seabury expressing anxiety for the unity of the church. Bishop Provoost had been bitterly hostile to Bishop Seabury because of his Toryism, but two years later (1789) Seabury was invited and accepted the invitation to attend the national convention and here the new constitution was adopted. Bishop Seabury was recognized, and thus was consummated the union of the Protestant Episcopal Church in the United States.

IV

No religious body was so well fitted to meet the new problems of independent America as the Presbyterians. They had supported the

Revolution with almost complete unanimity; they had an American-educated and able leadership, imbued with the American spirit. For these reasons the task of forming a national organization was comparatively simple. Nor had any church grown more rapidly. Between 1758 and 1789 two hundred and thirty new ministers had been ordained and new presbyteries were forming in the West and South. Redstone Presbytery in southwestern Pennsylvania was founded in 1781 while at the close of the war two Kentucky presbyteries were organized, Transylvania and Lexington. The Synod of New York and Philadelphia was the most important Presbyterian body in the country, though there were several other Presbyterian bodies, such as the Associate and Associate Reformed synods, two conservative bodies representing the Covenanters and the Seceders and also the German and Dutch Reformed churches.

In the process of reorganization Dr. Witherspoon, president of the College of New Jersey, was the leading spirit, though Duffield and Ewing of Philadelphia and Rodgers of New York gave powerful assistance. At the meeting of the synod of New York and Philadelphia in 1785 he headed a committee to devise a system of general rules for the government of the synods, presbyteries and churches, which was to report at the next yearly meeting. The next year (1786) the boundaries of the presbyteries were rearranged, so that the number was increased from twelve to sixteen, and these were grouped into four synods, while it was provided that there should be a General Assembly consisting of ministerial and ruling elders, elected annually by the presbyteries. At this session of the synod also a committee was appointed, again headed by Witherspoon, to prepare "a book of discipline and government . . . accommodated to the state of the Presbyterian Church in America." This committee met in September (1786) and prepared and published a draft of their government and discipline, which was distributed through the church, for consideration, in preparation for its discussion the following year. The next year (1787), after full discussion, some alterations were made and again copies of the amended instrument were sent to the presbyteries and churches for further discussion. Finally at the Synod of 1788 the Confession of Faith, somewhat amended in the matter of the civil magistrate's relation to the church, the Larger Catechism also somewhat amended, the Shorter Catechism, the Directory of Worship and the Form of Government and Discipline, were adopted. Thus by 1788, the year in which the Federal Constitution was being ratified by the states, the Presbyterian Church had adopted a form of government for a great national church.

It has sometimes been suggested that there is an intimate relationship between the constitution of the Presbyterians and the Federal Constitution. The constitution making period in the Presbyterian Church and in the nation covers the same years, 1785 to 1788; both constitutions were formulated in the city of Philadelphia, while it is undoubtedly true that such well-informed men as James Madison and James Wilson must have been familiar with the Presbyterian forms of government. But it is also true that the Episcopalians were likewise engaged in constitution making at the same time, and in the same place, and a like claim might be made for their influence. As a matter of fact, there must have been a large interplay of influence, which we are not now able to trace definitely but which any fair inference is justified in assuming.

V

The constitution making period in the Dutch Reformed Church was between the years 1784 and 1792. At the close of the war the governing bodies of the church assumed titles which indicated their independence, and in 1788 a committee was appointed to translate and publish the creeds and articles of church government and in so doing it was found necessary to modify the articles in order to adapt them to the American Church. This work was completed in 1792 and was adopted.

The German Reformed body were slow in breaking their Old World connections, because of the lack of leadership and also because a majority of their ministers were still receiving financial assistance from the Holland authorities. An important step was taken in 1787 in the founding of Franklin College at Lancaster, Pennsylvania, which began as a joint institution under the auspices of both the Lutheran and Reformed bodies and received the name Franklin because Benjamin Franklin had given the largest sum for its establishment. When the American Coetus in 1789 informed the Holland Classis that steps must be taken to form a national organization, the suggestion was ignored, but three years later, no word having come from Holland, a committee was appointed to draw up rules for a national church, which were adopted the next year, when the new synod met at Lancaster. The name chosen was "The Synod of the Reformed Church in the United

States." In 1795 the Heidelberg Catechism was reissued and the first edition in English was published in 1810.

When the Revolution began the elder Muhlenberg was supervising seventy Lutheran congregations in Pennsylvania and adjacent colonies, while in other sections there were some thirty other congregations. A semisynodical organization, known as the Ministerium of Pennsylvania —which had no formal constitution—had been formed in 1748 designed to include Lutheran ministers throughout the colonies, while in 1781 a constitution was adopted, providing for clerical representation only. In 1792 a new constitution was adopted and amended in 1796, providing for lay representation in the synodical **meetings, an indication** that the Lutherans were being influenced by the democratic spirit of the new nation. At the same time the name "German"—which had not previously been used—was attached to their official name, an indication of a fear that English influence might become dominant. Later the language question caused a bitter fight in the denomination and even today it has not been completely solved. The adoption of this constitution also marks the end of European control of the American Lutheran churches. The movement toward gathering the Lutheran churches into separate state organizations was begun in 1786 with the formation of the Ministerium of New York; was continued in 1803 by the formation of the Synod of North Carolina, in 1818 by the Synod of Ohio and in 1820 by the Synod of Maryland and that of Tennessee. In the latter year the first General Synod, uniting four state synods, was organized, which was the only general Lutheran body in America to the Civil War.

The small body of American Moravians were hampered at the close of the war and for a number of years afterward by the domination of the governing board in Germany and by the continuance of the use of the German language in their worship, while the laymen had no voice in the management of the affairs of the church. There was also a lack of well-qualified ministers. For these reasons the Moravians failed to grow, and the Moravian Church is the best example among the churches of the folly of resisting the rising spirit of nationalism in America as it manifested itself in the years following the Revolution.

The Quakers also continued their connection with the mother church in England and in 1784 there were ten Americans present at the London Yearly Meeting. This relationship, however, did not really affect the independence of the American Friends in their Yearly Meeting, but was largely for the purpose of spiritual encouragement and advice.

VI

At the close of the Revolution the number of Catholics in the United States numbered some 24,000, the great majority being found in Maryland and Pennsylvania. There were 24 clergy, most of them former members of the Society of Jesus, for when the order was suppressed in 1773 the individual members became diocesan priests. The nominal head of the American Catholic body was the Vicar Apostolic in London, but he was completely inactive and in order to secure their property in America the American ex-Jesuits formed themselves into a legal corporation. The American Catholics, being a small body throughout the colonial period, were naturally favorable to religious toleration and had become thoroughly imbued with the growing idea of the separation of church and state. They gave almost unanimous support to the War for Independence and a number of their leaders had taken a conspicuous part in the Revolutionary cause in Maryland, especially the Carroll family.

With the close of the war the Vicar Apostolic of London declared that he would no longer exercise jurisdiction in the United States, and the American priests began at once a movement, largely led by John Carroll, to form an American Roman Catholic organization. John Carroll was a member of the well-known Maryland Carrolls, and was born in 1735 in Prince George county. His education was received in a Jesuit school in Cecil county, Maryland, and he was later sent to St. Omer's College in France. After studying in several Jesuit institutions he became a priest of that order at the age of twenty-eight and for fourteen years was a professor in Jesuit institutions at Liége and Bruges. When his order was suppressed he returned to Maryland where the opening of the Revolution found him.

The first action looking toward a plan of government for the American Catholics was a meeting held at Whitemarsh, Maryland, June 27, 1783, where a plan was drawn up and submitted to the priests of Maryland and Pennsylvania. Later in the same year two other meetings were held and a committee was named to petition the Pope to appoint the Rev. John Lewis as Superior with power to confirm, bless chalices and impart faculties to the priests in the mission. The petition was referred to the "Congregatio de Propaganda Fide," the organization in Rome having in charge the missionary activities of the church. Instead of appointing Lewis, John Carroll, to his surprise, was appointed Superior, the reason being the great age of Lewis and the influence exercised by Franklin, the American minister in Paris. Franklin had become involved in a scheme to subordinate the American Catholic Church to the French, but the American Congress, by refusing to act in a matter of religion, fortunately caused the scheme to fail.

With Carroll's appointment (June 6, 1784) the English jurisdiction over the American Church ceased. Carroll's power as Superior was limited and though at first inclined to decline such a doubtful honor he was finally led to accept. Accompanying his letter of acceptance he enclosed a description of religious conditions in the United States, in which he gives the number of Catholics in the country as 15,800 in Maryland, 1,500 in New York, 7,000 in Pennsylvania, and 200 in Virginia. There were 19 priests in Maryland and 5 in Pennsylvania. The authorities in Rome, replying to this letter, informed Carroll of the intention of the Pope to appoint him as first bishop, which was done November 6, 1789, after he had been selected for that office by the American priests as a special concession from the Pope. They were also allowed, in this case, to name the seat of the first American See, and Baltimore was the choice. On August 15, 1790, Carroll was consecrated in the chapel of Lulworth Castle, England, by the Vicar Apostolic of London. With Carroll's return to America in December, 1790, the American Catholics had secured as their first bishop a leader admirably fitted for the peculiar task which America presented.

VII

Strange to say, New England Congregationalism seemed to be little affected by the nationalizing tendencies and centralizing influences of the period, in spite of the fact that federalism was more strongly intrenched in New England than perhaps in any other section of the country. The Congregational leaders, such as Nathaniel Emmons and Jonathan Edwards the younger, were emphasizing the pure democracy of Congregationalism, and in Massachusetts particularly the tendency was to reassert the old emphasis upon the independence of each congregation. Emmons had trained in his home more than one hundred young men for the ministry, and no one exercised greater influence in Congregationalism. In 1803 in his fight to oppose the establishment of state associations in Massachusetts he stated:

Association leads to Consociation; Consociation leads to Presbyterianism; Presbyterianism leads to Episcopacy; Episcopacy leads to Roman Catholicism; and Roman Catholicism is an ultimate fact.

Even in Connecticut the decentralizing tendency was abroad and in 1784 the law establishing the state association was repealed. This failure on the part of Congregationalism effectively to unite in these years of national expansion proved a blow to the growth of the denomination. Later there arose an impulse to unite into voluntary missionary societies, but such organizations were no match for the more highly developed denominational machinery of the Presbyterians and Methodists and even of the Baptists.

The Baptists in the period of the Revolution and during the years following had developed a distinct national spirit and to a certain degree a national organization. This had come about, in spite of Baptist theory of the complete independence of each congregation, because of their leadership in the fight for religious liberty and the separation of church and state. In order to carry on this fight effectively an organization that was strong enough to bring pressure to bear upon the new state governments was found necessary. Thus there arose the Warren Association, made up of the Baptist churches in New England. In Virginia a General Committee of Baptists was in existence from 1784 to 1799 which was made up of delegates from the several Baptist Associations. This General Committee was responsible for effecting a union between the Regular and Separate Baptists in Virginia, and carried on correspondence with Baptist churches all over the United States. In a sense this committee represented the Baptists in the United States and in that capacity sent an address to the newly elected president, and President Washington in his reply addressed the Baptists all over the nation. This was also a period of great activity in the organization of Baptist associations and between 1774 and 1789 nineteen were organized and the movement continued as Baptist people moved westward into the new regions beyond the Alleghanies.

CHAPTER XIV

✣   ✣   ✣

THE WESTERN MOVEMENT OF POPULATION AND
THE RISE OF THE POPULAR CHURCHES

THE treaty which closed the Revolution fixed the western boundary
of the United States at the Mississippi River, but in this vast expanse
of territory there was only a very narrow line of settlements, with many
breaks between, scattered along the eastern seaboard from Maine to
Georgia. In the first general census taken in 1790 it was found that
there were in round numbers 4,000,000 people in the United States,
and the enumeration revealed that population was moving rapidly
westward in three distinct streams. One stream, made up largely of New
England people, was pushing out along the valley of the Mohawk, a
second passed through southern Pennsylvania and Maryland, while a
third was observed going westward through the Valley of Virginia and
by way of the passes over the Blue Ridge into Kentucky and Tennessee.
These were largely Virginians and North Carolinians. The census also
showed that 5 per cent of the total population were already living west
of the mountains, in southwestern Pennsylvania, in western Virginia,
and in the present states of Kentucky and Tennessee.

This western movement, noted in the first census, continued with
increasing momentum for the next four decades. Previous to 1795 the
largest percentage of population was going into the region south of the
Ohio. The general economic distress along the eastern seaboard following the Revolution set in motion this westward movement. In the
northern and middle states the movement was soon checked by the
return of better times, due to the restoration of credit and the opening
of the West Indian trade, which called for such products as fish, lumber,
horses, wheat flour and other foodstuffs, the staple products of these

states. As a result wages were good and work plentiful and the discontent which always produces emigration largely disappeared. But in the South hard times continued, for the people here were neither ship-owners nor shipbuilders, while the products of the South were similar to those of the West Indies. For these reasons emigration from Virginia, Maryland, and the Carolinas continued over the passes of the Blue Ridge, which soon furnished to Kentucky and Tennessee a population sufficient for their admission into the Union, Kentucky in 1792, Tennessee in 1796.

When the Ordinance of 1787 was adopted, which created a government for the territory north of the Ohio River, known as the Old Northwest, population began to move into that region. In the year previous to the adoption of the famous ordinance a land company, called the Ohio Company, had been organized in one of the taverns of Boston by a group of New Englanders. This company purchased a large section of land in what is now southeastern Ohio, and there in 1788 at the mouth of the Muskingum their first settlement was formed and called Marietta. The first settlers were New Englanders and were typical representatives of the New England movement westward.

The great movement of population into the region north of the Ohio, however, did not begin until after General Wayne's victory over the Miami Confederacy at the Battle of Fallen Timbers, August 20, 1794, and the signing of the Treaty of Greenville the next year. This treaty opened up more than half of Ohio and a narrow strip in southeastern Indiana to settlement. The second census revealed that in the ten years from 1790 to 1800 an immense movement of population had taken place; Kentucky now had a population of 220,955; Tennessee, 105,602; Ohio, 45,365; while Indiana had more than 5,000; and Mississippi territory, the region south of Tennessee, contained more than 8,000. The town of Lexington, Kentucky, boasted 1,750 souls, Cincinnati, 500, while Pittsburgh claimed more than 1,500. The early movement west-ward was made up largely of native Americans, for the non-English strains, except for the Scotch-Irish, had been largely absorbed except in Pennsylvania as there had been little immigration from Europe in the previous twenty years.

The third census (1810) showed that westward emigration had gone steadily forward, especially from Massachusetts and Connecticut in New England, and from New York, Pennsylvania, Virginia and the

Carolinas. The Ohio River was the great highway to the West, people floating down the river in great flatboats, filling up all southern Ohio, which had already been admitted to statehood (1803), raising Indiana to a territory of the second grade, overrunning Tennessee and Kentucky and pushing southward into northern Alabama. The New England element had also filled more than half of the "Western Reserve" along the south shore of Lake Erie, while their Marietta settlements were greatly extended, and other New Englanders were now to be found here and there scattered through central and southern Ohio.

But the greatest movement of population westward was yet to come. This began with the passage of the embargo (1808) and continued with little interruption throughout the War of 1812, until indeed the return of good times in the East, which did not come until about 1820. Nothing like it had ever been seen before. The roads westward swarmed with wagons, cattle, sheep and horses. Through one Pennsylvania village lying on the road to Pittsburgh, toward the end of 1811, 236 wagons and 600 Merino sheep had passed on the way to Ohio in one day. Old settlers in central New York declared that they had never seen "so many teams, and sleighs loaded with women, children and household goods" on their way to Ohio, as in the winter of 1814. All winter long the movement westward continued and throughout the next summer, all journeying to Ohio, which was then but another name for the West. During the month of July, 1814, 6 wagons with 70 persons, all from Massachusetts, passed through Newburgh bound for the West, while from Lancaster, Pennsylvania, came the report that 100 families had passed through that town in one week; at Zanesville, Ohio, 50 wagons crossed the Muskingum in one day. "All America," said a European observer in 1817, "seems to be breaking up and moving westward."

Towns sprang up in the new country almost overnight, while the older states were beginning to become alarmed at the great loss of population. In North Carolina in 1815 the assembly appointed a committee to investigate the matter, as did also Virginia. It is estimated that in 1816, 42,000 settlers came to Indiana alone, while the increase in population in the 5 states of the Old Northwest from 1810 to 1830 was sixfold. In 1816 Indiana was admitted to the Union with a population of 63,897 and two years later a census in Illinois placed the population at 40,258. Again as in 1814 even winter weather failed to stop the movement westward. Some of the settlers went on foot, drawing their small belongings in carts while during this winter (1817) a train of 60 wagons carrying 120 souls, men, women and children, carrying their minister with them, journeyed to Indiana, where they planned to buy a township. These are but examples of the many thousands who set their faces westward during the years between 1808 and 1820.

The fourth census (1820) was startling to the eastern states. New York had become the most populous state in the Union, crowding out Virginia from that distinction, and had added 413,000 people. Ohio came next in the total increase of population, adding 351,000, and now ranked fifth among the states in the Union, while Kentucky was sixth, having added a population of 158,000. In 1821 the total number of states in the Union numbered 25, and of the 12 new states, 10 were west of the Alleghanies. These were critical years in the history of the American churches, for the future of the nation as well as the future of religion in America was largely to be determined by the way in which organized religion met the problem of the new West. And the churches which met this problem most adequately were the ones destined to become the great American churches.

THE PRESBYTERIANS AND CONGREGATIONALISTS

Of all the American churches at the opening of the national era, the Presbyterian was the most strategically located for an immediate advance into the West. The Scotch-Irish constituted the last great wave of emigration previous to the Revolution, and by 1760 Scotch-Irish Presbyterian churches were to found scattered along from "the frontiers of New England to the frontiers of South Carolina." In 1766 the Rev. Charles Beatty and Mr. Duffield were appointed by the Synod of New York and Philadelphia to visit the frontier inhabitants in western Pennsylvania; they reported the following year that they had found on the frontiers "numbers of people earnestly desirous of forming themselves into congregations, and declaring their willingness to exert their utmost to have the gospel among them." Year by year other ministers were appointed to spend longer or shorter periods "over the Alleghany Mountains." In 1772 the synod instructed the Donegal Presbytery, then the farthest west of the presbyteries, "to send either Mr. Craighead or Mr. King to Monongahela and other places adjacent, to supply as long as they can," while in 1775 a Mr. Forster was appointed to supply six Sabbaths in the frontier parts of Pennsylvania. Thus occasional ministers visited the region over the mountains for a number of years before regular ministers were settled over churches in the West. Between 1776 and 1781 there came to be four regular ministers in the southwestern corner of Pennsylvania, among them John McMillan, and in the latter year the Redstone Presbytery was formed, the first west of the mountains. Each of the four early preachers had two churches under their charge from eight to twelve miles apart, though there were fifty places calling for ministers and needing aid. Frequently in responding to these calls the ministers would travel many miles, often with no road to follow, and many times were compelled to be away from their families for days together, while the danger from Indian raids filled the absent minister with constant alarm for their safety. It was not until Wayne's victory at Fallen Timbers (1794) that dread of Indian forays was removed.

Meanwhile Presbyterian people were finding their way from Virginia and North Carolina into Kentucky and Tennessee. The father of Kentucky Presbyterianism was David Rice. Rice, a native of Hanover county, Virginia, had been the pastor of three Presbyterian congregations in Virginia, and like many another of that time was the father of a large family of children. In 1783 Rice decided to visit Kentucky with the idea, if the country pleased him, of removing thither in order to secure cheap land for his "rising family." After his return to Virginia he received a call, signed by three hundred men, inviting him to return to Kentucky and officiate as a minister among them. The next year he took up his residence in Kentucky, settling on a farm near Danville where he became the minister of three congregations, Danville, Cane Run and the Forks of Dick River. The next year a church was built for him in Danville, the first Presbyterian church in the present state of Kentucky. Rice was also instrumental in forming several other churches such as that at New Providence on Salt River, organized in 1785, where a log house was erected to serve the double purpose of school and church. Five years later this building gave place to a large hewn log building, which again in 1803 was enlarged, and sometime within the next twenty years gave way to a brick building "substantially built and handsomely and commodiously finished."

By 1785 there were as many as twelve Presbyterian congregations in Kentucky and steps were taken to form a presbytery. The Synod of New York and Philadelphia at its meeting this year authorized the dividing of the Abingdon Presbytery and the formation of the Transvl-

vania, which was to include the district of Kentucky and the settlements on the Cumberland. The first meeting of the new presbytery was
held in the courthouse in Danville, in October, over which David Rice
presided as moderator. "But the blighting curse of schism," to quote one
of the early Presbyterian chroniclers, "was soon to retard the healthy
and triumphant march of evangelical truth." The perpetrator of this
unfortunate split was the Rev. Adam Rankin, the second Presbyterian
minister to come to Kentucky, who had in 1784 become the minister at
Lexington. The presbytery finally found it necessary (1792) to expel
Rankin on account of his virulent opposition to Watts' Psalmody and
his general "pugnacious propensities." The following year Rankin was
admitted to the ministry of the Associate Reformed Presbyterian
Church and proceeded to organize some congregations of the Covenanter communion from among his followers. Eventually there came
to be several of these congregations in Kentucky, but by 1818 most of
them had disappeared.

Meanwhile other congregations and presbyteries in the new West
were in process of formation, and in 1802 when the Synod of Kentucky
was organized it consisted of three presbyteries, Transylvania, West
Lexington and Washington. The same year a separate presbytery was
formed of the churches on the Cumberland, consisting of six ministers,
among them James McGready and William McGee whose names had
become well known throughout the whole western country as leaders
in the Great Revival.

Of great significance to the growth of Presbyterianism in the West
was the adoption of the "Plan of Union" of 1801 by which the Congregationalists and the Presbyterians agreed to combine their forces in
the great work of carrying religion to the new settlements. Since the
adoption of the Saybrook platform in 1708 by the Connecticut Congregationalists, the trend toward Presbyterianism had been noticeable,
so that the names Congregational and Presbyterian were used more or
less interchangeably. After the Great Awakening there was a considerable intermingling of the two bodies, evidenced by the coming of Jonathan Edwards to Princeton, while from 1766 to 1775 the Synod of New
York and Philadelphia and the associations of Connecticut sent representatives to meet together in an annual convention to oppose the
establishment of an American episcopate. These meetings were interrupted by the Revolution, but soon after peace was signed steps were

again taken to bring about closer coöperation between the two bodies. In 1791 an agreement was reached by which the General Assembly of the Presbyterian church and the General Association of Connecticut should each be represented in the other body by delegates and after 1794 these representatives were given the right to vote in the meetings. Within a few years following the Congregational state organizations of Massachusetts, New Hampshire and Vermont entered into similar agreements with the Presbyterian General Assembly.

The Plan of Union was proposed by Jonathan Edwards the younger in the Connecticut General Association in 1800 where he was sitting as a delegate of the Presbyterian General Assembly. The next year the Plan was adopted by both bodies. It provided a scheme whereby Congregational and Presbyterian settlers in a new community might combine to form a single congregation, and might call a minister of either denomination. If the majority of the members were Presbyterian they could conduct their discipline according to that church even if their minister were a Congregationalist, and vice versa. In case of disagreement between pastor and church the matter could be referred to the presbytery or association of which the pastor was a member or, if this was not agreeable, to a committee consisting of equal representatives of each group. Appeals were to be taken to the presbytery in case the minister was a Presbyterian, but if a Congregationalist the male members of the church were to be the final court. Later the other New England state associations approved the plan.

The plan as formulated evidently called for the organization of Congregational associations as well as presbyteries in the regions where it was to operate, but as a matter of fact it worked in almost every instance to the advantage of the Presbyterians. It was in the region north of the Ohio River, where the New England migration had centered, that the Plan of Union largely operated, and in central western New York, Ohio, Illinois and Michigan many churches which began as Congregational became Presbyterian. The founding of the First Presbyterian Church in Chicago furnishes an interesting example. The first minister, Jeremiah Porter, was a New Englander, educated as a Congregationalist in a Congregational college and was ordained by a Congregational association, while a large majority of the first members—indeed, twenty-six of the original twenty-seven—were Congregationalists, and yet the church was organized as Presbyterian. Another example is that of the church at Jacksonville, Illinois. Here there was a mingling of Presbyterians, largely from Kentucky, and New England Congregationalists. Illinois College was founded by a group of Yale graduates, known as the Illinois Band, but the first church to be established was the Presbyterian, though the Congregational influence was so strong in Jacksonville that soon afterward a Congregational church was also organized—one of the few to come into existence in the region where the two churches were coöperating.

That the Presbyterians were more tenacious than Congregationalists of their denominational standards there can be no doubt, and they were likewise more assertive of their denominational spirit. There was undoubtedly also a feeling, largely held among Congregationalists at this time, that their form of organization was not suited to new and unformed communities, a fact which led the American Home Missionary Society (organized in 1826), supported by Congregationalists as well as Presbyterians, to advise all young men going out as missionaries to the West to receive Presbyterian ordination.

As might be expected the first schools and colleges in the new West were those established either by Congregationalists or Presbyterians. In February, 1785, a school was opened in the house of the Rev. David Rice at Danville; this had been provided for by the Virginia legislature five years previously when 8,000 acres of land had been set aside for the purpose, while in 1783 an endowment of 12,000 acres had been added for the new Transylvania Seminary. In 1788 the seminary was moved to Lexington, where, according to Davidson, the prejudiced historian of the Presbyterians of Kentucky, it fell into the hands of the liberal element, and the Rev. Harry Toulmin, a Unitarian minister of English birth, "a known disciple of Priestley," became the head and the Presbyterians lost control. The Transylvania Presbytery, foreseeing this result, took steps in the spring of 1794 to found a school of their own which would be under their direction, with the provision that half the trustees should always be ministers of the presbytery. "Father" Rice was sent to the legislature to secure the charter and "The Kentucky Academy" was launched, the legislature granting it 6,000 acres of land as an endowment. The ministers of the presbytery collected £1,000 in Kentucky, while the commissioners to the next General Assembly were authorized to collect money in the East, where they secured nearly $10,000, among the donors being George Washington and John Adams.

Meanwhile the presbyterians had opened a grammar school at Pisgah, near Lexington, and in the fall of 1797 an academy began operations at the same place. Transylvania Seminary in Lexington had failed to prosper under the management of the liberals, and the citizens of Lexington now proposed that the two schools be united, promising that the majority of the trustees should be Presbyterians. This was done by act of legislature in December, 1798, under the imposing title of "Transylvania University," and medical and law schools were made a part of the university, besides the usual college and academy. For a time the university prospered, but gradually, as vacancies occurred in the trustees, these were filled by "prominent political characters" until finally the Presbyterians found themselves in a hopeless minority. The crisis came in 1818 when the Rev. Horace Holley was chosen president. Holley was a graduate of Yale and was evidently a man of attractive personality, and although he was suspected of holding liberal views his administration began auspiciously; even "the intractable Presbyterians were reduced to silence." It was soon reported, however, that the president was holding up to ridicule the doctrine of human depravity and denied the "real personality of the devil" or that the world was created in six days. This was too much for the Presbyterians and steps were taken by the Kentucky Synod to establish a school in which orthodox teaching would be assured. After some delay a charter for Centre College was secured and the college opened at Danville in 1823. President Holley's popularity meanwhile had waned and he was forced to resign in 1826, becoming the head of a college at New Orleans, where his health soon broke and he died at sea while journeying northward in search of health.

While the Presbyterians south of the Ohio were busy founding schools their brethren in western Pennsylvania and Ohio were likewise engaged. The first Presbyterian ministers in western Pennsylvania conducted schools in connection with their churches, one of which was that of the Rev. John McMillan in the Redstone country, who like William Tennent conducted a "log" college. Among his early pupils was James McGready. An academy was established at Canonsburg in 1794 partly under Presbyterian patronage, which in 1802 became Jefferson College. The Congregationalists also early founded academies in the Northwest Territory, that at Marietta being established in 1790 and later developing into Marietta College.

The Presbyterians and Congregationalists made the largest contributions to the educational and cultural life of the frontier, though they did not succeed in gaining large numbers for their churches. Both the Baptists and Methodists far surpassed them in this respect. The census of 1820 placed the population of Kentucky at 563,317 while the church population for the same year was but 46,730, or 1 in 12. Of the total church membership the Baptists and Methodists had about equal numbers, 21,000 each; the Presbyterians had but 2,700 and the Cumberland Presbyterians another 1,000 while all others numbered 500. These figures are typical of conditions generally on the frontier. The average Presbyterian clergyman ministered as a rule to not more than three churches, and usually to but two, while he spent some weeks of each year on preaching tours through the new settlements under the direction of the presbytery. In most cases, however, it would seem that the initiative in the formation of new churches came from laymen, and ministers were not settled until there were enough Presbyterian members in a given community to provide for his support. Then too the Presbyterians were a particularly rigid body in both doctrine and polity, and every innovation to meet the peculiar needs or problems of a new country was always strongly opposed.

Unlike the Methodist circuit rider and the Baptist farmer-preacher, to whom all frontier communities were alike, the Presbyterian preacher was inclined to limit his responsibility to people of Presbyterian background. In other words the average Presbyterian preacher on the frontier went forth seeking Presbyterians and Presbyterian settlements made up of people of Scottish and Scotch-Irish descent. This difference in approach to frontier society is doubtless partially responsible for the slower progress of frontier Presbyterianism in comparison to the more rapid growth of the Baptists and the Methodists. A second factor which slowed down the Presbyterians in the trans-Alleghany West was their system of congregations calling ministers. In a new region where there were no congregations, the method the Presbyterians adopted in forming new congregations was a slow and often painful process. Two or three congregations generally had to unite to call a minister and this caused still further delay. On the other hand the Methodist circuit rider was not called, but was sent to the people to form classes and churches, while the Baptist farmer-preacher was one of the people and moved out with the settlers. Or to put it concisely, the Presbyterian preacher was called; the Methodist preacher was sent; the Baptist preacher simply came with the people. A third cause for the less rapid growth of the Presbyterians in the West was that a large proportion of their early preachers became school teachers, combining schoolteaching with their preaching. Thus a large proportion of their time was taken up with their daily round as teachers. A fourth factor was that his preaching tended to be more theological than practical, and with little emotional appeal.

THE BAPTISTS

Among the early emigrants across the Alleghany Mountains into Kentucky and Tennessee were numerous Baptists from Virginia and North Carolina. Generally speaking they belonged to the class, economically, which would be attracted by the lure of cheap land. The pure democracy of Baptist church government would also tend to attract them to the freer life and the greater democracy of the frontier. Their preachers came from the people, and were self-supporting, and were themselves, indeed, farmers on the lookout for better land. Thus the Baptists were particularly well suited in their ideas of government, in their economic status, and in their form of church government to become the ideal western immigrants.

The first Baptist church west of the Alleghanies was the Severn's Valley Church, which was formed in 1781. It is still in existence and its early records may still be seen. An interesting example of Baptist migration into the West is that of the Gilbert's Creek Church in Kentucky. This church came out to Kentucky in a body, with its pastor, Lewis Craig. Its organization was kept up in the march over the mountains; the pastor preached as they camped along the way, while several baptisms were performed in the clear mountain streams. On their march westward they heard the news of the surrender of Cornwallis at Yorktown and made the hills ring with the firing of their rifles in their glad rejoicings. Finally reaching the place of their new settlement in December, 1781, they gathered for worship "around the same old Bible they had used back in Spottsylvania," in Virginia.

Of all the Baptist preachers who crossed the Alleghany Mountains to bring the Baptist gospel to the pioneers, John Taylor takes first rank. This is not only because he was a recognized and resourceful leader among frontier Baptists, but also because he has left us in his

History of Ten Baptist Churches,[1] by far the most illuminating description of how the Baptists functioned in the West. A native of Virginia of Anglican background, Taylor was converted under the preaching of William Marshall, a Baptist farmer-preacher, an uncle of the future Chief Justice of the United States. He married a Baptist wife in 1782 and the next year set out for Kentucky. The trip down the Ohio on a flatboat and through the wilderness on horseback took three months of painful travel. He settled in Woodward County, where he, with other Baptist preachers in the settlement, formed the Clear Creek Baptist Church, which he served for nine years as pastor. At the same time, he, with his sons and slaves, cleared a large farm, and he became a man of importance in the whole region. He helped form seven other Baptist churches in Kentucky as well as others in western Virginia, North Carolina and Tennessee. It was his lifelong custom to set out from his home in the latter part of the summer and visit eight or ten Baptist Associations, and throughout the year he always found places to preach every Sabbath. All this labor was performed of his own volition and without compensation or overhead direction. But this was not peculiar to John Taylor; rather he is a prototype of the fearless and self-reliant farmer-preachers who planted Baptists churches throughout the length and breadth of the new West.

By 1785 six Baptist churches in Kentucky sent "messengers" to the house of Lewis Craig and there formed the first Baptist association west of the mountains, called the Elkhorn Association. In October of that same year four other little backwoods churches, in the settlements to the west, formed the second western association, called the Salem, while two years later the South Kentucky Association was organized by the Separate Baptists; the two earlier associations being Regular Baptists. In 1801 this distinction was abolished when the two bodies agreed on terms of union.

In like manner the western migrations had brought Baptist people into eastern Tennessee, where at Boon's Creek a church was formed in 1781. These were Baptists from the Sandy Creek Association in North Carolina and by 1786 seven churches had been organized and the Holston Association was formed. In the Cumberland settlements in

---

[1] John Taylor, *History of Ten Baptist Churches* (Frankfort, Kentucky, 1823). See also Chapter VI. "Extracts from the History of Ten Baptist Churches" in W. W. Sweet, *Religion on the American Frontier*, Vol I, *The Baptists* (New York, 1931); also article "John Taylor" by W. W. Sweet in *Dictionary of American Biography*.

central Tennessee Baptists were among the first settlers; in fact, in most instances Baptists were first on the ground in the western settlements, for their preachers came with the settlers and the formation of a church was a comparatively simple matter.

The typical Baptist preacher on the frontier was a settler who worked on his land five or six days each week, except when called upon to hold weekday meetings or funerals. He was generally without much formal education, for there was a deep-seated prejudice against educated and salaried ministers, though some of the preachers received some support, which in the early days was paid in kind. There were two types of frontier Baptist preachers, *licensed and ordained,* and sometimes there were several ministers in a congregation, though generally one was designated as the pastor of the flock. Licensing a preacher was the first step in the making of a minister after he had been permitted to "exercise his gifts" by vote of the church. When chosen to take charge of a regular congregation he was then ordained. Frontier Baptists generally accepted a mild form of Calvinism, and there was little doctrinal discord among them though out-and-out Arminianism was strongly condemned. The initiative in the formation of a frontier Baptist church came generally from a licensed or ordained farmer-preacher settled in a new community. Sometimes there were several preachers living in the vicinity and all would take a hand in the organization, as John Taylor tells us was the case of the Clear Creek Church in Kentucky.

The churches once organized held business meetings once each month with the minister as moderator, and a large share of the business had to do with the disciplining of members. A random turning of the pages of any of the old record books of the early frontier churches will soon convince one that the church was a large factor in maintaining order in these raw communities. Discipline was meted out to members for drinking, fighting, harmful gossip, lying, stealing, immoral relation between the sexes, gambling and horse racing. Even business dealings and intimate family affairs, such as the relation between parents and children, were considered matters for church discipline. In the region south of the Ohio particularly all the churches had slave members, and the churches watched over the slaves with as much care as over the white members, and in some cases the slave members were permitted a voice in church matters.

Practically all the early frontier Baptist churches were named after creeks, runs, valleys or rivers, which simply means that the frontier settlements were located along the streams and that the first geographic names which became familiar to the settlers were those of rivers or creeks. Thus every one of the first churches constituting the Elkhorn Association took its name from a stream: Gilbert's Creek, Tate's Creek, South Elkhorn, Clear Creek, Big Crossing and Limestone. Of the seven churches constituting the Illinois Association in 1807 five were named for streams or valleys: Mississippi Bottom, Silver Creek, Wood River, Kain Spring and Richland Creek. The first Baptist places of worship were the rude cabins of the settlers, which as a rule served for the first several years after a church was formed, for the membership of the early churches was small. Numerous churches were formed with no more than six to ten members, and probably the average was not more than twenty. The first meetinghouses were of round logs, to be followed in a few years, if the church prospered, with a house of hewn logs with a fireplace and chimney built of brick. Such a building Thomas Lincoln helped to build on Pigeon Creek, Indiana, in 1819. The period of the better meetinghouses, frame or brick, came fifteen or twenty years after the formation of the average congregation.

THE METHODISTS

The most successful of the American churches in following the population as it moved westward, especially in the earlier years, were the Methodists. Both in organization and in doctrine they were well suited to the frontier. The circuit system had been devised by Wesley for his English societies, but once introduced into America by Francis Asbury it proved especially adaptable to the needs of a new country where settlements were scattered and far between. All the early Methodist preachers were itinerants, that is, they had no one place or congregation to which they ministered, but traveled circuits varying in size according to the number of settlements. Thus, if the country was new the circuits were very large, requiring from four to five weeks for the circuit rider to make the rounds. At convenient places he established "classes" over which "class leaders" were appointed and on the average circuit there were twenty to thirty such classes. The circuit rider preached almost every day, with the possible exception of Monday, nor was he particular where he preached; a log cabin, the barroom of a tavern and out under the trees were all alike to him. Nor did he delay his visits until Methodists moved into a community; his task was not so much to find Methodists among the settlers as to make Methodists of the raw material which he found on the frontier. Often he made his appearance before the cabin of a settler was completed, or before the mud in the stick chimney was dry.

The doctrine preached by the Methodist circuit riders was also well adapted to meet the hearty acceptance of the frontiersmen. It was a gospel of free will and free grace, as opposed to the doctrines of limited grace and predestination preached by the Calvinistic Presbyterians, or even the milder Calvinistic Baptists. The frontier Methodist preachers brought home to the pioneers the fact that they were the masters of their own destiny, an emphasis which fitted in exactly with the new democracy rising in the West, for both emphasized the actual equality among all men.

The Methodist system of lay or "local" preachers was likewise one which lent itself easily to the spread of Methodism in a new country. A young man who gave any evidence of ability in public speaking was urged by the class leader and by the circuit preacher to "exercise his gifts," and if he proved useful, when the presiding elder came around to hold the "quarterly meeting conference" the young man was recommended to receive an "exhorter's license." Some of these lay preachers joined the "conference" and became regular traveling preachers, but many of them remained lay preachers, preaching frequently in the vicinity of their homes, and were often instrumental in organizing classes in new settlements. These men, like the Baptist farmer-preachers, had little learning but were full of zeal and earnestness. It was, indeed, two local preachers, Francis Clark and John Durham, both from Virginia, who were responsible for founding the first Methodist classes in Kentucky.

It was in 1782 that the first regularly appointed circuit rider was sent over the mountains, to the Yadkin country, and the next year both Yadkin and Holston are listed among the Methodist circuits. In 1784 the Redstone circuit in southwestern Pennsylvania appeared, and by 1789 there were ten Methodist circuits in the new West, four in Tennessee, three in Kentucky and three along the waters of the upper Ohio. The number of circuits increased as population grew; the circuit preachers followed the moving population across the Ohio, with the close of the Indian wars, so that by the end of the century there were more than two thousand Methodists in Kentucky and Tennessee, while in the Northwest Territory there were four circuits, and also one—the Natchez—in the region of the lower Mississippi.

The administration of the church in every section of the United States was placed upon the shoulders of Bishop Francis Asbury. Nor was he an absentee supervisor, directing the work from a comfortable seat east of the mountains. Again and again he crossed the Alleghanies from 1788 to 1800, holding conferences of the preachers, assigning them to their circuits, preaching and advising. In 1790 he passed over the mountains from western North Carolina into eastern Tennessee, where he found the preachers "indifferently clad, with emaciated bodies." Returning to the East, he again in the same year recrossed the mountains into Kentucky, "over mountains, steep hills, deep rivers, and muddy creeks, and thick growth of reeds for miles together."

There was early objection to Asbury's supreme appointing power which resulted in 1792 in a serious schism. The leader of the malcontents was James O'Kelly, a prominent Virginia preacher of strong character and with a following numbering several thousands. Those who withdrew called themselves "Republican Methodists" and there were a number of adherents among the Kentucky and Tennessee Methodists. It is, indeed, passing strange that the highly centralized Methodist system of government could win its way in the new West, the most democratic society in the world. The Methodists, however, preached a democratic gospel while they were under a monarchical form of church government; on the other hand, the Presbyterians and Baptists had a more democratic form of church government but preached a monarchical gospel. The arbitrary Methodist system, however, was greatly tempered by the fact that the early bishops moved about the country, from north to south, from east to west; stayed in the rude cabins on the frontier, preached at camp meetings and received the same salary as the humblest circuit rider.

The name "Western Conference" was applied to the great region west of the Alleghany Mountains from 1800 to 1812. In 1800 all the western circuits were gathered into one district and placed under the supervision of William McKendree, who for a number of years, until his election as a bishop in 1808, was the major general of the Methodist forces on the frontier. When the century began there were 2,622 white Methodists and 179 colored in the whole western country; in 1812 there were 29,093 white and 1,648 colored, while the circuits had increased from 9 to 69. In 1830, instead of 1 conference west of the Alleghanies, there were 8, while the membership had grown from

30,000 to more than 175,000, and among these were nearly 2,000 Indians and more than 15,000 negroes.

THE PRIVILEGED CHURCHES

It is a significant fact that the two most privileged churches of the colonial period, the Episcopalians and the Congregationalists, failed to deal adequately with the problems created by the western movement of population, and both lost at least their numerical standing among the American churches. As has been noted in a previous chapter, the Episcopalians were under a cloud for nearly a generation after independence, and except in a few cases failed even to hold their ground in the older sections of the new nation. In a few instances rugged and courageous individuals, such as Philander Chase, planted Episcopal churches in the trans-Alleghany West, but the church at large deserves none of the credit for what was done. What Chase accomplished was due to his own devotion and energy and not to any policy which his church had devised. It was not until 1835 that the Episcopal Church adopted a definite policy for the West, when Jackson Kemper was consecrated a bishop for the vast western area, a diocese without boundaries.

The Congregationalists likewise failed to develop a national organization, simply because their leaders were sectional-minded, and did not have a national view of their task. Consequently, through the operation of the Plan of Union, they allowed the Presbyterians to absorb a great proportion of the New England people moving westward. It was not until 1852 that the Congregationalists adopted a national organization and by that time the religious pattern of the West had been fixed. A glance at the church membership figures for the year 1850 tells the story. The Methodists, who had been the smallest religious body in the new nation at the achievement of independence had a membership in 1850 of 1,324,000 and ranked first among the American churches; the Baptists, who had ranked third in numbers, were now second with 815,000 members; the Presbyterians came third with 487,000, changing places with the Baptists; the Congregationalists, who had stood at the top of the list in 1783 were now fourth with 197,000 on their membership rolls; while the Lutherans and the Disciples were ranked fifth and sixth respectively with 163,000 for the former and 118,000 for the latter. The Episcopalians, formerly the fourth in point of numbers, were now seventh, with a membership of 90,000. In other words the numerical importance of the churches was determined by the effectiveness with which each of them met the problems of the people moving west.

THE CATHOLICS

Among the settlers in the new West there was early a sprinkling of Roman Catholics, mostly from Maryland, who were occasionally visited by itinerant priests. The old French settlements along the Mississippi and about the Great Lakes were supplied with priests by Bishop Carroll, among them being the Rev. Benedict Joseph Flaget who was sent in 1792 to Vincennes on the Wabash. He found there "a very poor log building, open to the weather and almost tottering. The congregation, if possible, in a still more miserable condition. Out of seven hundred souls, only twelve could be induced to approach holy communion during the Christmas festivities." In like manner Kaskaskia and Cahokia, in Illinois, and Detroit were supplied with faithful missionary priests. The first priest ordained for Kentucky was the Rev. Stephen T. Baden and with his coming the Catholic Church had its real beginnings in this region. Other priests also came, among them Charles Nerinckx, a native of Belgium, who was active in forming churches and created a sisterhood, while the Dominicans established a convent and a college.

By 1808 the Catholic growth in the West had increased to such an extent that it was thought necessary to erect a new diocese, known as that of Bardstown (Kentucky), which included besides Kentucky and Tennessee all the Northwest Territory. Benedict Joseph Flaget, who for several years had been the priest at Vincennes, was named the first bishop. He came down the Ohio in a flatboat and reached his diocese in June, 1811. Four years later he reported 19 churches in Kentucky and 10 priests; he estimated the number of Catholics in Kentucky at 10,000; the number of Catholics in Ohio at 50 families without a priest; 130 Catholic families in Indiana; 3 Catholic parishes in Illinois with 120 families, while in Detroit there were some 2,000 Catholics. By 1817 the work of supervising this vast diocese had become so burdensome that Bishop Flaget asked for a coadjutor and the Rev. John Baptist David was appointed in July of that year. In 1815 the diocese of Louisiana and the Floridas was erected, and in 1829 the diocese of Cincinnati.

C H A P T E R   X V

✣　✣　✣

THE SECOND AWAKENING AND THE FRONTIER SCHISMS

THE famous Marquis of Pescara once said to the papal legate, "It is impossible for men to serve Mars and Christ at the same time." "It is possible for individuals," suggests J. Franklin Jameson, "but it is difficult for a whole generation."[1] It will not be surprising, then, to learn that the decade and a half following the close of the American Revolution was one of spiritual deadness among all the American churches. A historian[2] of the Episcopalians has characterized the period from the close of the war to 1812 as one of suspended animation. Nor was this true of the Episcopalian body alone. It was, indeed, "the period of the lowest ebb-tide of vitality in the history of American Christianity." At this period deistic influence was particularly strong, described by the orthodox as "the spirit of half belief or unbelief." This influence had come from both England and France and there were soon numerous Jacobin clubs and societies of the Illuminati throughout the country, devoting their energy to ridicule of Christianity and to the bringing in of the *Age of Reason.*

Lyman Beecher, who was a student at Yale College in 1795, describes in his interesting *Reminiscences* the religious conditions in the college at that time. He says:

"The College was in a most ungodly state. The college church was almost extinct. Most of the students were skeptical, and rowdies were

---

[1]J. Franklin Jameson, *The American Revolution Considered as a Social Movement* (Princeton, 1926), p. 148 ff.

[2]C. C. Tiffany, *A History of the Protestant Episcopal Church in the United States of America* (New York, 1895), pp. 388-390. "Virginia was the most flagrant illustration of decline; but other regions of the South were not much more hopeful," p. 390.

plenty. Wine and liquors were kept in many rooms; intemperance, profanity, gambling, and licentiousness were common." Tom Paine was the great vogue among the young men, and boys came to college boasting of their infidelity and addressing one another as Voltaire, Rousseau, d'Alembert, etc.

So low were the fortunes of the Protestant Episcopal Church at this period that even some of the bishops looked for it to die out with the old colonial families. So hopeless did Bishop Provoost of New York consider the religious situation that he ceased functioning, while Bishop Madison of Virginia, we are told, shared the conviction of Chief Justice Marshall, himself a devout churchman, that the church was "too far gone ever to be revived." William Meade, later Bishop of Virginia, tells us that when he offered himself for ordination at Williamsburg in 1811, universal surprise was expressed that a college-bred man should apply for orders. And on the way to the dilapidated Williamsburg church, where the ordination services were to be performed, they met a party of students with dogs and guns, all of whom passed the church scornfully by, having recently debated the question "whether Christianity had been beneficial or injurious to mankind." In 1813 when a special convention was called in Virginia to elect a successor to Bishop Madison, who had died the previous year, only seven clergymen and eighteen laymen were present.

In the Presbyterian Church there was likewise reason for concern. The college at Princeton, which but a generation before was noted for its evangelical fervor, had in 1782 but two students who professed themselves Christians. In 1798 the General Assembly thus describes religious conditions in the country:

We perceive with pain and fearful apprehension a general dereliction of religious principles and practice among our fellow-citizens, a visible and prevailing impiety and contempt for the laws and institutions of religion, and an abounding infidelity, which in many instances tends to atheism itself. The profligacy and corruption of the public morals have advanced with a progress proportionate to our declension in religion. Profaneness, pride, luxury, injustice, intemperance, lewdness, and every species of debauchery and loose indulgence greatly abound.

The Baptists had been so busy fighting for the separation of church and state that they too, in the words of Robert Semple, the historian of the Virginia Baptists, "suffered a very wintry season. With some exceptions," says he, "the declension was general throughout the state. The love of many waxed cold. Some of the watchmen fell, others stumbled, and many slumbered at their posts." The Methodists also suffered a decline and for a number of years reported a steady decrease in membership.

If moral and religious conditions were at low ebb along the eastern seaboard they were even more deplorable in the new West. The pioneer Baptist preacher, John Taylor, who visited Kentucky for the first time in 1779, was distressed by the low state of religion which he found there, while David Rice, the first settled Presbyterian minister in Kentucky, states that when he came to the West (1783) he "found scarcely one man and but few women who supported a creditable profession of religion. Some were grossly ignorant of the first principles of religion. Some were given to quarreling and fighting, some to profane swearing, some to intemperance, and perhaps most of them totally negligent of the forms of religion in their own houses." Peter Cartwright tells us that Logan County, Kentucky, was called "Rogues' Harbor" and was the refuge for escaped murderers, horse thieves, highway robbers and counterfeiters. People from the East who visited the West were shocked by the swearing, fighting, gouging, Sabbath-breaking and general lawlessness which prevailed.

To quote the words of a recent interpreter of this period,

However great the apathy which had fallen upon the spirit of American religion, it would surely recover, as the nation itself gradually recovered from the ravages and injuries of war. A nation inspired by the sense of a career of future greatness can seldom fail to develop active religious life in some form, and it was certain that America would sometime become religious, even if it were not so in the years immediately after the Revolution.

Nor was a revival of religion in America to be long delayed.

I

Times were, indeed, ripe for a renewed emphasis upon vital religion throughout the nation. The movement in this direction was first noticed in the East. Almost imperceptibly people began to take a larger interest in matters of religion and in numerous New England communities especially, churches were strengthened by the addition of new members, while new churches were established. The revival in New England was, no doubt, partly due to the introduction of Methodism, with its strong evangelistic emphasis. In 1789 Bishop Asbury appointed Jesse Lee, a tall Virginian, to the first Methodist circuit in New England, and he preached his first sermon in the New England metropolis standing on a deal table on Boston Common in 1790. Six years later the New England Conference was formed with three thousand members, while a network of circuits soon covered all the New England states.

The changing attitude is well illustrated by what was taking place at Yale College. Timothy Dwight, the grandson of Jonathan Edwards, became the president in 1795, and under his administration the whole moral and religious atmosphere of the college was changed for the better. He met the students on their own ground and in a series of frank discussions both in the classroom and in the college chapel treated such subjects as "The Nature and Danger of Infidel Philosophy," "Is the Bible the Word of God?" while he preached a notable series of sermons in the college chapel on "Theology Explained and Defended," in which he grappled with the principles of deism and materialism. Soon he had won the admiration of the students and in 1802 a revival began in which a third of the student body professed conversion, to be followed at frequent intervals by other awakenings. Dartmouth, Williams and Amherst Colleges experienced similar religious awakenings, while the movement spread into the middle states and into the South, especially among the Presbyterians.

The spread of infidelity was effectively checked and out of the renewed interest in religion came the beginnings of home missionary effort as well as the foreign missionary enterprise. The founding of numerous academies and colleges was another result, and it also furnished the impulse for the founding of the first theological seminaries for the special training of ministers. The first two decades of the nineteenth century saw likewise the founding of numerous interdenominational societies and philanthropic organizations, as well as the beginning of religious journalism, all of which was largely the result of the new emphasis upon religion which characterized this period. So important were these new organizations that they deserve special consideration in a separate chapter.

II

The western phase of the second awakening was far different from the quiet spirit of revival which largely characterized its eastern progress. In the East there were no prominent leaders or evangelists, nor was there great excitement engendered. On the other hand, the revival in the West was attended by such excitement and by such strange manifestations as were never before seen in America.

The outstanding leader at the beginning of the revival in the West was James McGready, a Presbyterian minister of Scotch-Irish parentage. Born in Pennsylvania, he moved with his parents at an early age to Guilford County, North Carolina, where as a youth he was particularly careful about his religious duties and early determined to study for the ministry. Accordingly he became one of John McMillan's first students at his Log College in western Pennsylvania and after the completion of his studies was licensed to preach by the Redstone Presbytery. He preached within the bounds of that presbytery for a time, but later went to the Carolinas where under his preaching a revival was soon begun. He has been described as exceedingly uncouth in his personal appearance, with small piercing eyes, coarse tremulous voice, and so unusual was his general ugliness as to attract attention.

He was accused in South Carolina of "running people distracted" and of diverting them from their occupations, and there soon developed fierce opposition to him and his preaching. Indeed, the opposition became so extreme that his pulpit was torn out of the church and burned, while a threatening letter was sent him written in blood. This opposition led him to visit the West in 1796, where after a short time he became the pastor of three Presbyterian churches in Logan County, Kentucky: Gasper River, Muddy River and Red River. It was here under his zealous and persuasive preaching that the great western revival began which came to be known as the Logan County, or Cumberland, revival.

Through 1797, 1798 and 1799 the religious interest increased, while several other Presbyterian and Methodist preachers united their efforts with those of McGready to carry the revival throughout the whole region. It was in the summer of 1800, however, that the Cumberland revival reached its culmination. In June of that year unusual excitement had attended a meeting held on Red River, which had been encouraged by a Methodist preacher, John McGee, who, overcome by his feeling, "shouted and exhorted with all possible energy." Numbers professed conversion, but the unusual excitement which attended the meeting filled some of the Presbyterian ministers present with amazement and others with resentment. The news of this meeting soon spread far and wide so that at subsequent meetings even greater crowds assembled to see the strange sights. It was at this period that people began to come to the meetings prepared to spend several days on the ground, bringing their provisions with them—which is undoubtedly the origin of the camp meeting. Other meetings with similar results were held at Gasper River, Muddy River and at a Methodist Quarterly Meeting in August at Edward's Chapel. This latter meeting lasted four days and nights and more than a hundred conversions were reported.

The revival now spread rapidly throughout Kentucky and Tennessee, into North and South Carolina, western Virginia and Pennsylvania and into the settled regions north of the Ohio River. Sacramental services were the occasions for some of the largest gatherings. In these meetings the Presbyterians and Methodists commonly united; the Baptists also held joint preaching with the others, but since they generally held to "close communion," would not unite in the communion services.

People traveled long distances to see for themselves what was going on at the Logan County meetings. Among the visitors was Barton W. Stone, the minister of two little Presbyterian churches in Bourbon County, Kentucky, who in the spring of 1801 journeyed to Logan County to investigate the religious situation. He soon returned fully convinced that the work was genuine and deeply affected by what he had seen. Immediately a revival broke out under his preaching at Cane Ridge, one of his churches, and the happenings in Logan County were duplicated in Bourbon County. Perhaps the greatest of all the single phases of the western revival was what has come to be known as the Cane Ridge meeting. This was a sacramental meeting held in August, 1801, which extended over several days and was attended by crowds variously estimated at from 10,000 to 25,000. There are numerous descriptions by eyewitnesses of this great meeting. One such eyewitness states:

I attended with 18 Presbyterian ministers; and Baptist and Methodist preachers, I do not know how many; all being either preaching or exhorting the distressed with more harmony than could be expected. The governor of our State was with us and encouraging the work. The number of people computed from 10, to 21,000 and the communicants 828. The whole people were serious, all the conversation was of a religious nature, or calling in question the divinity of the work. Great numbers were on the ground from Friday until the Thursday following, night and day without intermission, engaged in some religious act of worship. They are commonly collected in small circles of 10 or 12, close adjoining another circle and all engaged in singing Watt's and Hart's hymns; and then a minister steps upon a stump or log, and begins an exhortation or sermon, when, as many as can hear collect around him. On Sabbath I saw above 100 candles burning at once and I saw 100 persons at once on the ground crying for mercy, of all ages from 8 to 60 years. . . . When a person is struck down he is carried by others out of the congregation, when some minister converses with and prays for him; afterwards a few gather around and sing a hymn suitable to the case. The whole number brought to the ground, under convictions, were about 1,000, not less. The sensible, the weak, etc., learned and unlearned, the rich and poor, are subjects of it.[3]

Camp meetings played a particularly important part in the western revival and they were soon being held in every section of the West. Bishop Asbury states in his *Journal* for 1811 that there were four hundred camp meetings held that year. The camp meetings at night were particularly impressive, for everything in the immediate surroundings combined to furnish those elements which would greatly affect the imagination.

The glare of the blazing camp-fires falling on a dense assemblage . . . and reflected back from long ranges of tents upon every side; hundreds of candles and lamps suspended among the trees, together with numerous torches flashing to and fro, throwing an uncertain light upon the tremulous foliage, and giving an appearance of dim and indefinite extent to the depth of the forest; the solemn chanting of hymns swelling and falling on the night wind; the impassioned exhortations; the earnest prayers; the sobs, shrieks, or shouts, bursting from persons under intense agitation of mind; the sudden spasms which seize upon scores, and unexpectedly dashed them to the ground; all conspired to invest the scene with terrific interest, and to work up the feelings to the highest pitch of excitement.

Meetings of this sort were held in many places as the revival spread. Through Kentucky and Tennessee the movement continued powerful, while from North Carolina and Georgia came reports of the progress of the revival. In 1803 a revival began among the Presbyterians on the upper Ohio and spread through all the churches of the Ohio Presbytery. Ministers from Kentucky crossed the river and carried the revival to the Ohio settlements, and by 1803 it had reached as far north as the Western Reserve.

[3] From a letter of the Rev. John Evans Finley, a Presbyterian minister in Kentucky, dated September 20, 1801, published in the *New York Missionary Magazine* (1802). See also John Lyle's account in C. C. Cleveland, *The Great Revival in the West, 1797-1805* (Chicago, 1916), Appendix V, pp. 183-189.

There were some among the Presbyterians especially who opposed the revival from the start. Stone tells of an attempt of some of the opponents to put a stop to a camp meeting in Paris, Kentucky, where for the first time a minister arose and opposed the work. This preacher proposed that the people go to a nearby town to worship in the church. Some of them responded to this suggestion and repaired to the church where the opposing minister, we are told, addressed the people in "iceberg style" and labored hard to "Calvinize" them. The meeting, however, was turned into a particularly warm revival by Stone, who began to pray at the close of the sermon. On this turn of affairs some of the opposing preachers jumped out of a window back of the pulpit and left the meeting to the revivalists.

The revival produced several peculiar bodily exercises, such as falling, jerking, rolling, running, dancing and barking. Perhaps the most common was the falling exercise which befell all classes "the saints and sinners of every age and of every grade." The subject would generally "with piercing scream, fall like a log on the floor or ground" and appear as dead, sometimes lying thus for hours at a time. All the eyewitnesses testify to the commonness of this occurrence. The jerking exercise affected different persons in different ways. Frequently one of the limbs only would be affected, sometimes the whole body, and often the head alone. It often happened that "sinners" were taken, cursing and swearing as they jerked. "Sometimes the head would be twisted right and left, to a half round, with such velocity, that not a feature could be discovered." Cartwright tells us the more the exercise was resisted "the more they jerked," and the only way to stop it was to pray earnestly.

To see [he further says], proud young gentlemen and young ladies, dressed in their silks, jewelry, and prunella, from top to toe, take the jerks would often excite my risibilities. The first jerk or so, you would see their fine bonnets, caps and combs fly; and so sudden would be the jerking of the head that their long loose hair would crack almost as loud as a wagoner's whip.

The other exercises were little more than variations of these already described.

The influence of the revival upon western society was both good and evil, with good predominating. The immediate effect upon western morals was undoubtedly good. "Father" Rice, whose attitude toward the revival was particularly sane, stated in a sermon before the Synod of Kentucky in 1803:

A considerable number of persons appear to me to be greatly reformed in their morals. This is the case within the sphere of my particular acquaintance. Yea, some neighborhoods, noted for their vicious and profligate manners are now as much noted for their piety and good order. Drunkards, profane swearers, liars, quarrelsome persons, etc., are remarkably reformed.

Another witness writing to an eastern correspondent thus describes the general effect of the revival:

On my way I was informed by settlers on the road that the character of Kentucky travelers was entirely changed, and that they were as remarkable for sobriety as they had formerly been for dissoluteness and immorality. And indeed I found Kentucky to appearances the most moral place I had ever been. A profane expression was hardly ever heard. A religious awe seemed to pervade the country. Upon the whole, I think the revival in Kentucky the most extraordinary that has ever visited the church of Christ; and all things considered, it was peculiarly adapted to the circumstances of the country into which it came.

In 1802 another witness wrote that the "revival has confounded infidelity, awed vice into silence, and brought numbers beyond calculation under serious impression." On the other hand, a more recent student concludes that there is reason to think

That the habits of impulsive social action, developed and fostered in the early years of the century by the Kentucky revivals, and imitated at intervals ever since, have played their unworthy part in rendering that section of our country peculiarly susceptible to highly emotional outbreaks of prejudice, passion and even criminality.

The effect upon denominational growth was particularly marked. Though the revival was largely Presbyterian in its beginnings, the Methodists and Baptists reaped the largest results in church membership. In two years during the time when the revival was at its height the Western Conference of the Methodists alone added more than 6,000 members. The Baptists also greatly increased their numbers. Between 1800 and 1803 more than 10,000 were added to the Baptist churches in Kentucky alone, and there were like increases pretty generally throughout all the western Baptist associations. The Presbyterians also added large numbers to their churches, but as a whole the revival was to prove detrimental to Presbyterian interests in the West, because of the serious schisms which occurred as a result of the extravagances, disorders and heresy disputes which soon arose.

III

Two serious schisms occurred in the Presbyterian Church in the early years of the nineteenth century, the first centering in the Cumberland region, resulting in the formation of the Cumberland Presbyterian Church, the second centering in north central Kentucky, which came to be known as the New Light schism. These were the two great centers of the Kentucky revival and produced the two outstanding revival leaders, James McGready and Barton W. Stone. In both sections serious opposition arose to the revival and to the "fervor, noise and disorder" which accompanied it. In the Cumberland country the ministers were evenly divided, five favorable and five against; in northern Kentucky six ministers were strongly revivalistic while the remainder opposed the "noise and false exercises," among whom was "Father" Rice, and thus there came to be two distinct parties among western Presbyterians.

The Cumberland schism was precipitated when the Cumberland Presbytery, which had been formed in 1802, began to license and then ordain certain men who lacked the required educational qualification for the Presbyterian ministry. This had been done to meet the increased demand for preaching which the revival had created. As early as 1801 the Transylvania Presbytery had given permission to four laymen to exhort and catechize in vacant congregations. When the Cumberland Presbytery was formed additional catechists were licensed, until there came to be seventeen, characterized by the strict Presbyterian party as "illiterate exhorters with Arminian sentiments." These exhorters traveled through the vacant congregations, which they called "circuits," in imitation of the Methodists, while the presbytery directed the churches to contribute toward their support. Meanwhile strong opposition to these innovations was developing among the opponents of the revival, and at the meeting of the Kentucky Synod in 1805, after a committee had found the records of the Transylvania Presbytery "defective, discordant and obscure; and abounding in evidences of the flagrant violation of the Rules of Discipline," the synod proceeded to appoint a special commission with full synodical power to visit the Transylvania Presbytery and to make an examination into its affairs.

This precipitated a crisis which soon brought about a schism. The commission summoned the members of the presbytery before it, but some of them refused to appear on the ground of its unconstitutionality. The commission also made accusations of heresy against three of the ministers, stating that they held doctrines contrary to those contained in the Confession of Faith, while others were cited to the next meeting of the synod. Twelve ministers were summoned to stand an examination as to their qualifications for the ministry, to which they refused to comply, while certain churches, presided over by untrained ministers, were declared vacant and the Cumberland Presbytery was dissolved.

When the commission had finished its work the revivalist members immediately formed themselves into a council, which at once made an appeal to the Transylvania Presbytery to act as a mediator. This was without avail. Next an appeal was made to the General Assembly of 1809 praying for redress, but this too was defeated. Nothing seemed to be left to the revivalists but to form themselves into an independent presbytery, and this was done, largely through the efforts of Finis Ewing and Samuel King in February, 1810, and there was created the Cumberland Presbyterian Church. By 1829 the church had grown to considerable proportions, there being at that time eighteen presbyteries, and in that year a General Assembly was formed. The rapid growth of the new church was due to the fact that it adopted the camp meeting as well as the circuit system, while its warm evangelical preaching of a radically modified Calvinism made a large appeal to the frontier people of the section where it ministered.

Equally unfortunate was the New Light schism which began at about the same time in north central Kentucky. Barton W. Stone, the outstanding leader of the revival in that region, had from the beginning of his ministry been troubled over the doctrines of election and predestination, doctrines which stand at the very center of strict Calvinism. At his ordination he had told some of the ministers of his doubts and had said to them that he was only willing to accept the Confession of Faith as far as he felt it consistent with the Word of God. Four other Presbyterian ministers who were intimately associated with him in the revival were all likewise troubled concerning the Calvinistic doctrines. These men were Richard McNemar, John Thompson, John Dunlavy and John Marshall. In their preaching they laid chief emphasis upon God's love for the "whole world" and upon the ability of all sinners to accept the means of salvation—doctrines flatly antagonistic to the Calvinistic system—which soon brought down upon them the censures of their orthodox brethren. At the meeting of the Synod of Kentucky in 1803 charges were brought against McNemar and Thompson for preaching erroneous doctrines and from the first it was apparent that the decision would go against them. Before matters could go farther the five preachers under suspicion held a conference and decided to withdraw from the jurisdiction of the synod, though not from the Presbyterian Church. After attempts to reclaim them on the part of a committee of the synod had failed, the synod suspended the five ministers and declared their pulpits vacant.

The five suspended ministers, together with several others who joined them, now proceeded to organize a new presbytery which they called the Springfield Presbytery, and for the course of a year carried on their **work under this name. By the end of a** year it became apparent to them that they were forming a new denomination, a thing that was furthest from their desire. Already they had published an *Apology* in which they maintained that all creeds and confessions ought to be rejected and that the Bible alone should be the bond of Christian fellowship. They now decided to dissolve the Springfield Presbytery, which was announced in what was termed, in a semihumorous vein "The Last Will and Testament of the Springfield Presbytery." This was accompanied by an address in which they explained the reasons for this action. Their chief motive, they stated, was their desire to promote the unity of Christian people, which they felt could not be done under the present organization of the churches. They adopted the name "The Christian Church," a name without sectarian bias, while they rejected all forms of organization, such as presbyteries, synods, conferences, sessions, etc., which did not have a Scriptural basis. The movement thus inaugurated spread rapidly through Kentucky and extended northward into Ohio, while Stone spent his time traveling extensively, preaching and organizing churches. The movement was retarded, however, by the defection of McNemar and Dunlavy to the Shakers, and by the return of Thompson and Marshall to the Presbyterians.

Shakerism was introduced into the West in the midst of the Great Revival, by three missionaries who had been sent out from their communities in the East. This peculiar communistic sect had originated in England in the middle of the eighteenth century and was brought to America in 1774 when Ann Lee, or "Mother Ann" as she was called with a small group of followers migrated to New York, where several small communities were formed. The Shakers repudiated marriage as the root of all evil and claimed that theirs was the only true church having all the apostolic gifts. In their worship they adopted a peculiar form of dancing and handclapping, in which they expressed their joy in the Lord and from which they received their name of Shakers. The three missionaries who now visited Kentucky were soon successful in winning a number of converts, both ministers and people, and eventually two Shaker communities were established in Ohio, two in Kentucky and one in Indiana. The orthodox churches in the West were soon united in their opposition to Shakerism. Cartwright tells us that the "Shaker priests" were successful in sweeping scores of "members of different churches away from their steadfastness into the muddy pools of Shakerism."

For some time the question of the mode of baptism disturbed the leaders of the New Light movement, but eventually immersion was accepted as the Scriptural form. The acceptance of immersion gave Stone and his helpers access to the Baptists and in numerous instances Baptist churches came over entirely into the Stonite movement, rejecting their confessions and associations and, as Stone expressed it, becoming "one with us in the great work of Christian union."

Hardly had the New Light movement gotten under way in Kentucky and southern Ohio before a similar movement had begun in western Pennsylvania and Virginia, under the leadership of Thomas Campbell and his more brilliant son Alexander. The Campbells were Scotch-Irish Anti-Burgher Presbyterians, the most conservative of all the Presbyterian bodies. The father was a minister of an Anti-Burgher church in County Armagh, Ireland, dividing his time between his church and a school which he conducted. Though belonging to this very conservative body the Campbells were in contact with more liberal groups arising in both Scotland and Ireland, such as the "Old Scotch Independents," the "Tabernacle Churches" which arose through the evangelistic activity of Rowland Hill and the Haldanes.

In 1807, on the advice of his physician, the elder Campbell came to America to seek his health, leaving his family behind, and his school in charge of his son Alexander. Landing in Philadelphia he found the Anti-Burgher Synod in session in that city, and on presenting his credentials was admitted and sent to the Presbytery of Chartiers in southwestern Pennsylvania. The Associate Synod, or the Anti-Burgher Synod in America, was even more conservative than was the parent body in Scotland and had, in 1796, passed an act prohibiting "occasional communion," or communion with other bodies of Christians. To this narrow ruling Thomas Campbell could not subscribe, and it was his custom to invite all Presbyterian parties who were without pastoral care to join his members in partaking of the sacrament. This gave offense to some of his brethren in the ministry and proceedings were soon begun against him in the presbytery The condemnation voted by the presbytery caused him to appeal to the synod, and in his letter to that body he set forth certain opinions which indicate his trend away from narrow creeds and theological formulas, and make the Scripture a basis of Christian unity. Though the synod set aside the judgment of the presbytery, yet an atmosphere of hostility and criticism remained, and rather than try to work under such strained relations he decided to sever his connection with the Seceder body and become a *free lance* in the western religious world.

Thomas Campbell now began to hold meetings wherever opportunity offered, in barns, groves and houses, and soon a considerable number of persons had placed themselves under his spiritual care. After a time these friends met and agreed upon a basis of coöperation calling themselves "The Christian Association of Washington." It was at this time that Campbell, in an address, stated a principle which was to become a "watchword" among his followers: "Where the Scriptures speak, we speak; where they are silent, we are silent," and in August, 1809, the association adopted a "Declaration and Address," prepared by Campbell, setting forth the purposes of the association. This has been termed the most important document in the entire history of the Disciples body although, like Stone, Campbell had no desire to form a new sect but hoped that all Christian people might unite upon the broad platform of the Scriptures.

Just as the "Declaration and Address" was issuing from the press the son, Alexander Campbell, arrived in America and he at once heartily accepted the principles laid down in the address. The next turn in events (1810) was the application of the elder Campbell to the (Regular) Presbyterian Synod of Pittsburgh to be taken into that body, together with the association. When this was refused the Christian Association organized themselves into the Brush Run Church (May 4, 1811) in which Thomas Campbell was appointed elder and Alexander was licensed to preach, while four deacons were chosen. Soon after the church was formed the question of baptism arose for discussion, and finally it was decided that upon the principles which they had adopted there was no place for infant baptism, and accordingly immersion was accepted as the only form of baptism allowed in the Scriptures. When the Redstone Baptist Association learned that the Brush Run Church had adopted the practice of immersion they were elated, and urged that it join their association. After full discussion among themselves, and after it was pointed out to the Baptists that their views were not entirely in harmony regarding the Lord's Supper or even regarding baptism, the Brush Run Church finally (1813) decided to unite with the Baptist body.

From 1813 to 1830 the Campbells and their followers were nominally Baptists. And from this time forward Thomas Campbell began to retire into the background, while his brilliant son became more and more the active leader of the movement. Up to about 1820 Alexander Campbell was chiefly occupied in establishing and conducting a seminary at Bethany, in western Virginia, but from 1820 to 1830 he became increasingly active in propagating his peculiar views, especially among the Baptists. Soon a party had formed, made up of his followers, called the "Reformers," advocating the "restoration of the ancient order of things." In 1823 he established a paper, *The Christian Baptists,* to promote his teachings, while he began to travel more and more extensively throughout western Pennsylvania and Virginia, Ohio and Kentucky, preaching and debating wherever he had opportunity. Campbell was an especially able debater, and both in his debates and in the pages of his paper attacked all human innovations which had crept into the churches, such as Sunday schools, missionary societies, synods, conferences, bishops, reverends, etc. Soon groups of Reformers were to be found in almost every Baptist congregation in the West, and by 1826 the Reformers began to separate from the Baptist churches to form congregations of their own. It has been estimated that in Kentucky alone more than ten thousand Baptist members withdrew to form Disciple congregations. Thus the movement which had begun as a protest against the numerous sects of Christians, instead of uniting them, had only succeeded in adding one more to the number.

By the year 1827 the followers of Stone began to come in frequent contact with the followers of Campbell and as they came to know more and more about one another, it became increasingly apparent that they had much in common. The churches of both groups were organized on a strictly congregational basis, and the only way to promote union between the two bodies was for individual congregations to unite. In 1832 two men, one representing the "Disciples" the other the "Christians," were sent out among the churches to bring about union in Kentucky, while similar coalitions took place between the two groups in the other states where they were numerous. There was an element among the Christians who did not welcome the union, however, and after uniting with the "Republican Methodists" formed what became known as the "Christian Connection Church," which in 1929 voted to unite with the Congregational churches. Since the union of the Christians and the Disciples the two names have been used interchangeably for the reason that there is no central body with authority to adopt an official name for the denomination.

While the Presbyterians and Baptists were suffering serious losses because of controversy and schism, the Methodists likewise were facing disruption. There is abundant evidence to show that although Francis Asbury was thoroughly devoted to the cause of advancing Christianity, he was also extremely arbitrary in his administration of the church. He demanded absolute obedience and was seldom willing to take advice from others. He has been characterized as "a born conservative and a born autocrat," and it is not at all strange that such arbitrary procedure should provoke rebellion. The O'Kelly schism of 1792 has already been mentioned, but in 1830 a far more serious split resulted after ten years of agitation to secure the election of presiding elders and the admission of laymen into the conferences. This movement had its largest following in Maryland, while Baltimore was the center of agitation. Those favoring these changes called themselves "Reformers" while their opponents termed them "radicals," and when the General Conference of 1828 refused to pass favorably upon their petition they began to withdraw in considerable numbers and in 1830 formed themselves into the Methodist Protestant Church. It may seem strange that this movement in the direction of greater democracy did not gain headway on the frontier but was confined so largely to the East. Perhaps the chief reason the new West did not rebel against the Methodist arbitrary system is that the personal popularity of such men as McKendree, who became a bishop in 1808, and the fact that in their lives the leaders of frontier Methodism showed themselves as simple and democratic as the people among whom they worked.

IV

The other religious bodies which arose in the early years of the nineteenth century were the "United Brethren in Christ" and the "Evangelical Association." Both were German revivalistic bodies and came out of much the same general background. Though contributing the principal Pietistic strain in colonial America, the Germans had little part in, and reaped only indirect benefits from, the colonial revivals. The principal reason for this was the language barrier, which limited the influence of such intercolonial revivalists as Whitefield and Gilbert Tennent to the English-speaking part of the population. This explains why revivalistic movements among the American Germans were delayed for a generation and did not begin until the emergence of German-speaking revivalists.

The founder of the United Brethren was Philip William Otterbein, who came out to America in 1752 as a missionary to the German Reformed people in Pennsylvania. He, like most of the other German missionaries, was Pietistic in his emphasis, and preached the necessity of an inner spiritual experience, and so strongly did he bear down upon this emphasis that he offended some of his people as well as his colleagues. At about the same time he came in contact with a Mennonite preacher, Martin Boehm, who was preaching in the same general region and emphasizing the same doctrines. Otterbein, in 1774, accepted a call to an independent Reformed church in Baltimore, and with Baltimore as the center continued his evangelistic tours among the German-speaking people of the surrounding states at the same time keeping in touch with Boehm. Meanwhile Otterbein had come into close personal touch with Francis Asbury, and when in 1784 Asbury was ordained in Baltimore as General Superintendent of the Methodist Episcopal Church, he requested that Otterbein assist in the ordination. Gradually there came to be a number of preachers associated with Otterbein and Boehm who were evangelistic in their emphasis, and they began to meet in informal conferences in 1789. It is quite probable that if the Methodists had made any adequate provision for work among the German-speaking people Otterbein and those coöperating with him might have united with the Methodists, but unfortunately this was not the case. In 1800 Otterbein, Boehm and eleven others felt it necessary to form a new church, which they called the "United Brethren in

Christ." The name was derived from the greeting "We are brethren" which Otterbein extended to Boehm after hearing him preach for the first time. The new church was organized along Methodistic lines and, like the Methodists, was Arminian in doctrine. In the first decade of the nineteenth century the United Brethren had crossed the Alleghany Mountains and soon established their work in Ohio, Indiana and Illinois.

The founder of the Evangelical Association was Jacob Albright, a Pennsylvania German of Lutheran background, who, after his conversion under Methodist influence, felt the call to preach to the religiously destitute German people in the German counties of Pennsylvania. Although licensed as an Exhorter by the Methodists, in 1800 Albright began to organize classes independently of the Methodists, and in 1803 five or six little groups had been formed who looked to him as their spiritual father. The same year an informal conference of his followers was held, at which Albright was ordained by two of his assistants, and they declared themselves an independent ecclesiastical body. This marked the beginning of the Evangelical Association, which later took the name the Evangelical Church. Both the United Brethren and the Evangelicals expanded westward, and although both bodies had their original centers in Pennsylvania, a majority of their members are now found west of the Alleghanies. They are now happily united into the Evangelical United Brethren Church with a membership of well over seven hundred thousand.

V

A schism which belongs to this period, but which has no relationship with the frontier, was that which resulted from the Trinitarian and Anti-Trinitarian controversy in New England. The beginnings of this controversy which have already been noted, occurred in the years immediately following the Great Colonial Awakening. King's Chapel, the oldest Episcopal church in New England, was the first to become openly Unitarian. This church had lost its rector and many of its members in the migration of leading Tory families to Nova Scotia, following the British evacuation of Boston in 1776. James Freeman, a young graduate of Harvard College, acted as lay reader in the absence of a minister, was finally chosen pastor and accepted lay ordination. For some time Freeman had been troubled about the doctrine of the

Trinity and had conducted discussions among his members on the subject of Christian doctrine. These discussions led finally to action on the part of the congregation to strike out of the order of service all references to the Trinity. This action was taken in 1785, and thus King's Chapel became the first American Unitarian church.

Of greater importance to the progress of Unitarianism in New England was the election in 1805 of an avowed Unitarian, Henry Ware, to the Hollis Professorship of Theology at Harvard. For a number of years Congregational ministers in and about Boston had been gradually accepting Anti-Trinitarian views, but there had been no open break. The election of Ware, however, aroused resentment among the orthodox and three years later Andover Theological Seminary was established as a protest at the defection of Harvard. The orthodoxy of Andover was protected by a provision that each professor was to sign periodically a statement of the seminary creed. The very year Ware was elected to his professorship *The Panoplist,* under the editorship of a young lawyer, Jeremiah Evarts, began publication in the defense of orthodoxy. A clean-cut alignment now began to appear between the two parties. Of the sixteen pre-Revolutionary Congregational churches in Boston, fourteen were tending toward Unitarianism, while the movement was spreading to the smaller towns in the vicinity. It was not, however, until 1815 and after, that the actual separation took place. Two influences contributed directly to the separation. One was the review of Belsham's *American Unitarianism* in the *Panoplist,* a pamphlet which had formerly circulated only among Unitarians. It was an English publication and described the progress of the liberal movement in Massachusetts, frankly discussing the actual situation and giving names and churches. The other event was a sermon preached by William Ellery Channing at the installation of Jared Sparks (1819) as the minister of a Unitarian church in Baltimore. The sermon was an arraignment of the orthodoxy of the time, which aroused the resentment of the great body of orthodox ministers and made Channing the recognized leader of the American Unitarians; and from this time forward the liberal churches began to assume their true position.

After separation had finally taken place it was found that the largest percentage of the people of wealth and position in and about Boston had gone into the Unitarian churches. Although calling themselves liberals in theology, this class was at the same time the most conservative element in New England society in every other respect, especially in their economic and political ideas. In 1820 the State Supreme Court of Massachusetts established in the Dedham case a ruling which gave to the Unitarians a large share of the property in dispute. It provided "that an orthodox majority of church members might be overruled in questions affecting church property by the 'society' or parish, in which the actual communicants might be and frequently were in the minority." This decision was a blow to the orthodox party, but it served to arouse them thoroughly to action, and within a few years a whole series of new orthodox churches was formed. To these new pulpits were called an especially able group of preachers, who, while accepting the substance of the old theology, were yet able to restate it in such a way as to give it a popular appeal. Of these new pulpits none was more influential than that of Hanover Street Church where Lyman Beecher, the most able of the orthodox ministers, was the pastor.[4]

---

[4] For a recent account of the Unitarian and Universalist movements see W. W. Sweet, *Religion in the Growth of American Culture, 1765-1840* Chap. V, "The Revolt Against Calvinism." (Volume in preparation.)

CHAPTER XVI

THE ERA OF ORGANIZATION AND THE RISE OF MODERN MISSIONS

THE first years under the Federal Constitution are frequently characterized as the period of nationality. This period marked the temporary decline of state powers and sectional interests, for in these early years of the nation's life the people had caught the vision of national need and were uniting in common national tasks. The great Chief Justice John Marshall was rendering his nationalistic decisions, and the principle of nationality was generally dominant. The churches likewise were imbued with the thought of national need and were uniting to carry on the great common Christian tasks. "Both church and nation felt themselves called at the same period to grapple with the same problem," that of securing harmonious coöperation among the states and among the churches. Coupled with the dominant idea of national need were the new religious energy and zeal which had been engendered by the Great Revival which had swept over the country in the closing years of the eighteenth and the opening years of the nineteenth century. While the revival resulted in several unfortunate schisms, yet in the early years of the century, especially, there had been a large growth of interdenominational good will, which soon manifested itself in concrete form by the formation of numerous interdenominational societies.

I

Naturally the revival greatly increased the desire of Christian people to spread the gospel among all classes, and especially among the many new settlements forming in the West, and among the American Indians. The early missionary societies which had been formed in England and

Scotland, such as the S.P.G. and the S.P.C.K., were organized to work primarily among the colonists of the far-flung British Empire. Beginning with the latter eighteenth century, however, emphasis began to be laid upon work for the so-called heathen, and in 1792 the English Baptists organized a society and sent William Carey to India. Three years later the London Missionary Society was formed by Presbyterians, Congregationalists and some adherents of the Church of England, while similar societies were springing up in the Netherlands and Scotland. A like movement began at about the same time in America influenced by their English brethren, and numerous missionary societies were formed in the New England and middle states, and among Congregationalists, Presbyterians, Baptists, Dutch Reformed and finally Methodists.

At first these societies were local in their scope and were primarily concerned with the conversion of the heathen in America—the Indians —and were generally interdenominational. Thus the New York Missionary Society, formed in 1796, was made up of representatives of Presbyterians, Dutch Reformed and Baptists and its immediate object was to carry the gospel to the southern Indians. In 1803 this organization received about $5,000 for its work and soon there were several auxiliary societies formed in other sections of the state and work among the New York Indians was enlarged. In New England there were numerous Congregational societies, the earliest being the Missionary Society of Connecticut, organized by the General Association in 1798. The purpose of this society was "to Christianize the heathen in North America, and to support and promote Christian knowledge in the new settlements within the United States." In 1800 it sent its first missionary, David Bacon, "afoot and alone, with no more luggage than he could carry on his person," to the region south and west of Lake Erie, where he was instructed to visit the wild tribes of that region, "learn their feelings with respect to Christianity, and, so far as he had opportunity, to teach them its doctrines and duties." The Connecticut society was the strongest of the early societies and was supported by numerous auxiliaries, and by 1807 it had a permanent fund of $15,000. Within the next few years at least eight such societies had been formed in the New England states, all of them with numerous smaller local societies as auxiliaries. Thus the Massachusetts Missionary Society was supported by the "Boston Female for promoting the Diffusion of Christian Knowledge"; "the Cent Institution" supported by Boston women, who promised to pay a cent a week for the purchase of Bibles, Psalms and hymnbooks, primers, catechisms, etc. Similar organizations were to be found in Rhode Island where Samuel Hopkins was the prime mover; in New Hampshire; in Maine and in Vermont.

Of great importance in the spreading of missionary propaganda was the missionary periodical which now began publication. *The Connecticut Evangelical Magazine* was the official organ of the Connecticut Missionary Society beginning in 1800, and for fourteen years, as the magazine quaintly states, communicated "instruction upon the great truths and doctrines of religion" in order "to comfort and edify the people of God and to interest the pious mind by exhibiting displays of the grace and mercy of God." Such were the objects of its work, "rather than to amuse the specialist and entertain the curious." *The Massachusetts Missionary Magazine* began to appear in 1803 and from the begining produced a profit for the Massachusetts Missionary Society. In 1805 *The Panoplist* was launched as a private enterprise for the purpose of combating Unitarianism, which in that year had gained its first great victory in the election of its candidate to the Hollis Professorship of Divinity in Harvard College. Three years later it was combined with the *Massachusetts Missionary Magazine* and has continued since 1820 as the *Missionary Herald*. The New Hampshire Society published *The Religious Repository* though it proved short-lived, while the Vermont Society supported as its official organ the *Vermont Evangelical Magazine* which continued its operation until 1815. By the latter date all the Congregational magazines had disappeared except the *Panoplist and Missionary Magazine*.

Organized missionary effort among American Presbyterians began with the incorporation of the General Assembly in 1799 with the power of holding property for pious and charitable purposes, and three years later a standing committee on missions was appointed to supervise the work of missionaries. Previous to this, missions had been supported by individual churches, presbyteries and synods. Several of the synods and presbyteries also organized as missionary societies, as did the Synod of Pittsburgh in 1802 when it formed the Western Missionary Society "to carry the gospel to the Indians and interim inhabitants." Early Presbyterian mission activities had four objectives: frontier communities, settled regions without churches, Indians and Negroes. From 1805 to

1809 *The General Assembly's Missionary Magazine or Evangelical Intelligencer* was published as their missionary organ. The Dutch churches also began to manifest interest in missions about the same time, and in 1800 were supporting six missionaries in Upper Canada.

The Baptists, before the formation of formal missionary societies, were missionary in purpose, and missionaries had been sent out by individual churches and associations as early as 1778, when the Warren Association of the New England Churches sent workers to the northern section of the country. With the opening of the new century (1802) the Massachusetts Baptist Missionary Society was launched, which was soon publishing a magazine. Within a few years Baptist societies were to be found in Maine, Pennsylvania, New York, all with their supporting organizations of the usual type. At about the same time the Friends also manifested a new interest in Indian missions which were carried on under the supervision of committees appointed by the Yearly Meetings.

The Methodists were several years behind the other churches in their formal missionary organization, the reason being that Methodism had from the beginning been missionary in character. During the latter years of Asbury's life he had collected money wherever he could, to supply the wants of the frontier preachers and their families. The sums collected were also used to extend the work of the church among the poor and the destitute. The early American Methodists, however, had done little for the Indians, and it was largely the aroused interest in Indian work which led to the formation of the Methodist Missionary Society in 1819. This interest was first awakened through the work of John Stewart, a freeborn mulatto who after his conversion at a camp meeting in Ohio felt the call to preach to the Indians. Stewart began his work among the Wyandots at Upper Sandusky, Ohio, in 1816, was licensed as a local preacher of the Methodist Church two years later, and the next year his work was taken over by the Ohio Conference and regular missionaries appointed. Meanwhile steps were being taken in New York to form a Methodist Missionary Society, the reasons for which were thus summarized by Nathan Bangs, one of the organizing committee and the first historian of Methodist missions: First, other denominations had organized missionary societies and so zealous were they that many Methodist people were contributing to them; second, it was evident that although the Methodist system is missionary in character yet there were many places, such as new and destitute settlements, which were incapable of supporting the gospel; third, work among the Indians was opening up; fourth, it might become the duty of Methodists to help "others in extending the Redeemer's kingdom in foreign nations"; and finally it was evident that such an organization could probably raise much more money and consequently do more good than under the present arrangement.

II

While the early American interest in missions was confined principally to work among the new settlements and the Indians, yet there was to be found at the same time a growing interest in the great "heathen world" outside America. New geographical and anthropogical knowledge was arousing the interest of an increasing number of American readers, while the work of early English missionaries was eagerly followed by the readers of the numerous American missionary magazines. Missionaries sent out by the London Missionary Society frequently made the voyage to the East by way of America. Such was the case of Robert Morrison, who sailed for China in 1807 by way of the United States. Here he met Presbyterian, Reformed and Baptist missionary leaders, who not only gave him assistance while here, but after he reached China continued to assist his mission. American interest in foreign missions, however, was brought to a head by the dramatic appeal of a group of students in Andover Theological Seminary in 1810.

The leader of this group was Samuel J. Mills, who had become interested in foreign missions through the efforts of Samuel Hopkins, the minister of the First Congregational Church at Newport, Rhode Island, to send two young Negroes as missionaries to Africa. Mills came to Williams College aflame with zeal to take the gospel to the non-Christian lands, and through his influence a group of students banded themselves together into a secret society, each pledging to devote his life to missionary service. On graduation from Williams College most of the group entered Andover Theological Seminary where three others joined them, Adoniram Judson, Samuell Newell and Samuel Nott, Jr. The burning desire of this group to engage in missionary work led them to petition the Congregational General Association of Massachusetts (1810) to inaugurate a foreign mission and offered themselves to go as missionaries. The time, evidently, was ripe for such an appeal, for immediately steps were taken by the association to carry out their desire, and the

American Board of Commissioners for Foreign Missions was formed (June, 1810). Immediately liberal donations began to flow to the board, four wealthy supporters gave $7,000; $4,000 came from auxiliary societies, while in 1811 a legacy of $30,000 came to them. Thus means were seemingly providentially provided for the sending out of the young missionaries, and in February, 1812, in Salem, Massachusetts, five young men were ordained and soon set sail for India.

Even more dramatic was the beginning of foreign mission organization among the Baptists. On the long voyage to India, two of the missionaries sent out by the American Board, Judson and Rice, though sailing on different vessels, were converted to Baptist principles through diligent study of the Scriptures, and on landing they and their wives were immersed, in the Baptist Church at Calcutta. The announcement of these dramatic conversions to Baptist views, and the fact that the converts offered themselves as ready to serve as Baptist missionaries seemed a providential happening to many leading Baptists in America. Rice returned to the United States to urge the appeal on their immediate attention, while Judson remained in Burma to establish the first Baptist mission. Luther Rice now entered upon his task of awakening American Baptists to their missionary responsibility and to his appeal there was an immediate response. His first work was an extended tour through the United States, establishing missionary societies in all the important Baptist centers. In May, 1814, there gathered in Philadelphia thirty-three delegates representing eleven states, and out of this gathering came the "General Missionary Convention of the Baptist Denomination of the United States of America for Foreign Missions." This event was notable, not alone because it was the first Baptist foreign missionary society, but because it was the first general organization of the Baptists in the United States.

Rice now became the field marshal of Baptist missions, and from this time until the end of his life in 1836 he traveled throughout the country furthering that cause together with education. At the meeting of the General Baptist Society in 1817 plans were laid for the beginning of home missions in the West, under the conviction that "western as well as eastern regions are given to the Son of God for an inheritance," and in that year John M. Peck and James E. Welch were sent to the Missouri territory. Though the General Society soon discontinued its support, Peck remained in the West and devoted the remainder of his life to missions and to education. After 1820 the Massachusetts Baptist Missionary Society gave him some support, though much of his work was carried on through local societies which he established. No other man in the early history of Illinois exercised a larger influence than did Peck, and it is stated that he did more than any other single individual to induce settlers to come to Illinois, through his publications, *Guide for Emigrants* (1831) and *Gazetteer of Illinois* (1834).

III

Baptist work among the Indians began the year Peck came to Missouri when Isaac McCoy was appointed a missionary to the Indians of Indiana and Illinois. In 1820 McCoy opened a mission at Fort Wayne where he conducted a school, for English and French Indians and negroes. Two years later he established a mission in southern Michigan to which he gave the name Carey, and here he and his wife labored for four years amidst privations and sickness, though with great success. In 1823 a United States exploring expedition under the command of Major S. H. Long, visited the mission and Long has left us a glowing account of Mc-Coy's work in his journal. Though the mission had been established but seven months at the time of Long's visit, yet he found "a large and comfortable dwelling house,—a schoolhouse, a blacksmith's shop, and other out houses—a large garden, pasture ground enclosed with a good fence, together with a large field of plowed ground planted with corn." The school contained about forty pupils, half of them the children of Indian parents, the others mixed breed. The girls were taught, besides the usual subjects, needlework, knitting and spinning, while the boys, besides the general branches of education, were taught the art of agriculture. The government appropriated $1,000 a year for the support of the mission, which was to be expended to provide a teacher and a blacksmith, while additional support came from the Baptist Missionary Society of Washington City.

From the year 1820 onward mission work among the Indians received great impetus through the announced policy of the Federal government of distributing annually a subsidy of several thousands of dollars among the missionary societies already engaged or prepared to engage in missionary work. This led to a rapid expansion of Indian mission activity among all the churches, and real progress was made toward civilization especially among the southern Indians. An excellent illustration of this growth is presented by the Indian work of the American Board of Commissioners for Foreign Missions. In 1817 their first missionary was sent to the Cherokee nation on the Tennessee, which by 1830 had grown to eight stations, the most important being Brainerd. At the latter station in 1822 the mission property was valued at $17,300 and consisted of four large buildings, including a mission house, two schoolhouses, a saw and grist mill and ten out buildings, while the mission farm was stocked with five yoke of oxen, thirty cows, one hundred young cattle, three hundred swine, twelve sheep and three horses with four colts, besides blacksmith and farm tools. In 1830 the board was supporting the following Indian missions: to the Cherokees one on the Tennessee and another on the Arkansas, Chickasaw, Choctaw, Osage mission on the Neosho, Osage mission at Maumee; mission among the New York Indians; and a mission in the Northwest. Similar expansions took place among the Presbyterians, Friends, Baptists, Methodists, Roman Catholics. The Methodists, for instance, in 1830 were maintaining Indian missions in Ohio, Tennessee and Mississippi and reported that year an Indian membership of 4,501.

The American Board of Commissioners for Foreign Missions was Congregational in its origin, but in 1812 it became interdenominational by the election of Presbyterians to its board, and four years later Dutch Reformed representatives were added. During the first thirty years of its existence the board sent out 694 missionaries, and among the most notable of its early achievements was the Christianization of the Hawaiian Islands, which was begun in 1820, and five years later the Ten Commandments were made the basis for the laws of the islands. Early mission work among the frontier settlements, as has been noted, was carried on by numerous local societies, among the several denominations, while the Indian missions were conducted under the early foreign mission boards. The first home missionary organization on a national scale was the American Home Missionary Society, formed in 1826, which like the American Board for Foreign Missions was interdenominational in character.

IV

The American Home Missionary Society became the principal agent in carrying out the Plan of Union of 1801. At first the society was largely Presbyterian in membership, but later the numerous Congregational local societies became auxiliary, and a large proportion of the missionaries sent to the West were young men from Congregational colleges and seminaries. The society did an immense work in spreading Christian institutions throughout the West, while it supported weak churches in every section of the country. Nine years after its formation (1835) the society was employing 719 agents and missionaries; 481 of these were settled pastors or employed as "stated supplies" in single congregations; 185 were placed over 2 or 3 congregations, while 50 were employed in larger districts. Twenty years later (1855) the society was employing 1,032 missionaries working in different states and territories. The other American churches soon organized their own home missionary societies to carry on work in the West. The societies of the Protestant Episcopal (1828) and the Methodist (1819) Churches at first served the double purpose of foreign and home missions, while the Baptists organized their national Home Missionary Society in 1832.

An example of the spirit of sacrifice and devotion to the cause of missions is illustrated by the "Illinois Band," a group of eleven students at Yale Divinity School, who in 1828 banded together and pledged themselves to seek service in Illinois as teachers and ministers. All but one of the number went to Illinois immediately on graduation, sent by the American Home Missionary Society, where some became ministers and others established Illinois College. One of the band, Julian M. Sturtevant, became the first instructor in the college, while Theron Baldwin, another of the band, after helping to found the college, assisted in forming the "Society for the Promotion of Collegiate and Theological Education at the West," and as secretary of this organization came to be known as "the Father of Western Colleges." Some years later Asa Turner, one of the Illinois Band, after a period as minister in Quincy, moved across the Mississippi into the "Black Hawk Purchase" which become in 1838 a part of the territory of Iowa. After establishing a Congregational church at Denmark, he was joined by a Yale friend, Reuben Gaylord, who organized a number of churches, while in 1843 a band of eleven young men from Andover Theological Seminary came to the territory. They were all ordained in Turner's little church at Denmark and then scattered through the territory to plant churches and found schools. Out of their work came Iowa College, first established at Davenport, later moved to Grinnell, and now known as Grinnell College.

V

Interest in missions, both foreign and home, gave rise also to many kindred organizations. The increased demand for missionaries led to the establishment of schools where they could be adequately trained. To aid in this important work education societies began to be formed, and a national organization known as the American Education Society was organized in 1815. This society had for its purpose the aiding of "all pious young men, of suitable talents, who appear to be called to preach Christ, and who belong to any of the evangelical denominations." In 1818 the Protestant Episcopalians established their own Education Society as did later the Baptists, Methodists and others.

To this period also belong the establishment of the first theological seminaries, as well as the first colleges among Baptists and Methodists. From 1818 to 1840 at least twenty-five theological seminaries were established by Congregationalists, Presbyterians, Baptists, Dutch Reformed and Unitarians. The first to be founded was Andover in 1808, which came about as a result of the seating of an avowed Unitarian in the professorship of Divinity at Harvard in 1805. In 1810 the Dutch Reformed Church established their seminary at New Brunswick; two years later the Presbyterian seminary at Princeton was opened, to be followed in rapid succession by Bangor (Maine) in 1816; by an Episcopalian Seminary in New York, 1817; Auburn in 1821; Yale Divinity School in 1822; Union Seminary in Virginia (Presbyterian) in 1824; in 1825, the Baptist Seminary at Newton, Massachusetts, and the German Reformed Seminary at York, Pennsylvania; and in 1826 the Lutheran Seminary at Gettysburg. Other seminaries were founded in the thirties and forties including several Catholic seminaries for the training of priests, while the first Methodist seminary was that at Concord, New Hampshire, established in 1847, and later removed to Boston. It is significant that all of the early theological seminaries were to be found in the East.

Of greater importance from the standpoint of general education in the West was the founding of numerous colleges during these same years. The establishment of the small denominational college generally came about in the process of settlement. This is particularly well illustrated in the states of Ohio, Indiana, Illinois, and Missouri. Indeed, almost any section of the United States will furnish illustrations of this process. Harvard College, for instance, was established while Massachusetts was in process of settlement, while Yale, Dartmouth, Williams, and William and Mary were frontier colleges at the time of their founding. And the history of these older institutions furnished inspiration to the founders of the colleges in the Ohio and Mississippi valleys. These colleges were manned almost entirely by ministers. The presidents were always clergymen, as were also a large proportion of the faculties.

As has been noted, the earliest colleges west of the Alleghanies were those established by Congregationalists and Presbyterians, but by 1830 Baptists and Methodists were giving increasing attention to education. In 1832 a Baptist institution was opened at Granville, Ohio, which in 1847 assumed the dignity of college, later becoming Denison University. John M. Peck's school, first established at Rock Spring, Illinois, was moved to Upper Alton in 1832 and in 1835 became Shurtleff College. The Baptists were also busy forming State Conventions, and State education Societies, and the slogan "every state its own Baptist college" was soon coming true in the establishment of Baptist institutions in most of the older states as well as in the newer communities of the West. The oldest of these state institutions was Colby College, Maine, which opened under Baptist patronage in 1820. The first permanent institution of college grade founded by the American Methodists was Wesleyan University, at Middletown, Connecticut, which was chartered in 1831; the next year Randolph-Macon College in Virginia was founded, while Dickinson College became a Methodist institution in 1833, although it had been chartered as a Presbyterian college fifty years before. Allegheny College dates from 1834. The oldest Methodist college west of the Alleghanies is that at Lebanon, Illinois, which opened as Lebanon Seminary in 1828 and became McKendree College in 1834. Three years later (1837) the Indiana Conference founded at Greencastle, Indiana, Asbury University, which later became DePauw University.

VI

The religious destitution of the frontier, the lack of Bibles and religious literature in the cabins of the early settlers, prompted the establishment of organizations in the East to print and distribute Christian literature. When Samuel J. Mills made his first missionary tours of the United States in 1812-1813 and again in 1814-1815 in which he covered nearly ten thousand miles, he reported these conditions in pamphlets published in 1814 and 1815. At Kaskaskia, then the capital of Illinois Territory, he found but five Bibles in one hundred families, and there was an amazing lack even in the older sections of the country. It was such conditions as these which led to the founding of the American Bible Society in New York in 1816, although there had been local Bible

Societies for several years previous. The national Bible organization in 1829-1830 made a systematic drive to place a Bible in every home throughout the country, while efforts were made to supply foreign immigrants with copies of the Bible as they entered the ports of the United States. In 1825 a kindred organization was formed in New York known as the American Tract Society. Like the American Bible Society this organization sought the support of Christians of all Protestant denominations, and its board of publication was composed of ministers representing the several orthodox churches. Among the larger publications of the Tract Society were the *Evangelical Family Library* of fifteen volumes and the *Religious Library* consisting of twenty-five volumes. The society published a paper called the *Christian Messenger* which soon had a large circulation throughout the country, while its agents of one kind or another were sent into every section of the nation, visiting towns and villages and supplying the poor with books and tracts. In 1855 the Tract Society had 659 colporteurs at work, 126 of whom were laboring among the Germans and immigrants; they visited in that year 639,193 families, 64,686 being Roman Catholic.

Besides this interdenominational distribution of literature throughout the country, most of the larger churches were soon engaged in publishing and distributing their own literature. The oldest of these denominational publishing houses was the Methodist Book Concern, established in New York in 1789, and every Methodist circuit rider became its agent distributing its publications throughout the network of the circuits. The American Baptist Publication Society (1840) grew out of the Baptist Tract Society organized in 1824, while the Presbyterians, Episcopalians, Friends, Lutherans and others likewise had their tract, Bible and publication societies. It would be difficult to overestimate the influence for good of this tremendous output of Christian literature which found its way into every nook and corner of the land.

The Methodists seem to have been the first to introduce Sunday schools in the United States, as early as 1786, the movement having already gained considerable impetus in England. By 1816 Sunday schools had been formed in various parts of the country and soon societies were organized in the larger cities, as New York and Philadelphia, for the publication of little books for the instructions of children, such as spelling and hymnbooks, and catechisms. Finally in 1824 there was begun a movement resulting in the organization of the American Sunday

School Union, composed of an association of men of all denominations, the board of managers being laymen, the greater part of them living in Philadelphia. Its twofold object was to promote the establishment of Sunday schools and prepare and publish suitable books and manuals for Sunday-school use, and also for libraries, which were intended to furnish children with suitable home reading. In 1839 the society resolved to establish a Sunday school in every neighborhood without one, in the West. Three years later it adopted the same resolution in regard to the southern states, and great efforts were put forth to carry out these resolves; large sums of money were collected and many new Sunday schools were established while the society employed agents and missionaries to travel through the country visiting the Sunday schools and establishing new ones.

VII

While the vast majority of Christian people of every denomination throughout the country were giving enthusiastic support to these many new societies, there was developing in the West an opposition which gained considerable headway, particularly among the Baptists. At first the Baptists in the West gave hearty support to the cause of missions, and when John M. Peck came to Illinois he was well received by the Illinois Baptist Association and the cause of missions recommended to the churches. But soon it became evident that opposition was developing especially among the old frontier Baptist farmer-preachers, and by 1825 antimission sentiment was to be found in almost every section of the West. The antimissions resolutions adopted by the Apple Creek Baptist Association of Illinois in 1830 are typical. They declare that "We as an association do not hesitate to say, that we declare an unfellowship with foreign and domestic mission and bible societies, Sunday schools, and tract societies, and all other missionary institutions." Further they emphatically state, "No missionary preacher is to have the privilege of preaching at our association," and they "advise the churches to protest against Masonic and missionary institutions, and not to contribute to any such beggarly institutions." In 1832 the Sugar Creek Association in Indiana placed in their constitution the following: "Any Church suffering their members to unite with any of the Mission Conventions, Colleges, Tracts, Bible, Temperance, etc., Societies, and failing to deal with their members, shall be considered of such a violation of the principles of the union, that the Association when put into possession of a knowledge of such facts shall punish such churches as being not of us."

In certain sections of the West the antimission movement made almost a clean sweep of the Baptist churches, and by 1846 there were more than 68,000 Anti-Mission Baptists in the United States, by far the largest majority being found in the West. A good share of the responsibility for the rise of this movement is due to the activity and influence of three men, John Taylor, the old pioneer Baptist preacher of Kentucky, Daniel Parker, likewise a Baptist preacher, first in Tennessee and later in Illinois and Indiana, and Alexander Campbell, who has been mentioned before as the leader of the "reform" party among the western Baptists from 1820 to 1830.

John Taylor struck the first blow at missions in 1819 when he published a pamphlet called "Thoughts on Missions." The assumption on the part of the missionaries that there had been no religious work done in the West previous to their coming aroused the old veteran's ire and he says: "To hear and read their reports it would seem as if the whole country was almost a blank as to religion" and that there was not a preacher in the country which deserved the name except missionaries. The arch-enemy of missions in the West, however, was Daniel Parker. In 1820 he published a pamphlet of twenty-eight pages called "A Public Address to the Baptist Society" in which he vigorously opposed the cause of missions, and four years later published another pamphlet in which he set forth his two-seed doctrine, which purports to furnish a theological basis for antimissionism. The third archopponent of missions was Alexander Campbell, who between the years 1820 and 1830 was particularly active in preaching, debating and conducting his paper, the *Christian Baptist,* and after 1829 the *Millennial Harbinger.* Campbell professed to be favorable to missions and to spread of the gospel, but he objected to all societies which did not have a Scriptural basis and authorization.

One of the chief reasons for Baptist opposition to the cause of missions and other societies was their objection to the centralization of authority. One of the fundamental principles of the Baptists is the complete independence of the congregation, and the formation of societies, with their officers and paid secretaries, with authority to send men here and there, seemed to some a complete violation of Baptist principles. Taylor states: "I consider these great men [the missionary secretaries], are verging close on an aristocracy, with an object to sap the foundation of Baptist republican government." Baptist objection to a paid ministry constituted another reason for their opposition. Taylor considered Rice a "modern Tetzel, and the Pope's old orator of that name was equally innocent with Luther Rice and his motive about the same," while Parker compared the missionaries to the moneychangers whom Christ drove from the temple, and he expected Christ would do the same thing for these modern traders in sheep and oxen. Undoubtedly also jealousy of the better educated missionaries on the part of the frontier preachers played its part in their opposition, while their contention that missionary societies were unscriptural was strongly stressed. This was the chief argument used by Campbell, and the columns of his paper were filled with bitter attacks upon all man-made societies. Parker in his pamphlet states that God did not send Jonah to Nineveh through a missionary society, nor was he "sent to a seminary of learning to prepare him to preach to these Gentiles; but was under the tuition of God, and was in no case under the direction of any body of men whatever, neither did he look back to a society formed to raise money for his support."[1]

The doctrinal basis of antimissionism was hyper-Calvinistic. It stated that God in His sovereign power did not need any human means to bring His elect to repentance. Nor was there need to preach to the nonelect, for all the preaching in the world could not bring them to repentance. Indeed, Parker held that sending the gospel to the nonelect, or to the devil's bona-fide children, as he called them, or giving them the Bible were acts of such gross and supreme folly that no Christian should be engaged in them. Campbell had become Arminian in his theology and did not accept this doctrine, but opposed missionary societies as being an unscriptural means of carrying the gospel. Later he gave up his opposition and in 1849 became the first president of the Missionary Society of the Disciples, though this move was strongly opposed by others, who got their best arguments against the society from the columns of the *Christian Baptist*.

[1] See W. W. Sweet, "The Anti-Mission Baptists, a Frontier Phenomenon," in *Religion on the American Frontier*: Vol. I, *The Baptists* (New York, 1931).

✦ ✦ ✦

CHAPTER XVII

RELIGION IN THE RESTLESS THIRTIES AND FORTIES

THE period from the adoption of the Federal Constitution to 1830 is usually called the era of nationalism; with equal appropriateness that from 1830 to the opening of the Civil War may be termed the era of sectionalism. This holds true both in politics and in religion. In both church and state the spirit of nationalism gradually gave way to that of sectionalism. Especially was this true after the question of slavery began to occupy the center of stage, until the country was divided into two distinct sections, each with its peculiar political and economic demands. So likewise was the trend in church affairs, resulting in divisions and subdivisions of the churches, while each denomination began to emphasize its own peculiar interest. Loyalty to a denomination comes now to be the great emphasis, just as loyalty to the South or the North became the catchword in politics. The period is characterized by quarrels and contentions and slanders among the churches. Protestants are arrayed against Catholics; the famous Plan of Union of 1801 between Presbyterians and Congregationalists is first rejected by conservative Presbyterians and then by the Congregationalists; the great popular churches divide over slavery and then contend with unchristian bitterness for the border, while acrimonious conflicts are waged within the Lutheran, Episcopalian and German Reformed Churches, and even the newly formed liberals, the Unitarians, find it impossible to agree among themselves.

New winds were blowing over the American people in the thirties and forties. A new democracy had arisen, manifesting its power by the elevation of Andrew Jackson to the presidency of the United States.

Rapid changes were taking place in the economic life of the people; indeed, an industrial revolution was under way comparable to that which had taken place in England a century before. New streams of population were pouring into the country, especially from Ireland and southern Germany, profoundly disturbing the whole economic, political and social equilibrium of the nation. And withal it was a period of immense optimism. This had come about with the elevation of the common people to place and power. Opportunity was the key word of this new era. "Few boys of that generation escaped being told that they might become president. Few were not told that in the matter of money the future was in their hands." To the American of the thirties and forties his country was a land of boundless opportunity, nor did he for a moment doubt his own ability to take full advantage of it. Naturally an individualistic attitude dominated the period, while emotionalism everywhere prevailed. We must not be surprised, then, to find in this period a great variety of new interests arising, new and strange sects, new movements in thought, reforms of one kind or another, many of them the result of individual vagaries.

I

The first of the great American churches to be torn by internal strife was the Presbyterian. The controversy which finally culminated in the schism of 1837-1838 came about largely as a result of the working of the Plan of Union and the operations of the American Home Missionary Society, which after 1826 became the chief agent in carrying out its provisions. Plan of Union churches had been formed numerously through central and western New York, in Ohio, Michigan, Indiana, Illinois and Wisconsin. In all of these churches there were large and influential New England groups, with their Congregational background, and influenced by the new theological currents coming out of New England. On the other hand, there was the large body of Presbyterians with their rigid Scotch-Irish background, who looked upon any change in the Calvinistic system as dangerous heresy. It was the presence of these two divergent elements in the church which was the fundamental cause of division.

The rift between these two elements began in New England, occasioned by a sermon preached by Dr. Nathaniel W. Taylor, of Yale Divinity School, at the Commencement of 1828. Taylor belonged to the new school of theological thought, farthest removed from the old strict Calvinism, while he was particularly severe on the doctrine of Original Sin. The following year the young and brilliant Presbyterian minister at Morristown, New Jersey, Albert Barnes, in a sermon before his congregation announced his agreement with the position of Taylor, admitting, however, that such a position was out of harmony with the Westminster Confession. The next year when Barnes was called to be the minister of the First Presbyterian Church of Philadelphia, the mother church of the denomination in America, his installation was opposed by conservative members of the presbytery. From this time on for a period of six years, Barnes was the storm center in the Presbyterian Church. The fact that his church was generally the meeting place of the General Assembly caused the controversy to assume a national significance. Year by year his case came before the General Assembly in one form or another, while in 1836 a new charge of heresy was lodged against him by Dr. George Junkin, a representative of the rigid Scotch-Irish group, and Barnes was suspended from his pulpit by action of the Philadelphia Synod, though the next General Assembly reversed the decision.

Another heresy trial of the period was that of Dr. Lyman Beecher, president of Lane Theological Seminary. Beecher had come from a brilliant pastorate of a Congregational church in Boston to take charge of the new Lane Theological Seminary in Cincinnati, a Plan of Union project. Charges of heresy, slander and hypocrisy were placed against him in 1835 by Dr. Joshua L. Wilson, one of the "war horses" of western Presbyterianism, but his acquittal by the synod, though Old School in its sympathy, was soon obtained by a large majority. Two years before, two of the professors of Illinois College and the president, Edward Beecher, were arraigned before the Presbytery of Illinois for teaching the "New Haven doctrines," and when they were acquitted their accuser appealed to the synod, though the case was not pushed further. All of these young men were Yale graduates and were working under the Plan of Union. The conservatives, by this time, were thoroughly aroused to the dangers of heretical teachings on the part of the "Congregationalized" Presbyterians generally and the slightest tendency in the direction of liberalism in religion on their part was sure to result in protest if not in accusation of heresy from the orthodox brethren.

Matters were now drifting rapidly toward a division in the church. In 1836 Union Theological Seminary in New York had been founded by the liberal, or New School, wing, independent of the control of the General Assembly. This was undoubtedly one of the factors which threw the Princeton Seminary influence toward the Old School position, and made their ultimate victory possible two years later. Of fundamental importance in the whole controversy was the Home Missionary Society, the agency through which the Plan of Union largely functioned. The Old School party contended that the Plan of Union churches established through the Home Missionary Society were not real Presbyterian churches. These churches, they contended, were lax in discipline, did not possess full presbyterial organization and were heretical in their doctrinal position, while a growing number of Old School leaders felt that abolitionism was gaining too strong a hold among the New School brethren. The rigid Old School party now began to advocate, more and more, the strengthening of their own denominational societies, and the repudiation of the agreement with the interdenominational Home Missionary Society and the American Board. This program they hoped to carry through the General Assembly of 1836. This they were unable to accomplish, however, as that assembly contained a New School majority, who carried through their own program with a high hand. This New School victory greatly alarmed the Old School party and led them to take steps, at once, to divide the church.

The crisis came in the General Assembly of 1837. In this assembly the Old School party, now joined by the moderates, or Princeton Seminary group, were in a decided majority, and having met previous to the convening of the assembly, were well organized with a fully laid out program. No religious body ever took such heroic measures to rid the church of what was considered heresy as did the Presbyterian body in 1837. Without hesitating a moment, 4 synods, and eventually 533 churches and more than 100,000 members were read out of the church by a strictly party vote. This having been accomplished the assembly then proceeded to separate the church from the voluntary and interdenominational societies and adopted the Western Missionary Society as the assembly's Foreign Mission Board, while it declared its own Boards of Education and Domestic Missions to be its only agents in those respective fields.

The New School party was taken completely by surprise, while many belonging to the Old School were indignant at the high-handed manner in which the church had been divided. In August, 1837, the New School body held a convention at Auburn, New York, where it was determined to stand by the Plan of Union and to make an attempt, at the next General Assembly, to regain their place in the church. They also drew up a document maintaining their doctrinal soundness. Their plan, however, to regain their place in the church was completely unsuccessful, for when the New School delegates presented their credentials to the assembly of 1838 the moderator refused to recognize them. There was nothing left now for the New School delegates to do but to withdraw, and steps were immediately taken to organize a separate church. After the formation of the New School body into a church, other synods and presbyteries outside the exscinded synods joined them, so that eventually the New School represented four-ninths of the ministry and membership of the old church. In many instances synods, presbyteries and churches were divided. The New School strength lay largely at the north, though the Synod of Eastern Tennessee and a few southern presbyteries adhered to them, but the overwhelming majority of southern presbyteries were Old School.

It is now definitely known that slavery played an important part in the Old School-New School controversy which divided the church in 1837, although none of the Presbyterian historians have noted that fact. By 1836 there had come to be antislavery and proslavery wings in the Presbyterian Church, as well as a large number of moderates who were antislavery in sentiment, but at the same time were anxious to rid the church of the "Presbygationalists" because of their looseness of doctrine and polity. Joshua L. Wilson of Cincinnati and R. J. Breckinridge of Kentucky, both men of large influence in the church, were antislavery, but at the same time were stanch opponents of loose doctrine and discipline. Previous to the meeting of the General Assembly of 1837 an Old School convention had been held in which it was agreed that the slavery issue should not be discussed on the floor of the General Assembly, since they feared that it would divide the Old School delegates and therefore defeat their purpose of purging the church of heresy and looseness in polity. In other words in order to keep the Old School men together on the one issue, it was necessary to avoid a discussion of slavery.[1] Since slavery did not appear as an issue on the floor of the Assembly it has been assumed that it had nothing to do with the division of the church. It is well known, however, that antislavery sentiment was much stronger among the New School party than in the Old School, and doubtless the large majority of the Old School delegates, from the South particularly, were immensely relieved to be rid of the radical New School influence for that reason.[2]

II

The epidemic of controversy which characterized the years under discussion in the American churches manifested itself among the Episcopalians in a bitter contest between the high church and low church parties. The outstanding influence in the early years of American Episcopalianism were decidedly low church, under the leadership of Bishop William White, but beginning with the consecration in 1811 of John Henry Hobart (1775-1830) as Bishop of New York, the high church party obtained an especially aggressive leadership, and a new period in the history of American Episcopalianism was begun.

By the close of the War of 1812 the Episcopal Church was no longer looked upon with suspicion by patriotic Americans, for "churchmen" had fought on the American side in the war, while in New England they naturally aligned themselves with the party fighting for the abolition of the privilege of the standing order. Thus they were identified with the rising popular party under the leadership of Thomas Jefferson. A new and energetic leadership within the church was also arising. Besides Bishop Hobart, three other bishops stand out in this period of renewed life and advance in the church: Alexander V. Griswold, Bishop of the

[1] See W. W. Sweet, *Religion on the American Frontier*: Vol. II, *The Presbyterians*, pp. 117-125. The following resolution passed by the Synod of North Carolina in September, 1837, furnishes an interesting side light on the slavery issue:
"Resolved, that this Synod regards the attempt to make Abolition a principal influence in bringing about that result [expelling the New School Synods] as making a false issue; & as it was not alluded [sic] to in the debate they believe it had little or no influence in bringing about the decision, but they believe the question [loose doctrine and discipline among the New School churches and ministers] was honestly debated & decided on its merits."

[2] See also "Abolitionism and the Presbyterian Schism of 1837-1838," by C. Bruce Staiger in *The Mississippi Valley Historical Review*, Vol. XXXVI, December, 1949, pp. 391-414.

Eastern Diocese (New England), Richard Moore of Virginia, and Philander Chase, the founder of the church in the great region west of the Alleghanies. Each of these leaders had distinctive characteristics. Hobart was the high churchman *par excellence,* Griswold was as emphatically low church, Moore was warmly evangelical, while Chase was the ideal leader of the pioneer forces of the church.

If the period to 1812 was one of suspended animation, that from 1812 to 1835 may be as truthfully characterized as one of almost feverish activity. If the old leaders lacked energy, the new leaders burned themselves out with their excess of toil. The work of Hobart is particularly significant. When he came to the New York diocese there were twenty-eight clergymen, at his death in 1830 the number had grown to one hundred and twenty-seven. He was the "embodiment of positive assertion and aggressive action." With his coming the Episcopal Church in New York ceased to exist on sufferance and became "self-conscious, self-confident and aggressive." He took openly and proudly the high church position, at the time when that position was unpopular in his own church and especially unpopular in the country. His church he considered the one channel of saving grace; to him the sacraments were the only vehicles of that grace, and valid only when administered by a priesthood ordained in proper apostolic succession. He would have nothing to do with interdenominational societies, fearing if he united with others he would thereby weaken the claims he made for his own church. But he organized numerous societies within the church, such as the Episcopal Tract Society, the Sunday School Society, the Bible Society and a Missionary Society, and missionaries were sent to the Indians in western New York, to whom he gave personal supervision.

The opposite of Hobart in his churchmanship was Bishop Griswold, who from 1811 to 1843 administered the affairs of the Episcopal Church in New England. Low churchman and a strong preacher he was a man of deep and simple piety, with an abundance of "moderation, good sense and careful equipoise." During his long episcopate he saw his original diocese divided and subdivided, as the number of churches grew, until at his death there were five dioceses in the original territory over which he presided at the beginning of his episcopate. When Bishop Moore was consecrated Bishop of Virginia in 1814 there were not more than five active ministers in Virginia; at his death in 1841 there were nearly a hundred ministers and one hundred and seventy churches. These three bishops were typical of the church of their time.

Bishop Chase was of pure New England stock and a graduate of Dartmouth College, where as a student he was brought into the Episcopal Church through the study of the Prayer Book. Soon after graduation he was ordained and became an eager and restless missionary and remained a frontiersman until the end of his life. His first parish was on the New York frontier. Thence he went to New Orleans, where he formed the first Episcopal church in that newly acquired region. Returning to New England in shattered health he stayed only long enough to regain his strength and then was off again, on horseback, in the middle of winter, for the Western Reserve of Ohio. Here he went about from house to house and from settlement to settlement gathering together the people of his church. Finally in 1818, largely through his pioneering work, there had come to be five clergymen in the state of Ohio, and in that year these five with nine laymen met and organized a diocese and elected Chase their bishop.

The number of Episcopalians on the frontier were few, and the people of the other denominations generally hostile, but none knew better than this frontier bishop how to overcome their prejudice. Perhaps the greatest monument to Bishop Chase's work is Kenyon College which was established on a beautiful ridge in the midst of a primeval forest in central Ohio in 1824. After Chase had determined to establish a college, he journeyed to England to raise money and in spite of opposition from other bishops in America he succeeded in his enterprise and came home with $20,000, largely obtained through the help of Lord Gambier and Lord Kenyon, and appropriately, to the town which grew up about Kenyon College he gave the name Gambier. In 1831 Chase resigned both his bishopric and the presidency of the college, because of disagreements which arose in his administration. For three years he combined farming with missionary labor in Michigan, but in 1835 a new diocese was formed in Illinois, and the three clergymen who constituted it called upon Chase to be their bishop. Here he duplicated his work in Ohio, even journeying to England in search of funds to found Jubilee College, while generous help was also received from American churchmen. Meanwhile two other western dioceses had been organized in 1829, Kentucky and Tennessee, and in 1835 the General Convention adopted the policy of sending out missionary bishops into the new country without waiting for any call for them, and in that year the first missionary bishop was elected in the person of Jackson Kemper, and largely through his apostolic labor his church was established in Indiana, Iowa, Minnesota and Wisconsin.

The Protestant Episcopal Church was expanding in spite of internal dissension. By about 1835 a line of cleavage had been run through the church, separating the two radically opposite parties, the high churchmen on the one hand and the evangelicals, or low churchmen, on the other. When Chase began his work in Ohio in 1817 he called "together his neighbors and his companions for the preaching of the Word, and the Prayers. When Breck and his companions laid down their packs under an elm tree in Minnesota, in 1850," they erected "a rustic cross," built "a rude altar of rough stones," and began "their work by the celebration of the Eucharist Feast." Thus is illustrated the radically different emphases of these two church parties.

The high church party adopted the name "Anglo-Catholic," by which they meant a halfway position between Roman Catholicism and Protestantism, but which many could not distinguish from Romish Catholicism. They stood for the authority of the church as opposed to the right of individual judgment. Through the influence of such leaders as Bishop Hobart, year by year this exaltation of the church was winning converts among the people and gradually the Protestant Episcopal Church "was becoming more sharply differentiated, not only from the world, but from the current forms of American Christianity." This movement, already under way, was tremendously augmented by the influence of the "Oxford Movement" which began in 1833, at Oriel College, Oxford, by a group of young men who formed an "Association for vindicating the rights of the Church and Restoring the Knowledge of Sound Principles." In a series of able tracts, largely from the pen of John Henry Newman, the *Via Media* between Protestantism and Romanism was set forth. Their influence in America soon swelled the high church movement into a flood, and from 1835 onward to the Civil War was a period of strife within the church. Those opposing the movement feared that the high church party were making of the Protestant Episcopal Church a training school for Rome, while able defenders set forth the Anglo-Catholic position. Each side formed its own societies to propagate its own views, and a pamphlet warfare was fiercely waged. Election of bishops brought on bitter party contests and the marvel is that the church did not split into fragments.

The church leader most responsible for preventing such an unfortunate result was William A. Muhlenberg who called himself an Evangelical Catholic. Muhlenberg, the great grandson of Henry M. Muhlenberg, had come to New York in 1847 as rector of a free church, the Church of the Holy Communion, built by his sister, having previously established the first Protestant Episcopal Church school in connection with his church at Flushing, Long Island. He later established the first order of deaconesses in the Episcopal Church and was the founder of St. Luke's Hospital, opened in 1856. This broad-spirited man consistently stood for "a broader and more comprehensive ecclesiastical system" and for a larger freedom of opinion within the church. He felt that the high and low church parties both had a legitimate place within the church. At the General Convention of 1853 these views were put in the form of a memorial and presented to that body where they were accepted by both parties and a reconciliation became an accomplished fact. The church parties, however, did not disappear, but from this time forward the "evangelical" party declined in influence until some thirty years later when the Reformed Episcopal Church was formed by a secession made up of discontented evangelicals.

III

The American Lutherans contributed their full share to the controversy of the period. A bitter dispute arose between two parties within the church, one advocating the Americanizing of the Lutheran Church and a liberal interpretation of the Confession, while a growing conservative party insisted upon the continued use of the German language and a strict adherence, not only to the Augsburg Confession, but to the symbolical books associated with it. The outstanding leader of the liberals was Samuel S. Schmucker who in 1826 had been the prime mover in the founding of the Lutheran Theological Seminary at Gettysburg and six years later of Pennsylvania College. Here he spent the remainder of his life as professor of theology and exercised widespread influence as a liberalizing force. In this respect he was the successor of Henry M. Muhlenberg, who had advocated the use of the English language and whose general outlook was particularly sane. Schmucker maintained that American Lutheranism had come out of a background of wholesome evangelism and he advocated the reincarnation on American soil of that spirit "which had characterized the school of Francke." On the other hand, he opposed that type of Lutheranism which had its background "in the sixteenth and seventeenth century confessional orthodoxy."

Dr. Schmucker might have swung American Lutheranism to his way of thinking if it had not been for the great wave of German immigration which set in about 1830 and continued until well past the Civil War. Up until the former year American Lutheranism had just kept pace with the growth of population in the country, but between 1830 and 1870 Lutheran increase was three times that of the general population. In the decade just previous to the Civil War nearly a million Germans came to America. Many of these German immigrants were Roman Catholics and a larger share were hostile to all religion, but perhaps the majority were Lutherans. The coming of this vast body of new fellow religionists placed a heavy burden upon the American Lutherans, but in many instances these new immigrants brought their own ministers with them and also their Old World conservatism and orthodoxy.

It was during these years that a number of extremely conservative Lutheran synods were formed: the Missouri Synod in 1846; the Buffalo Synod in 1845; the Iowa Synod in 1854. The recognized leader among these extremely conservative Lutherans was C. F. W. Walther who had come out as a young pastor with a number of immigrants from Saxony in 1839. These immigrants had left Saxony largely because of the growing rationalism in the state church and were strict Lutherans of the extreme orthodox type. After a period of uncertainty, during which one group advocated their return to Germany, Walther succeeded in restoring confidence among the colonists, and eventually gave them a new idea of the church, which characterizes the Missouri Lutherans to this day. He became the pastor of their church in St. Louis and in 1844 began the publication of *Der Lutheraner* which became a powerful influence in maintaining Lutheran orthodoxy as it was interpreted by Walther. He advocated the establishment of parochial schools and the acceptance of all the symbolical books as "the pure and uncorrupted explanation and statement of the Divine Word," and led in the establishment of colleges and seminaries for the training of its ministry.

The decade and a half just previous to the Civil War saw also the beginning of a large immigration of Norwegians and Swedes. Illinois early attracted this immigration and in 1853 the Norwegians organized an American Synod. The Swedes at first united with the General Synod and received help from eastern Lutheran bodies and were even assisted by the American Home Missionary Society, but in 1860 under the leadership of Lars Paul Esbjörn they withdrew from that body and formed the Augustana Synod and organized their own college at Rock Island, Illinois. Both of these Lutheran bodies helped swell the volume of Lutheran conservatism in the country and played their part in the controversy of the period.

While this Lutheran immigration was resulting in the formation of these several new bodies, it was at the same time exerting an increasing influence in the older Lutheran organizations. In 1820 a General Synod had been organized which had come out of the growing sense of need of closer coöperation, as the church expanded westward and southwest. Schmucker for many years was the leading influence in this general body, and worked consistently for "American Lutheranism" and also for a closer coöperation among the American churches. In 1838 he issued an appeal for the reunion of the churches on "the apostolic basis" and was one of the strongest advocates of the "Evangelical Alliance," organized in 1846. By the middle of the century, however, the conservative wing in the General Synod had become the larger party, Schmucker's influence steadily declined and more conservative leaders came into the ascendancy. In these years numerous Lutheran periodicals began publication advocating one side or the other of the issue, while within the synods controversy went on often resulting in lasting divisions and in in the formation of new synods.

IV

Somewhat similar to the controversy among the American Lutherans was that which went on within the German Reformed Church. The language controversy was particularly severe in Philadelphia, resulting in the withdrawal of those advocating the use of the English language and the formation of congregations of their own. But far more important was the controversy which arose over the so-called "Mercersburg theology."

The first theological seminary of the German Reformed body was established at Carlisle, Pennsylvania, in 1825, but ten years later it was removed to Mercersburg, and the same year Marshall College was

founded in the same place. In 1840 Dr. John W. Nevin, a former Presbyterian of Scotch-Irish ancestry, was chosen to a professorship in the
Mercersburg Seminary, and in 1844 Dr. Philip Schaff, a young Swiss
scholar, was elected professor of historical and exegetical theology.
Both Nevin and Schaff were scholars of high rank and were thoroughly
familiar with the new German theological currents. It was not long
until the more conservative ministers began to find cause for alarm in
the teachings of these two brilliant professors, and the "Mercersburg
theology" was attacked in the church papers and in some instances there
were withdrawals from the church. Both Nevin and Schaff were particularly active in their scholarship and a series of scholarly books came
from them during this period of controversy that have been equaled by
few if any among American scholars.

V

Of greatest importance from the standpoint of the rapid growth of
Roman Catholicism in the United States from 1830 to the Civil War
was the Irish and German immigration. The Irish had been coming to
America for years previous to 1845, but after that date two causes
account for its rapid increase: one was the greatly improved means of
ocean transit, the other was the potato-rot famine in 1845-1846. By this
time the potato had become the great Irish staple. In the former year
a blight, which destroyed the potato plant overnight, swept over the
island and the next year (1846) again the crop was destroyed. This
brought on a famine, most devastating and terrible in its consequences,
and resulted in a mighty wave of Irish immigration to America which
has continued more or less down to the present time. These Irish immigrants, who were 100 per cent Roman Catholics, were mostly peasant
farmers with slender resources, which were soon exhausted after their
arrival in an American port. This meant that they must settle down
where they landed, and Boston, New York, Philadelphia and Baltimore
early became centers of Irish Roman Catholic influence.

As has been noted in connection with Lutheran growth, emigration
from southern Germany was particularly large after the unsuccessful
revolutions of 1830 and 1848. These immigrants were better financed
than were the Irish and settled mostly in the newer sections of the
country north of the Ohio or beyond the Mississippi, Missouri and
Wisconsin becoming great centers of German influence, though many

Germans came to Cincinnati, and to the other cities along the Ohio, such as Evansville and Madison, Indiana. Perhaps a third of these Germans were Roman Catholic.

The large Catholic emigration to the United States prompted the organization of missionary societies among European Catholics to aid their coreligionists in the United States. The two most important of these societies were the Lyon (France) Propaganda, organized in 1822, and the Leopold Society of Austria, formed in 1829. In 1828 the Lyon Propaganda sent to the United States more than 100,000 francs and in 1846, 660,207 francs were distributed among the 21 bishoprics and missions in America. From the time of its organization to 1850 this society alone sent nearly 9,000,000 francs to the United States. Other European societies also sent large sums, amounting in some years to as much as 1,000,000 francs.

Of considerable importance to American Roman Catholicism was the resuscitation (1805) of the Jesuits, who had been suppressed by the Pope in 1773. Of even greater importance in many respects was the founding of the Order of Sisters of Charity at about the same time, and the beginning of the work of religious women of other orders, such as the Ursulines, Carmelites and Sacred Heart, with their numerous schools, convents and religious houses. By 1835 every large city in the United States contained houses of these orders. Meanwhile, year by year new dioceses were established; Charleston, South Carolina, in 1820; Richmond in 1821; Cincinnati in 1823; Mobile in 1824; St Louis in 1826; Detroit, 1832; and between 1834 and 1847, Vincennes, Dubuque, Little Rock, Nashville, Natchez, Pittsburgh, Milwaukee, Chicago, Hartford, Oregon City, Albany, Buffalo, Cleveland and Galveston. Thus by 1850 practically every considerable city in the United States had become the head of a diocese.

The two outstanding American Catholic leaders in the period from 1820 to the Civil War were Bishop John England who became, in the former year, the first Bishop of Charleston (1820-1842), and Bishop John Hughes of the diocese of New York. These two great Irish Catholic bishops were men of decided character and great ability, bold, fearless and independent. Bishop England's diocese covered a territory eight hundred miles in length and from two to three hundred miles inland. He traveled through this vast territory continuously in his carriage, administering the sacraments, preaching, and instructing; made fre quent trips to Rome where he was known as the "steam bishop;" and in the midst of all these activities found time to prepare catechisms, establish "Book Societies," deliver lectures and write books. About the name of Bishop John Hughes two great Roman Catholic controversies center, that of "Trusteeism" and the "Common School question."

The struggle over trusteeism began in 1785 in New York City when the "Trustees of the Roman Catholic Church in the city of New York" purchased a site for a church and were incorporated. The trustees claimed the right to appoint and dismiss their pastors, as well as to administer the property. This was opposed from the start by the Catholic authorities, but it was not until Bishop Hughes took charge of the diocese that the matter was finally settled. Because of the long controversy between the trustees and the bishop, five of the eight New York churches became bankrupt, and when they were sold at a sheriff's sale, were bid in by Bishop Hughes on his own right, and by skillful management and an appeal to European Catholics for aid he finally succeeded in paying off the large debts. In Philadelphia a similar struggle over trusteeism occurred. In 1831 Bishop Kendrick of Philadelphia issued an interdict against St. Mary's Church, forbidding all sacred functions until the trustees were willing to disclaim their pretensions to authority. This severe measure was finally successful and the trustees gave way.

The public school question likewise centered in New York, and arose in 1823 when "The New York Public School Society," an organization formed in 1805 for the education of poor and neglected children, objected to the distribution of public school funds to church schools. This practice had been going on for a number of years and several denominations had been securing funds annually from the state. On the protest of the Public School Society the Protestant churches gave way, but the Roman Catholics, headed by Bishop Hughes, continued to insist upon state appropriations for their schools and other benevolent work. In 1840 Bishop Hughes brought the school matter to a head by appearing before the corporation of the city in behalf of the Catholic schools, and later a petition was presented asking that seven Catholic schools be permitted to share in the public school fund. This was finally denied by the corporation. The Catholics then took the matter to the legislature, where the Catholic petition was again defeated, though the lower house favored their demands. This discussion created great excitement throughout the country and was one of the factors which led to the Know-Nothing, or Native American, movement which swept over the nation in the forties and fifties.

The Native American party began in 1837 primarily to emphasize the necessity of limiting immigration and advocating the passage of more stringent immigration and naturalization laws, and demanded that a residence of twenty-one years be made a condition for obtaining citizenship. A few years later, however, it became frankly an anti-Catholic movement. In 1845 an organization of Native Americans was formed claiming a membership of 100,000, while in 1850 it became a secret organization under the name, known only by its members, as "The Supreme Order of the Star-Spangled Banner," which later came to be known as the "Know-Nothing party." To be admitted to the lodges of this organization the candidate had to be a native-born American citizen, reared under Protestant influence, and neither himself, his wife, nor his parents Roman Catholics. In the initiation of members the president thus addressed the candidates: "In every city, town and hamlet, the danger has been seen and the alarm sounded. And hence true men have devised this order as a means . . . of advancing America and the American interest on the one side, and on the other of checking the stride of the foreigner or alien, of thwarting the machinations and subverting the deadly plans of the Jesuit and the Papist." The Know-Nothing movement was unjust and ill-timed, while such methods as it pursued are always under suspicion, and can only lead to disorders and rioting and a vast increase of ill feeling.

In spite of such attempts to resist the growth and influence of Catholicism in the United States, their numbers were increasing by leaps and bounds. In 1830 there were in round numbers, 600,000 Catholics in the United States; 20 years later (1850) they were numbered at 3,500,000, while on the outbreak of the Civil War they had increased another million.

VI

So far in this chapter the controversies and outstanding happenings among some of the larger American churches have been considered. The strange and unusual religious movements which so crowd this restless period will now be treated. A bare catalogue of these many movements with their founders would more than fill a page, and would include names of men and women long since forgotten, but who at the time of their activity were household words in many sections of the United States. It will be possible to discuss only a few of the more important of these movements, such as Mormonism, the Millerite Movement, spiritualism and some of the more successful communistic experiments. Along with the many strange religious phenomena which characterize the period, there also arose numerous other reform movements, such as temperance and other humanitarian societies of one kind or another. These movements, although differing radically among themselves, sprang usually from a common background of revivalism, influenced by disturbed economic conditions.

From the beginning of the century to 1845 was a period of revivalistic emphasis throughout the country, but if there was one section where the revival emphasis was stronger than anywhere else and the excitability of the people greater, it was in central western New York, which came to be known as the "burnt-over district" because of the repeated revival waves which swept over this region. These counties had been settled by New Englanders, the first wave being of "rather unsavory fame," though they were followed by an intelligent and industrious class from eastern New York and New England. The mingling of these two classes gave a peculiar psychological character to the people, producing on the one hand, sane and progressive social movements, and, on the other, tendencies toward fanaticism. Added to this was the tendency, which seems to be in New England blood, toward "eccentricity of opinion and extremity of temper," which has made of New England a "fertile seed-plot" for fads and extravagances. In this territory originated the anti-Masonic agitation in 1826; a few years later it became one of two chief centers of the Millerite craze; here lived the Fox sisters who were responsible for the beginnings of the spiritualistic movement; while the greatest of all, in its permanent influence, Mormonism, likewise originated in this region. This region also produced the greatest revivalist of the time in Charles G. Finney, who, though a native of Connecticut, was taken in childhood by his parents to Oneida County, New York, and later moved farther westward into the country about Lake Ontario. John Humphrey Noyes, one of Finney's converts, became the founder of a new religious cult, which established one of the most successful of the communistic communities—the Oneida Community—in this same region.

It was from the revival-singed soil of western New York that Mormonism arose. Its founder, Joseph Smith, known to the Mormons as Joseph the Prophet, was born of penniless parents, who had, after much moving about in New Hampshire and Vermont, finally come into western New York to the town of Palmyra. The father was a seer of visions and a digger of hidden treasure and was accustomed to locate proper places to dig wells by a sort of divining rod. The family seem to have had numerous contacts with the frontier religious bodies, but whether or not they became members of any of them is in doubt. Joseph Jr. at an early age also began to have visions, the first occurring in 1820. He professed that the angel Moroni appeared to him and told him that the Bible of the Western world lay buried in a hill near by, but that he must not attempt to unearth it until the angel gave permission. This was given, and on September 22, 1827, he dug up a stone box in which was a book made of thin golden plates, covered with characters, which he states was the "reformed Egyptian tongue." With the golden plates were found two stones by the aid of which he was able to read the characters. For three years he was engaged in translating the golden book, employing at different times four helpers, among them his wife, to whom he dictated through a curtain. In 1830 the Book of Mormon was printed at Palmyra, accompanied by the sworn statement of three witnesses, as to the manner in which the golden plates were found and translated. Soon after this the golden plates, as Smith stated, were removed by the angel who had told him of their existence.

The Book of Mormon professes to be a history of America from its settlement by a company of "Jaredites," a people who had been dispersed at the Tower of Babel. These first settlers eventually destroyed one another. Later a company from Jerusalem settled on the coast of Chile, and these too after a period of years fell to quarreling among themselves, one group becoming known as the "Lamanites," an idle and warlike people with dark skins. These were the American Indians. The other group were the "Nephites," or God's chosen people. Between these two peoples wars ensued for many centuries. The Nephites finally fell away from the true faith and were nearly destroyed in A.D. 384, in a battle in Ontario County, New York, only Mormon and his son Moroni and a few others escaping. Moroni collected the sixteen books of records of his people into one volume with some personal recollections and buried them in a hill where, he was told, a true prophet would eventually find them.

There has been much discussion, among non-Mormons as to the origin of the Book of Mormon. Some claim that it was based on an unpublished novel by an eccentric Presbyterian minister, Solomon Spaulding, in which a fanciful description of the origin of the American Indians is given. Others credit Sidney Rigdon, an able ex-Baptist and ex-Disciple minister, who joined the Mormon movement soon after the publication of the Book of Mormon, as having an influential part in it. More recently the Book of Mormon has been studied as a purely frontier production.

But whatever the origin of the Book of Mormon, the Prophet Joseph and his new revelation were soon accepted as genuine by numerous followers and a church was formed at Fayette, in Seneca County, in April, 1830. In October the first missionaries were sent out by the Prophet. The early conversion of Sidney Rigdon was of large importance, and it has been conjectured by non-Mormon students that he furnished a good share of the doctrinal content of the new religion. From 1831 to 1837 Kirtland, Ohio, was the Mormon headquarters, the Mormon removal to the locality being due to the fact that Rigdon had a church there. Here Smith and Rigdon established a general store, a tannery and a sawmill, and a large stone temple was built and dedicated in 1836. It was here that the most dynamic of Mormon leaders joined the movement in the person of Brigham Young, and within a short time he became one of the "Twelve Apostles. " Lawsuits against Smith and Rigdon for their violation of the law against unchartered banks caused them to flee to Jackson County, Missouri, where a Mormon outpost had already been established. Mormon immigration to Missouri now became large, and Far West in Caldwell County became their center. Trouble arose between the Mormons and the Missourians, which came to a climax as a result of a Fourth of July sermon preached by Rigdon and a new revelation delivered by the Prophet, to the effect that the "saints" were to buy up all the land in the vicinity. A war of extermination was begun against the saints by the Missourians which did not cease until 15,000 Mormons had turned their backs upon Missouri (1839) and had crossed the river into Illinois.

From 1840 to 1846 Nauvoo, Illinois was the Mormon "New Jerusalem." The Illinois politicians of both major parties welcomed the Mormons hoping to secure their vote in the hotly contested presidential election of that year, and a charter was easily obtained making the Mormon town of Nauvoo practically independent of state control. The town grew rapidly; a university was established; a finely equipped military organization was formed with Smith as lieutenant general, and Nauvoo was soon the largest city in the state. The downfall of this flourishing community came soon after Joseph Smith received a revelation (July, 1843) authorizing polygamy. Although not officially announced at the time, it became known in the town and a party formed opposing Smith and his new revelation, while a paper called the *Expositor* was begun to oppose Smith and his supposed immoralities. The editors of the paper were arrested, their printing press destroyed, and a general uprising against the Mormons and Smith ensued. The state militia was called out, the Nauvoo Legion surrendered and the Prophet and his brother Hyrum were arrested and placed in jail at the county seat on a charge of treason. Here on the night of the twenty-seventh of June, 1844, a mob with the evident collusion of the militia broke into the prison and the two brothers were brutally shot. Two years later under Brigham Young's leadership the Mormons left Nauvoo and started in a body across the plains to the Valley of the Great Salt Lake in what is now the state of Utah. Thus was begun one of the most successful colonizing endeavors in the history of the United States.

The story of the economic and political development of the "State of Deseret;" the introduction of large-scale irrigation; the success with which Brigham Young molded the Mormon Church into a magnificent social and economic institution, and his carrying on for a period of twenty years practically independent of Federal control, constitute an exceptionally interesting phase of the history of the United States. The missionary policy of the Mormon Church was responsible for winning many converts outside the United States.

VII

During the same years in which Joseph Smith, Jr. was gathering his Mormon Church, another religious movement was sweeping over the eastern and middle states, under the preaching of an honest and earnest New England farmer of Baptist background, William Miller. The doctrine which won so many followers from among all the churches, and which so profoundly stirred many communities in different sections of the country, was the setting of the exact time when Christ should return to the earth and make an end of the world. All the evangelists of the time had been preaching the second coming of Christ, but none of them had fixed the exact date of that coming. This is just what Miller did, by the study of certain passages from the books of Daniel and Revelation.

The year of the second coming he fixed at 1843, and the day around the twenty-first of March.

It was in August, 1831, that Miller began his great mission to warn the people of the United States of the approaching end of all things. At first he preached his simple message among the villages near his home whenever and wherever opportunity offered. In 1839 he was invited to preach in the Chardon Street Baptist Church of Boston and his message now became of more than local importance. He soon was invited to speak in many of the larger churches in the cities of the East, and calls began to come from many sections of the country for preachers and literature setting forth the great message. Soon Second-Advent journals began publication: *The Signs of the Times* in Boston, *The Midnight Cry* in New York, the *Philadelphia Alarm* and others were soon spreading the new gospel.

The number of Miller's followers at the height of the movement has been variously estimated at from 50,000 to 1,000,000, the former number being perhaps more nearly correct. At first there was no attempt to gather them into a single organization, and most of them retained their membership in their respective churches. But as the "craze" increased, and as preachers of less sanity began to advocate the new doctrine, clashes between them and the orthodox naturally resulted. Excitement grew as the time approached for the supposed end of the world. Great meetings were held in churches, tents, public buildings, and in the fields and groves, and finally when the year 1843 dawned the emotions of the believers were of white heat. In some instances insanity resulted, while under the stress of their emotions people fell to the floor and professed seeing visions and hearing heavenly voices. With the coming of the eventful year Miller thus addressed his followers:

> This year . . . O glorious year! the trump of jubilee will be blown, the exiled children will return, the pilgrims reach their home, from earth and heaven the scattered remnants come and meet in the middle air . . . fathers before the flood, Noah and his sons—Abraham and his, the Jew and the Gentile,—This year! the long looked-for year of years! the best! it has come!

As March 21 dawned people in many places went out into the open fields or climbed to hilltops to await the coming of the Lord, but the day passed and nothing unusual occurred. Then Miller reminded his followers that he had never definitely fixed the exact day, but it might occur any time within the next year. The awful day was surely coming, and for another year the believers waited in nervous suspense. But the year passed and March 21, 1844, came, but still things went along as usual. Miller was now almost prostrated with disappointment and dis-may at the failure of his careful calculations. But some of his followers revised the figures and fixed another date, in the fall of the same year, for the coming of the Lord, and again there was excitement and prepara-tion among the believers; stores were closed, homes were broken up, while the minds of the most credulous gave way, and even murders were committed under the excitement. Again the new day of prophecy dawned, October 22, 1844. Some people sought the graveyards as an ap-propriate place from which to ascend; others climbed to the housetops; some arrayed themselves in their best clothes, but it was all to no avail; Christ did not appear in the clouds and the day passed.

This ended the prophecy of the exact day, but still the leaders did not give up their belief in the eventual second coming. But the old authority was gone, and with it went the old accord. In 1845 a loose organization was perfected of all Adventists but in 1846 the Seventh Day Adventists separated from the main body on the question of the observance of the Jewish Sabbath; in 1861 the Advent Christian Association was organized, separating over the question of immortality of the soul, while other divi-sions came in 1864 with the formation of the Life and Advents Union; in 1866, the Church of God was formed and in 1888 a number of small adventist bodies organized an association called the Churches of God in Jesus Christ.

VIII

In this era of religious chaos the rise of spiritualism must not be over-looked. In 1855 it was claimed that there were nearly two million people who were believers in spiritualism in the United States. As early as 1837 spiritualistic phenomena began in the several Shaker communities but the occurrences which created the greatest stir in the country began in a little house in western New York in 1847, not far from Palmyra where the Book of Mormon was first printed. The Fox sisters, Margaret and Kate, lived in this house with their parents; and in the above year they began to be disturbed by rapping noises, which were discovered to be directed by some intelligence. Within two years the Fox sisters had suc-ceeded in convincing Horace Greeley and other leaders that there was "something in it" and spiritualism was not six years old when a petition was presented to Congress signed by 15,000 signatures, most of them of educated people, asking for a Federal investigation of the spiritualists' claims. About this time one of the sisters confessed to a committee of physicians that the raps had been produced by "cracking the joints" of the knees. But other such phenomena occurring at different places over the country could not be accounted for by fraud, and table-tipping, rappings, and automatic writing continued to attract the attention not only of the ignorant and credulous, but of such men and women as Bancroft, Cooper, Bryant, N. P. Willis, Poe, Theodore Parker and Harriet Beecher Stowe. In 1857 a list of sixty-seven books and magazines on spiritualism were listed in the *Practical Christian* and belief in spiritualism was undoubtedly widespread throughout the country. The chief apostle and clairvoyant was Andrew Jackson Davis, while Robert Dale Owen and many original communists, phrenologists and mesmerists and innovators of one kind or another came into the spiritualist associations.

IX

Of the communistic experiments with which this period is crowded only three can be briefly mentioned: the Rappite Community, first at New Harmony, Indiana, and later removed to Economy, Pennsylvania, the Oneida Community under the leadership of John Humphrey Noyes; and the Brook Farm Community made up of New England transcendentalists. George Rapp, a native of Würtemberg, was the founder of the New Harmony community, on the lower Wabash in Indiana, in the year 1814. Rapp, a peasant farmer of strong character became the leader of a group of Pietists who refused to remain within the state church and for that reason were subject to persecution. Because of this he and some three hundred of his followers determined to seek a land where they could enjoy religious freedom. The Rappites began their migration to America in 1803, settling first in western Pennsylvania. Here within a few years they established a prosperous community and were raising large crops of corn, wheat, oats, potatoes, flax and hemp and other products. But the community was twelve miles from a navigable stream and the country was not suited to fruit raising. For these reasons and also because they desired a warmer climate they removed to the lower Wabash. Here they founded New Harmony, which soon became the largest town in Indiana Territory. Soon the Rappite fertile fields were yielding abundant crops; log, frame and brick buildings were erected;

and orchards and vineyards planted. Everybody worked. An entire block was given over to manufacturing purposes, and here were woolen, grist and sawmills; and soon great flatboats of Rappite products were floating down the great river to New Orleans and other markets. New Harmony "became a garden of neatness" with its gable-roofed buildings and vine-covered hills, its stately church and fruitful orchards.

Nor was the life of the Rappites out of harmony with the beauty and neatness of their community. Simplicity, neighborly love, self-sacrifice, prayer and worship, with their regular and persevering labor made up their lives. Father Rapp required confession to him of all transgression, nor were quarrels allowed to remain uncompromised. Regular religious services were conducted on Sunday and on Thursday, and four religious holidays observed throughout the year. Celibacy was practiced by all in the community and even hostile critics have found nothing to indicate any irregularities.

Because of the prevalence of malaria in the Wabash valley the Rappites sold out their large holdings in 1824 to Robert Owen, the English social reformer, for $150,000 and moved to the banks of the Ohio, 17 miles below Pittsburgh. The new community was called Economy. Here a prosperous town was soon established, duplicating what had already been done at New Harmony. In 1827 there were 522 members in the community; in 1844 it had dwindled to 385. Some years since, when only 3 members remained, a Pittsburgh syndicate purchased the town and all it contained for several millions of dollars.

Equally successful economically, but far different in respect to the relation of the sexes, was the Oneida Community established in 1847 by John Humphrey Noyes. Noyes, a graduate of Dartmouth College, studied for the ministry at both Andover and Yale. Previous to his entering college he had come under the influence of the great evangelist, Charles G. Finney, and had professed conversion. While at Yale he made a profession of perfection, and because of his peculiar doctrines was asked to leave the school and his license to preach was revoked by the New Haven Association. He soon became a leader of a movement in which perfectionism was the central doctrine. Indeed, at this period perfectionists were many, especially in those regions over which numerous revival waves had passed, which as has been noted was particularly true of central and western New York. Noyes finally came to hold that direct divine guidance was above Scripture and that true Christians are not subject to sin. As might be expected, such teachings soon led to the wildest excesses on the part of many who accepted these views. For a period of about ten years (1836-1847) Noyes was gradually gathering together a group of people at Putney, Vermont, into a community, which he called a "Bible School," where he taught an entirely new ethical and doctrinal system. The basis of this new system was sexual promiscuity. The new society which he hoped to establish was to have everything in common including a community of women.

In 1848 this system was put into operation at Oneida, New York, where for thirty years he and his followers followed the practice of "complex marriage." In 1879, the practice was given up, because of aroused public opinion. Economically the community was a success, based largely on the manufacturing of traps for the catching of fur-bearing animals. When a visitor suggested that the making of traps for the killing of animals was a strange way to bring in a "terrestrial kingdom of heaven" he was told by a communist that the earth was under a curse of which vermin are a consequence and that by destroying them they were helping to bring nearer that time when the earth might be perfect. Soon other manufacturing was going on, such as silk-making machinery, traveling bags, sewing and embroidery silks, hardware, and eventually the famous Community silver. When in 1881 the community was transformed into a stock company an issue of $600,000 was made.

The best known of all the community experiments in the United States, and one of the most dismal failures, was that at Brook Farm in eastern Massachusetts. This was an outgrowth of a schism which took place in American Unitarianism in 1832 when Ralph Waldo Emerson, then the pastor of Second Church in Boston, preached a sermon in which he proposed a radical change in the observance of the Lord's Supper. When the church refused to agree to this proposed change, Emerson resigned and retired "to his literary seclusion at Concord" where he brought forth books and pamphlets in which he set forth his objections to all fixed forms of belief and rejected all restrictions upon the freedom of intellectual action. Soon Emerson became the intellectual leader in a group of New England Unitarians who became known as Transcendentalists. A Transcendental Club was formed in Boston in 1836, made up of a group of brilliant idealists, such as James Freeman Clark, A. Bronson Alcott, Margaret Fuller, Elizabeth Peabody and Theodore Parker. This group formed the Brook Farm Association in 1841 for the purpose of bringing cultivated and thoughtful people together, and a farm was purchased where speculation was to be put into practice. But the members proved far better speculators than farmers, and after seven years the experiment came to an unhappy end and the farm was sold.

X

The chief revival movements of these years may be appropriately gathered about the name of Charles G. Finney.[3] Finney was a New Englander born in Connecticut, but brought up in the "burnt-over" district in western New York. While still a young man he revolted against the strict Calvinism of the Presbyterians, and soon after his quiet conversion in 1820 resolved to preach a gospel of "free and full salvation." Largely self-taught, Finney's admission to the ministry was opposed by some of the members of the presbytery, but in 1824 he was finally licensed to preach and from this time until his death he was a flaming evangelist. Beginning his ministry in Jefferson County, New York, he began to preach a type of gospel that aroused the whole community and soon brought down upon him the censures of his brethren in the ministry. Very soon he gave up a settled ministry and began to hold meetings in various sections of the country; in New York State, Pennsylvania, Ohio and throughout New England. His most remarkable revivals were those in Rochester, New York, where in the thirties, forties and fifties great campaigns were conducted and nearly three thousand converts were secured. Boston and New York City were also favorite areas for his activity, while campaigns were conducted in Scotland and England. In 1834 Broadway Tabernacle was built in New York, with the understanding that Finney was to be the pastor, but the next year he was called to the new school organized in Oberlin, Ohio, and later became its president. Here he divided his time between the college and revival campaigns throughout the country.

Finney's doctrine and revival methods were not long in arousing opposition, and the more staid Presbyterians and Congregationalists determined to curtail his activities. Dr. Lyman Beecher was particularly active in his opposition to Finney and his type of revivalism, but Finney went on to the end. After 1843 Finney, during a revival at Oberlin, began

3For an account of the Finney revival methods and the opposition they aroused see Sidney E. Mead, *Nathaniel William Taylor, 1786-1858: A Connecticut Liberal* (Chicago, 1942), pp 203-210.

to advocate a doctrine of Christian perfection, denying, however, that there was any relationship between his doctrine and that of Noyes. Thus from its beginning Oberlin became widely known as a revival center, while in many instances reform movements of one kind or another followed in the wake of the revivals. It is significant that in those regions where the revivals had been most successful, the temperance and anti-slavery movements found largest support.

Many of these strange religious movements were the unhealthy offspring of the revivals of the thirties, forties and fifties. But along with the rise of Mormonism, Adventism, perfectionism and all the other "isms," the great Protestant churches were adding tens of thousands of sane Christians to their membership, were busily planting new churches in the ever advancing frontiers, founding colleges, expanding their missionary work to the Indians, especially in the Northwest, while their mission work beyond the seas was receiving increasing attention.

CHAPTER XVIII

✦ ✦ ✦

SLAVERY CONTROVERSY AND SCHISMS

NOWHERE else in the world has Negro slavery exercised such a large influence upon the Christian Church as in the United States. All of the great American churches grew up in more or less intimate contact with the institution of slavery and all of them were of necessity greatly affected by it. The most important of the many schisms which have occurred among the American churches were those growing out of Negro slavery, while some of the most difficult problems facing the churches today are due to the Negro and the bitter conflicts which have arisen in the churches because of him.

Indian slavery early arose in New England and grew out of the ordinary course of the Indian wars. The sanctioning of Indian slavery led to a ready sanction of Negro slavery. The New England Calvinist considered that he was God's elect and that to him God had given the heathen for an inheritance, and by enslaving the Indians and trading them for Negroes he was doing nothing more than entering into his heritage. As long as this type of theology prevailed in New England, the New England churches could not be expected to raise any protest against the institution. And it is a significant fact that it was not until their Calvinism was radically modified that New England's oppositon to slavery began. Many of the most influential Congregational ministers were slave owners, as were John Davenport of New Haven, Ezra Styles, president of Yale, and even Jonathan Edwards. It is also true that Congregational ministers were early interested in the conversion of slaves, as was Cotton Mather, and several of the New England churches had Negro members and gave instruction to them, but there was no settled policy developed nor organized work among them.

As is well known, New England and especially Rhode Island became the center of the slave trade during the eighteenth century. The first English slave voyage was that of John Hawkins in 1562, when this famous English captain secured a cargo of slaves on the west coast of Africa and sold them to the Spanish colonies in the West Indies, then the only slave market. About a hundred years later (1672) the Royal African Company was organized, with the Duke of York at its head, which eventually came to trade primarily in slaves. For twenty-five years this company had a monopoly of the trade and prospered greatly, but after 1697 private traders were permitted to share in the trade of the Guinea coast by paying the company a percentage on the value of its cargoes. It was during this period that the New England slave trade arose and by the middle of the eighteenth century the company was driven out of existence by the private traders. Hand in hand with the New England slave trade went rum-making, for the best article of trade on the African coast was rum. By 1730 Rhode Island alone was sending eighteen or more vessels each year to Africa to trade in slaves, carrying at least eighteen hundred hogsheads of rum. The most respected of New England's citizens invested in the early slave voyages; the well-known Boston merchant, Peter Faneuil, owning an interest in the famous slave ship *Jolly Bachelor*. The ethics of the slave trade are well illustrated by the following instructions of the notorious privateer, Peter Potter: "Make ye Cheaf Trade with the Blacks and Little or none with the White people if possible to be avoided. Worter ye Rum as much as possible and sell as much by the short measure as you can. Also order them in the Bots to worter thear Rum, as the proof will Rise by the Rum standing in ye Son."

Slaves, though never numerous in New England, were to be found in every New England colony. Massachusetts had the largest number, there being nearly six thousand at the opening of the Revolution while Connecticut had almost as many. The most effective influence in colonial New England against slavery and especially the slave trade was that exercised by Dr. Samuel Hopkins, who became the minister of the First Congregational Church at Newport, Rhode Island, in 1769. Although he had himself been a slaveholder, what he saw in Newport soon made him a bitter foe of the institution and he began preaching against the evils of the slave trade. He saw the so-called best people, his friends, the wealthiest men in the town engaged in the slave trade, and he determined, no matter what it might cost him, to obey his conscience and denounce the whole slave business. In 1770 he preached a sermon against kidnaping, purchasing and retaining slaves. The people of Newport were astonished and one wealthy family left the church, but most of his members were surprised that they had not long before seen the evil of the system. Hopkins went from house to house urging people to free their slaves, while his antislavery influence was soon widespread throughout New England. His most influential antislavery publication appeared in 1776, called "Dialogue Concerning the Slavery of the Africans," while the same year he published an address to slave owners. Opposition to slavery became common among Congregational ministers in the period of the Revolution and their influence was almost unanimously exerted in the direction of emancipation, and they were undoubtedly a large factor in bringing about the emancipation acts which were passed by the New England and middle states, during and immediately following the war.

The only colonial church which had a definite program as far as religious work among slaves and other Negroes was concerned was the Anglican. This work was carried on by the Society for the Propagation of the Gospel, which from its organization (1701) looked upon "the instruction and conversion of the Negroes as a principal branch of their care; esteeming it a great reproach to the Christian name, that so many thousands of persons should continue [pagans] under a Christian government and living in Christian families as they lay before under, in their own heathen countries." Although the Established Church was the most active in work among the slaves, nowhere do we find it denouncing the institution itself. The Scotch-Irish Presbyterians were largely nonslaveholders in the colonial period, largely because of their location and economic condition. Some of their preachers, however, such as Samuel Davies, preached to the Negroes in Virginia. The early Baptists likewise did not generally belong to the slaveholding class and therefore had little intimate contact with the institution.

The largest antislavery influence wielded by any religious body in the colonial period was that exerted by the Quakers. Protests against both the slave trade and the holding of slaves began in the latter seventeenth century and continued until the institution was completely outlawed in every Friends' Yearly Meeting in the United States. George Fox in his visit to America in 1671-1672 urged slaveholders to "deal mildly and gently with their negroes, and not use cruelty toward them . . . and

that after certain years of servitude they would make them free." Slavery
was recognized by the charter of Pennsylvania, yet there were provisions in the charter that slaves should be freed under certain conditions after fourteen years of service. From the beginning the question
of slavery was discussed in the Friends' meetings, but the matter was
handled very cautiously. The most aggressive in its antislavery position
was the Quarterly Meeting of Chester, Pennsylvania, where as early as
1711 a minute was passed discouraging the enslavement of any more
Negroes. Year by year from this time on the Chester Quarterly Meeting
and the Philadelphia Yearly Meeting discussed the question, particularly of buying and selling slaves. Indeed, it was not until after the
middle of the century that the matter of holding slaves began to be
seriously considered, and this forward step was largely due to the agitation carried on by several individuals, among them Benjamin Lay,
William Southby, Ralph Sandaford, but particularly Anthony Benezet
and John Woolman.

Anthony Benezet, the son of a Huguenot refugee, came to Philadelphia as a teacher and about 1750 became especially interested in the
cause of the slave. His significance in the antislavery agitation among
the Quakers is that he used every form of publication, such as newspapers, almanacs, pamphlets and books, to spread his ideas. Clarkson,
the great English antislavery apostle, states that his interest in the cause
of the slave was first aroused by reading one of Benezet's booklets. But
the greatest of all the Quaker antislavery advocates and the one chiefly
responsible for the final disappearance of slavery from among the American Quakers was John Woolman. After 1743 Woolman gave his time as
an itinerant preacher among the Quakers, visiting Friends' meetings in
every section of the colonies, urging upon them the iniquity of slave-
keeping. He also wrote an influential tract called "Considerations on
Keeping Negroes Recommended to the Professors of Christianity of
every Denomination," while he has left in his *Journal* one of the most
beautiful and simple revelations of a great human soul.

The Philadelphia Yearly Meeting between 1758 and 1776, by a series
of regulations passed from year to year, provided for the complete elimi-
nation of slaveholding. In 1775 the Yearly Meeting directed that "such
members as continued to hold slaves be testified against as other trans-
gressors are by the Rules of our Discipline of other immoral, unjust and

reproachful conduct," which meant exclusion of slaveholders from the society. In the other Yearly Meetings similar action was taken in the years following: in the New England Yearly Meeting in 1783; the New York in 1784; while the Maryland, the Virginia and the North Carolina Yearly Meetings had completed the work by 1787. The work of freeing the slaves met many handicaps in the southern Yearly Meetings. In North Carolina a law was enacted by the state legislature forbidding the manumission of slaves "except for meritorious services" which were to be adjudged and allowed by the court. Acting under this law forty slaves which had been freed by the Quakers were seized and sold. The Friends took the case to court and finally won their case on the ground that the law under which the freed negroes had been seized was ex post facto. The antislavery action in the Yearly Meetings led to a large migration of southern Friends to Ohio, Indiana and Illinois, especially from Virginia and North Carolina.

II

During the latter eighteenth century two forces were at work, among English-speaking people particularly, which were to exercise large influence in affecting public opinion in regard to the institution of slavery. One such influence was the great humanitarian impulse which grew largely out of the evangelical revival and resulted in such enterprises as the founding of the colony of Georgia for debtors, in the prison reform movement, and in the amelioration of the penal code. As a whole, people were becoming more sympathetic and humanitarian in their attitude toward the unfortunate and the downtrodden. This was the chief influence back of the crusade led by Thomas Clarkson and William Wilberforce in England against the slave trade, which eventually resulted in the abolition of slavery throughout British dominions. A second influence was the diffusion of liberal ideas, which constituted the philosophy of the American Revolution. Such statements as that all men are created equal, and that all have a right to life, liberty and the pursuit of happiness, and that "all men are by nature free and independent," were commonly made and believed, and found expression in the Declaration of Independence and the Virginia Declaration of Rights. These ideas were propounded not only by the French political philosophers of the eighteenth century, but by such English leaders as John

Wesley, Adam Smith in his *Wealth of Nations*, by Edmund Burke, Charles James Fox and William Pitt; while in America they were proclaimed and believed by all the Revolutionary leaders.

Under such influences the first antislavery society was formed in America, the Philadelphia Society (1775), of which Franklin was the first president; all the states north of Delaware and Maryland provided for the immediate or gradual abolition of slavery; the antislavery clause was written into the Ordinance of 1787, while the southern states prohibited the further importation of slaves from Africa. Indeed, at the close of the War for Independence the leadership of the new nation was practically a unit in its opposition to the institution of slavery. Jefferson, though a large slaveholder, denounced slavery as endangering the very principle of liberty on which the nation was founded. Patrick Henry declared: "I will not, I cannot justify it! I believe a time will come when an opportunity will be offered to abolish this lamentable evil," while Washington wrote in 1786 that it was one of his chief desires that some plan might be devised "by which slavery may be abolished by slow, sure and imperceptible degrees."

This widespread antislavery sentiment also found expression in the formation of numerous antislavery societies, especially in the border states, as Kentucky, Tennessee, Ohio, Maryland and North Carolina, which were supported in many instances by slaveholders themselves. Indeed, these early societies were to be found in every state of the Union except New England, a few of the extreme southern states and Indiana. A national organization was formed in 1794 called "The American Convention of Delegates from Abolition Societies," which after 1818 became the "American Convention for Promoting the Abolition of Slavery and Improving the Condition of the African Race." In the conventions half of the delegates came from southern states lying nearest the border. Every phase of the slavery question was freely discussed in the societies, while they were active in supporting antislavery publications and addressing petitions to state legislatures and to Congress.

As might be expected, during this period in which antislavery opinion was commonly held throughout the nation the American churches were likewise active in passing strong antislavery resolutions, and in some cases even made the attempt, though unsuccessful in most instances, to rid their churches of slaveholding members. From the Revolutionary period onward both Methodists and Baptists were particularly active in carrying on religious work among Negroes and in 1795 there were 17,644 negro Baptists in the states south of Maryland, while in 1800 there were 15,688 negro Methodists throughout the country.

At the Christmas Conference in 1784 when the Methodist Episcopal Church was formed, a rule was adopted providing that every slave-holding member must within a year execute a legal instrument agreeing to free his slaves, while the preachers were required to keep a record of all transactions in their circuits. All members were required to comply with this ruling within a year or withdraw from the church. This was the most extreme antislavery legislation enacted by the Methodist Epis-copal Church until the outbreak of the Civil War. It was soon found, however, to be too extreme, for in less than six months it was necessary to suspend the rule. The following year (1785) Bishop Coke, because of his antislavery utterances, almost met physical violence in Virginia, and Asbury soon learned, to his sorrow, that any mention in the South of antislavery views might lead to evil consequences for the church. In 1796 a new rule was adopted and an attempt made to restrict slavery within the church. It provided that official members must agree to eman-cipate their slaves, while slave sellers were to be expelled. Preachers were to surrender their positions at once if they refused to free their slaves where it was legal to do so. Under these provisions there is evidence that a considerable number of slaves were emancipated, but year by year it became increasingly difficult to carry out its provisions, especially after the southern states, one by one, passed legislation prohibiting their emancipation.

In 1789 the General Committee of Virginia Baptists, representing all the Baptist churches in the state, passed a resolution declaring that "slavery is a violent deprivation of the rights of nature and inconsistent with a republican government and therefore recommend it to our brethren to make use of every legal means to extirpate this horrid evil from the land." The same year the Philadelphia Baptist Association gave its endorsement to societies working for abolition of slaves and recommended that Baptist churches form societies of their own. But perhaps the most active antislavery sentiment in this early period was to be found among the Baptists of Kentucky and a little later in Illinois. From the beginning the most influential leaders in Kentucky neither desired nor expected slavery to continue long in their state and among these early antislavery leaders were several Presbyterian, Methodist and

Baptist preachers. In the Constitutional Convention of 1792, of the six ministerial members who voted against slavery three were Baptists. The slavery issue was also early introduced into the Baptist associations, and in 1807 an antislavery association was formed, called the Friends of Humanity Association, which adopted a set of antislavery regulations, known as Tarrant's Rules, rigidly excluding all slaveholders from their churches.

A much larger antislavery movement among Baptists was that in Illinois, organized under the guidance of James Lemen who claimed that Thomas Jefferson had financed his removal from Virginia to Illinois to help in the antislavery struggle. Eventually several Friends to Humanity Associations were formed in Illinois and Missouri and the Baptists played a considerable part in the critical slavery controversy in Illinois before 1818, and also a few years later when the slavery issue was again before the people of the state.

The Presbyterians, like the Methodists, and Baptists went on record during this first period of general antislavery agitation, against the institution of slavery. As early as 1787 the Synod of New York and Philadelphia passed resolutions approving the "general principles in favor of universal liberty, that prevail in America; and of the interest which many of the states have in promoting the abolition of slavery" and recommending that slaveholding members give their slaves "such education as may prepare them for the better enjoyment of freedom." The resolution on slavery passed by the General Assembly in 1818 takes the strongest antislavery position of any Presbyterian declaration. Members are urged to use "honest, earnest and unwearied endeavors to correct the errors of former times, and as speedily as possible to efface this blot on our holy religion, and to obtain the complete abolition of slavery **throughout Christendom, and if possible throughout the world.**"

Great importance has been attached to the unanimity with which, in 1818, the General Assembly of the Presbyterian Church adopted the above antislavery resolutions. Recent researches, however, have made clear that these resolutions do not reflect the views of the majority of the members. It is now known that the friends of slavery came to the Assembly with one fixed purpose, and that was to effect the deposition from the ministry of George Bourne. Bourne was an indefatigable antislavery advocate who had exasperated his opponents by his persistent condemnation of the institution of slavery. This finally led to his expulsion from the ministry by his presbytery. His case had been in process for more than three years, and was now before the Assembly for final action. The Assembly affirmed his deposition and the proslavery members felt that they had won a great victory. The passage of the strong antislavery resolutions came on the last day of the session, after many of the members had already left. Since the "slaveites" had accomplished their design in expelling the obnoxious Bourne, they were now willing to let the antislavery resolutions pass with the nominal sanction of the whole Presbyterian Church. In other words the Assembly was definitely proslavery when it expelled Bourne from the ministry, and nominally antislavery on the last day of the session. These facts raise a large question as to the sincerity and real significance of the Resolutions of 1818.[1]

An organization which had the hearty endorsement of the churches from its organization in 1816 was "The American Society for the Colonization of the Free People of Color of the United States." The immediate plan of this organization was to carry the free Negroes out of the country and colonize them in Africa. But it was generally thought that the net influence of colonization would be in the direction of the ultimate abolition of the institution of slavery. Interest in this movement was large, particularly between 1820 and 1830, when the first settlement was made in Liberia, and this society absorbed most of the public interest in the Negro whether slave or free and was one of the causes which accounts for the dying out of the early abolition societies.

By 1830 the first period of antislavery agitation had come to an end, and a new and more aggressive movement was about to begin. The antislavery sentiment in the churches was now quiescent and their voice was no longer heard in protest. This first antislavery movement had been largely negative. Its leaders were, no doubt, sincere in their desire to promote the ultimate abolition of slavery, but to most of them abolition was a theory to be held rather than a fact to be accomplished. Thus slaveowners could and did belong to these early antislavery societies, while slaveowning church members were found willing to vote for resolutions calling for the abolition of slavery.

[1]These facts were brought out in a paper by Dr. J. W. Christie read before the American Society of Church History in Cleveland, Ohio, in December, 1947. See George Bourne, *Picture of Slavery in the United States,* and the *Minutes of the Assembly* for 1818.

III

The passing of the first phase of the antislavery movement was due, first, to the revolution in southern agriculture which was taking place between 1790 and 1830. The rise of a new cotton market in England, due to the invention of spinning and weaving machinery, and the opening of new markets for cotton cloth in India and China, created an increased demand for cotton, while Whitney's cotton gin (1792) made possible the profitable growing of the short staple cotton in the upland South. A few figures showing the rapid increase in southern cotton production will tell the story. Between 1791 and 1795, 5,200,000 pounds of cotton was produced; between 1826 and 1830, 307,244,400 pounds; in 1820 cotton constituted 22 per cent of the nation's exports, in 1860, 57 per cent. In 1790 good Negroes might be purchased for $300; the same Negro in 1830 would bring $1,200, and in 1860 $1,500 to $2,000. In other words, slavery was vastly more important economically both to the South and to the nation as a whole between 1830 and 1860 than it was between 1775 and 1830. Cotton had become king: the most important American product; it made up more than half of our exports; and by 1830 southern leaders were convinced that the welfare of the nation depended upon cotton culture.

A second factor which brought a change in the whole slavery situation in America was the rise of a new and aggressive antislavery leadership, especially in New England and in those sections which had been settled by New England people. Under the lash of such extreme abolition propagandists as William Lloyd Garrison with his *Liberator*; of Wendell Phillips with his eloquent appeal for the downtrodden slave; of John G. Whittier and his numerous antislavery poems, and many others who joined in the new crusade, thousands of converts were soon made to the new gospel of freedom. This new gospel of abolitionism was very different from the older negative antislavery doctrine and called for immediate action. Once more antislavery societies were numerously formed, and in 1833 the American Anti-Slavery Society was organized. In contrast to the older antislavery societies, these new organizations were to be found most numerously in New England and the central states, and were also numerous and active in northern Ohio and southern Michigan. Thus at the very time the institution of slavery was becoming more important to the economic life of the South, a bold and aggressive abolition movement began in the North. With this background we are prepared to understand the conflict over slavery which now began in the great democratic churches and which eventually brought schism and bitterness.

The new antislavery movement found ready support among church people, and it was not long until the question of slavery became a church issue of prime importance. The antislavery societies at their meetings took frequent action regarding the relation of the churches to the antislavery movement. In 1837 the New England Anti-Slavery Society passed a resolution urging the necessity "of excommunication of slaveholders, and a solemn consideration of the question whether the churches remaining obdurate, it is not the duty of the advocates of truth and righteousness to come out from among them and be separate." Two years later at the national antislavery convention it was decided to push the slave question in the churches, to abolitionize them if possible, and if not successful to secede from them. Soon antislavery societies sprang up in the churches, and champions of the cause came forward, while Baptist associations and Methodist conferences and other religious bodies, particularly in New England, began to pass strong antislavery resolutions. Thus the Maine Baptist Association declared in 1836: "Of all the systems of iniquity that ever cursed the world, the slave system is the most abominable." In 1853 both the New England and the New Hampshire conferences of the Methodist Episcopal Church formed antislavery societies, while such ministers as Orange Scott and LeRoy Sunderland were tireless in their antislavery agitation.

This radical antislavery agitation in the churches in the North was met by proslavery defenders in the South. The southern ministers were not long in finding arguments based on the Scriptures which confirmed them in their proslavery position. Thus the clergy at Richmond, Virginia, passed resolutions deprecating the unwarrantable and highly improper interference of the people of any other state with the domestic relations of master and slaves, and they quoted the example of Christ and his apostles in not interfering with the question of slavery as one which should be followed by all ministers of the gospel. Ministers of such prominence as Dr. Furman (Baptist) of South Carolina in 1833 proclaimed that "the right of holding slaves is clearly established in the Holy Scriptures both by precept and example" while similar views were widely held by southern ministers of all denominations.

A phase of the antislavery movement, hitherto little known, was presented in 1933 by Gilbert H. Barnes in his *The anti-Slavery Impulse*, which throws much new light, especially on the relation of the churches to the movement. The extremes to which Garrisonian abolitionism went in its "rancorous denunciations and brawling ferocious abuse" lost the support of large sections of the northern church people. This led Garrison and his cohorts to denounce the preachers as black-hearted traitors, and the antislavery society which Garrison had been chiefly instrumental in forming was rapidly losing its members and influence among church people. While this was going on in the Northeast where Garrisonian abolitionism had arisen, a new antislavery movement was arising in the central states, centering in Ohio. The leader of this movement was Theodore Dwight Weld, one of Charles G. Finney's converts and a graduate of Hamilton College (Oneida Institute), who, after his conversion, devoted himself to the promotion of temperance and other reforms. When Lane Theological Seminary opened in 1832 under the presidency of Lyman Beecher, Weld was one of the students. In fact, a good share of the first students at Lane Seminary were Finney converts. Lewis Tappan, a wealthy New York importer and a devout supporter of good causes, was the largest benefactor of Lane Seminary. He was an ardent antislavery advocate, and was anxious that the students at Lane Seminary be won over to that cause. Weld was commissioned by Tappan to undertake that work. So persuasive was Weld that in a relatively short time practically the entire student body, which included a number of southerners, was won over to abolitionism. The students were now bent on putting their abolitionist views into immediate practice by attempts to elevate the blacks of Cincinnati. This resulted in the mingling of the Lane students with the colored population, and it was not long until ugly rumors were afloat.

In the absence of the president, Lyman Beecher, who was in the East attending the meetings of the numerous benevolent societies, the trustees of the seminary attempted to handle the matter. Resolutions were passed abolishing the students' antislavery society and outlawing any further discussion of the slavery question. This eventually led more than fifty of the students to withdraw from the seminary with two of their professors. After carrying on for a time in a rented house in Cincinnati, secured for them by a young lawyer, Salmon P. Chase, the majority eventually transferred (spring of 1835) to Oberlin College, then just getting a feeble start. The students agreed to come to Oberlin on condition that Charles G. Finney be invited to become professor of theology. Asa Mahan, the only Lane trustee to stand by the students, accompanied the Lane rebels, and became Oberlin's first president. Most of these young men were soon engaged in zealous antislavery activities as agents of the antislavery society, under Weld's general agency. They made the antislavery cause identical with religion and used the Finney revivalistic methods in winning converts. Their activities covered central and western New York, western Pennsylvania and Ohio. Each "converted community" became a center of contagion, the converts continuing the work through other towns and countrysides.

Mr. Barnes has shown that instead of New England being the principal center of the abolition movement, and Garrison its accepted leader, the influence exerted by Weld and the other "Lane rebels" far outweighed, at least after 1836, the older New England influence. Another of the antislavery views long held as orthodox, which Mr. Barnes has overthrown, is that the liberal groups, Unitarians and Universalists, with the Congregationalists, were responsible for sustaining the cause in New England. By a study of the membership of the antislavery conventions held in New England, he has shown that more than two-thirds of the abolitionists of New England were Methodists and Baptists, and that antislavery sentiment was strongest in the rural towns and the countryside, rather than in urban centers.

Weld and his associates worked with, and through, the churches, receiving their chief support from the New School Presbyterians. It was in the region where the Weld crusade was the most successful, in northern Ohio and southern Michigan, that the first abolitionists were elected to Congress, while the first abolition governor was Salmon P. Chase of Ohio, who, as has been noticed, was stirred by the Lane Seminary incidents.[2]

IV

It will be necessary from this place forward to trace separately the steps leading to schism in the great democratic churches. Naturally those churches were most affected by the slavery controversy which were the

[2]Gilbert H. Barnes, *The Anti-Slavery Impulse, 1830-1844* (New York, 1933). The story from the Oberlin angle has been recently told in Robert Samuel Fletcher, *A History of Oberlin College from its Foundation through the Civil War* (Oberlin, Ohio, 1943), Vol. I.

most evenly distributed throughout the nation North and South. This was particularly true of the Baptists, the Methodists and the Presbyterians. The Congregationalists were generally antislavery, but they were largely confined to the northern states with practically no slaveholding membership.

One of the fundamental principles of the Baptist denomination is the independence of the congregation, but these independent congregations may unite in certain voluntary organizations, such as associations, state conventions and missionary societies. The oldest and most prominent general Baptist organization in the United States, at the period of the slavery controversy, was the "General Convention of the Baptist Denomination in the United States for Foreign Missions." This had been formed in 1814 with headquarters in Boston but drew its support from Baptist churches throughout the country. A Baptist Home Missionary Society had also been formed in 1832, likewise supported by Baptist churches both north and south. Both societies met together triennially, and the meeting was known as the Triennial Convention.

At the meeting of the Triennial Convention in 1841, which met at Baltimore, slavery was a prominent issue and both sides were fully alive to it. At this convention certain southern associations sent up protests against the antislavery activities of their northern brethren. One such protest came from the Savannah River Association, stating that the conduct of Baptist abolitionists is "censurable and meddlesome" and demanded of their northern brethren whether "they can acknowledge these fanatics as their co-workers," while they informed the convention of the impossibility of further coöperation of Georgia Baptists unless the abolitionists on the Board of Managers of the convention were dismissed. Particularly obnoxious to the Southerners was the Rev. Elon Galusha, vice-president of the Board of Foreign Missions, who was an active abolitionist, and the southern delegates came to the meeting determined that he should be removed. This they accomplished through the coöperation of the northern moderates, and the Rev. Richard Fuller of South Carolina was named in his place. The meeting came to an end without further disturbance, for the moderates of both sections were in control, and an understanding was reached that slavery was a subject which should not be discussed by the convention. The southern delegates went home with the feeling that their views had triumphed, which was thus expressed by one of them: "And now if we of the South and they of the

North, whose sympathies are with us, shall be mild, I am satisfied that abolitionists will go down among Baptists." "All the leading men," states another southern delegate, "are sound to the core on this vexed question."

But abolitionism did not "go down among Baptists" as the southern delegates had hoped. Rather the years from 1841 to 1844, the latter the year of the next meeting of the Triennial Convention, were filled with increased antislavery agitation among northern Baptists, particularly in New England. Antislavery Baptists were growing rapidly in numbers and influence. In May, 1843, an American and Foreign Free Baptist Missionary Society was projected in Tremont Temple, Boston, where a pledge was signed by all friends of the movement promising to separate themselves "from all connection with religious societies that are supported in common with slaveholders," if the coming Triennial Convention did not take steps to throw off their partnership with slaveholders. Thus secession was threatened by northern abolitionists as well as southern radicals.

In 1844 the Triennial Convention met in Philadelphia, with 456 delegates present, only 92 of whom were from slaveholding states. But again the moderates were in control and Francis Wayland, president of Brown University, was chosen president and Dr. J. B. Taylor, of Virginia, secretary. Dr. Richard Fuller, the leader of the southern moderates, took a prominent part in the discussions on slavery and declared that he was not convinced that slavery was a sin but he regarded it as a great evil. It was the opinion of the majority that slavery did not concern the convention, and a resolution to this effect was finally.passed, which declared: "That in coöperating together as members of this convention in the work of Foreign Missions, we disclaim all sanction either expressed or implied, whether of slavery or antislavery, but as individuals we are perfectly free both to express and to promote our own views on these subjects in a Christian manner and spirit." This simply laid the whole matter on the table. The Home Missionary Society met also at Philadelphia at the same time and they too discussed slavery pro and con and came to the same conclusion and passed the same type of resolutions as did the General Convention. Thus the solution of the vexing problem was again avoided and left to the boards of the two societies finally to determine the issue.

The slavery question came up for final decision first before the Home

Board. The Georgia Baptist Convention in April, 1844, instructed its executive committee to recommend for appointment as a missionary Mr. James E. Reeves, at the same time stating that he was a slaveholder. This was intended to be a test case, the letter accompanying the applica-tion stating: "We wish his appointment so much the more as it will stop the mouths of gainsayers. . . . There are good brethren among us, who notwithstanding the transactions of your society at Philadelphia, are hard to believe that you will appoint a slaveholder a missionary, even when the funds are supplied by those who wish his appointment." A de-cision on this question was not reached by the board until October, but meanwhile the question was discussed by associations and churches, North and South. The Michigan *Christian Herald* stated: "The religious sentiment of the North and West are fast setting against the vile system of American slavery," while the Wisconsin Baptist Association pro-claimed that "The great ecclesiastical bodies and church organizations which are in communion with slavery, 'sanction and sanctify' the sum of all villainies, and present the greatest obstacle in the way of eman-cipation." Southern sentiment favored continued coöperation with the society if the board would act fairly with the South and appoint southern as readily as northern men as missionaries. When the board finally reached its decision it declared that the application to appoint Reeves introduced the subject of slavery, in direct contravention of the letter and purpose of the constitution, and they therefore were not at liberty to entertain the application of Reeves. The net result of this decision was the withdrawal of the southern associations from the old Board of Home Missions and the formation of a Board of Domestic Missions sup-ported by Baptists at the South.

Of greater importance was the decision of the Foreign Board regard-ing the question of the appointment of slaveholding missionaries. In the fall of 1844 a member of the Alabama Baptist Convention raised the question: "Is it proper for us in the South to send any more money to our brethren at the North for missionary and other benevolent purposes before the subject of slavery be rightly understood by both parties?" This question led the Alabama Convention to pass a series of resolutions, the second of which demands that the authorities in control of the bodies receiving funds from the Baptist churches state whether or not "slave-holders are eligible and entitled equally with non-slaveholders to all the privileges and immunities of their several unions." To this question the board gave answer on December 17,1844, and declared that in thirty years no slaveholder had applied to be a missionary and since the board does not send out servants it could not send out slaves. Further they state: "If, however, any one should offer himself as a missionary, having slaves, and should insist on retaining them as his property, we could not appoint him. One thing is certain, we can never be a party to any arrangement which would imply approbation of slavery."

Under the conditions prevailing such a decision could lead to nothing short of the withdrawal of the southern Baptists from participation with their northern brethren in the cause of missions, and steps looking toward separation were soon taken. The Virginia Baptist Foreign Missionary Society led the way, withdrawing from further connection with the Boston Board and recommended a southern convention, while southern churches and associations generally passed resolutions favoring this move. The convention met at Augusta, Georgia, May 8, 1845, with 377 delegates present, representing 8 slaveholding states. The following day it was resolved in the interest of "peace and harmony and in order to accomplish the greatest amount of good" to separate from their northern brethren and organize their own society. Dr. Fuller, however, stated that this action "did not divide the Baptist Church: that could not be separated, it was independent and republican, having no general head, and only associated for a general purpose." The next day a constitution was presented for the "Southern Baptist Convention," the purpose of which was to promote foreign and domestic missions. Thus did the great Baptist denomination divide over the slavery issue, and one of the great spiritual ties binding the Federal Union was broken.

In the Methodist Episcopal Church, as among the Baptists, the moderates led by the bishops, the general secretaries and editors of the official church papers, were in control during the thirties and early forties. The bishops as they traveled from conference to conference tried to discourage discussion of slavery, while two of the bishops in 1835 united in a pastoral letter to New England Methodists pointing out the evils which had already resulted from slavery discussion and warning them of even greater disasters if the discussion were continued. At the General Conference which met in Cincinnati in 1836 abolitionism was roundly condemned, when two delegates from the New Hampshire Conference attended and addressed a meeting of a local antislavery society. The address of the bishops to the church in 1836 counseled their brethren that abolitionism be not discussed and pointed out the fact that the church was opposed to radical movements. But instead of allaying discussion the action of this General Conference simply furnished ammunition for explosions in the annual and quarterly conferences. In the antislavery conferences the preachers were determined that an expression of their strong antislavery views should be placed on record, while the presiding bishops were equally determined that this should not be done. At the New England Conference in 1837 the presiding bishop was told that several petitions were to be presented bearing on the slavery question and they wished these to be referred to a committee for action. The bishop refused to hear the petitions on the ground that the General Conference had condemned abolitionism. He thus appealed to the conference:

Will you, brethren, hazard the unity of the Methodist Episcopal Church . . . by agitating those fearfully exciting topics, and that too in opposition to the solemn decision and deliberate conclusion of the General Conference? . . . Are you willing to contribute to the destruction of our beautiful and excellent form of civil and political government, after it has cost the labor, treasure and blood of our fathers to establish it? . . . I would that it [slavery] were obliterated from the earth; but in view of the terrible consequences that are likely to follow the agitation of those exciting topics, at the present I cannot consent to be participant in any sense or degree, in those measures which are advocated by modern abolitionists.

In many instances the advice of the General Conference of 1836 against abolitionism was followed, and for ten years in the Philadelphia Conference every young minister applying for admission was asked the question "Are you an abolitionist?" and if the reply was in the affirmative he was not admitted. The Ohio, Baltimore, New York, Pittsburgh, Michigan and other conferences passed resolutions expressing regret at the proceedings of abolitionists, while many abolition leaders among the preachers suffered the heavy hand of discipline because of their activities. But the struggle went on, and gradually new converts were made to the cause of abolitionism among both ministers and laymen. As the General Conference of 1840 approached, discussion as to its probable action became rife and the radicals began to hint at possible withdrawal from the church if the oppressive measures which had silenced them in the annual conferences should be continued. When the General Conference met, the great question before it was the matter of the power of a president of a quarterly or annual conference in declining to put a question or receive a petition. The conference went on record as recognizing this right to exercise gag rule, and the whole contention of the abolitionists was thus denied and the radicals seemed to be defeated at every point.

Following the General Conference of 1840 abolitionism throughout the United States, both in and out of the church, fell upon evil days. Among the Garrisonian party there was internal strife, and a new antislavery society was formed. The Methodist abolition leaders were discouraged and inactive. Sunderland had withdrawn from the church and repudiated orthodox Christianity, while Scott stated in 1842 there was no choice "but to submit pretty much to things as they are or secede." And this is exactly what took place the following year. A group of radical leaders gathered in Albany and there decided definitely to withdraw from the Methodist Episcopal Church, giving as reasons the attitude of the old church on the question of slavery, its aristocratic government, and its uncharitable attitude toward the dissenting brethren. A second meeting convened at Andover, Massachusetts, in February, 1843, and in May of the same year the Wesleyan Methodist Connection was organized at Utica, New York, with 6,000 members. The new church prohibited slavery and intoxicating liquors, provided for lay representation in the conferences and allowed conferences to elect their own presidents. Though the secession was ridiculed and its principles misrepresented, yet it had an immediate effect upon the Methodist Episcopal Church in developing and crystallizing the latent antislavery spirit in the church. The official papers became more outspoken on the question of slavery, and several Methodist conventions were held which took radical antislavery ground; all of which greatly alarmed the Methodists of the slaveholding states.

The crisis in the controversy was reached in the General Conference of 1844, when 180 delegates, representing 33 annual conferences and the best talent of the church, met in New York in May. From the beginning of the month's session slavery was the burning issue, and an appeal of a slaveholding minister, who had been suspended from the Baltimore Conference for refusing to free his slaves, brought the question to the center of the stage. Eventually, after long debate in which the whole slave issue was reviewed, the conference voted, overwhelmingly, to uphold the decision of the Baltimore Conference. This decision revealed the antislavery temper of the majority of the conference and presaged their decision on the more important question as to what was to be done with Bishop James O. Andrew of Georgia, who by a second marriage had become the possessor of a few household slaves and thus became the first Methodist slaveholding bishop.

What was to be done with a slaveholding bishop? Some of the anti slavery brethren said either let him rid himself of his slaves or resign Southern delegates stated that the bishop had violated no rule of the church; northern delegates contended that he might be tried under the general phrase "improper conduct." The Southerners claimed that the bishops were beyond any such interference as the conference contem plated; as the bishops were a coördinate body with the General Con ference. The debate lasted eleven days but was carried on in the best of temper. Compromises were proposed; delay for another four years was suggested, but all to no avail, and when finally the vote was taken on the resolution asking the bishop to desist from his episcopal labors until he should rid himself of his slaves, it was carried by a large majority, 111 yeas to 60 nays.

The conference occupied itself in the closing days of the session draw ing up a Plan of Separation, suggested by Dr. William Capers of South Carolina. A committee of nine was appointed to bring in a plan for separating the church if the southern churches found it necessary to divide. The Plan as reported and adopted provided a method of estab lishing a boundary between the parts of the church if separation was to take place; "it allowed ministers to choose without blame the church to which they would adhere;" recommended modification of the constitution to permit a division of the property of the Book Concerns, and suggested certain rules for the division and transfer of property. It was, indeed, a most generous and Christian provision, "enacted," as Norwood suggests, "in a fit of Christian generosity during the dying hours of the General Conference." Perhaps the drawing up of the Plan was a bid to the South to withdraw. At any rate the day after the General Conference adjourned the southern delegates met and there determined to call a convention of the southern churches to meet in Louisville, Kentucky, on May 1, 1845, and issued an address to the ministers and members of the southern states and territories setting forth the situation as they saw it.

The southern annual conferences one by one took favorable action on the question of the division of the church and appointed delegates to the Louisville Convention. The convention met at the appointed time and place and was completely harmonious. On the second day it voted by an overwhelming majority to separate, and then and there steps were taken to form a new church. The Plan of Separation was their Magna Charta, while the church in every respect was modeled closely after that of the Methodist Episcopal, even keeping the name Methodist Episcopal Church with "South" added.

While these steps were being taken by the southern brethren, opinion in the North was fast crystallizing in opposition to the Plan of Separation, which had been so generously offered in 1844. The very men who had urged its adoption were now demanding its repudiation. It was characterized as unconstitutional; it was urged that the South had violated the Plan, while others claimed that it was entirely unnecessary. Perhaps it was too much to expect of human nature, even among a body of Christian ministers, that they should stand by their generous proposals especially after they had been so bitterly assailed by southern partisans. Sad to relate, at the General Conference of 1848 the Methodist Episcopal Church repudiated the Plan of Separation by a large majority and refused to receive the fraternal delegate sent to them from the Methodist Episcopal Church, South.

From 1848 to the opening of the Civil War was a period of growing bitterness between the two branches of American Methodism. One cause was the border conflict, since both churches immediately made plans to retain the border, and conflicts were thus inevitable in Maryland, Kentucky, western Virginia and Missouri, where the two churches met. Misunderstanding and conflict resulted also from the attempt of the Southern Church to gain its share of the Book Concern properties. Leaders in the North took the view that they were under no obligation to divide the property and funds, and no steps were taken to satisfy the demands of the Southern Church. Finally two suits were brought in the Federal courts, one in New York involving the New York branch of the Book Concern, the other in Ohio involving the Western Book Concern at Cincinnati. The New York suit was decided in favor of the South, while the Ohio suit was decided for the North. The South appealed the Cincinnati case and it was brought before the Supreme Court of the

United States in 1854, where a unanimous decision was handed down in favor of the South. Eventually a settlement was reached and the property was divided to the satisfaction of the South.

In tracing the slavery controversy among the Presbyterians the New School body will first be considered. At the time of the schism (1837-1838) the two Presbyterian bodies were nearly equal in size, but the Old School was from the beginning in far better condition for future growth. The Old School had been granted the general property by the courts, while the New School was further weakened by the withdrawal of churches which became Congregational. The large New England element in the New School body would presage a larger interest in the antislavery cause and explains the legislation which finally brought schism in 1857.

Slavery discussion occupied much of the time of every New School General Assembly and at every session numerous petitions and memorials on slavery were presented, and there seems never to have been any attempt to stop discussion. The General Assembly of 1846 adopted by an overwhelming majority a declaration stating that they considered slavery a wrong and urging the churches to put away the evil. In 1847 there was a secession of some radical antislavery churches in Ohio which formed the Synod of the Free Presbyterian Church, but this movement developed only in the Middle West, and in 1862 when it reunited with the New School embraced five presbyteries and forty-three ministers. In 1849 the General Assembly again sternly condemned slavery and stated: "It is the duty of all Christians . . . as speedily as possible to efface this blot on our holy religion" but adds this statement, "where freeing is impossible, there are other duties of instruction and preaching to attend to." Meanwhile abolition sentiment was growing in the church and in 1853 the assembly ordered that a census be taken to determine the number of slaveholders in the church, the number of slaves held by them, to what extent the slaves are held by unavoidable necessity, and what provision is made for their religious well-being.

In seeming open defiance of the action of the Assembly of 1853 the Presbytery of Lexington, Kentucky, reported that a number of its ministers, elders and members held slaves "from principle" and "of choice," believing it to be right. Twenty-seven antislavery memorials were presented to the General Assembly of 1857 and after days of discussion the assembly adopted resolutions exhorting "all our people to eschew" such doctrines as that "slavery is an ordinance of God" and that in the United

States it is "Scriptural and right." They express pain at the action of the Presbytery of Lexington, and declare that such doctrines and practices cannot be tolerated in the Presbyterian Church. The southern delegates protested the passage of this measure, but in spite of their protest it passed by an overwhelming majority. The southern delegates then issued a call to all Presbyterians for a convention to constitute a General Assembly in which slavery would not be introduced. This movement resulted in the formation of the United Synod of the South, made up of six synods, twenty-one presbyteries and about fifteen thousand communicants.

Of greater importance, but more difficult to understand was the position taken by the Old School body in regard to the all-absorbing question of slavery. Year after year its assemblies adopted the policy of laying all memorials on slavery on the table without debate, but this policy aroused vigorous protest on the part of a growing number of antislavery advocates. In 1844 twenty memorials on slavery were presented, and at the Assembly of 1845 so large was the number of petitions and memorials that definite action on the subject was necessary. A special committee was appointed to consider these memorials and prepare a report on slavery, of which Dr. N. L. Rice was made chairman, a man characterized as the ablest "fencewalker" in the church. The report submitted to the assembly and passed by a large majority denied every demand of the antislavery delegates and virtually accepted slavery as a legitimate Christian institution, since Jesus did not denounce it. In 1849 in response to protests against its action of 1845 the General Assembly resolved "that in view of the civil and domestic nature of this institution, and the competency of our secular Legislatures alone to remove it . . . it is considered peculiarly improper and inexpedient for this General Assembly to attempt to propose measures in the work of emancipation," and thus like Pontius Pilate they washed their hands of the whole matter.

The conservative party represented by Dr. N. L. Rice determined the policy of the Old School body, as far as slavery was concerned, to the opening of the Civil War. In his letters on slavery Rice thus sets forth the position of his church:

> The Presbyterian Church has stood at an equal remove from the extremes of Abolitionism and Pro-slaveryism. She has refused to pervert God's word to make it either denounce or sanction slavery. She has regarded it as a great evil, but as an evil inherited, an evil of long standing, and so interwoven with the very texture of society, that, like a chronic disease, it must require much time,

and patience, and kind treatment, to eradicate it. She is fully persuaded, that for the evils under which mankind suffer, the Gospel is the great and only remedy. Refusing, therefore, to mingle in heterogeneous conventions, and to sanction their vague and unmeaning resolutions, she goes forward on her sublime mission, preaching the Gospel alike to master and slave, saying openly and boldly all the apostles said, and refusing to say a word more. And today she stands ready to compare notes, as to results, with her traducers.

Thus the necessity of defending its middle position drove the Old School Presbyterian Church to take a position almost if not quite proslavery. And in taking this position the Old School leaders felt that they were set apart from others, who could not see how profoundly Christian it was. They felt that their church was the last great spiritual influence binding the Union together, and pride in this fact we find expressed again and again.

As might be expected the Old School Presbyterians furnished the most able defenders of slavery on Scriptural and moral grounds. Dr. J. H. Thornwell, of South Carolina, in a sermon preached in 1850 at a dedication of a negro church, defined slavery as an obligation to labor for another determined by the providence of God. The master, he stated, has a right to the labor of the slave, but not to the man. Slavery is inconsistent with the perfect state, yet it is a natural evil which God has visited upon society. Class distinctions are an evil of the same kind, but in our world absolute equality would lead to stagnation. Though founded on a curse, slavery may not be inconsistent with the spirit of the gospel, as that spirit operates among "rebels and sinners," in a degraded world, and under a dispensation of grace. The Christian beholds in his slave, not a tool, not a chattel, not a brute or a thing, but an immortal spirit assigned to a peculiar position in this world of wretchedness and sin. Not greatly unlike Thornwell's position was that held by Dr. Charles Hodge of Princeton Theological Seminary as set forth in several articles in the *Biblical Repertory,* of which he was the editor.

There was however, considerable antislavery sentiment in the Old School church, especially in Ohio, led by Dr. E. D. MacMaster. MacMaster was the son of a minister of the Associate Reformed Presbyterian Church which had excluded slaveholders in 1831. As early as 1845 MacMaster and Rice had differed on the slavery issue and when MacMaster became a professor in the New Albany Theological Seminary (1849-1857) the seminary became involved in the dispute. The seminary was finally moved to Chicago where it took the name McCormick Theological Seminary because of a gift of $100,000 by Cyrus McCormick.[3] McCormick was proslavery in his sentiment and was a member of the church in Chicago of which Dr. Rice was the minister.

The position of Alexander Campbell on the question of slavery well illustrates the changes which were taking place among southern church leaders between 1830 and 1850. Campbell had been a member of the Virginia constitutional convention of 1830 and had been one of the antislavery leaders. In 1832 he declared in his *Millennial Harbinger* that slavery was an economic evil in Virginia; in 1845 he had come to the conclusion that the relation of master and slave was not unchristian.

VI

After the great popular churches had reached a definite position on the question of slavery there was a rapid increase along all lines of church activity in both North and South. "Revivals, educational movements, and missionary zeal were the fruits of the reformation." Within ten years after the great split the Southern Baptists were as numerous as the united church had been in 1844, and contributed within the first thirteen years after the division seven times as much for home missions as they had given in the same number of years preceding. The same activity characterized the Methodists, South, and within ten years they had added a net increase of 150,000. Especially were the Southern Methodists active in work among the Indians and negroes. The old restraint in the matter of their attitude toward slavery which existed before 1844 was now completely thrown off, and the churches in both sections became aggressive and denominationally conscious, to an exaggerated degree.

While the slavery controversy was at its height the Presbyterian and Methodist churches were busy establishing the first Protestant missions in the Pacific Northwest. Attention of Christian people was drawn to the Oregon country by an appeal made to General William Clarke of St. Louis on the part of four Indian chiefs who had journeyed all the way from the Oregon country, asking that they be given the "white man's Book from Heaven." The appeal caught the imagination of the Methodists and in 1833 Jason Lee was appointed to head a mission to the Oregon country, and in September, 1834, he preached his first sermon at Fort Vancouver. Lee soon saw the larger aspects of his task and became active

[3] William T. Hutchinson, *Cyrus H. McCormick* (New York, 1930.)

in securing funds and bringing settlers to Oregon and within a period of ten years Methodism was firmly established, especially in the Wil lamette valley. The leader of Presbyterian work in the Northwest was Marcus Whitman who was sent by the American Board to the Oregon country in 1836. Near the present site of the city of Walla Walla, Whit man and his wife with one associate and his wife labored among the Indians and soon a prosperous mission was established. In 1842 Whit man made his famous ride to Boston and Washington. There has been much controversy in regard to Whitman's motives in making this long journey, crossing the Rockies in the midst of winter. Years afterward it was claimed by those closely associated with him, that he had two pur poses, one to urge upon the Federal government the necessity of doing something to save Oregon to the United States, the other to persuade the board to rescind the order closing the Oregon mission. Lee died in 1845 after he had been removed by the Methodist Board from the super intendency of the mission, and Whitman and his wife with twelve others were brutally murdered in 1847 by the Indians whom they were trying to serve, but the labor of these two pioneers was not in vain.

At the same time that Protestant missions were being established in the Northwest, the first Catholic missionaries also began their work in the region. Father DeSmet was successful in founding missions at vari ous places, especially in the Willamette valley. The Catholics were more successful in their Indian work than were the Protestants and it is claim ed that in six years six thousand Indians had embraced the Catholic faith.

VII

In August of the year 1857 a financial panic was precipitated by the failure of the Ohio Life Insurance and Trust Company, caused by over speculation and investment in railroads and mines. The panic was pri marily due to financial dislocation and affected the banks in the large cities particularly where it caused great distress. This financial panic had much to do with starting one of the most unusual revivals in the history of religious awakenings in America. It was from start to finish a lay movement and its impact was principally urban. It began sudden ly in the financial center of New York City, in an upper room in the old North Dutch Church on Fulton Street, which the janitor of the church of his own accord opened for noonday prayer meetings. At first only a few attended, but the number grew and other rooms in the same building were opened to take care of the increasing number of businessmen who wished to have a part in this modern Pentecost. By the spring of 1858 twenty daily union prayer meetings were being held in different parts of the city. The movement quickly spread to other cities, and similar meetings were held in Philadelphia and Boston and eventually every large city and town in the North experienced similar awakenings. The ministers of the evangelical churches were drawn into the movement, and preaching services were held in downtown theaters adjoining business houses. The great city newspapers gave the revival wide publicity and the meetings were reported as important news.

The Young Men's Christian Association, just getting started in the United States, played a large part in the movement. Though the revival produced no outstanding revival preachers, it was responsible for raising up an extraordinarily able group of lay leaders who were to play a prominent part in the religious life of the cities, some of whom gained national prominence. Among them were Dwight L. Moody of Chicago and John Wanamaker of Philadelphia, both of whom, in 1858, started Sunday schools of their own in their respective cities, which grew into large and flourishing institutions. Other lay leaders produced by the revival were to have the principal part in forming the numerous voluntary religious and philanthropic agencies which served the armed forces during the Civil War, such as the United States Christian Commission and the United States Sanitary Commission. It has been estimated that at least 100,000 professed conversion within 4 months after the Fulton Street prayer meeting began, and that the final total ingathering of new members into the churches throughout the country as the direct result of the revival was more than 1,000,000.

Looking backward, it is instructive for us to raise the question how the church could have passed through the decade of the sixties without the spiritual reinforceemnt that came to it amid the pentecostal scenes of 1857 and 1858.[4]

[4]L. W. Bacon, *History of American Christianity*, p. 344.

CHAPTER XIX

THE CHURCHES NORTH AND SOUTH AND
THE CIVIL WAR

IN THE last formal speech made by John C. Calhoun in the United States Senate, in the great debate over the Compromise of 1850, he stated: "The cords which bind the states together are not only many but various in character. Some are spiritual or ecclesiastical; some political, others social." Of these cords the strongest are those of a religious nature, and they have begun to snap. In the powerful Methodist Episcopal Church, "The numerous and strong ties which held it together are all broke and its unity gone." Instead of one church there are now two hostile bodies. "The next cord that snapped was that of the Baptists, one of the largest and most respectable of the denominations." That of the Presbyterians is not entirely snapped, but some of its strands have given way. The Episcopal Church "is the only one of the four great Protestant denominations which remains unbroken and entire." It was the explosive force of slavery agitation which broke these cords, and, he stated, if the agitation goes on every cord will snap, political and social as well as ecclesiastical, and then there will be nothing to hold the states together except force. The snapping of the ecclesiastical cords had undoubtedly a large influence in creating the final breach between North and South. Indeed, there are good arguments to support the claim that the split in the churches was not only the first break between the sections, but the chief cause of the final break.

The long agitation carried on in the great churches over the slavery issue prepared them to take a definite stand when the Civil War began. And no war in modern times, not even excepting the two Great Wars, received such unanimous support from the churches. Baptists, Catholics,

Methodists, Lutherans, Congregationalists, Moravians, German and Dutch Reformed, Old and New School Presbyterians vied with one another in their determination to give support to the Federal government. Only in the Protestant Episcopal and Old School Presbyterian Churches were there protests against the passage of patriotic resolutions, and in these churches the protestors represented but a small minority.

I

The General Assembly of the Old School Presbyterian Church at its session in 1861 adopted resolutions acknowledging and declaring obligation to promote and perpetuate "the integrity of these United States, and to strengthen, uphold and encourage the Federal Government in the exercise of all its functions under our noble Constitution." These resolutions were introduced by Dr. Gardiner Spring, of the Brick Presbyterian Church in New York, who throughout the slavery controversy had been on the side of the extreme conservatives and whose utterances on the slavery issue had mostly been in the form of denunciation of abolitionism. In 1862 the resolutions on the "State of the Country" were introduced in the assembly by Dr. R. J. Breckinridge, of Kentucky, and as might be expected were much more outspoken in their denunciation of disloyalty, affirming: "This whole treason, rebellion, anarchy, fraud, and violence is utterly contrary to the dictates of natural religion and morality, and is plainly condemned by the revealed will of God," while he exhorts all "who love God or fear his wrath to turn a deaf ear to all councils and suggestions that tend towards a reaction favorable to disloyalty, schism, or disturbance either in the Church or in the country."

The Methodists were particularly proud of their 100 per cent loyalty, though at the opening of the war there had been a considerable loss of members from the border conferences to the Church South. At the General Conference of 1864 held in Philadelphia a special committee was formed to prepare an address to the President of the United States and a deputation of five members was sent to bear the address to Washington. The address stated that the Methodist Church had sent thousands of its members and many of its ministers into the Union armies to maintain the cause of God and humanity, and they pledged to the President all appropriate means to suppress the cruel and wicked rebellion. To this President Lincoln made the following reply:

Gentlemen: In response to your address, allow me to attest the accuracy of its historical statements, indorse the sentiment it expresses, and thank you in the nation's name for the sure promise it gives.

Nobly sustained as the Government has been by all the Churches, I would utter nothing which might in the least appear invidious against any. Yet without this, it may fairly be said that the Methodist Episcopal Church, not less devoted than the best, is by its greater numbers the most important of all. It is no fault in others that the Methodist Episcopal Church sent more soldiers to the field, more nurses to the hospitals, and more prayers to heaven than any! God bless the Methodist Episcopal Church! Bless all the Churches! And blessed be God, who in this our trial giveth us the Churches.

(Signed) A. LINCOLN

The patriotic resolutions passed by the Ohio Baptist Convention in 1862 were typical of many others enacted by their numerous associations and conventions. They avowed it to be their right and duty as Christian citizens to tender sympathy and support to those intrusted with the government and they promised to uphold the armies "in their endeavors to crush the wicked rebellion" and to "offer up" their "prayers and supplications daily" in this behalf. They heartily approved the proclamation of the President declaring liberty to the slaves, and promised support in carrying out that proclamation "till our beloved country shall be purged of the accursed blot" which they declared to be "both the cause of the war and the chief means in our enemy's hands of carrying it on."

During the first year of the war the Church periodicals were very critical of the administration because of its failure to take immediate steps to free the slaves which fell into the hands of the Union forces. When General Frémont issued his proclamation freeing the slaves in the department of the Missouri in August, 1861, he, and General Benjamin F. Butler, who had declared the slaves within his lines contraband of war, were hailed by the church press as "the day stars to our Nation." When President Lincoln recalled Frémont's unwise order, one editor of a church paper in the Northwest states: "Never had a brave man such difficulties thrown in his path as Frémont . . . yet he has held to his way. . . . The people are incensed." It is one of the ironies of history that these two Union generals, Frémont and Butler, probably the two most incompetent and corrupt commanders of high rank in the Union army, should have received such high praise at the hands of the northern church people.

II

During the summer of 1861 delegates from the Old School synods and presbyteries in the Confederate States met in Augusta, Georgia, and there formed the Presbyterian Church in the Confederate States of America, and elected as its first moderator Benjamin M. Palmer of South Carolina, who from the beginning had been one of the most ardent and eloquent advocates of secession. In a long address setting forth the cause of their separation they declare that the only condition upon which the two churches could have remained together was "the rigorous exclusion of the questions and passions of the forum from its halls of debate." Their attitude toward slavery is thus summarized: "We venture to assert that if men had drawn their conclusions only from the Bible, it no more would have entered into any human head to denounce slavery as a sin, than to denounce monarchy, aristocracy or poverty." To the next General Assembly (1862) the committee on the State of Religion reports that Presbyterian congregations without exception in the southern states evince "the most cordial sympathy with the people of the Confederate States" to maintain their rights against the despotic power which is attempting to crush them. And they are convinced that "this struggle is not alone for civil rights, and property and home, but the religion, for the Church, for the gospel." In 1864 the United Synod of the South, which had separated from the New School in 1857, united with the Presbyterian Church in the Confederate States and thus by the end of the war southern Presbyterianism was completely united.

The Southern Baptist Convention in 1861 adopted a series of resolutions on the State of the Country, prepared by Dr. Richard Fuller, of South Carolina. After recounting the steps taken by the South in separating from the Federal Union, in which, he stated, they but desired a fair and amicable adjustment but which the government at Washington insultingly repelled, and since the United States government insists "upon letting loose hordes of armed soldiers to pillage and desolate the entire South," and since the northern churches and pastors, whom he had hoped would interpose and protest against the appeal to the sword, are "breathing out slaughter and clamoring for sanguinary hostilities," therefore be it resolved that the formation of the Confederate States of America be approved; that the Divine direction be invoked upon those who rule over them and that the Confederate States and also the Kingdom of Jesus Christ may prosper; that the President of the Confederacy and the Confederate Congress be assured of their sympathy and confidence; that every principle of religion and patriotism calls them to resist invasion; and that prayer be offered for those from their families who are in the armies "to cover their heads in the day of battle, and give victory to their arms." They would also pray for their enemies, "trusting that their pitiless purposes may be frustrated" and that blessing and prosperity may be restored under the two governments. Baptists throughout the South are called upon to observe certain fast days, and are enjoined to follow the example of Baptists during the Revolution and the War of 1812 in which they "bated no jot or heart or hope for the Redeemer's cause."

Of all the American churches none handled the delicate situation created by the war more tactfully than did the Protestant Episcopal. This was largely due to the fact that the Episcopalians had taken no stand on the slavery issue previous to the War, and had not divided into northern and southern bodies. Although there were ardent patriots on both sides among the bishops, yet there was an absence of bitterness which speaks well for their Christiantiy. After the secession of the cotton states a convention, made up of delegates from those states, was held at Montgomery, Alabama, July 3, 1861, and there it was unanimously determined that the formation of the government of the Confederate States made necessary an independent organization of the dioceses within the seceded states. After drawing up a draft of a constitution, the convention adjourned to meet in October at Columbia, South Carolina, where the Protestant Episcopal Church in the Confederate States was formed. Bishop Polk of Louisiana was the most ardent of the southern cause, and was the first to urge the necessity for a separate organization. Soon after the war opened, Bishop Polk, who had been educated at West Point, was made a major general in the Confederate army, and was killed during the course of the war.

The Protestant Episcopal Church in the United States had never recognized the withdrawal of their southern brethren, and at the General Convention of 1862 the roll call included the names of the southern dioceses. At the next convention three years later (1865), again the roll call included the southern deputies. Such courtesy and deference was shown to the southern bishops who attended the convention that their hesitation was soon overcome and thus most fortunately unity was restored to the church with the end of the war, and all traces of strife and bitterness soon vanished. This easy solution of the problem of separation was made possible by the fact that the Protestant Episcopalians had never taken sides on the slavery issue and there was therefore no prewar bitterness to overcome.

III

The need of chaplains in the army was early recognized by the War Department and at the opening of the war a general order was issued allowing to each regiment one chaplain, specifying that he must be a regularly ordained minister. Later Congress passed an act ratifying this order of the War Department. It was soon called to the attention of President Lincoln that chaplains were also needed for hospitals, and in May, 1862, Congress authorized the appointment of chaplains for each permanent hospital. The war had not progressed long, however, before complaint was made that some very unworthy men were occupying the position of chaplain. To safeguard the office Congress passed an act (July 17, 1862) requiring that only a regularly ordained minister of good standing in his denomination, who had recommendations for his appointment from an authorized ecclesiastical body or from not less than five accredited ministers belonging to his denomination, should receive appointment to the office. All the churches coöperated in providing chaplains to the army and navy; the Methodists alone furnishing nearly five hundred. Frequently a regimental church was formed which held regular services, and if the chaplain was an evangelical a long stay in camp was likely to be improved by holding a revival meeting among the soldiers. In a New York regiment a revival meeting was kept up for thirty nights in succession in a tent furnished by the commanding general and more than a hundred soldiers professed conversion. The chaplains often kept in touch with friends in the North and made appeals for literature, provisions and comforts for their men, and also acted as distributing agents of the American Bible and Tract Societies.

Religion in the Confederate armies was even more conspicuous than in the armies of the Union. Both Generals Lee and Jackson were men of strong religious conviction and gave great encouragement to the work of the chaplains among their soldiers. One Confederate officer testified that "I seldom heard an oath in the Confederate camps, and I had every opportunity, from second lieutenant to the command of the regiment. Our camps often resounded at night with hymns and spiritual songs;

arrests for drunkenness were very rare." In the years 1863-1864 a great revival swept through the army of northern Virginia and thousands Episcopalians were all active in their coöperation in religious work in the Confederate army. The Episcopalians furnished nearly a hundred chaplains, the Southern Methodists more than two hundred while Baptists, Catholics and Presbyterians sent their full quotas. The following quotation from the diary of a chaplain in the Confederate Army will give some idea of the feverish interest in religion prevailing among the southern soldiers:

May 17, 1863, 10 A.M., I preached in the Presbyterian Church: house crowded with officers and soldiers; serious attention. At three o'clock, I preached in Bates' brigade: a very good time; revival in the brigade. May 19th, I preached in Johnson's brigade: thirty to forty mourners; glorious work in this command. May 20th. I preached in General Polk's brigade: many mourners; several conversions. May 21st, I preached in General Wood's brigade: forty to fifty mourners; fifteen or twenty conversions. May 22nd, I spoke in General Riddle's brigade: a great work here; already more than one hundred conversions in this command.

IV

At the battle of Chickamauga this chaplain remained on the battle-field eleven days, "nursing the sick, ministering to the wounded, and praying for the dying. The sight was awful. Thousands of men killed and wounded. They lay thick all around, shot in every possible manner, and the wounded dying every day."

The churches coöperated in supporting a number of organizations which were working among the soldiers and sailors. Most important of these were the Christian Commission, the American Bible and Tract Societies, and the several Freedmen's Societies which came into existence during the course of the war. The Christian Commission was formed in New York in 1861 to supply comforts and supplies to the armies not furnished by the federal government. It received its support largely through the churches, and made its appeals through ministers and church papers, as the commission published no organ of its own. During the four years of the war it received more than $2,500,000 in cash, besides stores and clothing of many kinds. At the Thanksgiving Day services in 1863, $83,400 were received by the commission. Those who carried on the work of the commission in the camps and on the field were called "delegates" and were voluntary workers drawn largely from the churches. Hundreds of ministers volunteered their services to the commission for short periods of time and rendered valuable service, circulating good publications in the armies, encouraging and helping soldiers to communicate with their friends, giving aid to surgeons, and comfort to sick and dying soldiers.

The American Bible Society was particularly active during the war, distributing Testaments and Bibles in both Union and Confederate armies. In 1864 the society received $429,464.12 and distributed during the year 994,473 copies of the Bible. The Christian Commission alone distributed more than half million copies in the Union armies and navies, while 50,000 copies were sent to the Confederate army under General J.E. Johnston and 50,000 to the army under General Bragg, besides 100,000 copies sent to the Board of Colportage of North Carolina. The Tract Societies were also unusually active during the years of the war, printing and distributing among the soldiers many thousands of tracts.

V

As the war progressed and as the Union armies pushed farther and farther into the South the number of Negroes dependent upon the care and protection of military commanders increased. To care for this situation several of the commanding generals organized Departments of Negro Affairs. Among the duties of those placed in charge of this work was to take a census of the Negroes in the region, provide food, clothing and medicines where needed; see that all the able-bodied had employment, while there was an effort also to establish schools. Early in the war the attention of religious organizations in the North was called to the growing need among freedmen, and by the end of 1861 the American Missionary Association had several representatives in the field. By the beginning of 1862 Freedmen's Relief Associations began to spring up in every section of the North, from Maine to Missouri. These societies received a large share of their support through the churches, but toward the end of the war the denominations began to form their own Freedmen's Societies. Thus the United Presbyterians of Ohio formed a Freedmen's Society in 1863; while the same year the Baptists, the United Brethren and the Reformed Presbyterians formed their own societies. The Protestant Episcopalians formed a Freedmen's Aid Society at their General Convention in 1865 and the same year the Congregationalists began their large work among the Negroes and called upon their churches for a quarter of a million dollars annually. The Methodist Episcopal Church continued to coöperate with the local Freedmen's Societies until 1866 when they too formed their Freedmen's Aid society. Work among negroes soon became one of the great benevolent enterprises of the church.

VI

A phase of religious activity on the part of most of the Protestant churches of the North, which left some unfortunate consequences, was their attempt to push into the South during the progress of the war. As a natural result of war, many localities throughout the Confederacy were soon without ministers and were thus deprived of regular Christian worship. After the capture of New Orleans in 1862 more than two score churches in that city were left without ministers. In the five Methodist churches in the city there was not a single minister habitually officiating and the same condition was true of the five Presbyterian churches. In Baton Rouge, Newbern, Vicksburg, Natchez, Pensacola and Memphis and in many other places throughout the South, large and small, like conditions prevailed. This situation was soon brought to the attention of the northern church officials. The chaplains with the armies of invasion wrote numerous letters to the northern church papers describing these conditions. Sometimes the chaplains used the vacant southern churches for their services and in that case the civilian congregation was invited to attend the services with the soldiers. Under such conditions it was but natural that there should be a movement started in the North to send missionaries into the South to take over these abandoned fields.

Before such work could begin it was necessary to gain the consent of the Federal government and to secure the protection of Union commanders. As early as 1862 an order was obtained from the War Department, signed by Secretary Stanton, directing the commanding generals of the several departments in the South to place at the disposal of certain designated bishops "all houses of worship belonging to the Methodist Episcopal Church, South, in which a loyal minister, who has not been appointed by a loyal Bishop of said church does not officiate." The order further stated that the government considers it a matter of great importance in order to restore tranquillity to a community "that Christian ministers should by example and precept, support and foster the loyal sentiment of the people." The commanders were instructed to supply the bishops designated (Bishop Ames in the departments of the Missouri, the Tennessee and the Gulf) "with transportation and subsistence when it can be done without prejudice to the service" and are to afford them "courtesy, assistance and protection." Later other northern Methodist bishops were given jurisdiction over Methodist churches in other southern military departments.

In 1864 similar orders were issued concerning the Baptist churches in the South, the military commanders being directed to turn over to the American Baptist Home Missionary Society all churches of the Baptist Church South "in which a loyal minister of said Church does not now officiate." Like orders were issued regarding the United Presbyterian Church and the Associate Reformed Presbyterian Church as well as both Old School and New School bodies. In every instance these orders were issued at the solicitation of some church official. The order issued to the United Brethren gives permission "to teachers and missionaries" to enter southern military departments, while in the case of the Presbyterians the agencies designed to work in the South were the Domestic Missionary Society and the Presbyterian Committee of Home Missions, these orders having been solicited by the secretaries of these societies.

Thus the way for considerable missionary activity in the South on the part of the northern churches was opened. In 1864 the Missionary Board of the Methodist Episcopal Church made an appropriation of $35,000 for this work and missionaries were soon to be found in numerous places. In Norfolk and Portsmouth, Virginia, all churches were placed under the provost marshal who was to see that the pulpits were filled by loyal ministers, and orders were issued requiring that the churches be opened to all officers and soldiers "white or colored" at the usual hour of worship and "at other times if desired."

This action on the part of northern churches in going into the South at this time and under these circumstances aroused great indignation on the part of the Southerners. The Presbytery of Louisville in 1864 passed resolutions of protest against the Board of Domestic Missions procuring the order from the War Department and called upon the General Assembly to "at once disavow the said act, so that the church may be saved from sin, the reproach, and ruin which this thing is calculated to bring upon her." In 1864 a convention of southern Methodist ministers from states within the Federal lines met at Louisville to protest against this activity.

They stated that they did not believe that the President of the United States approved of this action, and characterized the procedure as "unjust, unnecessary and subversive alike of good order and the rights of a numerous body of Christians."

These southern ministers were right in their surmise that President Lincoln did not approve of such interference with the churches. The President's attitude in regard to the military interferences with the churches is brought out in connection with the famous McPheeters case of St. Louis. Dr. Samuel B. McPheeters was the minister of an important Presbyterian church in St. Louis and in December, 1862, the commanding general of the department of the Missouri deposed McPheeters from his pulpit and ordered both him and his wife to leave the state within ten days. This was done because of the refusal of McPheeters to declare his loyalty to the United States, and also on the ground that his influence greatly encouraged the enemies of the government, while his wife had openly avowed that she was a rebel. McPheeters wrote a long letter of protest to the Attorney General of the United States, which led to a long discussion covering more than a year, into which the President was eventually drawn. The President writing to the commanding general at St. Louis in January, 1863, stated:

I add that the United States Government must not, as by this order undertake to run the Churches. When an individual, in a Church or out of it, becomes dangerous to the public, he must be checked; but let the Churches, as such, take care of themselves. It will not do for the United States to appoint Trustees, Supervisors, or other agents for the Churches.

Later in a letter to McPheeters President Lincoln wrote:

I have never interfered, nor thought of interfering as to who shall or who shall not preach in any Church, nor have I knowingly or believingly tolerated any one else to so interfere by my authority.

Up to this time the President had not heard of the orders issued by the War Department giving military commanders the right to seize churches and turn them over to the loyal agents of the northern bodies. His attention was brought to the situation by a Missouri Methodist preacher, the Rev. John Hagan, claiming to represent the loyal members of the Methodist Episcopal Church, South in Missouri. When President Lincoln heard of the orders he wrote at once to Secretary Stanton, stating:

After having made these declarations [in reference to the McPheeters case] in good faith and in writing you can conceive of my embarrassment at now having brought to me what purports to be a formal order of the War Department, bearing date November 30, 1863, giving Bishop Ames control and possession of all the Methodist Churches in certain Southern military departments where pastors have not been appointed by a loyal bishop or bishops . . . and ordering the military to aid him against any resistance which may be made to his taking such possession and control. What is to be done about it?

The Secretary of War wrote at once, modifying the order, exempting all loyal states from its operations. Even then the President feared it was liable to abuses, but he stated, "It is not easy to withdraw it entirely and at once."

Writing in March, 1864, to the military commander at Memphis, who had interfered with the churches in that city, the President stated:

If the military have need of the church building, let them keep it, otherwise let them get out of it, and leave it and its owners alone, except for causes that justify the arrest of any one.

Still the church squabble continued in Memphis and two months later the President again wrote the military commander:

I am now told that . . . the military put one set of men out of and another set of men into the building. This, if true is most extraordinary. I say again, if there be no military need of the building leave it alone, neither putting one set in or out of it, except on finding some one preaching or practicing treason, in which case lay hands on him, just as if he were doing the same thing in any other building, or in the street or highway.

Such vigorous words well illustrate the clear-sightedness with which the President saw the situation, and also indicate how much his patience was taxed by these petty squabbles.

It is difficult to find justification for the action of the northern churches in entering the South in the midst of the war, and starting their work in regions where the southern churches were at their mercy. The argument that this would help strengthen the Union cause was frequently used, while the northern church leaders stated that they were simply performing their Christian duty of taking the gospel where it was not preached, that they were following Christ's injunction by going "into all the South and preach the Gospel to every creature." In both North and South patriotism became the chief theme of the pulpit and the church press, and too often the Christian ideal of forgiveness and the Golden Rule gave way to a bitter vindictiveness.

VII

During the course of the war the United States government asked certain church leaders to go abroad as unofficial representatives to explain the Federal policies to European peoples, who were prone to be critical. In 1863 Henry Ward Beecher, who had already won great fame, both for his eloquence and for his advocacy of the cause of the slaves, was sent to England. In the face of much irritating heckling he toured England and through his efforts helped change public opinion in that country toward the United States. Archbishop John Hughes, of New York, was likewise sent to France in 1861 where through interviews with members of the ministry, high Catholic officials and finally with Napoleon III, he succeeded in placing before them the true situation of affairs in America. Dr. John McClintock, a Methodist minister, was from 1861 to 1863 the pastor of the American Church in Paris and both in France and in England exercised no little influence in favor of the cause of the Union, especially through articles which he sent to both French and English papers.

Bishop Matthew Simpson, of the Methodist Episcopal Church, was a close personal friend of President Lincoln's and was one of the most eloquent preachers in the country. Through his patriotic lecture entitled "Our Country" delivered in every section of the North during the war, Bishop Simpson often produced telling effects. *Harper's Weekly*, describing the effects of this lecture in Pittsburgh, in October, 1864, stated:

Toward the close [of the address] an eye witness says: "laying his hand on the torn and ball-riddled colors of the Seventy-third Ohio, he spoke of the battle fields where they had been baptized in blood, and described their beauty as some patch of azure, filled with stars, that an angel had snatched from the heavenly canopy to set the stripes in blood." With this description began a scene that Demosthenes might have envied. All over the vast assembly handkerchiefs and hats were waved, and before the speaker sat down the whole throng arose as if by magic influence and screamed, and shouted, and saluted, and stamped, and clapped, and wept, and laughed in wild excitement. Colonel Moody sprang to the top of a bench and called for "The Star-Spangled Banner," which was sung or rather shouted, until the audience dispersed.

This moving lecture was delivered in the Academy of Music in New York on November 3, 1864, where it played an influential part in the winding up of the presidential campaign.

VIII

The Civil War period saw the rise of charities on a larger scale than had ever before existed in the United States. Increased giving is noted to Home and Foreign Missions, to Bible and Tract Societies and for the aid of the poor and the homeless. Men of wealth vied with one another in their giving to every good cause. The American Home Missionary Society at the close of the war was maintaining 800 missionaries, 200 fewer than 5 years before, but the Baptist Home Missionary Society doubled both its number of missionaries and its receipts. All the benevolent enterprises of the Methodist Episcopal Church showed a steady increase throughout the years of the war. The Protestant Episcopal, the Old and New School Presbyterians maintained their activities at least on the prewar level and the general need in all the churches was for more men rather than for more money. In 1864 the receipts of the American Board of Commissioners for Foreign Missions showed that the receipts of the society had increased more than 50 per cent since the opening of the war and that old deficits were wiped out and a surplus created. In 1860 the Methodist Episcopal Church reported $270,000 for home and foreign missions; in 1865, $607,000. In the New School Presbyterian Church the amount contributed for foreign missions in 1860 was $80,000, in 1865, $112,000; in the Old School Church the figures were $137,000 in 1860 and $180,000 in 1865, while missionary giving in the Baptist denomination increased from $88,000 to $153,000. In 1865, 26 missionary societies, home and foreign, gave $3,000,000 to the cause.

But in spite of all this increased giving the cause of vital religion and morals undoubtedly suffered as a result of the war. Membership in the churches generally showed a decrease for the war years, while many a minister could subscribe to the following complaint:

The sound of the drum calling for volunteers, the training of soldiers, companies leaving for the seat of war, are but scenes of every day's occurrence. Amid the excitement consequent upon such a state of things, you can readily understand the difficulty of sustaining the institutions of religion. In fact tne pastor and his church are continually in danger of having their feelings more deeply interested in the fearful conflict between the North and the South than in their own growth in grace, or in the winning of soldiers for Christ.

From Albany, New York (1862), came the report:

Of the general state of religion in this city and neighborhood, I regret to say that our worst fears in regard to the effects of the war are realized. Ever since the calamitous conditions of the country became the all-engrossing subject of thought and conversation, the higher interests of Christ's kingdom have been thrown proportionately in the background. The additions to most of our churches have been few; the interest in our week-day meetings has diminished; the preaching of the gospel has not excited the accustomed power; in short, the humiliating confession must be made that the church and world seem to a great extent, to have fallen into a common slumber. And the saddest thing is that our condition in this respect seems to be but too faithful a representation of the conditions of nearly the whole church.

Toward the end of the war religious conditions began to show some improvement in various sections of the country. From Massachusetts, Michigan, New Jersey and other states came reports of revivals, while in many cities new branches of the Young Men's Christian Association were being formed and new churches were being erected. The high tension of feeling brought on by the opening of the war; the terrible bloodshed of the first great battles; the hospitals filled with wounded and dying men; all this had stunned men's finer feelings and as a result suffered. But as the war progressed a readjustment came and the spirit of religion again asserted itself. But the brutalizing effects of the four bloody years, the resulting increase of drunkenness and human selfishness generally, were to exercise their blighting influence upon the life of the nation for years to come.

CHAPTER XX

✤ ✤ ✤

THE CHURCHES IN THE PERIOD OF
RECONSTRUCTION

I

THE Civil War was considered by church people in both North and South as primarily a moral and religious struggle, and it appealed more strongly to religious zeal than any war in modern times. The great northern churches, which had given an almost unanimous support to the government during the stress of war, felt that they not only had a right, but that it was their duty, to take a hand in the solution of reconstruction problems. Hence in the period following the war we find the influence of the churches in politics considerably on the increase. As has been suggested, loyalty to the government had become almost a part of the creed of the great body of northern church members. In Missouri every minister admitted to orders in the Methodist Episcopal Church had been compelled to take the oath of allegiance to the United States, and throughout the North, Methodists and Baptists especially were considered as practically 100 per cent Republican. The missionaries who had gone into the South during and following the war realized that the success of their work there depended upon the continued triumph of the Republican party, and especially of that wing of the party which supported radical reconstruction.

In the struggle between President Andrew Johnson and Congress over the policy of reconstruction church people of the North generally supported Congress. A Baptist editor, in October, 1865, gave this solemn warning, "Let the military be withdrawn, and the Union men will be slaughtered like sheep by these unhung traitors." A southern missionary writing to a church paper in 1866 stated that if President Johnson's policy succeeded "Union men, missionaries and the teachers of the freedmen" would be in danger, and every church and schoolhouse established in the South would be destroyed, and asserted: "If Congress fails we fail: if Congress suceeds we succeed." The Methodists especially were accused of political activity and were active in their hostility to President Johnson whom they accused of moral corruption and drunkenness. Gideon Welles, Secretary of the Navy in both the Lincoln and Johnson cabinets, in his *Diary*, accuses Bishop Simpson of having "brought his clerical and church influence to bear" in order to bring about the conviction of the President. The Methodist Episcopal General Conference which met in Chicago in May, 1868, during the progress of President Johnson's trial, set aside an hour of prayer that the country might be delivered from the "corrupt influences" which were being exerted to prevent the conviction of Johnson, while the African Methodist Episcopal Church at their conference session in Washington likewise prayed for the President's conviction.

II

The missionary work begun in the South by the northern churches during the war was carried forward with increasing momentum during the period of reconstruction. The Freedmen's Aid Societies soon had numerous negro schools in every section of the South. The Presbyterian and Congregational societies were particularly active in their educational work, resulting in the intellectual and moral uplift of the freedmen rather than in winning members to their own churches. On the other hand, the Methodist Episcopal Church, through their Freedmen's Aid Society, soon had not only many schools in operation but also by 1869 had formed ten new annual conferences in the late slaveholding states, working among both Negroes and whites. They were much more successful, however, in winning Negroes than whites and by 1871 their membership was twice that of the white.

The southern churches, though in a greatly disorganized condition, recognized their obligation to their ex-slaves and were making plans to meet that obligation. Thus the Alabama Baptist Convention in 1865 stated: "The condition of our colored population appeals strongly to the sympathy of every Christian heart and demands, at the hands of all who love the Saviour, renewed exertions for their moral and religious improvement," and recommended the establishment of Negro Sunday schools and that means be provided for more adequate preaching of the gospel to them. The Protestant Episcopal Church took like action the same year, the Bishop of North Carolina pointing out in his pastoral letter the ignorance and inexperience of the colored people, and warned his members of the danger of the Negro falling into mischievous hands; he urged the formation of Negro congregations in the towns and that means be provided for the religious training of Negro children. Likewise the Methodist Episcopal Church, South recognized their obligation to the negroes and by 1866 had outlined a plan for their colored members. They were to be formed into separate charges with their own quarterly conferences; colored persons were to be licensed to preach, and where conditions justified, colored districts were to be organized, and later to be formed into Annual Conferences, and when there came to be two or more Annual Conferences they were to be assisted in forming a separate church. Thus in 1870 the Colored Methodist Episcopal Church was organized, consisting of the Negro members who had remained in the Methodist Episcopal Church, South.

But the efforts of the southern churches for the Negro were more or less in vain. The Negroes were now free and many of them, if for no other reason than to put their freedom to the test, were anxious to separate themselves from the churches of their former masters. In many cases the Negroes were suspicious of the intention of the southern churches, in which they had formerly worshiped under the eye of their white masters, with the result that the Negro membership of the old southern churches rapidly decreased. The Negro membership of the Southern Presbyterian Church decreased 70 per cent within a few years following the war, the majority going into the independent Negro churches. In 1860 the Methodist Episcopal Church, South had 207,000 negro members; by 1866 only a few more than 78,000 remained. Organization of negro Baptist churches went on rapidly throughout the South during the years from 1865 to 1870, frequently aided by the whites. Thus in Montgomery, Alabama, the white Baptists of that city assisted the Negro Baptists in the organization of their church and in the erection of a building. The ease with which a Baptist church could be organized largely accounts for the great number formed among Negroes, though the practice of baptism by immersion which the Negro made into an appealing outdoor pageant, likewise attracted Negroes to that church. The independent negro Methodist churches also grew with amazing rapidity during the years following the war. The African Methodist Episcopal Church, which had been formed in Philadelphia in 1816, and until the Civil War had existed only among northern Negroes, by 1880 had nearly 400,000 members, mostly in the South. The African Methodist Episcopal Zion Church, organized in New York in 1820, in 10 years during this period grew from 26,746 members to nearly 200,000.

At the close of the war the Negroes were enthusiastic for education and religion. The Freedmen's Bureau organized by the Federal government emphasized Negro education while northern benevolent and missionary agencies coöperated. Frequently Negro schools were taught by negro preachers, and especially was this true of the northern negro ministers who had come into the South with the close of the war. Naturally the freedmen had strange ideas regarding freedom, many thinking it meant freedom from work, and thousands forsook the plantations and flocked into the towns and cities. Idleness among the Negroes gave them plenty of opportunity to exercise their religious desires and it is reported that baptizings among the Negroes were as popular as were operas among the whites.

Unfortunately the Negro churches and schools soon began to be used by unscrupulous politicians for their own ends. Religion and politics were naturally blended in the mind of the Negro at this period. He could see no distinction between his political and religious interests and emotions. His religion was tinged with political thought and his political thought shaped by religious conviction. He could not understand why he should not bring his politics into the church, or why the Union League or the Lincoln Legion should not hold their meetings there. Unprincipled carpetbaggers, both white and colored, frequently took advantage of this situation and used Negro churches for the political organization and control of the Negro. One such carpetbagger in Florida is thus described: "He preached to the blacks in their churches, kissed their babies and told them that Jesus Christ was a Republican." Numerous negro ministers were elected to office during the period of Negro rule, along with a long list of dishonest and corrupt carpetbaggers. It is to be regretted that the independent Negro churches should have had their rise in the South in this particular period of our history, but it was seemingly inevitable that these should have been formed.

As far as his church organization is concerned the Negro has been largely an imitator of his white brother. According to the latest figures (1948) there were in the United States thirty-four exclusively colored denominations, with more than 52,000 churches and more than 8,000,000 members.[1] Besides, there were more than 600,000 colored members in 30 white denominations, making a total of 8,600,000 negro-church members in the United States. Of this number the Negro Baptists alone make up at least two-thirds of the total, while the number of Negro Methodists total 1,770,000. Thus there are nearly 10 times as many Negro Baptists and Methodists as there are Negro members of all other denominations.

The Roman Catholics have been giving increased attention to the winning of Negroes to the Catholic fold in recent years. In 1945 there were 330,000 Negro Roman Catholics and 351 churches for the exclusive use of negroes, while several thousand Negroes are found in racially mixed Catholic congregations. In the above year there were 520 Catholic priests, 30 Brothers and 1,900 Sisters devoting themselves exclusively to work among American Negroes. There were 227 Catholic grammar schools for Negroes, 61 high schools, 13 boarding schools, 1 college and 1 theological seminary, with a total enrollment of 58,294.[2] Of the priests serving Negro Catholic churches 22 were Negroes.

As might be expected, the Negro churches have displayed shortcomings. Frequently in their churches worship is subordinated to amusement, due largely to the poverty of the race in social institutions. Too frequently also, the Negro church has tolerated lax morals among both ministry and membership especially in financial and sexual matters, facts which Negro leaders themselves admit, though investigation shows that in this respect slow gains are perceptible. The Negro church is still used by unprincipled leaders for political purposes, especially in the large northern cities such as Chicago, to which vast numbers of southern Negroes have come since 1915. Sometimes the Negro church has opposed the best colored leaders, a fact most unfortunate to the best interests of the colored race, while until very recent years the Negro churches have not lived up to their opportunities in dealing with the fundamental social problems either in the cities or in rural communities.

His long slave experience has furnished the Negro the central theme for his religion. Even today his religion is dominantly reminiscent of his long servitude, and he is still well aware that he is not yet completely

---

[1] Florence Murray (Ed.), *The Negro Handbook 1946-'47* (New York, 1947), pp. 153-155.

[2] *St. Augustine's Messenger*, Rev. Clarence J. Howard, Ed. quoted in Florence Murray, *op. cit.*, pp. 157-159.

free. A relatively recent study of the Negro church has shown that over three-fourths of the sermons stenographically reported in urban Negro churches were predominantly otherworldly, and that this was true to an even larger extent in the rural churches. For this reason the Negro has little encouragement in applying his religion to his everyday life, and there seems to be little relation in his mind between religion and morality. The otherworldly nature of the Negro's religion is shown most strikingly in the spirituals in which the central theme is death and heaven. This is particularly true of the best known and most loved among them, such as "Deep River" "Swing Low, Sweet Chariot", many of them coming directly out of their slave experience. Dean Sperry has well stated that "the Negro spirituals are perhaps our most moving statement of an inescapable fact and a serene hope."[3]

The Negro's church has undoubtedly meant more to him than any other of his institutions, for he has made it what it is. It may have many faults and failings, but it is his, and there he finds the chance fully to express himself. One of the reasons, if not the principal reason, why **seven-eighths of the Negro church** members are either Baptists or Methodists is that they give him a larger opportunity for self-expression and lay leadership.

III

Lowering of the standards of conduct in both public and private life was one of the unfortunate consequences of the Civil War. The country's wealth was increasing with an alarming rapidity in the midst of political and social confusion while the war brought to prominence a class of rough, unscrupulous men, with low standards of personal conduct, who too frequently were permitted to gain leadership in both business and politics. Out of such a general background came an era of wholesale corruption in politics which affected every section of the nation and every department of government. The use of money in buying elections was but one of the many forms of political corruption. Votes were bought and sold in more than one state capital as commonly as meat in the market; governors' signatures to bills intended to create private fortunes

[3]Benjamin E. Mays and Joseph Nicholson, *The Negro's Church* (New York, 1933), especially Chap. 4, "The Message of the Minister." See also B. E. Mays, *The Negro's God* (Boston, 1921).

were purchased with sums which reached into the tens of thousands. New York City was being robbed of millions by the famous "Boss" Tweed ring, while at the national capital well-known Congressmen and leaders of national prominence were involved in transactions which brought to them eventual disgrace and humiliation.

Corruption in business was even more common, if possible, than in government. Defalcations, wildcat stock selling, oil speculations, fraudulent railroad projects were some of the ways in which dishonest adventurers robbed the unwary. Unscrupulous methods of destroying business competitors were common, well illustrated by the "war" carried on between Cornelius Vanderbilt on the one side and Daniel Drew and Jay Gould on the other for the control of the Erie Railroad. Even while this disgraceful affair was in progress, Vanderbilt "maintained an air of high respectability" and was giving large sums of money to found Vanderbilt University, while Daniel Drew professed a deep interest in religion, having a few years before promised large gifts for the establishment of Drew Theological Seminary. Even the business of the church did not entirely escape the corruption of the time and serious frauds were uncovered in the conduct of the great publishing business of the Methodist Episcopal Church. A few years later the Augustinian Fathers, of Lawrence, Massachusetts, having borrowed large sums from parishioners for the erection of church edifices, through extravagance and bad management became hopelessly insolvent, causing serious loss and scandal.

The liquor evil, which had been considerably checked in the forties and fifties by the Washingtonian movement and the adoption of temperance legislation by a number of the states, attained greatly increased proportions during and following the Civil War. The Federal tax on liquors, which had been enacted as a war measure for the purpose of revenue, was continued after the war and gave to both liquor drinking and the liquor business an added respectability. The amount of capital invested in the liquor business grew from $29,000,000 in 1860 to more than $190,000,000 in 1880. The situation brought into existence the Prohibition party in 1869, and in 1874 a convention of Christian women met in Cleveland, Ohio, and formed the Women's Christian Temperance Union; five years later Frances E. Willard became its president. This organization from the start was closely allied with the churches and was soon a powerful influence in the temperance cause.

IV

Immigration was one of the factors which accounts for the rapid growth of the liquor traffic and for the important part the liquor interests soon began to play in politics. In 1873 the editor of a brewer's journal pointed out that the foreign-born citizens and their children were strong enough at that time to turn the scale in favor of one or the other political parties. He claimed that in some states the German vote alone could do it, and urged the liberal people to unite to give the deathblow to puritanical tyranny. "The future," he stated, "is ours! The enormous influx of immigration will in a few years overreach the puritanical element in every state in the Union."

From 1865 to 1884 more than seven million immigrants entered the ports of the United States, nearly 50 per cent of whom came from Ireland and Germany. This immigration was mostly Catholic, Lutheran or rationalist and its influence upon American Protestantism is most important. The Germans, both Lutheran and Catholic, brought with them the "continental Sabbath," and in many places used the day as one of general merrymaking, which soon became a cause for alarm among the evangelical churches. Ministers throughout the seventies denounced the growing tendency to forsake the Puritan Sabbath and warned their people that the very foundations of the Republic were being undermined. In 1872 when the Germans of Chicago opened their Turner Hall they boldly announced that they were giving to Chicago "the honor and fellicity of an European Sabbath," while a Baptist editor described Chicago on Sunday as a "Berlin in the morning and a Paris in the afternoon." By the eighties, however, even strict Sabbatarians began to admit that the maintenance of the Puritan Sabbath was impossible and began to adjust themselves to the change.

The increase of foreign-speaking people and the rapid growth of cities following the Civil War created new problems for the American churches. Both Methodists and Baptists had begun working among the Germans in the eighteen-forties and after 1865 this work was greatly increased. The Baptist Home Mission Society reported in 1867 that they had forty-nine ordained "foreigners" who were laboring among Germans, Hollanders, French, Welsh, Norwegians, Swedes and Danes, while foreign-language departments were opened at three Baptist theological seminaries for the training of ministers for this work. Similar work was carried on by the Methodists, Presbyterians, Congregationalists and other denominations. Strong city churches began to establish missions in needy sections where foreign populations were predominant. Thus in 1870 the First Baptist Church of Chicago was working among the Welsh, Swedes, Danes, and Germans while it maintained missions in four different localities in that city. During these years home mission work in the cities assumed large proportions and was carried on most effectively by all the larger denominations.

V

Serious efforts to meet the new religious problems presented by the rapidly growing cities were made by laymen in such interdenominational organizations as the Young Men's Christian Association. The rise of the Y.M.C.A. was largely a city affair. The first organization of the kind was formed in London in 1844, where under the leadership of George Williams a little group of young men engaged in the draper's trade banded together for "the improvement of the spiritual condition of young men engaged in the drapery and other trades." The purpose was soon widened to include young men generally and by 1851 there were twenty-four such organizations in Great Britain. In that year the first organization was formed in Boston. In 1861 two hundred organizations had been formed in the United States and during the Civil War the Y.M.C.A.'s in the northern cities were active in caring for the soldiers and sailors and in supporting the Christian Commission. In 1869 a businessman made a trip through Ohio, New York, and Pennsylvania, where he found the Y.M.C.A. in nearly every city enjoying the full confidence and sympathy of the churches. Full membership in the Y.M.C.A. was granted to members in regular standing of an evangelical church.

Dwight L. Moody, the most effectual evangelist of the postwar period, was a layman and began his career as a religious worker in the city of Chicago. He came to Chicago in 1856 where he joined Plymouth Church and was soon renting four pews which were filled each Sunday by young men whom he invited as his guests. Soon he had organized a Sunday school in one of the neediest sections of the city, persuading an influential Chicago merchant to become its superintendent. In 1860 he gave up business and devoted himself to city missionary work and during the Civil War to labors among the soldiers. Between 1865 to 1869 he served as the president of the Chicago Y.M.C.A. and collected funds for the erection of the first Y.M.C.A. building in the country. In 1871 he was joined by a remarkable evangelistic singer, Ira D. Sankey, whose singing added greatly to the effectiveness of Moody's preaching. From this time until his death Moody was occupied in revivalistic efforts. He made three extensive trips to England and Scotland, where amazing results were accomplished, such as had not been witnessed since the days of Whitefield and Wesley. Moody and Sankey held great meetings in every leading city in the United States and Moody was undoubtedly the outstanding evangelist in the English-speaking world. His sermons were simple but full of conviction and point. He had intense sympathy for and insight into the individual and great practical skill and tact. His singular largeness and sweetness of spirit and his consuming passion for mending souls gave him a unique place as a religious worker.

For a generation following Moody's death in 1899, big-time city revivalism flourished, making its principal appeal to people who had come to the cities from small towns and rural districts, and had left their church and religion behind. Modern psychology has given considerable attention to the study of conversion and the revival, especially since the publication of Starbuck's *Psychology of Religion* and William James' *Varieties of Religious Experience*.

VI

During and following the Civil War population continued to move westward. Kansas was admitted to the Union in 1861, and two years following the close of the war Nebraska became a state. During the sixties and seventies the great mining boom brought an increasing number of people into the Rocky Mountain region, which by 1876 was sufficient to raise Colorado to statehood and led to the organization of the territories of Nevada, Arizona, Idaho, Montana, Wyoming, New Mexico and Dakota. The building of railroads west from Chicago, Omaha and Kansas City offered inducements for the rapid settlement of the prairie states, while streams of covered wagons brought large numbers into western Kansas, Nebraska, the Dakotas and regions farther westward.

The churches were fully alive to the opportunities as well as the problems presented by the rapid occupation of the trans-Missouri regions and were eager for the conquest of these new areas.[4] The Baptist

4D. W. Holter, "The Role of the Church in Trans-Missouri," *Church History*, Vol. IV, pp. 134-146.

Home Missionary Society obtained a pledge from the Union and Central Pacific railroads to deed to them land sufficient for a meetinghouse and parsonage in every city and town along their extended routes and in some cases they obtained whole blocks. The Methodists organized a Church Extension Society in 1864 as the task of erecting new churches in the new states and territories was too great for the Missionary Society. This society not only assisted in the erection of churches by direct gifts but established a loan fund, which stimulated the erection of thousands of churches. From 1868 to 1884 "Chaplain" C. C. McCabe was the assistant secretary of the Church Extension Society. One day while riding on the train he saw in the newspaper that at a "freethinkers'" convention, Robert G. Ingersoll in an eloquent speech before the convention had stated that "the churches were dying out all over the land." At the next station McCabe got off the train and sent this telegram to Ingersoll:

Dear Robert: 'All hail the power of Jesus name'—we are building more than one Methodist Church for every day in the year, and propose to make it two a day! C. C. McCABE

This incident caught the imagination of Methodists throughout the land and Chaplain McCabe went from ocean to ocean singing:

> The infidels, a motley band,
>   In council met and said:
> "The churches die all through the land,
>   The last will soon be dead."
> When suddenly a message came,
>   It filled them with dismay:
> "All hail the power of Jesus' name!"
>   We're building two a day.

VII

One of the unfortunate consequences of the pushing of settlers into the trans-Missouri region and the building of the transcontinental railroads was the unrest produced among the western Indians. At the close of 1865 at least twenty-five thousand troops were on the frontiers of Minnesota, the Dakotas, Kansas, and in Arizona and New Mexico holding the restless Indians in check, keeping open the mail routes, guarding the telegraph line from Omaha to Carson City and protecting the settlers thronging westward. This general situation was particularly hard on Indian missions, for many missionaries were compelled to flee for their lives, and religious and economic conditions among the Indians were

rapidly going from bad to worse. Meanwhile a rising humanitarian sentiment in the country found expression in memorials and petitions to
Congress from religious and philanthropic organizations asking that the
policy of the Federal government be changed to meet the urgent needs
of the critical Indian situation. In April, 1869, an act was passed providing a fund of $2,000,000 for immediate Indian relief, while a board of
Indian Commissioners was to be appointed, made up of ten intelligent
and philanthropic men who were to have joint authority with the Secretary of the Interior in administering this fund. This board was in
hearty sympathy with the efforts of missionary organizations, and served
as an intermediary between the government and the religious bodies
working among the Indians. "The Peace Policy" as this new plan of dealing with the Indians was termed, has produced on the whole good results,
though for the first few years after its inauguration Indian wars continued.

The government now spends about $4,000,000 yearly for Indian
education, and has established several types of schools, all, however,
laying large emphasis upon industrial training. Besides the work carried
on by the government, sixteen Protestant denominations and the Roman
Catholics are engaged in educational and religious work among them.
Religious instruction and services are not only conducted in the mission
schools, but in many of the government reservation and nonreservation
schools parts of the buildings are assigned to the workers from the several
churches, who hold Sunday services and conduct weekday religious instruction. Under this influence the American Indian has made rapid
progress from a barbarian to a civilized man, especially when one considers "that it has only been within the last half century that intensive
training along educational lines had been given by missionary societies."

In 1904 the Indian population of South Dakota was about 20,000,
and of this number 4,000 were communicants of the Protestant Episcopal
Church and in that year contributed more than $8,000 to the support of
their churches. One Indian congregation in Arizona had a membership
(1904) of 525 and is one of the churches formed by Charles Cook. In
1870 Cook was the pastor of a German church in Chicago, when he
heard an army officer describe the condition of the Pima Indians. He
resigned his church and started to Arizona without pledge of support
from any organization and for ten years supported himself as a trader.
He learned the Indian language and gradually won the confidence of

the Indians. In 1904 there were more than 100 Christian Indians under his care, and his work required 9 helpers, 6 of whom were Indians.

In 1923 reports of the United States Indian office showed that there were 650 missionaries engaged in missionary work among the Indians; of these 410 were Protestant and 240 Catholic. There were 41,072 Protestant and 52,316 Catholic churchgoing Indians attending 991 churches. Not included in these statistics are the 5 civilized tribes of Oklahoma, which are largely Protestant.

VIII

By 1869 the causes for the division between Old and New School Presbyterians had largely disappeared and in that year a reunion of the two bodies was happily consummated, and the next year (1870) the first united assembly met in Albert Barnes' church in Philadelphia. Thus the northern Presbyterians were united just in time to meet the increased demands of the new West. Previous to the reunion both churches had maintained societies for promoting church building and at the reunion both these organizations were merged into the Board of Church Erection. The Presbyterian Board of Home Missions was active in sending ministers into Kansas, Nebraska and the Dakotas and on westward, while the Board of Church Erection aided in the building of churches in the new communities.

The years following the Civil War constituted an era of denominational awakening among Congregationalists. This movement was inaugurated before the war when a group of Congregational leaders began to express impatience with the Plan of Union and the willingness of Congregationalists to subordinate the well-being of their own denomination to plans of coöperation in which other churches reaped a large share of the advantage. This feeling finally culminated in the unanimous rejection of the Plan of Union at a national convention of Congregationalists which met at Albany in 1852. This meeting also mapped out a comprehensive plan of Congregational advance, and in 1853 the American Congregational Union was formed, to unite the energies of the church throughout the country. Among the functions of this new organization was to coöperate in the building of meetinghouses and parsonages. Out of the Albany convention also came numerous new enterprises, among them the establishment of Chicago Theological Seminary (1855). Following the war Congregationalism advanced into the new prairie and mountain states and continued its educational tradition by establishing colleges—Washburn College in Kansas in 1865, Carleton in Minnesota in 1867, Colorado College in 1874, and others in Nebraska, South Dakota and Washington.

Strong competitors of the Methodists and Baptists in the new West were the Disciples who in 1883 established a Church Extension Fund to be loaned to churches needing help. A few years later a Board of Church Extension was created and located at Kansas City. By 1904 this board had aided in the erection of more than eight hundred churches; one of the policies instituted was the purchasing of strategic sites for future church building purposes and by 1904 the board was holding such sites in fifty-six cities and towns in the United States.

IX

The churches which benefited most largely from the postwar immigration were the Catholic and Lutheran. In 1890 the Roman Catholics in the United States embraced immigrants from nearly all the countries of western Europe, and had a membership of 6,231,417. There were 13 archdioceses and more than 60 dioceses with property valued at nearly $120,000,000. In this year the Catholic population in New England exceeded the Protestant communicants by more than 200,000 and all the great cities throughout the country had become centers of Catholic influence and power.

Of greatest importance to American Lutheranism was the large Scandinavian immigration which entered the United States in the reconstruction years. From 1870 to 1910, 1,750,000 Northmen came to American shores, one-half of whom were Swedes, while Norway furnished one-third and Denmark one-sixth of the total. Minnesota became their chief home, which by 1900 had a Scandinavian population of more than 1,000-000. Wisconsin, the Dakotas, Illinois, Michigan, Iowa and Kansas also received large numbers. This great body of sturdy people was potential material for the Lutheran Church in America, but unfortunately the American Lutheran bodies were unable to meet fully the problems presented by their coming and a large majority were lost to the church. It has been estimated that only 7 per cent of the Danes joined any church; not more than 20 per cent of the Swedes and less than 30 per cent of the Norwegians.

This failure on the part of American Lutheranism to embrace fully its great opportunity was due in part to the fact that from 1860 to 1870 was a period of disruption among the American Lutherans. The first rupture came in 1860 when the Swedes and Norwegians withdrew from the General Synod and formed the Augustana Synod. The second break came in 1862 as a result of the war, when the southern Lutherans withdrew and formed the United Synod of the South, which embraced more than 20,000 members. Meanwhile strained relations continued between the conservative element in the church and the more liberal group, finally culminating in 1867 in the withdrawal of the conservative element and the organization of the General Council of the Evangelical Church in America, which soon became a larger body than the General Synod.

The first national organization of Jewish congregations was formed in 1873, called the Union of American Hebrew Congregations, and in 1875 established Hebrew Union College in Cincinnati. Many German Jews had come to America in the great migrations of 1830 and 1848; this soon produced a new and aggressive leadership, out of which came largely the Jewish Union and Reform movement. The leader in this movement was Isaac M. Wise, who was rabbi of congregations first in Albany and later in Cincinnati. He was prime mover in the Union movement and became the first president of the Hebrew Union College. The Reformed Jews accept the moral laws of the Mosaic code only and reject all ceremonial and rabbinical regulations, which they deem not suitable to modern life. This interprets the Messianic hope as the dawning of a new era rather than the coming of a person, while it emphasizes the universal aspects of Judaism rather than the restoration of the Jewish state and the return to Palestine. The great majority of Jewish congregations in the United States, however, have remained orthodox, and the number of orthodox Jews has been greatly increased by the large Jewish immigration from Russia and Poland which began in 1882 and has continued to the present time. In 1877 there were 278 Jewish congregations in the United States and a Jewish population of 230,000. By 1890 the population and also the Jewish congregations had doubled; in 1926 there were 3,118 congregations and a total population of more than 4,000,000. In polity each Jewish congregation is independent, and there are no conferences, synods or hierarchy which in any way control the ritual or customs of the congregation. At the present time there are three federations of synagogues, one representing the reformed, the second the conservative and the third the orthodox.

X

At the end of the Civil War the great churches in the United States were thoroughly orthodox and conservative, but there were at work certain influences which were soon to bring about far-reaching changes in religious thinking. One such influence was that exercised by Horace Bushnell, a Congregational minister at Hartford, Connecticut. Without attempting to set up a complete theological system, and with little thought of combating any of the old theological positions, Bushnell in his sermons and writing became the inspirer of new religious thought and experience. His work was largely that of emancipating American Christianity from unchristian conceptions. This is well illustrated by his little book *Christian Nurture* which first appeared in 1846, and in its final form in 1861. American revivalism had largely ignored the law of Christian growth and in this book he sharply criticized the practice of the revivalistic churches in their insistence upon a conscious emotional experience and maintained "that the child is to grow up a Christian and never know himself as being otherwise." This would be possible, he maintained, if the life in the home was truly Christian and if the child was given his proper place in the church. This volume was one of the strong influences which turned the attention of the churches toward the more adequate training of youth. Bushnell also repudiated the old mechanical theories of the atonement then in vogue, and advanced what was known as the "moral influence theory," by which he tried to show that the atoning work of Christ falls under the law of self-sacrifice. Of all the preachers of his time in America, Bushnell was the most successful in relating the truths of religion in terms of human life and experience.

At first he was attacked by his ministerial brethren as a dangerous heretic and his association attempted to bring him to trial before the consociation. Pulpits were closed against him, but his own church stood by him and finally withdrew from the consociation. Ill health caused him to resign his church at Hartford in 1861, but for fifteen years thereafter he continued his writing; his influence steadily grew with the years, and at his death he was recognized as the foremost citizen of Hartford as well as the chief inspiration of the new liberalizing movement in religion and theology. The more widely acclaimed ministries of Henry Ward Beecher and Phillips Brooks were largely inspired by the essentials of Bushnell's message which through them reached Christian people in every section of the nation.

It was in this period also that the church began to be disturbed by the principle of evolution which had been announced by Charles Darwin, because it seemed to conflict with the Biblical account of creation. Most Christian people in the United States at this time were literalists as far as the Scriptures were concerned and to many earnest people evolution seemed to strike at the very foundation of Christian belief. There soon arose, however, several able defenders of the position that evolution is not necessarily subversive of religion. John Fiske was one of the most successful popularizers of these ideas, and in a series of widely read volumes performed a useful service for both science and religion. Henry Drummond's *Natural Law in the Spiritual World* and his *Ascent of Man* also exercised a wide influence, especially on young men, and were widely read in America. Another influential Christian evolutionist was Lyman Abbott, the successor of Beecher at Plymouth Church, Brooklyn, who proclaimed that creation is "a process not a product," and that " 'God is not merely a Great First Cause,' but the one Great Cause from whom all forms of nature and of life continuously proceed." As the editor of the *Independent* and a lecturer, he performed a great service to multitudes of people who were perplexed as to the relations of science and religion.

The church was also divided during the latter quarter of the nineteenth century into liberal and conservative groups by controversy over what was called the "higher criticism." In 1881 a revision of the New Testament was published, the aim of the combined English and American committee being to "adapt the King James' version to the present state of the English language without changing the idiom and vocabulary," at the same time utilizing the further knowledge which Biblical scholarship through three hundred years had made available. Four years later the revised version of the Old Testament appeared. In 1901 an American revision was published containing the readings preferred by the American committee, and since that time other translations have appeared, some of them "based upon the new knowledge of the differences between classical and hellenistic Greek."

The revisions of the Bible naturally led to discussions of creedal revisions which became especially intense among the Presbyterians, resulting in a decided reaction toward conservatism. The questions of the inspiration of the Bible and the errancy or inerrancy of the Scriptures were warmly discussed in every section of the church, and resulted in a number of unfortunate heresy trials. The trial which attracted most attention was that of Professor Charles A. Briggs, a distinguished Hebrew scholar in Union Theological Seminary. Some member of the New York Presbytery took exception to some of his views. The case was finally brought to the General Assembly in 1893, which by a large majority found him guilty of the violation of his ordination vows and suspended him "from the office of a minister in the Presbyterian Church." Soon after this Briggs withdrew from the Presbyterian Church and took orders in the Protestant Episcopal Church. About the same time another distinguished Presbyterian scholar, Henry Preserved Smith, of Lane Theological Seminary was brought to trial on a similar charge, of denying the inerrancy of the original manuscript of the Scriptures, and was also convicted. A few years later Professor A. C. McGiffert of Union Theological Seminary was accused of heresy, the accusation being based upon certain statements in his book, *Christianity in the Apostolic Age.* The General Assembly referred the case to the Presbytery of New York, of which the accused was a member, but rather than cause further disturbance in the church, McGiffert announced his withdrawal from the Presbyterian ministry. Altogether these famous heresy trials served no other purpose than to rid the church of its most distinguished scholars and create differences and divisions which still persist.

CHAPTER XXI

✣　✣　✣

THE CHURCH AND THE CHANGING
ECONOMIC ORDER

I

THE most significant single influence in organized religion in the
United States from about the year 1880 to the end of the century and
beyond, was the tremendous increase in wealth in the nation. This
influence manifested itself among the American churches in various
ways. In the first place the more comfortable ways of living which growing wealth was making possible was rapidly doing away with the crudi-
ties in religion, which had been typical of the frontier stage of our religious development. As the log house gave way to more comfortable
dwellings in town and country, no longer were church members willing
to worship in crude and ugly meetinghouses and an era of church building was the natural consequence. It was a period also of educational
advance not only in the nation as a whole, but among church people in
particular, and the denominational colleges throughout the land
flourished as never before, in spite of the new state universities which
were springing up west of the Alleghanies. The rising cultural and
educational standards in the ministry and among church people generally brought in its train, as a natural consequence, the questioning
of the old orthodoxy; and the hard and overemotionalized religion
which had characterized the frontier, was gradually giving way to a
more easygoing religion. The great popular churches, which had achieved such phenomenal success in following population westward, and
which had been proud to be known as poor men's churches, were rapidly
being transformed into churches of the upper middle class. As a con-

sequence many among the great body of the poor, who are always with us, were compelled to seek their religious expression outside the older and well-established churches.

An interesting illustration of the general changes taking place in the popular churches, largely due to the increased well-being of their members, is that furnished by the transformation of the old camp-meeting grounds, first, into Chautauqua assemblies and later into middle-class summer resorts. During the later two decades of the last century many of the old camp-meetings were still being held throughout the country, but the rows of tents were rapidly giving place to streets of substantial frame cottages. No longer were the religious services held out-of-doors, under the trees, but instead great frame tabernacles had been erected, and the old camp-meeting revival was rapidly giving place to lectures on moral, cultural and religious subjects. The Chautauqua movement which had its birth at the camp-meeting grounds on Lake Chautauqua in 1874 under the leadership of Lewis Miller and Dr. J. H. Vincent, soon spread throughout the country and the old camp-meeting facilities were increasingly being utilized for lectures and entertainments.

The general pattern of revivalism which had been the principal technique of all the evangelical churches in meeting the needs peculiar to the frontier was still being extensively followed to the end of the century and even beyond. Practically every Baptist, Methodist, Presbyterian, Disciple and Congregational church as well as the numerous smaller revivalistic bodies, such as the United Brethren, and the Evangelical churches, throughout the eighties and nineties, had, as a part of their regular yearly programs a two weeks' revival, generally held during the winter months. Revival meetings were also a part of the yearly program of the denominational colleges which still maintained their relationship to the revivalistic churches.

Revivalism, though under increasing criticism, indicated by the appearance of such books as Davenport's *Primitive Traits in Religious Revivals* in 1902, reached its high-water mark during these years in the career of Dwight L. Moody. He had won his remarkable reputation as an evangelist in the seventies in his great meetings in the British Isles and later in the United States, but his work continued seemingly undiminished throughout the eighties and nineties, and at the time of his death in 1899 he was engaged in an evangelistic campaign in Kansas City, speaking to great audiences in a hall with a capacity larger than that of any in which he had ever spoken. These years were also the heyday of the professional evangelists. Most of them were imitators of Moody, though some of them lacked, unfortunately, his complete disinterestedness.

Among these later evangelists was Wilbur Chapman, whose genius for organization made his campaigns in the great cities astonishingly successful, and literally thousands professed conversion under his preaching. Another conspicuous evangelist of the time was Reuben Torrey who conceived of a world-wide evangelism, and prayed and preached around the world. The last of the spectacular revivalists, who utilized almost to perfection the technique of big business in organizing his campaigns, was the Rev. William A. Sunday, who stormed up and down the country during the first two decades of this century, gaining headlines in newspapers wherever he went. His denunciations of alcohol and the saloon played a conspicuous part in his evangelism, and undoubtedly his influence had much to do in making America dry. It is an interesting fact that practically all the conspicuous individual revivalists in the history of American revivalism, from Jonathan Edwards to "Billy" Sunday have been either Congregationalists or Presbyterians.

Revivalism still continues in many parts of the United States, especially in the South and in rural areas throughout the country, but it is no longer the universal technique of the evangelical churches. The conditions which produced it have been gradually passing, and will doubtless continue to do so. Most of the churches which formerly depended upon the revivalistic method for winning converts are now in the throes of trying to find new methods of approach.[1]

II

An outstanding factor in the development of the United States since the Civil War has been the tendency toward the consolidation of political and economic institutions. In politics this is illustrated by the steadily growing power of the Federal government at the expense of the states; in business, by the rise of the great corporations and the consolidation of management, at the expense of the individual operator. This is well illustrated by the history of the American railroads. Previous to and during the Civil War the railroads were short lines controlled by numerous independent companies; in 1900 there were more than 198,000 miles of

[1] W. W. Sweet, *Revivalism in America* (New York, 1944), "Revivalism on the wane."

track in the United States directed by a few powerful corporations. Before the Civil War there were fifty telegraph companies operating in the United States; today there are but two. There were, at that time more than four hundred coal mines operating under independent management. Today such great corporations as United States Steel, the American Telephone and Telegraph Company, the great oil corporations, the American Tobacco Company, are but typical of American business organization. In 1919 the corporations constituted only 31.5 per cent of the total business organizations in the country, but they employed 86 per cent of the wage earners and produced 87.7 per cent of the total value of the products.

Many of the men who were leaders in the creation of these great business organizations were at the same time stanch church men. The well-known banker and principal financier of the Civil War, Jay Cooke, was a loyal Episcopalian, a tither, and gave liberally to charitable causes. For many years he taught a Sunday-school class, and at the time of the failure of his great banking house, which precipitated the panic of 1873, he was entertaining a group of clergymen at his suburban home. Throughout his long life John D. Rockefeller was a devoted Baptist, and looked upon himself as a steward of the Lord and his wealth as "God's Gold." He once made the remark to a Baptist friend that he did not know how good a Christian he was, but he knew that he was a good Baptist. Cyrus H. McCormick, the principal creator of the great farm machinery corporation, was a devoted Presbyterian and gave large sums to church and educational enterprises. The Swifts were Methodists, as was Daniel Drew, while Philip D. Armour, James J. Hill, J. Pierpont Morgan and the Vanderbilts gave large endowments to church educational institutions. Of this group, only Andrew Carnegie seems to have been tinged with skepticism, but that did not deter him from giving millions of dollars for church organs.

It was not strange that the successful businessman became the symbol of modern America and that his ideals and methods began to permeate every phase of American interest and life. Nor was it strange that the church soon was responding to this influence, and there began to be an emphasis placed upon efficiency, system and organization, while more and more responsibility was delegated to committees and boards. The admission of laymen to the General Conference, the governing body of the Methodist Episcopal Church, in 1872 is an indication of the rising influence of laymen, while the appointment of successful business-men to church boards became increasingly common in all the churches. Better business methods in the conduct of the individual church became a matter of discussion in church assemblies. At the Illinois Christian Convention in 1868, an annual interdenominational gathering at Bloomington, the great subject for discussion was Christian efficiency, and complaints began to be heard that business meetings were taking the place of prayer meetings and that churches were more and more being controlled by little groups of individuals, constituting committees who were applying modern business methods to the affairs of the "king-dom." In city churches particularly, men with business ability were more and more sought after as church officials.

Laymen's organizations in the church soon appeared, at first con-fined to local churches. Among the earliest were the social unions. The first Baptist social union was formed at Tremont Temple, Boston, in 1864, but ten years later such organizations were to be found in many of the larger churches, and in 1874 a convention was called of delegates from all the Baptist social unions of the country to meet in Brooklyn to discuss the place of laymen in the denominational movements, their responsibility to the churches, the education of the ministry, the en-dowment of colleges and other subjects of interest to the denomination as a whole. This movement eventually developed into the Baptist Con-gress which met annually from 1881 to 1912 and performed a most valu-able service to the loosely organized Baptist denomination, in that it brought together the best minds of the denomination, both lay and cleri-cal. At these meetings it was frequently urged that the great business en-terprises of the churches be placed under the control of laymen, and from this time on the treasurers of Baptist national societies, almost without exception, were outstanding businessmen of the denomination. In 1908 the Northern Baptists took an additional step in the direction of further-ing their unity and efficiency by the formation of the Northern Baptist Convention. Dr. Harry Pratt Judson, President of The University of Chicago, was its first president.

The introduction of lay representation in the General Conference in 1872 led at once to a more active participation by laymen in the manage-ment of the great business concerns of the Methodist Episcopal Church. An example of this is found in the appointment of several prominent businessmen and lawyers on the committee to examine into the affairs of the publishing interests of the church, as a result of accusations of fraud made by one of the agents. This brought things to a head in the affairs of book concerns and provision was made for permanent lay participation in their management.

III

Not only was the business administration of the churches falling more and more into the hands of laymen, but to an even larger degree was this true of the denominational colleges. Men of wealth began to make princely gifts to educational institutions already established, or provided for the founding of new colleges and universities. George Peabody added to his many benevolent givings $3,000,000 in 1867 to stimulate education in the South; Matthew Vassar, a wealthy brewer and merchant, gave $800,000 to found a woman's college where a curriculum could be developed under Baptist influences, suited to the needs of women in the modern world. On the first board of trustees was Henry Ward Beecher. Other women's colleges, Wellesley, Smith and Bryn Mawr followed in rapid succession. In 1882 John F. Slater, a wealthy Connecticut manufacturer and a Congregational layman, created a fund of a million dollars to "uplift the lately emancipated people of the South," while Booker T. Washington, aided by northern philanthropists, opened Tuskegee Institute in 1881 where Negro students could be trained in the arts of self-help. John P. Crozer, a rich Baptist manufacturer, devoted all his later years to philanthropies. He gave large funds to the Baptist Publication Society; established a professorship at Bucknell University; gave $50,000 for missions among colored people, and after his death his wife and children established Crozer Theological Seminary as a memorial to him. In 1884 Indiana Asbury University was transformed into De Pauw University as a result of large gifts and larger promises on the part of Washington C. De Pauw, a glass manufacturer and an influential Methodist layman. Cornell University, established through the munificent gifts of Ezra Cornell, whose fortune was built on the development of the telegraph, was opened in 1868 with Andrew D. White as the president. The Leland Stanford Junior University was founded in 1885, backed by the vast Stanford railroad fortune. The princely giving of John D. Rockefeller began in the seventies. The first Rockefeller gift to the University of Chicago was $600,000, but at the time of his death some $78,000,000 had been contributed to the super-

Baptist University from the Rockefeller funds, though some years before his death the Baptists had surrendered exclusive control of the University. In 1887 the Catholics established the Catholic University of America in Washington, D. C., the first pontifical university in the United States, which has become the most important educational enterprise of the American Catholics. And finally (1924) a part of the Duke fortune, built on tobacco and electric power, was devoted to the transformation of Trinity College in Durham, North Carolina, into Duke University.

As a result of all this munificent giving to education, every denominational college president in the country began to dream of finding some merchant prince, oil magnate, or railroad baron who might endow his institution. Places on boards of trustees formerly largely held by ministers, began to be filled, more and more, by wealthy laymen, and in many instances wealth rather than church affiliation was responsible for such appointments. As endowments and equipment of colleges developed, the administrative end of the colleges increased in importance accordingly. Presidents of even the smaller colleges no longer had time to teach, as had been commonly the case previous to 1890, but more and more gave their entire attention to administration. Thus the office of president of the college became primarily that of a business director, while the number of administrative officials, such as registrars, comptrollers, treasurers, field agents, cataloguers, alumni secretaries and stenographers increased enormously, until in some instances the budget for administration in the denominational colleges equaled that devoted to teaching.

Another direct influence of growing wealth was the building of costly churches and larger giving to all benevolent causes. In the cities and larger towns Methodists and Baptists vied with Presbyterians, Congregationalists, Episcopalians, Lutherans and Catholics, in the size and elegance of churches which were rising on important corners. Church architecture also showed a change for the better during these years, the nondescript type of church edifice giving way to Gothic, Romanesque, and Classic structures, some of them vying in beauty and solidity of their construction with the great churches and cathedrals of England and the continent of Europe. The value of church property of the five leading denominations in the fourteen slaveholding states in 1860 as compared with the value in the same states in 1890 shows an astonishing increase in spite of the terrible destruction and poverty of the Civil War and reconstruction years. The properties of Catholics, Episcopalians and Presbyterians were doubled, while the value of Baptist and Methodist properties were quadrupled.[2]

IV

As the great denominations came more and more to be controlled by business methods, and dominated by men of wealth, as the services tended to become more formal and as ministers and choirs donned their robes, and cushions were placed in the pews. people of limited means began to feel more and more out of place and complaints began to be raised that "heart religion" was disappearing. Beginning about 1880 and continuing until the close of the century the so-called "holiness" question agitated the several churches of the Methodist family particularly. Wesley's doctrine of Christian perfection had become little more than a creedal matter among the main bodies of American Methodists.

The economic cleavage noted above, which was under way in all the evangelical denominations, was a factor in creating "holiness" groups in numerous congregations, since the doctrine of the "second blessing" was most frequently held by those whose material blessings were meager. The "holiness" advocates claimed that they were simply holding to the doctrine of Christian perfection as preached by John Wesley and that they were trying to get the church to return to the true Wesleyan position. On the other hand, the intellectual leaders in both branches of Episcopal Methodism as well as in other churches disparaged the movement. The growing tendency of the principal leaders among the evangelical churches to accept modernistic views was a cause for alarm among the more conservative leaders, many of whom had not had large educational advantages. The inevitable result was that as these people felt increasingly ill at ease in their association with those who had no sympathy with their "holiness" emphasis, they began to withdraw and form independent religious bodies. This movement was undoubtedly as much economic and social as it was doctrinal and religious.

		1860	1890
[2]	Methodist	$10,050,139	$38,167,259
	Baptist	7,227,123	29,008,657
	Presbyterian	6,930,991	16,120,097
	Catholic	7,387,582	15,010,250
	Episcopalian	5,151,830	12,159,973

H. D. Farish, *The Circuit-Rider Dismounts* (Richmond, Va. 1938), pp. 379-383.

Between 1880 and 1926 at least twenty-five holiness and pentecostal bodies came into existence, most numerously in the Central West where their chief feeders, the Methodistic bodies were the most numerous. But they were by no means confined to any one section. Though largely rural, where their work was carried on in the open country or in small towns among the underprivileged particularly, yet such bodies as the Church of the Nazarene which came into existence through a combination of eight smaller groups in 1894, has made decided progress in the cities. Between 1926 and 1937 this active body increased from 63,000 to more than 125,000. The depression years have proven particularly fruitful for these churches of the underprivileged.

Closely related to the rise of these protest groups was the rural church problem which had grown to major proportions by the end of the century. During the last two decades of the nineteenth century the number of rural churches greatly declined, and by the end of the century the larger Protestant denominations were fully alive to the seriousness of the situation. The Roosevelt Commission stated in its report on country life that the time had "arrived when the church must take a larger leadership, both as an institution and through its pastors, in the social reorganization of rural life." Soon the churches began to create agencies both to study and meet the situation. Home missionary boards gave special attention to the rural problems. A literature arose giving the results of surveys and suggesting solutions; professorships of rural sociology were established in colleges, agricultural schools and theological seminaries; summer schools for the training of a better rural leadership were conducted; the Federal Council of the churches of Christ in America (1910-1912) inaugurated a bureau of research, information and promotion touching the church and country life interests, while state agricultural schools, the Federal Department of Agriculture, and the Bureau of Education have coöperated in awakening the national consciousness to the importance of maintaining the country church as a conserving force in American civilization

V

Organized labor was one of the inevitable accompaniments of the rise of the great corporations. Combinations of capital were not only a powerful factor in producing labor organizations, but also constituted one of its principal justifications. The history of labor organizations in the United States properly begins with the formation of the Knights of

Labor in Philadelphia in 1869. The organization included all branches of labor, and its aims were to improve the economic, moral, social and intellectual condition of its members. By 1885 it had become a powerful body with more than 700,000 members. One of the champions of the Knights of Labor was Cardinal Gibbons, who expressed concern "at the prospect of the church being represented as the friend of the powerful rich and the enemy of the helpless poor." The bishops in Canada obtained from the Holy See a condemnation of the Knights of Labor for Canada, but Cardinal Gibbons, after consulting with the Roman Catholic head of the order, T. V. Powderly, and calling upon him to explain the secrecy phase of the order before the twelve American archbishops, succeeded in warding off a similar condemnation for the order in the United States. It has been suggested that if the president of the Knights of Labor had not been a loyal Roman Catholic the outcome might have been different.

After 1890 the Knights of Labor declined, while its place was gradually taken by the American Federation of Labor which had been organized in 1881. By 1890 the new organization had 100,000 members; ten years later more than 500,000, and in 1914, 2,000,000. By 1890, 500 newspapers devoted to the cause of labor, were published in the United States, and the formation of organizations among the farmers, especially in the Middle West, indicates the growing tendency of the less powerful classes to unite.

The latter seventies and eighties were a period of industrial strife throughout the United States. Chicago particularly was the center of disturbance, where on May 1, 1886 occurred the famous Haymarket riot. But this was only the climax of a long series of labor disturbances. During the year 1886 there were nearly 1,600 controversies involving more than 600,000 men and causing an estimated financial loss of $34,000,000. In 1892 came the violent strike at the Carnegie Steel Company's works at Homestead, Pennsylvania, which came about because of the reduction in wages and the refusal of the company to recognize the Steel Workers' Union. Two years later the most disastrous of the strikes of the period was precipitated among the employees of the Pullman Palace Car Company of Chicago when the Company made a 30 to 40 per cent reduction in wages. Eventually the American Railway Union and all the railroads entering Chicago were involved and the property loss, together with the loss in wages, totaled more than $80,000,000.

Such was the immediate economic background out of which came the beginnings of the emphasis among the American churches upon the social teachings of Jesus. The bitter contests between capital and labor, coupled with the fact that the churches and church institutions were the recipients of large gifts from capitalists and seemed to be largely under their control, brought the frequent accusation that they were the agents and tools of the rich. Generally speaking, these labor disturbances were roundly condemned by middle-class people, the class making up the largest proportion of church membership. The vast waste involved seemed to them wicked, a violation of their Puritan notions of thrift, and they blamed labor rather than capital for the loss of life and the destruction of property. The disturbances, instead of eliciting their support for better wages for the laboring man, blinded them to the injustices against which labor was in revolt. The church papers frequently voiced these anti-labor sentiments.

All the evangelical churches through the years had laid chief emphasis upon the salvation of the individual. The church leaders generally considered it the principal business of the church to deliver individuals from sin and spiritual death. But as the conception of religion broadened, many saw that there needed to be a change in the concept of salvation. An increasing number began to feel and to express the belief that to bring about needed reforms in the social and industrial world there was something more needed than a revival of religion in the old sense of that term. Not only must individual sins be forgiven, but something must be done about the sins of society. "Poverty, intemperance, extortion, irresponsible use of wealth, unhealthful and indecent conditions of life, ignorance, social ostracism, despair, lust, cruelty, laziness, dishonesty, untruthfulness" were social sins which must concern the church. But there were many, of course, who still held to the belief that "conversion will cure all ills; that if everybody were converted, this would solve the social and all other problems." To this contention came the reply that "many slaveowners professed conversion, but did not give up their slaves" or make any attempts to do so.

As a result of the lack of sympathy on the part of church people for the demands of labor, there began to develop a clearly discernible cleavage between labor and the church. The membership of the Protestant churches was made up largely of employers, salaried persons, farmers, and those engaged in personal service for such persons, and as a result naturally had the employers' viewpoint. But on the other hand there were also influences at work both within and without the church which were slowly creating a different point of view. Among such influences were the liberal tendencies coming from the theology of Channing and Bushnell; the new emphasis upon social studies and the giving of sociology a place in the curriculum of the colleges and universities; and the rise of a group of economists, such as Ely, Commons, Henry George, and Bellamy, none of whom were clergymen, but were all writing "with religious presuppositions." Such were the forces which now began to challenge the church and there soon emerged a new type of church leadership, as a result, which advocated not only the promoting of charity but also the furthering of economic justice.

Among the forerunners in this new religious emphasis were Washington Gladden, a Congregational minister in Columbus, Ohio, Josiah Strong, minister of the Central Congregational Church in Cincinnati, Francis G. Peabody of Harvard, and Walter Rauschenbusch of Rochester Theological Seminary. Gladden in a succession of volumes—such as *Workingmen and Their Employers*, 1876; *Applied Christianity*, 1887; *Tools and Men*, 1893—exercised a determining influence upon the rising generation of young ministers. Strong popularized the conception of the Kingdom of God as a social ideal, while Walter Rauschenbusch through his three important books, *Christianizing the Social Order*, 1912, and the *Theology of the Social Gospel*, 1917, probably did more than any other single man to carry the social gospel message over to the church as a whole.

The Divinity School of the University of Chicago became perhaps the most important center for the presentation and application of the social teaching of Jesus, under the leadership of Shailer Mathews, A. W. Small, and Charles R. Henderson. At the same time Graham Taylor, as Professor of Christian Sociology at the Chicago Theological Seminary, was doing pioneering work in applying the social teaching of Jesus at the Chicago Commons. By the end of the century Christian sociology or courses in social service were being offered in many of the theological seminaries, while numerous settlements had been established in all the larger cities, not only as institutions for the carrying on of social work but as laboratories where students of sociology might receive practical training in dealing with the problems of society. Interest in social Christianity has steadily grown and all the larger churches have not only adopted social creeds but have established organizations to put those creeds into practice. In 1908 the Federal Council of the Churches of Christ in America adopted the Social Creed of the Churches, an exceedingly able and commanding declaration which has exercised a large influence upon the social thinking of all the Protestant churches. It has also brought down upon the head of the Federal Council accusations of being a radical organization.

VI

Throughout the last decades of the nineteenth century and continuing through the early years of the twentieth, foreign missionary interest increased among all the American churches, Protestant and Catholic alike. One of the factors in this increasing foreign missionary interest was the Spanish-American War and the new imperialistic policy adopted by the United States government as a result. Though the Spanish-American War lasted scarcely more than a hundred days, yet its consequences were long extended and highly significant both for the nation and the churches. Long before the war began the humanitarian interests of the American people had been profoundly stirred by the cruel policy adopted by the Spanish authorities in attempting to crush the recurring insurrections in Cuba. As a consequence it was relatively easy to secure church support for the war with Spain once it was declared, though the church press was practically unanimous in denouncing the "yellow" journalism which played such a prominent part in fomenting it. The following editorial statement from the *Christian Advocate* (April 28, 1898) represents the majority opinion of American Protestantism:

> As long as the war was not declared, any citizen, without exposing himself to just imputation upon his patriotism, could oppose it and urge strenuously in favor of a favorable use of peaceful arts of diplomacy. But war having been resolved upon . . . loyalty to the country now requires every citizen to support "the powers that be". . . . Public attempts to show that the war was ill-advised and unnecessary are now out of place.

The Catholics took a like position as indicated by the following excerpt from a circular letter issued by the American archbishops to be read in all churches:

> We, the members of the Catholic Church, are true Americans and as such are loyal to our country and our flag, and obedient to the highest decrees and the supreme authority of the nation, and it calls upon the faithful to beg the God

of battles to crown their arms on land and sea with victory and triumph, to stay unnecessary effusion of blood, and speedily to restore peace by glorious victory for our flag.

The spectacular victories of Admiral Dewey at Manila Bay and the speedy crushing of Spanish resistance, on land and sea, convinced the majority of the American clergy that the hand of God was in the nation's conflict.

The war brought out a veritable flood of war sermons, which varied, according to the *Outlook* (June 23, 1898), all the way from denouncing the war as a mistake, if not a crime, to the strong conviction that the war was conceived in righteousness and that God's blessing was upon American arms. On the Sunday following the victory at Manila one minister announced as his subject, "The Dewey Days of May."

With the close of the war, the decision of the government to retain the Philippine Islands and Porto Rico met with favor among the American Protestant churches generally, especially those with extensive foreign missionary programs. This too was considered a providential happening, opening doors for humanitarian and evangelizing enterprises. The great American churches, unlike the nation, were already equipped to occupy the newly acquired regions, and their leaders were seldom found among those advocating withdrawal. But it was an "Imperialism of Righteousness" which they advocated, though most were not adverse to expansion of American trade at the same time. All the missionary-minded Protestant churches made effective propaganda use of the "corrupt friar" administration of Catholicism in the Philippines as indicating how sorely needed were Protestant missionaries in the former Spanish possessions.

The Protestant churches, however, did not enter the new fields as competitors. At a meeting of representatives of the major denominations held in New York under Presbyterian auspices on July 13, 1898, plans were projected whereby the evangelical denominations agreed to a friendly coöperation and a division of responsibility in the former Spanish colonies, which were about to become American possessions. And it is heartening to notice that in the various comments in the Protestant press, now and again a good word is spoken for the accomplishments of Spain, especially in the early days, and in the coöperative spirit shown by some of the Catholics. This was particularly true of Father Sherman in Porto Rico (the son of General W. T. Sherman), one Protestant journal stating that:

... any special religious revival in Porto Rico must come through the medium of the Roman Catholic Church; and ... that there was vastly greater hope in the missionary efforts of a large hearted priest, like Father Sherman than ... in the mission of any Protestant who might carry confusion of thought and sectarian distinctions.

No single factor has been more influential in developing interdenominational understanding and coöperation than has the cause of missions. The absurdity of Christian competition in foreign fields brought about the formation in 1893 of the Foreign Missions Conference of North America, which includes all the Protestant missionary societies and boards in the United States and Canada. This body functions through a Committee on Reference and Council, which maintains a permanent staff, while the Conference meets each year to discuss common problems. Coöperation has also worked admirably in certain foreign fields. In China there are more than twenty educational institutions under interdenominational control, while in all the important mission fields numerous coöperative enterprises are in operation. In the Philippine Islands an Evangelical Union of the Philippines was early formed, made up of Baptists, Congregationalists, Disciples, Methodists, Presbyterians and United Brethren. The union has prevented duplication of work and has served to unite Christian forces in a great common cause. The Committee on Coöperation in Latin America formed in 1913 is another interdenominational missionary agency, which through representatives of the mission boards which compose it, maintains an office and a permanent staff in New York. It has conducted two important congresses on Christian work in Latin America, the first at Panama in 1916 and a second at Montevideo in 1925.

One of the most far-reaching and effective interdenominational agencies for missionary work was the Student Volunteer Movement which had its inception at a meeting of missionary workers at Northfield, Massachusetts in 1886. The movement at once caught the imagination of Christian students throughout the world, and student volunteer bands made up of students in preparation for foreign service were formed in all the church colleges and in many of the state universities. In 1888 John R. Mott became the chairman of the executive committee of the movement, and in this connection he soon became an international figure, and the most important man in the world from the standpoint of Protestant Christian missions. By 1915 the Student Volunteer Movement had been instrumental in finding, training and sending to the foreign field through the several mission boards more than five thousand young men and women from the American colleges. The great Student Volunteer conventions held every four years were events of national and even international importance. The Missionary Education Movement inaugurated in 1902 to promote missionary education in all Protestant denominations has carried on continuously until the present time. Its editorial work and the publication of missionary literature for the forty-seven coöperating denominations has been its most important activity. The Laymen's Missionary Movement, an offshoot of the Student Volunteer Convention held in Nashville in 1906, formed a permanent organization for the purpose of stirring up the intelligent laymen of American Protestantism to a larger interest in and support of the missionary cause. Altogether it was a period of tremendous optimism, and there was a great hope that through the combined efforts of Protestant Christian forces the "Evangelization of the World in This Generation" could be accomplished. This was the title of a book published by John R. Mott in 1900 and that title became the watchword of the militant forces of Protestant Christianity.

VII

In 1880 the United States still contained much home missionary territory. Western Kansas and Nebraska, the Dakotas, much of Colorado, New Mexico and Arizona, Idaho, Nevada, Wyoming and Montana were still in process of settlement, while the present state of Oklahoma was not opened to white settlement until 1889. The gold rush to Alaska which began in 1897 soon brought a large increase of population into "Seward's Ice Box," which gave the region favorable attention. In 1912 Alaska was given territorial status. Besides these regions home missionary activities were being carried on in the South, among the Negroes and mountain whites, and after the Spanish-American War and the annexation of Hawaii, both Porto Rico and Hawaii were considered home missionary territory. The American Missionary Association, a Congregational agency, in 1917 was maintaining six colleges, three theological seminaries, and thirty-two secondary and elementary institutions for negroes; had three mission districts in Puerto Rico; Indian missions in Nebraska, North and South Dakota and Montana; was carrying on missions among the Chinese and Japanese in California and Washington; and was working in Hawaii and Alaska. The total amount received during this year for their work was $498,163. All the large Protestant bodies were equally active in this type of enterprise.

The most famous home missionary of these years was Sheldon Jackson, who under Presbyterian home missionary auspices ranged over the Rocky Mountain section from 1870 to 1882. Journeys from 1,000 to 2,000 miles were not unusual to him. During one period of 16 days he formed 7 churches. In the prairie states, where lumber was scarce, the problem of securing church buildings was acute. To meet this dilemma Jackson had church buildings shipped in sections from Chicago. Summarizing the results of his work, his biographer states that in the 9 states and 3 territories where he labored there had been organized (1906) 6 synods, 31 presbyteries, 886 churches, which at that time had 77,005 communicants.

But the most thrilling part of Sheldon Jackson's career was the work he performed in Alaska. From 1882 to his retirement in 1907 Alaska was the scene of his principal activities. In 1877 he visited Alaska for the first time, and on his own initiative started religious work there. At first he had no official connection with the work in that territory, but in 1884 he was appointed missionary to the church at Sitka and the same year the Department of the Interior authorized him to establish a public school system for the territory. The most romantic episode in his colorful career was his introduction of reindeer into Alaska. This he did, on his own initiative, after convincing himself that the Eskimo population would soon be extinct if a new food supply were not speedily provided. In 1892 he imported the first reindeer herd, numbering 171, from Siberia. The following year Congress made an appropriation of $6,000 for additional animals, and eventually 1,280 reindeer were brought in. In 1928 there were 675,000 head of reindeer in the country, the natives owning about half the number. In the extent of territory covered and in the diversity of services rendered to mankind Sheldon Jackson is without a parallel in modern times.

In the type of work performed in Oklahoma during the period of settlement of that territory, the churches followed more or less the frontier patterns of the earlier day. The Presbyterians and Congregationalists, through the medium of their home missionary agencies, were active in many places throughout the territory, but they were no match for the Baptists, Disciples and Methodists; the first two denominations carrying on largely through their self-supporting lay ministry, while the Methodists used the circuit system to full advantage. The Congregationalists, particularly, through the American Home Missionary Society literally poured money into the new territory, but their work continued to be largely dependent upon eastern support. An indication of the failure of the Congregationalists to take root in Oklahoma is shown by the fact that in 1894 of the thirty-five Congregational churches, only eight were being served by Congregational ministers, while Methodists were serving ten, Presbyterians nine; six were in charge of United Brethren and two of Evangelicals. Kingfisher College, which opened in 1890 as an academy, soon developed into the best institution of higher learning in the state and continued its promising career for several years. But in 1922 financial difficulties compelled its suspension; the principal reason being that the college, like the churches, did not spring out of Oklahoma soil and when outside support failed there was nothing to do but to suspend operations.

VIII

Representatives of all the various branches of Eastern Orthodoxy have now been transplanted to American soil. The Eastern Orthodox churches took on increased importance in the United States during, and following World War II, and they now constitute a distinct religious group among the American churches. During the war the Eastern Orthodox people in the United States identified themselves with the American cause, and gave full support in the struggle against totalitarianism.

The oldest of the Orthodox churches in America is the Russian, which dates from the Russian occupation of Alaska. After some missionary work had been done among the natives, in 1792 the Russian Church sent a group of monks to Alaska with instructions to organize Christian work there. Two years later a bishop was consecrated for Alaska, but on his way out from Siberia he and his whole party were drowned. Not until 1840 was another bishop sent. Meanwhile, however, work had been carried on by the most important of the early Orthodox missionaries, the Rev. John Veniamienoff, who had come out to Alaska in 1824. He invented an Aleutian alphabet, taught the natives to read, and translated the Bible and other books into the native language. With the purchase of Alaska by the United States in 1867, a new period began in the mission work there. A bishop was appointed over all Russian Orthodox churches in America with his episcopal residence at Sitka, where a cathedral was erected. The Russians now began to move southward along the Pacific Coast and the church followed. This led to the removal of the Episcopal See to San Francisco in 1872. The large immigration to the United States from eastern and southern Europe after 1880 resulted in the formation of Eastern Orthodox churches in the eastern part of the United States. This caused the transfer of the Episcopal See to New York and the creation of an archiepiscopal office with two suffragan bishops, one to supervise the work in Alaska, the other with his residence in Brooklyn, to have charge of the work in the United States proper.

The Russian Revolution of 1917 brought new and serious problems to the Russian church in America, which eventually led to its complete autonomy. Previous to the Revolution the American churches were under the Holy Synod of Russia, and they also received an annual allowance of $77,850 from Russia for the maintenance of their work in America, besides an annual contribution of $1,481 for the carrying on of missionary work. This was now cut off. In 1919 the first general convention of the *Sobor* of the American Russian church met in Pittsburgh, and now became the supreme agency for church administration in America. In the *Sobor* of 1924 the episcopal head of the Russian churches in America was given the title of "Metropolitan of All America and Canada." In 1940 there were nine dioceses under his jurisdiction, with something near 500 churches and more than 500,000 communicants. Attempts by a small group to tie up the Russian churches in America to the so-called "Living Church" in Russia, which had been formed under Soviet direction, failed to gain any large support.

Ranking next to the Russian Orthodox Church in America in point of numbers is the Greek Orthodox, which, according to the Federal census of religious bodies in 1936 had 190,000 members. The first Greek church formed in America was that in New York in 1867, and other congregations were founded as immigration raised the number of Greeks in the United States. Unlike the Russian immigrants, who were largely laborers, the Greeks tended to establish small business enterprises in the cities, such as restaurants, candy stores and flower shops, and well supported Greek churches are now found in numerous large cities. In 1908 the Patriarchate of Constantinople assigned the jurisdiction over the Greek churches in America to the Holy Synod of Greece, with the understanding that they were to be formed into an American diocese. This, however, was delayed, because of the political upheavals in Greece after World War I and the fact that the American Greeks took sides in the political controversies going on in the mother country. In 1921 Archbishop Meletios, who had been deposed as archbishop of Athens when King Constantine displaced Venizelos, now as the Patriarch of Constantinople took over the affairs in America, and in 1930 sent to the United States Metropolitan Damaskenos of Corinth to bring order out of chaos. This was successfully accomplished when the warring factions were united into a province under a Metropolitan, who as archbishop is now the recognized head of all Greek churches in America.

Other Eastern Orthodox Churches in America are the Serbian, the Syrian, the Roumanian, the Albanian, the Bulgarian and the Ukrainian. The Ukrainians were largely Uniates in their native land; that is, they gave allegiance to the Pope, who in turn allowed them to conduct the Mass in their own vernacular, and permitted their priests to marry. When the Ukrainians transplanted their churches to America the Roman hierarchy objected to their married priests, numbers of whom were suspended, and attempted to Latinize their worship. This started a movement back to the Orthodox fold, resulting in the formation of the independent American organization of the Ukrainian church in 1927.

Another Uniat body which has broken away from the Roman Catholic Church in recent years is the Carpatho-Russian Greek Catholic Orthodox Christian Church, U.S.A. They came from a region formerly a part of Hungary, and were Eastern Orthodox in their religion. They became Uniats under Roman Catholic domination in 1649. Rome conceded to them the retention of their Eastern rites and their married clergy, as well as the election of their bishop, subject to the approval of Rome. When these Ruthenians, or Little Russians, came to the United States they began to revert to Eastern Orthodoxy, and numerous congregations broke away from Roman control. This movement went forward until in 1937 these former Uniat churches began to take steps for a permanent organization. They declared themselves independent and formed themselves into a self-governing body. A bishop was elected and the following year he received consecration at the hands of the Patriarch of Constantinople.

The Roumanian church in America dates from 1918, with the erection of a diocese with headquarters at Youngstown, Ohio. This was later (1943) moved to Grass Lakes, Michigan. The president of the Roumanian council, the Very Rev. S. Mihaltian, gives the number of communicants in America at 80,000. The Serbian Orthodox Churches in America were under the jurisdiction of Russia until 1921 when an independent Serbian diocese was formed and the first bishop for America appointed. The Syrian Antiochian Church, like the Serbian, had been subject to Russia, but they too established an independent organization in 1927. In 1936 the first American Syrian Archbishop was consecrated by the Patriarch of Antioch with his archiepiscopal residence in New York.

Besides the orthodox bodies noted above, there are three native American orthodox churches, all of which are attempting to make Eastern Orthodoxy attractive to native Americans and to integrate it "with American Christianity in general." The first of these bodies is the Holy Eastern Catholic and Apostolic Church; the second, The Holy Orthodox Church in America, and the third is the American Holy Orthodox Catholic Eastern Church. All of these bodies are of recent origin. The Holy Orthodox Church in America conducts its services in English.

Though hierarchial in their organization, all of the Eastern Orthodox bodies in the United States conduct their affairs on all levels—local, diocesan and national—democratically, and with a large degree of lay participation. In most cases the priests are chosen by the congregations. St. Mary's Russian Orthodox Church in Gary, Indiana, with a membership of some twelve hundred, furnishes an illustration. The congregation meets annually to elect a committee of twelve members whose business it is to direct the business affairs of the church for the year. The committee must be approved by the bishop. The priest and the president of this committee represent the congregation at all meetings of the diocese, as well as of the national body, the *Sobor*. The Greek Orthodox congregation in Gary carries on with much the same type of congregational participation.

Schools for the religious training of children have been set up by most, if not all, the Eastern Orthodox bodies. The Greek church maintains by far the best educational program, which reaches a large proportion of the children. Most of the churches have church publications, some of which are national and others diocesan. The Russian Church publishes a monthly magazine in New York called the *Russian Orthodox American Messenger*. The Greek arch diocese publishes a biweekly called the *Orthodox Observer*. Most of the papers are bilingual. Some of the priests are well trained and are men of broad culture, most of whom were educated in the Old World. Since the end of World War II several of the Protestant Theological Seminaries in the United States have established scholarships for Eastern Orthodox students studying for the priesthood. The Greeks particularly have taken advantage of these opportunities, which does not mean, however, that they are necessarily turning Protestant. There has now been established in New York St. Vladimir's Theological Seminary, with a faculty of Russian Orthodox scholars to train priests for the Russian Orthodox churches in America.

Though not a member of the Eastern Orthodox family of churches, the Armenian or Gregorian Church shares with Eastern Orthodoxy certain characteristics and was transplanted to America in the flow of immigration from eastern Europe and Asia Minor in the latter years of the nineteenth and early years of the twentieth centuries. Influenced by several excellent schools established by the American Presbyterians and Congregationalists in Asia Minor after the eighteen forties, numerous Armenian students began coming to America to further their education. As the persecutions and massacres of the Armenians continued the number of Armenian immigrants increased and in 1889 a bishop was sent from Constantinople and two years later the first Armenian church in the United States was erected in Worcester, Massachusetts. The greatly increased Armenian immigration following the massacres of 1894 led to consecration of a permanent bishop for America. The policy of extermination of the Armenians adopted by the Turkish government following World War I in which a million and a half Armenians were slain, and 250,000 driven into the Arabian desert, aroused indignation among the American people and led to the formation of the Near East Relief, and Americans became more and more aware of the Armenian people. In America many Armenians have gone into business and the professions; some have become teachers of distinction in our colleges, universities and theological seminaries.

In 1936, the last figures available, there were 37 Armenian churches in the United States with a membership of 18,787. The government of the Armenian Church is democratic, but at the same time it is strictly hierarchical. The Catolicos of Etchmiadzine in Armenia is the supreme head of the Armenian Church throughout the world, though the Armenian Church in America carries on with a large degree of independence. Several thousand American Armenians have joined Protestant churches, particularly the Congregational and the Presbyterian, but the great majority adhere to the ancient Gregorian or Armenian Church.

IX

At the close of the Colonial period there were something near a thousand Jews in the United States.[3] By 1800 their numbers had increased to at least 2,500, and Jews had won the right to citizenship. In the celebration of Independence Day in Philadelphia when the Constitutional Convention was gathering in 1787, one of the features of the day was a great parade, and it was noted that "the clergy of the different Christian denominations with the rabbi of the Jews walking arm in arm." That was a symbol of a new day for the Jews not only in America but in all the democracies of the world.

Most of the early American Jews were Spanish or Portuguese, who had established a number of synagogues in the larger cities of the eastern seaboard, in which their ancient ritual, the Sephardic, was used. German Jews began to come to America after the failure of the German revolution in 1848. They were treated with disdain by the older Jewish Americans, and the result was the formation of German congregations. This was the first break in the religious unity of American Judaism. Meanwhile, other Jews from other parts of Europe were arriving in America with varying rituals. This led to an attempt on the part of Isaac Leeser (1806-1868), a German Jew, who became the minister of a congregation in Philadelphia, to persuade all the Jews in America to adopt a common ritual, the Sephardic, since it was the oldest in the United States, and he considered it the most dignified. These plans and hopes were not realized at that time, nor have they been to this day. Thus did the Jews follow the general pattern already established by numerous other religious bodies of transplanting their differences to the New World.

In the period following the Civil War a new generation of native American Jews had arisen, and they were faced with the problem of shaping Jewish life and religion to meet the peculiar American needs. In 1843 the Independent Order of B'nai B'rith was formed to unite all of the Jews in America, though differing widely in their religious views, for social, cultural and philanthropic purposes. The order spread rapidly and has continued to the present day, a powerful agency in promoting charitable and welfare work, especially in the large cities. More important for American Judaism was the emergence of the reform movement, headed by Isaac M. Wise, a native American of German back-

[3] Abram V. Goodman, *American Overture: Jewish Rights in Colonial Times* (Philadelphia, 1947).

ground. Wise was distressed by the disunity of American Judaism and the growing ignorance among them of their ancient religion. While a rabbi of a congregation in Albany, New York, he introduced mild reforms. When in 1854 he became the rabbi of a Cincinnati congregation, he became more active in urging union among the American Jews and led in the formation of the Union of American Hebrew Congregations, and opened the Hebrew Union College, which was the first important training school for American rabbis. In 1885, at a meeting of rabbis in Pittsburgh, a platform of reformed Judaism was adopted. This platform stressed the teaching of the Old Testament rather than the Talmudic regulations; declared that the ancient dietary laws no longer applied, since the situations which had produced them no longer existed; rejected the idea of a return to Palestine; denied the expectation of a personal Messiah, substituting the hope for an era of peace and perfection which would come through cultural and scientific progress; and asserted that the mission of the Jews in the modern world was to spread godliness among the peoples of the world. Later, English was substituted for Hebrew in worship, while the conduct of the service of the synagogue is not greatly different from that in the Protestant churches.

For more than a generation, during the middle years of the nineteenth century, a new day seemed to have dawned for the Jews of Europe. Germany and Italy had achieved unification, and France had overthrown the reactionary monarchy and had established the second republic based on the democratic ideals of the Revolution. Even Spain, in 1869, had revoked the decree expelling Jews that had been issued the year Columbus discovered America, and invited the Jews to return. The Western powers had on several occasions protested against the unjust treatment of Jews in various places, and there were indications that there was in process of formation a world sentiment that would eventually put an end to anti-Semitic outbreaks, which were now considered as a blot on Christian civilization. But the hope was soon blasted by a series of occurrences in Austria, in Russian Poland, and even in Germany and France, where the Jews had completely identified themselves with the people. The worst situation was that in Russia, where in 1881 bloody riots (pogroms) occurred in which hundreds of Jews were murdered and their property destroyed, resulting in the adoption of a policy confining the Jews to a Pale of Settlement. Here, because of overcrowding and lack of ways of making a living, many Jews were starved to death.

Under Bismarck the German liberal attitude toward the Jews underwent a change and anti-Semitism began to find favor in the highest circles. And finally the Dreyfus case in France, in the eighteen nineties, though it eventually blew up when Dreyfus was cleared of the charge of treason, convinced many Jews of the Continent that their rosy hope for a new day was but an illusion.

Because of the new tide of anti-Semitism arising in Europe noted above, Jewish immigration to the United States increased to a veritable flood. Between 1881 and 1898 a half million Jews entered the United States; between 1899 and 1907, 700,000 came, while 600,000 had entered the country between 1908 and 1914, and by the latter year the total number of Jews in the United States had risen to 3,000,000. It was during this period of vast Jewish immigration to the New World that Emma Lazarus' poem was caused to be inscribed by the United States government upon the pedestal of the Statue of Liberty:

> "Keep, ancient lands, your storied pomp!" cries she
> With silent lips. "Give me your tired, your poor,
> Your huddled masses yearning to breath free,
> The wretched refuse of your teeming shore,
> Send them, the homeless, tempest-tost to me,
> I lift my lamp beside the golden door."

It was also during this period of Jewish persecutions in Europe that Zionism arose, a plan to restore Palestine as a home for the homeless Jews of the world. In the eighteen seventies and eighties, Jewish colonies began to be established in Palestine. The real father of the back to Palestine movement was Theodore Herzl (1860-1904), a Hungarian Jew, who became a distinguished newspaper correspondent in Vienna and Paris. The Dreyfus case convinced him that the only solution for the Jews of Europe was to form a Jewish state. In 1879 the first Zionist Congress was held in Basle, where it was decided to set up a permanent Zionist organization in every land, and to hold annual congresses. Opposition to Zionism developed in western Europe and America, especially among the Reformed Jews, but it found strong support among the Jews of eastern Europe. Isaac M. Wise called upon the American Jews to fight Zionism with all their energy. Many Jews opposed Zionism on the ground that they wished the Jews to be assimilated; others objected on the ground that there was no reason for a Jewish state because of the substantial progress made toward their emancipation.

The tragic story of the Jews under Nazi domination hastened the formation of the state of Israel, which has now been accomplished. But even in the face of that accomplishment, largely due to American Judaism's financial support and the good will of the United States government, there still remain different attitudes toward Zionism on the part of American Jews. Many Jews, though not Zionists, and though they have never belonged to any Zionist organization, yet look with satisfaction on the achievement of a national home for the many homeless Jews of the world. Others fear that the formation of a Jewish nation might affect their standing as citizens in the lands where they live. Thus the Jews are divided into three distinct groups on the question: The Zionists, the anti-Zionists and the non-Zionists. The non-Zionists have given support to the movement, and believe that much good can be done by making Palestine a home for persecuted Jews, but they would never consider becoming citizens of the new Jewish state.

Judaism in America is divided into three distinct religious groups—the Reform, the Conservative and the Orthodox. Each of these groups has developed its own institutions in America. The Reform group have already been described; the Orthodox hold to the ancient forms of worship and the Talmudic rules of conduct, whereas the Conservative hold a position about halfway between the two extremes. The Conservatives have the Jewish Theological Seminary in New York, the Reform body have their Hebrew Union College in Cincinnati, while the Orthodox have established the Yeshiva University, which has as one of its departments a theological seminary for the training of rabbis. Hebrew theological colleges have also been established in Chicago and other centers. In 1922 the Jewish Institute of Religion was established in New York to train rabbis to serve any one of the three religious groupings. All of them are independent of Europe, and have a common "desire to root their faith in American soil."

A movement among American Jews which has gained considerable support is known as Reconstructionism. Its philosophy and program are summed up in three statements: Judaism is necessary to the American Jews; Judaism as it is, is inadequate; therefore Judaism must be made what it should be. The Jews cannot solve their problem by escapism, such as changing names or otherwise trying to hide their identity. Such tactics undermine self-respect and mental health. The attempts to maintain Judaism in its present three forms has destroyed Jewish community, and present-day American Judaism is devoid of all social structure. The solution is to make Judaism what it should be—a religious civilization with a program consisting of *community, culture and religion.*

A recent Jewish writer has characterized Jewish religious life in contrast to Christianity as stressing deed rather than creed. Both believe in deed as well as creed, but they differ as to their relationship. The Christian seems to say that if you have the right belief you will arrive at the right action; the Jew comes at it the other way around, if you begin with the right action you will come to the right belief. Christianity begins with the abstract and arrives at the concrete; Judaism begins with the concrete and arrives at the abstract. The Jew says, we will do, and then we will hear; the Christian says, we will hear and then we will do. For this reason changes in practice among the Jews have greater significance than in any other faith.[4]

The Nazi anti-Semitic frenzy resulted in the destruction of 6,000,000 Jews, one-third of the total Jewish population of the world. The 500,000 Jews in Germany in 1933 were almost exterminated by the end of the war; the 200,000 in Austria were reduced to a few thousand. The Jewish populations of Roumania, Hungary, Czechoslovakia, Poland, France, Holland, Belgium and Italy, the countries occupied by the Nazi conquerors, which had numbered about 6,000,000 in 1933, were reduced in 1945 to less than 1,000,000. The details of Nazi cruelty and sadism are past description. Today there are 5,000,000 Jews in the United States, the largest Jewish population of any nation. Russia ranks next with 3,000,000. There were, at the war's end, 250,000 Jewish refugees. The tragic experience through which world Judaism has passed has stirred the American Jews to a greater concern for the preservation of their ancient faith and their culture. There is a new and widespread interest in Jewish Education, and all-day Jewish schools have been established in numerous cities, and their leaders have shown a desire to find a better adjustment between Jewish and American cultural values.

4Solomon B. Freehof, *Reform Jewish Practice and its Rabbinic Back-Ground* (Cincinnati. 1944), pp. 3-4.

CHAPTER XXII

✢ ✢ ✢

THE CHURCH AND THE RISE OF THE CITY

I

ONE of the marvels of the eighties was the astonishing growth of cities. The rapid rise of Chicago, Cleveland, Detroit, Milwaukee and the Twin Cities in the Middle West are but typical. For the urban movement was not confined to any one section alone but was everywhere manifest, but throughout the North particularly. So great was the movement of population from the countryside to the cities in such states as Iowa, Indiana, Ohio, Illinois, and Michigan that many rural districts were dangerously depleted. Between 1880 and 1890, 755 townships out of 1,316 in Ohio declined in population; 800 out of 1,424 in Illinois, though the total population of these states showed a substantial increase for these years. The growth of cities, however, was not alone due to the influx of population from the rural areas. The vast immigration from northern Europe—Germans, Swedes and Norwegians—during the eighties, and the influx of Russian and Polish Jews, Italians, Greeks and other Eastern Europeans, generally designated as the "new immigration," and the steady, continuing stream of Germans and Irish immigrants, swelled urban population. Although the Scandinavians generally preferred agriculture to city trades, yet in 1890, 70,000 of them were to be found in Chicago and nearly as many in the Twin Cities.

New England, of course, had long suffered from the movement of population from the farms to manufacturing centers, such as Manchester, New Hampshire, Lowell and Lawrence, Massachusetts, or to better opportunities in the West, but these years saw even a larger decline in rural New England population than formerly. Throughout the nation as a whole one-third of the population in 1890 were living in towns of 4,000 or more inhabitants, while there were 272 cities with a

population of more than 12,000. In 1900, 40 per cent of the total population of the nation were urban dwellers; in 1910 they had increased to
45.8 per cent; in 1930, 56.2 per cent of the total population were living
in cities.

The rapid rise of the city in American life brought in its train a whole
series of new problems for organized religion. The movement of population away from the rural areas endangered the life of countless country
churches; the increased immigration from Roman Catholic countries in
Europe into the cities, where they generally settled in congested areas,
forced the native-born population to move to other sections of the cities,
or to suburban districts, generally taking their church organizations with
them. The growing secularization of the Sabbath, noticeable at this
period, was largely also a city phenomenon. The rapid increase of the
number of Roman Catholics in the United States, especially in the cities,
constituted a challenge to the Protestant forces, and in an attempt to
meet the changed situation the city gave birth to new forms of church
organization, such as the institutional church, and brought to America
the Salvation Army.

II

The rapidly changing American city was responsible for creating
the institutional church. It was an attempt to give the church a wider
function, in the face of the growing needs for social and moral help-
fulness in congested city areas. As foreign population crowded into the
cities, and the older population moved out to newer residential sections,
many large churches were left practically without congregations or con-
stituencies. The father of the institutional church idea seems to have
been William A. Muhlenberg, an Episcopal clergyman and the great-
grandson of Henry M. Muhlenberg, the father of American Lutheranism. As the rector of the Church of the Holy Communion in New York
City on Sixth Avenue and Twentieth Street from 1846 to 1858, he
surrounded his church with various charitable enterprises. Among the
social agencies created were the Sisterhood of the Holy Communion and
St. Luke's Hospital. Grace Episcopal Church in 1868 introduced numerous social activities in connection with its work, and other churches
followed in rapid succession.

Thomas K. Beecher, one of the most individualistic sons of Lyman
Beecher and the pastor of the First Congregational Church of Elmira,

New York, from 1854 to his death in 1900, introduced institutional features in his church in 1872 at the time of the erection of the present building, equipping it with a gymnasium, lecture rooms, a library and other facilities for carrying on a social program. So new was it at the time that Mark Twain gave it a place in his *Curious Dream* where it is described under the title, "A New Beecher Church." One of the most conspicuously successful of the institutional churches was St. George's Episcopal Church in New York. In 1882 when it started its institutional features it had 75 communicants; in 1897 it had a membership of more than 4,000. Russell H. Conwell's Baptist Temple on Broad Street in Philadelphia adopted institutional features in 1891. Besides social clubs, sewing classes, reading rooms and a gymnasium, a night school for working people, with volunteer teachers, was inaugurated. That school has now become Temple University and in Conwell's lifetime (he died in 1925) more than 100,000 students had attended the institution.

The latest development in the institutional church idea is the Goodwill Industries which had their origin at the Morgan Memorial Methodist Church in Boston in 1907. The plan was to give people without employment, particularly old people past the employment age, a chance to earn a living by revamping old clothes, shoes and furniture discarded by the well-to-do, and selling the repaired product to the poor at a small price. Their plan is to use the waste of society to restore wasted humanity. The movement has grown to astonishing proportions. In 1929 there were forty Goodwill Industries in as many cities under the control of the Methodist Episcopal Church alone, and twenty or more under other church auspices. All the Goodwill Industries also conduct religious and social activities. During the ten years 1920 to 1930 Goodwill Industries through sales or contributions raised $14,500,000 for current expenses and buildings, and during that time paid out more than $6,000,000 in wages to aged, needy and handicapped people.

Two years after the founding of the Salvation Army in England (1878) it made its appearance in America under the direction of Commissioner George Railton and seven women officers. In ten years it had marched across the continent and was working in practically every large city in the country. Many respectable people think of the Salvation Army in terms only of the little groups of blue-uniformed men and women with their drums and horns, singing gospel hymns on a street corner, or of shivering Salvation Army lassies ringing bells to attract

Christmas shoppers to throw small coins into a pot suspended on a tripod on a busy street. A few statistics, however, of its activities for a typical year will give a truer picture of what the Salvation Army is and what it does.

In 1910 it was maintaining 896 corps with 3,875 officers and employees; it was conducting 75 workingmen's hotels, 4 women's hotels, 20 food depots, 107 industrial homes, 3 farm colonies, 20 employment bureaus, 107 second-hand stores, 4 children's homes, 4 day nurseries and 23 slum settlements. In that year 309,591 persons were given temporary relief, 3,972 mothers and 23,373 children were given summer outings, millions of pounds of ice and coal were distributed free among the poor, while employment was found for 65,124 men and 5,355 women. Doctrinally it is orthodox Christianity with a fundamentalist emphasis but without sect distinctions, and it works primarily to bring about conversion and the rebuilding of people who have met defeat in the struggle of life. The rescuing of fallen women is one of the most successful phases of its work, and in its total influence for good it has won the respect and support of tens of thousands.

III

Belonging in a peculiar sense to the era of big business and prosperity and the rapid rise of the city is the Church of Christ, Scientist, better known as the Christian Science Church, which has been described as the "outgrowth of a well-fed and prosperous society," and as the religion of the comfortable. The recognized founder of this new religion was a remarkable woman, Mrs. Mary Baker G. Eddy, a native of New Hampshire who from childhood had been afflicted by a strange nervous malady, which has never been fully explained. After the failure of every attempt on the part of regular physicians to afford her relief, she at last heard of a certain "Dr." P. P. Quimby who was achieving some marvelous cures in Portland, Maine, some hundred miles away, by methods of mental healing. She went to Portland and placed herself under his care and at once found relief if not an entire cure. She now became a pupil of Quimby's and was permitted by him to copy his manuscripts, which she used for a number of years after his death in 1866 in carrying on mental healing. The Christian Science textbook *Science and Health* first appeared in 1875, and has gone through many editions. Mrs. Eddy stoutly denied her dependence upon Quimby, but whatever it was, it is certain that she gave to healing a spiritual and religious significance which Quimby's entirely lacked. However, at Quimby's death Mrs. Eddy paid this tribute to him:

> Rest should reward him who hath made us whole,
> Seeking, though tremblers, where his footsteps trod.

The official life of Mrs. Eddy, *The Life of Mary Baker Eddy* (Boston: Christian Science Publishing Society, 1907), by Sibyl Wilbur, devotes a chapter to the Quimby manuscripts in which Mrs. Eddy is quoted as stating that she denounced Quimby's method, calling it merely Animal Magnetism, while she was the discoverer of the Science of Mind Healing, (pp. 94-101).

Christian Science, as it developed into a religion, taught that matter has no real existence, nor has evil, sickness, sin or even death. Disease is caused by mind alone and any type of disease can be cured just in proportion as the mind is able to expel a belief in disease. This can be done only as the mortal mind works in harmony with the Eternal Mind as revealed in Jesus Christ.

Organized Christian Science began in the city of Lynn, Massachusetts, where Mrs. Eddy had gone to carry on her teachings and where she gathered her first disciples. Here she had but meager success, as the few followers whom she succeeded in winning came largely from among the factory workers. The first Christian Science organizations, however, date from this period. In 1875-76, the Christian Science Association was organized and in 1881 the Massachusetts Metaphysical College. In 1882 came Mrs. Eddy's decision to move to Boston, and from that time forward Christian Science has had its principal development and growth in the large cities. What is known as the Mother Church in Boston was formed in 1892 with twelve members, who had succeeded in 1895 in building a great edifice costing more than $200,000, and since that time an even more magnificent structure has been added to the earlier building. The national organization consists of the Mother Church and its branches, called either churches or societies, which in 1930 numbered 2,451, with a reported membership in 1937 of 202,098. Mrs. Eddy lived to a great age, and although retiring more and more from public view the control of her great organization was never for a moment out of her hands. At the time of her death in 1910 Mrs. Eddy had accumulated a large fortune, largely through the sale of her book, *Science and Health*, and the numerous Christian Science publications.

Many outside the Christian Science fold have testified to its usefulness from the standpoint of its therapeutic psychology. Among those who have rendered such testimony are Dr. William Mayo of the Mayo Clinic and Dr. Richard C. Cabot of Harvard Medical School. It has undoubtedly also stirred leaders in other denominations, particularly among the Episcopalians, to see the importance of developing a renewed interest in spiritual healing. And perhaps the growing interest in psychiatry as a new technique is not unrelated to Christian Science.

Like most religious movements in America, Christian Science has suffered from schism. Mrs. Augusta E. Stetson led one such movement, although her withdrawal from the parent organization in 1909 was due in large measure to Mrs. Eddy's jealousy of her success as the head of the Christian Science organization in New York. Her $100,000 house, with its marble staircase, expensive rugs and tapestries, and six grandfather clocks no doubt played a part in her excommunication. After her expulsion Mrs. Stetson's students stood loyally by her and her movement came to be known as the "Church Triumphant." New Thought, another related group, looks to P. P. Quimby as the pioneer in their movement. The Church of the Higher Life, its first organization, was formed in Boston in 1894. The same year a New Thought convention met in San Francisco. Its emphasis is upon health, happiness and success, and does not profess to be a church. The Society of Silent Unity with headquarters in Kansas City is a good example of a New Thought organization using Christian Science methods.

Theosophy, in the words of its expounders, was brought to America by "messengers of the guardians and preservers of the ancient wisdom-religion" of the East. The principal messenger was Helena P. Blavatsky, a Russian noblewoman with a turbulent past who landed in New York in 1875 and, with William Q. Judge and Henry Steel Olcott and fifteen others, formed the Theosophical Society. Its purpose was to further universal brotherhood without distinction of race, color, sex, caste or creed; to further the study of ancient scriptures; and to investigate the "hidden mysteries of nature," and the psychic and spiritual powers latent in man. Though Madam Blavatsky left the United States in 1878 to found Theosophical societies in England and India, the movement has persisted and in 1937 reported 5,900 followers in Theosophical lodges. Other groups, drawing their inspiration from Hindu sources, are the Vedanta and the Yogoda-Sat-Sanga Societies which date from the World's Parliament of Religion held in connection with the World's Fair in 1893. The Yogoda societies teach the gospel of "getting-on;" the Vedanta groups "aim at the suppression of the body and the exaltation of the spirit." Both have flourished in cities and appeal almost exclusively to women.

Among the bizarre figures turned up by the World's Fair in Chicago was John Alexander Dowie. Beginning his career as a Congregational minister in Australia, he soon withdrew from that communion to found an independent church at Melbourne where he won a reputation as a reformer and a divine healer. The opening of the Fair in 1893 found him in Chicago, where he had come after touring the country on a healing mission. He soon found that Chicago furnished him the materials he needed for the carrying on of his "work" and by 1895 he had won so many followers as to justify his securing the great Chicago Auditorium as a meeting place. Such was the beginning of the Christian Catholic Apostolic Church in Zion. In 1901 a Zion City was under way, located forty-two miles north of Chicago along the lake shore, where nothing defiled was to be allowed to enter. Tobacco and liquor were forbidden; no physician could carry on his nefarious practice; drug stores were considered an equal abomination; and the use of pork was banned. Converts flocked to the new faith, and money flowed in in unbelievable amounts. Dowie was an autocrat, every industry in the town being under his control. With his long white beard and general benevolent appearance, Dowie looked like an Old Testament prophet. Indeed he designated himself as Elijah the restorer, which led one of the Chicago newspapers to propound the question, "What is the difference between Elijah the first and Elijah the second?" To which the answer was given, "Elijah the first was fed by the ravens; Elijah the second is fed by the gulls." An attempt to take his new gospel to New York City in 1903, where Madison Square Garden was rented, proved a complete failure and left the church bankrupt. Dowie's leadership was repudiated by his followers in 1905. He was succeeded by Wilbur Glenn Voliva, an ex-Disciple minister whose chief claim to fame is his stanch advocacy of the theory of a flat world. He carried on in Zion City until his death, though with a declining following.

IV

Of all the American religious bodies the Roman Catholics made by far the largest numerical gains from 1880 onward. A great proportion of this gain was due to immigration. From 1881 to 1890 Catholic increase from immigration alone was 1,250,000; from 1891 to 1900 it was 1,225,000; from 1901 to 1910, 2,316,000, making a total of 4,791,000 for the three decades.[1] The total Catholic population estimate for 1890 was 8,909,000; for 1900 it was 12,041,000 and for 1910, 16,336,000. About 5,000,000 of this increase from 1880 to 1910 was due to immigration. The countries from which the great majority of these Catholic immigrants came were Austria-Hungary, Germany, Italy, Poland, Canada, Mexico and Ireland. The polyglot nature of American Roman Catholicism is shown by a glance at the situation in the diocese of Scranton, Pennsylvania in 1890, where there were 7 Polish churches, 7 German, 4 Hungarian, 1 Lithuanian, 1 Polish and Lithuanian, 1 Italian, besides the English congregations. In the city of Chicago in 1929 there were 124 English Catholic churches, 35 German, 8 Bohemian, 12 Italian, 38 Polish, 4 Croatian, 9 Lithuanian, 10 Slovak, 5 French and 8 others, such as Mexican and mixed, making a total of 253.

This great influx of Roman Catholics during the eighties gave rise to one of the periodic anti-Catholic movements known as the American Protective Association. This oath-bound organization had its rise in Clinton, Iowa in 1887 under the leadership of a local lawyer, H. F. Bowers. Thus the movement flourished in the heart of the agricultural section of America, and was in a sense a phase of the growing antagonism on the part of the rural sections of the country against the cities into which the new Roman Catholic immigration was pouring. The dominance of the Irish Catholic politician in such cities as Boston, New York and Chicago, and the corrupt municipal governments which so often resulted from this control aroused real fear on the part of many that American institutions were in danger.

[1]These figures are taken from a Roman Catholic source: Gerald Shaughnessy, *Has the Immigrant Kept the Faith?* (New York, 1925), pp. 162-178. There is considerable discrepancy in the estimates of church membership in the United States. One of the reasons for this is the different meaning of the word "member" on the part of the several religious bodies, and also because of the peculiar statistical methods used by several of the bodies. There has never been an accurate Catholic census taken in the United States; the Catholic church has never made any attempt to enumerate its followers other than by estimates of pastors and bishops. (Ibid., p. 33.)

One of the methods used to gain A.P.A. membership was the circulation of certain forged documents purporting to have come from high Catholic sources urging Catholics in the United States to exterminate heretics. The most notorious of these documents was the papal encyclical ascribed to Pope Leo XIII which first appeared in an A.P.A. paper in Detroit on April 8, 1893. Among other things it absolved all Catholics who had taken the oath of allegiance to the United States from that oath, and called upon faithful Catholics to exterminate all heretics within the jurisdiction of the United States at the time of the convening of the Catholic Congress at Chicago in September, 1893. The oath of the American Protective Association, which was published in the *Congressional Record* on October 31, 1893, pledged the waging of continuous warfare against ignorance and fanaticism; promised to use all possible power to "strike the shackles and chains of blind obedience to the Roman Catholic Church from the hampered and bound consciences of a priest-ridden and church-oppressed people;" pledged never to aid in building or maintaining any Catholic church or institution; and promised never to countenance the nomination or election of any Roman Catholic to any office in the gift of the American people.

The order ran the usual course of such movements in America. It flourished chiefly in areas where Catholics were least numerous, as in Iowa, Nebraska, Kansas, Missouri, Illinois and Ohio. It got into politics and held the balance of power in numerous local elections and in some instances controlled state legislatures. But by 1896 it had run its course. Organized opposition to Catholics was by no means ended, however, but was kept alive by such organizations as the Guardians of Liberty, the Knights of Luther, the Covenanters and the American Pathfinder. For a time such anti-Catholic papers as the *Menace* and the *Yellow Jacket* flourished and many honest people were carried away by their propaganda. As one Catholic writer states, such movements generally serve to strengthen Roman Catholicism, since they tend to "arouse sleeping sentinels, to infuse new vigor and enthusiasm among the rank and file."

The rapid increase of Catholic population made necessary a like increase in bishoprics and archbishoprics in the United States. In the thirty years from 1881 to 1911 forty new bishoprics were created while the number of archdioceses rose to sixteen. The growth of Catholic religious orders of both men and women in the United States is astonishing. In 1930 the number of religious orders of women was placed at 215, a majority of them being small diocesan organizations. Such orders as the Ursulines are nation-wide and have about 3,000 members carrying on educational work chiefly. The Sisters of Charity have some 2,000 members and engage in educational, hospital and social service work. The largest of the women's orders is the Sisters of Mercy with some 10,000 members, centering their attention on hospital and educational activities. It is significant that at least half the hospitals in the United States are under Catholic control and management.

While the orders for men are not so numerous as are those for women, numbering some fifty, yet their work is widely extended throughout the country. In the archdiocese of Chicago, for instance, there are 33 religious communities of men and 26 monasteries and novitiates. None of the orders are more active or influential than the Jesuits, numbering about 5,000 in the United States at the present time. In 1921 the American Catholics were conducting 43 standard colleges for men and 24 for women, 1,552 high schools, 309 normal training schools and 6,551 elementary schools, while the total attendance in schools of all kinds conducted by Catholics was placed at nearly 2,000,000.[2]

The outstanding Catholic leader in the United States from 1880 to his death in 1921 was Cardinal James Gibbons. A native of America (b. 1834) and American educated, Gibbons was made the Archbishop of Baltimore at forty-three (1877) and was appointed by Pope Leo XIII the second American Cardinal in 1886. While in Rome to receive his red hat, in 1887, he delivered an address in which he gave expression to his gratitude for being a citizen of a country "where the civil government holds over us the aegis of its protection, without interfering with us in the legitimate exercise of our sublime mission as ministers of the gospel of Christ." He had previouly definitely expressed the view that the future of the Catholic Church was to be largely among peoples with democratic governments, and he never missed a chance to express his love for America and for her institutions. As has been already noted, during his stay in Rome he had succeeded in warding off Papal condemnation of the Knights of Labor, and had used his influence to prevent Henry George's book *Progress and Poverty* from being ecclesiastically condemned. He

2These figures are from Catholic sources largely taken from Rev. James H. Ryan, *A Catechism of Catholic Education* (National Catholic Welfare Council, 1922). See also *The Official Catholic Directory* (New York, 1937); James J. Walsh, *American Jesuits* (New York, 1934).

also favored the speedy blending of immigrant peoples with the native population, stating in a sermon in Milwaukee that "God and our Country" should be the watchword of all in America regardless of origin. It was particularly fortunate that the American Catholics should have had such wise and patriotic leadership at the time that Catholic immigration was pouring into the country in such unprecedented streams.

In 1927 Governor Alfred E. Smith of New York, then the candidate of the Democratic party for the presidency of the United States, in order to answer the question then much in the minds of the American people, "Can a Roman Catholic be a loyal American?" published in the *Atlantic Monthly* the following as his creed as an American Catholic:

I summarize my creed as an American Catholic. I believe in the worship of God according to the faith and practice of the Roman Catholic Church. I recognize no power in the institutions of my Church to interfere with the operations of the Constitution of the United States or the enforcement of the law of the land. I believe in the absolute freedom of conscience for all men and in equality of all churches, all sects, and all beliefs before the law as a matter of right and not as a matter of favor. I believe in the absolute separation of Church and State and in the strict enforcement of the provisions of the Constitution that Congress shall make no law respecting an establishment of religion or prohibiting the free exercise thereof. I believe that no tribunal of any church has any power to make any decree of any force in the law of the land, other than to establish the status of its own communicants within its own church. I believe in the support of the public school as one of the cornerstones of American liberty. I believe in the right of every parent to choose whether his child shall be educated in a public school or in a religious school supported by those of his own faith. I believe in the principle of non-interference by one country in the internal affairs of other nations and that one should stand steadfastly against such interference by whomsoever it may be urged. And I believe in the common brotherhood of man under the common fatherhood of God.

It has been suggested that since Governor Smith was not censured by Catholic authorities for the above statement, this would indicate that American Catholics, for all practical purposes, have departed from the political theory enunciated by Pope Pius IX in his "Syllabus of Errors" and by Pope Leo XIII in his "Christian Constitution of States." Professor C. H. Moehlman, in his *The Catholic-Protestant Mind* contends that there has arisen in America a peculiar type of Catholic mind which is willing to compromise with the situation as it exists in the United States;

to recognize the complete separation of church and state; to admit the equality of all churches before the law and even to endorse the public schools. Professor W. E. Garrison in his book *Catholicism and the American Mind* (1928) is not so sure that there has been any change in the Catholic position and points out that the kind of public schools Governor Smith believes in is different than that in which most Americans believe. It is also pointed out that Catholics have one position in regard to toleration and the relation of church and state when their church is in the minority, but that they consider it a duty to take quite a different view when their church is in a position where it can control the situation. On the other hand, one of the editors of the influential Catholic periodical *The Commonweal* has stated:

The great majority of Catholics in the United States have only the vaguest notion of the Syllabus of Pius IX; and I wager that none of those who do understand it has ever fancied, with certain zealous one hundred per cent pamphleteers, that it condemned democratic governments, freedom of inquiry or comment, and genuine modern progress.

That religious body which profited most from immigration next after the Roman Catholics were the Jews. The cruel anti-Semitic persecutions in Russia, Roumania, Austria-Hungary and Poland in the latter seventies and throughout the eighties, largely engendered by greed for Jewish treasure, led to a vast movement of Jewish people to the United States. It is estimated that 225,000 Jewish families left Russia within sixteen months after the Russian Czar had issued his ukase in 1890, ordering the return of Jews to those provinces where they had formerly been allowed to settle, and expelling all foreign Jews. In Poland, where the Jewish population was larger than in any other country, except Russia, anti-Semitism developed as a result of Jewish opposition to Polish nationalism, while economic factors also played their part. Becoming almost entirely city dwellers in the United States, and often settling in already congested areas, the Jews became large factors in complicating the problems confronting the older city Protestant churches. In 1890 there were in the United States 533 Jewish congregations with 130,496 communicants. The Jewish Year Book for 1905 gave the number of Jews in the United States as 1,253,213. In 1906 there were 1,152 Jewish Congregations in the United States; in 1916 there were 1,619; in 1926, 3,118. In the latter year the number of Jews in communities where there were congregations was placed by the Federal Census at 4,081,242.[3] Of this large number of Jewish people in the United States, less than 20,000 were listed as living in rural areas. Since the turn of the century Judaism has become one of the major religious bodies in America.

Another of the rapidly growing religious bodies in the United States during the last several decades is the Latter-day Saints, or the Mormons, though their increase has not been due so largely to immigration, as formerly. In 1906 the two Mormon bodies, the Church of the Latter-day Saints and the Reorganized Church, had together a membership of 256,647; in 1926 they reported 606,561, or more than a 100 per cent increase in missionary work and have more than 2,000 missionaries continuously in the field, working in every state of the union and in many foreign countries. The Utah church particularly is highly organized and centralized. It conducts numerous church schools, seminaries and Latter-day Saint Institutes in connection with high schools and state institutions. There are few churches in the country which mold and influence the daily life of its membership more than does the Mormon. It looks after the sick and the poor, provides education and amusement, and is closely identified with the economic life of the people. Their coöperative enterprises are numerous and successful and Mormon life generally presents an attractive and prosperous aspect. It has been pointed out that though there is not a state in the Union in which Roman Catholics or Jews constitute a majority of the total population, the Mormons, however, constitute four-fifths of the population in Utah, though they no longer are a unit in their political affiliations, nor for that matter are the Catholics and Jews.

In 1916 there were at least 2,700,000 persons of pure Scandinavian stock living in the United States, which represents a flow of immigration covering a period of about 90 years. But the vast majority came after 1880. This great influx of Swedish, Norwegian and Danish people swelled the ranks of American Lutheranism and raised to a place of growing influence the Augustana (Swedish) Synod, the Norwegian Lutheran Church, and the Danish and Finnish religious bodies. In 1949 the membership of the principal Scandinavian bodies in the United States was: Augustana Synod, 333,367; Norwegian Church, 514,304;

---

[3] There was no attempt to find the actual number of communicants in the Jewish congregations. The above figure is probably twice the actual number of communicants. *Religious Bodies,* 1926, Vol. II (1929), pp. 645-664.

United Danish Lutheran Church, 31,489. The Norwegian Lutheran Church did not achieve a united organization until 1890. All the American Lutheran bodies profited greatly from immigration, there being more than 2,000,000 foreign-born Germans in the United States in 1910, whose coming not only swelled Roman Catholic ranks, but also fed the conservative Lutheran bodies, such as the Missouri, the Wisconsin and the Iowa Synods.

The Roman Catholics, the Jews and the Lutherans were not the only bodies to profit from European immigration. All the revivalistic churches began work among the immigrants and with considerable success. The Baptists and Methodists particularly were successful in gaining a following among the Scandinavian and German immigrants, while the Presbyterians have had the largest success among the Italians. Among the American Swedes, the Mission Friends, which began as a lay movement in the state church in Sweden, developed into an independent religious body in America and in 1926 had a membership of some 37,000. It has recently adopted the name, the Evangelical Mission Covenant Church of America. The complete religious freedom in the United States helps to account also for other like schisms from transplanted European churches.

The end of the century and for a decade beyond saw organized religion in America advancing rapidly and in an optimistic mood for the future. From 1880 to 1890 the Baptist family had grown from 2,500,000 to 3,700,000; the Methodists from 3,500,000 to 4,500,000; the Presbyterians from nearly 1,000,000 to 1,300,000; the Disciples from nearly 600,000 to nearly 700,000; the Episcopalians added 250,000 to their 1880 membership, bringing it well beyond the half million mark, while other smaller churches had increased in like proportion. From 1880 to 1895 the annual total increase of church membership in the United States was more than 350,000.

V

Perhaps at no period in the history of the American pulpit had there been so many outstanding preachers as in the last two decades of the nineteenth century. Henry Ward Beecher's remarkable career came to an end in 1887 with his death, and he was succeeded at Plymouth Church, Brooklyn, by Lyman Abbott. Although never as great a preacher as Beecher, yet Lyman Abbott exercised an influence of great importance for the period, in helping many to adjust their religion to the new science and the new views of the Bible. At the Central Presbyterian Church in Brooklyn was T. De Witt Talmage, who, in 1890, at the height of his fame, was preaching to larger audiences than any other preacher in America, while his sermons were being published in 3,500 newspapers throughout the English-speaking world. Though called a pulpit clown and a mountebank by his critics, because of his startling pulpit manner and his unusual illustrations, he had many admirers. At the Marble Collegiate Dutch Reformed Church in New York was David James Burrell, preaching the old-fashioned evangelical theology, but doing it so effectively that his well-planned, fervent, well-illustrated and widely published sermons became the model for many a young man entering the ministry. At the First Baptist Church in Chicago (1882-1891) and after 1903 at Tremont Temple, Boston, P. S. Henson was attracting crowded audiences by his eloquent presentation of the fundamental truths of the gospel. Bishop Matthew Simpson, the most eloquent preacher among the Methodists, had died in 1884. At the Old South Church in Boston was George A. Gordon (1884-1929), "a philosopher who knew how to preach, and a theologian with religious insight and fervor." Preëminently a teaching ministry, his appeal was primarily to thoughtful people, and exercised large influence upon other ministers.

But the recognized prince of the American pulpit of the period was Phillips Brooks whose ministry at Trinity Church, Boston, began in 1869. Six feet four inches tall and broad in proportion, with a perfectly smooth face lighted by luminous brown eyes, he weighed in his prime three hundred pounds. A poet by nature, rapid of speech, with fervent piety and deep conviction, his preaching perfectly illustrated his own definition given in his Yale Lectures on Preaching (1877), "Preaching is the bringing of truth through personality." Though not strikingly original in thought, he possessed the ability of catching up the finest spiritual ideas of his time and putting them into glowing words so that everyone was able to catch their spiritual significance. Broad in his sympathies as well as in his churchmanship, Phillips Brooks exercised a wide influence outside his own communion. Dr. S. Weir Mitchell, his intimate friend in Philadelphia, wrote: "[he is the] only man I ever knew who seemed to me entirely great." Elected bishop of Massachusetts in 1891, his consecration was delayed because of accusations of unsoundness in doctrine and a too broad churchmanship, on the part of the Anglo-Catholic party. His death in 1893 was considered a public calamity. As one of his biographers has well said, "Phillips Brooks' supreme contribution to the country was himself."

VI

A movement which has grown to large proportions in all the Protestant churches is that known as religious education. It began with the opening of the century when a group of outstanding leaders in Protestantism in America began to realize the growing danger arising from the omission of religious teaching in the public schools. This meant that the religious training of American Protestant children must depend upon the Sunday schools, together with what training might be received in the home. The Roman Catholics and the Missouri Synod Lutherans, particularly, had already met the situation, at least to their own satisfaction, by the development of parochial school systems. Because of the fact that they were educating so many children, which otherwise would have been the duty of the public schools, the Catholics have always maintained that they should, in justice, receive government assistance in the maintaining of their parochial schools. The Lutherans, however, not only oppose such government assistance, but would refuse it if it were offered. On the other hand Catholics have always opposed the reading of the Bible in the public schools, or any religious instruction whatever, unless it be given under Catholic auspices. As a result all religious instruction has disappeared from public schools where Catholics are influential.

The Protestant churches had already learned coöperation in their Sunday-school work, the American Sunday School Union, an interdenominational organization, having been formed in 1824, and interdenominational Sunday-school conventions were held from time to time thereafter. In 1872 the Fifth National Sunday-school Convention adopted a system of uniform Sunday-school lessons, largely through the efforts of Dr. John H. Vincent and B. F. Jacobs, a businessman of Chicago and an enthusiastic Sunday-school superintendent. Thus it was arranged that all Sunday schools were to study the same Scripture lessons at the same time. There quickly arose an interdenominational Sunday-school literature for the promotion of this movement. Though the Sunday schools were enthusiastically supported and grew to large proportions, Sunday-school buildings began to be built for the better accommodation of classes, and teacher training courses were planned at Chautauqua and other places, yet by the end of the century the glaring incompetence of the average Sunday school began to be more and more recognized and deplored.

In the year 1903 William Rainey Harper, president of the University of Chicago, together with some of his colleagues in the University and an impressive list of religious leaders in the country, issued a call for a convention to meet in Chicago to form a national organization to promote the religious and moral instruction of youth. This was successfully accomplished and the Religious Education Association was organized. Its purpose was, through its boards and secretaries, to encourage and assist existing religious and moral educational agencies to improve their effectiveness; to make scientific investigations in order to define more closely the true relation of religious and moral instruction to other branches of instruction; to determine more clearly the place of the Bible in such instruction; and to carry on experiments in adapting moral and religious instruction to different stages of mental, moral and spiritual development. In other words, its purpose was to bring progressive educational ideas into the service of the cause of religious instruction.

In 1922 the Interdenominational Council of Religious Education was formed, the purpose of which was to bring about larger educational cooperation among the Protestant churches. Many of the larger churches installed directors of religious education, and state directors of religious education, both denominational and interdenominational are not uncommon. Standards of church-school work have been decidedly raised and weekday and vacation church schools are now commonly conducted, the latter being often interdenominational in character. Denominational colleges and theological seminaries have installed departments of religious education for the purpose of training competent workers in this new field. In more recent years the religious education movement has aroused considerable criticism, often based on the tactless and half-trained directors of religious education, who were strong on technique but weak on content and common sense. Shailer Mathews in his *New Faith for Old* (p. 251) well summarizes the counts against the religious educationist:

> The chief of these seemed to be the tendency to minimize churches as institutions. to hide God behind a smoke screen of psychology, to neglect theology

by those who had had no thorough theological training, an inadequate use of the Bible, and an overemphasis upon techniques and questionnaires.

But perhaps like all new movements in the church the tendency to claim too much for religious education, led to an overoptimism as to results.

One of the major weaknesses of American Protestantism has been its inability to speak with a united voice on any great issue of moral and religious concern. The very principles upon which Protestantism proceeds makes any unanimity difficult to attain. This is one of the problems which is as old as Protestantism itself. But is division and disunion a necessity of Protestantism? As my former colleague, John T. McNeill, so well points out in his *Unitive Protestantism* (1930), the union idea was strongly present among the reformers and has never been lost in the centuries which have followed. A long step in the direction of overcoming this handicap was taken in 1908 with the formation of the Federal Council of the Churches of Christ in America.

The beginnings of church federation go back to the formation of the Evangelical Alliance in London in 1846. This body was constituted of some fifty different evangelical bodies of England and America, and branches were soon established in nine European countries. Dr. Samuel S. Schmucker of the Lutheran Theological Seminary at Gettysburg, Pennsylvania, was the principal American leader in the movement. The purpose of the Alliance was to promote evangelical union in order to increase the effectiveness of Christian work, to promote the cause of religious freedom, and to advance the cause of Christ everywhere. The slavery controversy and the Civil War prevented the formation of a branch Alliance in the United States until 1867, but from that time until the close of the century it carried on successfully, furthering many coöperative enterprises. Toward the close of the century, however, it became less active and other interchurch organizations were formed, while several states organized state federations of churches. In addressing a meeting of representatives of the churches of New York State in 1900, which had met for the purpose of forming a state federation, Theodore Roosevelt stated, "There are plenty of targets that we need to hit without firing into each other."

In 1905 the constitution of the Federal Council of the Churches of Christ in America was drawn up, and three years later (1908), after ratification by the thirty denominations constituting its first membership, it began operations. The Council had to proceed cautiously, but

it found from the beginning a wide area of service, not seriously involving ecclesiastical differences, with which it could deal, such as the relation of the church to modern industry, Christian education and
family life. The most important thing accomplished at the organizing
meeting was the adoption of the Social Creed of the Churches, which has
exercised a determining influence on public opinion in the United
States. The Creed called for equal rights and complete justice for all
men in all stations of life; for the abolition of child labor; for adequate
regulations of the conditions of toil for women; for the suppression of
the "sweating system"; for the gradual reduction of hours of labor to the
lowest possible point, making possible leisure time for the attaining of
the highest human life; for one day of rest in seven; for the right of all
men to the opportunity of self-maintenance; for the right of workers to
some protection against the hardships resulting from industrial change;
for a living wage as a minimum in every industry, and for the highest
wage that each industry can afford; for adequate protection of workers
from dangerous machinery and occupational diseases; for a suitable
provision for old age and for those incapacitated by injury; for the
principle of conciliation and arbitration in industry; for the abatement
of poverty; for the more equitable division of the products of industry.

The social emphasis in American Protestantism has greatly changed
the tone of the American pulpit. According to Gaius Glenn Atkins it
has been a "life preserver" for twentieth-century preaching, though in
more recent years congregations have tended to become increasingly
tired of too much "harping on the same string." But it is an influence
which needs to be retained as a vital part of Christianity, for many leading laymen are still largely unconvinced that the church has any legitimate right to deal with economic matters. Such men are great supporters
of "spiritual religion." They hold that the noise and clamor of the world
should be halted at the church doors. But it must be understood that
the social gospel does not embrace all the Christian message. Perhaps the
main criticism which could be laid at the door of preachers of the social
emphasis is that they tend to an oversimplification of problems about
which they have only a superficial knowledge. This often tends to make
them advocates of foolish panaceas.

CHAPTER XXIII

✧ ✧ ✧

WORLD WAR I: PROSPERITY AND DEPRESSION

IN his book *Religion in Our Times,* Gaius Glenn Atkins had characterized the American churches in the decade and a half previous to World
War I as "the Crusading Church at Home and Abroad." This characterization, however, is not only apt for the years just preceding the war, but
continues to be applicable to the American churches throughout the
war itself and for a short period thereafter. In fact if the churches had
not already become imbued with the crusading spirit in promoting
such enterprises as the Men and Religion Forward Movement, Prohibition, the Laymen's Missionary Campaign, the World Student Christian Federation, the Student Volunteer Movement, Church Unity and
World Peace, the American churches might not have become such enthusiastic supporters of the war itself, with its program of making the
world safe for democracy, and of fighting a "war to end war." For after
all there was as much probability of making the world safe for democracy
and of making an end of all war by winning the war against German
autocracy, as there was of evangelizing the world in this generation, or
of making Christianity triumphant in America and the world by the
methods which were being enthusiastically supported by all the prominent Protestant church leaders of the prewar years.

Another fact which has significance is, that from the close of the
Spanish-American War, American Christian people were becoming increasingly internationally-minded. In the Protestant churches generally
the foreign missionary interest was the dominant interest. John R. Mott
and Robert E. Speer, with their dynamic personalities and their visions
of the speedy world triumph of Christianity, were the favorite speakers
before college and university bodies, and there were few sincere Christ-

ian young men and women in the colleges during those years who did not consider the question of giving themselves to some type of foreign Christian service, either under the auspices of some church board or under the Young Men's or Young Women's Christian Associations. Everywhere throughout the college world Student Volunteer Bands flourished. So well recognized was the wide knowledge and influence of John R. Mott in the Far East that President Woodrow Wilson urged him to accept the United States ambassadorship to China. This invitation Mott declined, evidently on the ground that he was engaged in a more important mission to the non-Christian peoples of the world.

II

At the end of World War I there arose in the English-speaking world particularly, a considerable number of able advocates of absolute pacifism, whose position was based upon what they considered the definite pacifism of Jesus. Among the oft-quoted passage of Scripture supporting this position was Matthew 5:38-41:

> Ye have heard that it hath been said, an eye for an eye, and a tooth for a tooth: but I say unto you, That ye resist not evil: but whosoever shall smite thee on thy right cheek, turn to him the other also. And if any man will sue thee at the law, and take away thy coat, let him have thy cloak also. And whosoever shall compel thee to go a mile, go with him twain.

Another passage frequently used by the modern pacifist is the account of the temptations of Jesus in which he refused to worship the devil in order to secure dominion over the earth (Matthew 4:8-10). The modern pacifist interpreting this passage would say that Jesus here rejected force, since he knew that it was by force only that the dominion of earth could be secured. A third Scripture passage used to support the absolute pacifist position is Matthew 24:15-22, in which Jesus pictures the "abomination of desolation," which was soon to come as a result of the revolutionary movements then under way in Palestine. Here Jesus tells the elect to flee to the mountains and to have no part in the defense of Jerusalem. There are other Scripture passages used by the modern pacifist, but these will serve to illustrate the method by which present-day Christian pacifism has reached its position. Besides these specific Scripture references modern pacificism has found support for it position in the total teaching and life of Jesus. These are love toward one's neighbor; the fatherhood of God; the infinite value he placed upon the individual soul; and finally the example Jesus set, especially his submission to the cross.[1]

The above summary seems to indicate that Jesus left no specific statement on the question of the Christian attitude toward war, just as he left no specific instructions in regard to the Christian attitude toward slavery. This fact has made it necessary for his followers to find their own answers to many similar puzzling questions which have arisen in the centuries that have followed, guided only by the "Spirit of truth."

It is definitely known that the early Christians disapproved of war. As late as the fourth century Lactantius describes Christians as:

> Those who are ignorant of war, who preserve concord with all, who are friends even to their enemies, who love all men as brothers, who know how to curb anger and soften with quiet moderation every madness of the mind. (Divine Institutions, V., xii, 4.)

The early Christians looked upon the world as only a temporary abiding place which was soon to be exchanged for a heavenly home and therefore they felt no obligation to take part in the ordinary organizational life about them.[2]

As time passed and as the expectation of the speedy end of the world began to dim, Christians took on gradually a different view as to the place they should occupy in the world. Naturally, also, with the gaining of legal status after Constantine and the making of Christianity the religion of the state the Christian's sense of obligation to society and the state increased. It has been commonly stated that as a result of this tendency the church became increasingly paganized and to a large degree secularized. Professor McNeill, however, corrects this view, stating that although compromises were inevitable, yet on the whole "Christian idealism was not surrendered."[3]

[1] The two best books on the bearing of the New Testament on war are C. J. Cadoux, *The Early Christian Attitude toward War* (London, 1919), and H. C. Macgregor, *The New Testament Basis of Pacifism* (London 1936). A convenient summary of the methods by which modern pacifists have come to their position may be found in Umphrey Lee, *The Historic Church and Modern Pacifism* (New York and Nashville, 1943.)

[2] Cadoux points out, however, that the ethics of Jesus cannot be explained on the basis of the expectation of the approaching end of all things. The ground for such commands as loving enemies, granting forgiveness and seeking the lost is based upon the nature of God and not upon anything that might come about "in the near or distant future." Cadoux, *op. cit.* p. 45.

[3] John T. McNeill, *Christian Hope for World Society* (Chicago, 1937), p. 9.

Gradually the church came to find a place for war, but only accepted it as a necessary evil. Augustine expressed the view, widely accepted, that what was bad in war was not so much the loss of life but the "moral evils let loose by war."

The Reformation resulted in the creation of a number of national Protestant churches, all of which had definite ties to the state. The most important single influence in determining American colonial church attitudes toward war came from John Calvin, exerted in America principally through the Congregationalists and the Presbyterians, the two largest colonial religious bodies. Full-fledged Calvinism was not only a creed, but also a system of government and implied a close partnership between the church and the state. According to Calvin the state was to be the protecting arm of the church; the kingdom of God was to be established by the church and state working closely together. The Christian was not only a member of the church but he was also a citizen and must take his part in carrying on the affairs of the state. But a Christian citizen may not take part in a war of aggression, but only in what Calvin termed, a "just war." He held that it was sometimes the Christian's *duty* to take part in war, but the only kind of warfare in which a Christian could engage was wars waged to preserve the tranquillity of a nation or to repel invaders. All persons participating in an invasion were to be considered as robbers and ought to be punished as such. In Calvin's thought civil order was a part of the divine plan and the means used to preserve order, such as courts, and wars to repel invaders or to put down internal disturbances, have a Christian sanction.

Luther's position toward war was not greatly different from that of Calvin. Luther held that the church occupied a separate sphere from that of the state: the state was duty-bound to protect true religion, but it was a negative rather than a positive duty. The Christian had duties toward the state as well as to the Church, one of which was to defend the state from invasion and to obey the powers that be. The Zwinglian movement was also closely tied to the State, indeed Zwingli met his death while participating in a war against the Catholic cantons of Switzerland. Generally speaking, the views of all the reformers were based on the principle that the Christian must live his life in the midst of organized society and must therefore assume the responsibilities and burdens of helping to maintain it. The Christian deplores war and is always depressed by a warring world, but he cannot escape his responsibilities to society.

Out of the Reformation there came also certain other groups which did not accept the views of the principal reformers in regard to church-state relationship, nor did they agree with their attitudes toward war. These groups are now designated as the left-wing phase of the Reformation. In the sixteenth and seventeenth centuries they were generally lumped together under the name Anabaptist. Though differing among themselves—at one time there were as many as forty kinds of Anabaptists, found principally in Holland, Switzerland and in southern Germany—they all held that the true church must be entirely separate from the state and from the world. Indeed they thought of themselves as reproducing the church of the early Christian centuries in respect to its relationship to government and to society. True Christians were to live apart from the world and were to have as little relationship to it and as little part in it as possible. Since government officials compelled men to use the sword, and participate in war, therefore no true Christian could have any part in government. The Mennonites, a name assumed by certain Anabaptist groups, insisted that all doctrine must have a New Testament basis, since the Old Testament permitted oaths, divorce, polygamy and war. The New Testament introduced a new dispensation and was God's complete revelation of his will to men.

The later Pietistic bodies, such as the Dunkers, the Schwenkfelders and the German Moravians, took the same position toward war, basing it on a literal following of the New Testament. The Dunkers adopted the principle of nonresistance and refused to take the oath of allegiance to the state, as did also the Mennonites, basing their refusal on New Testament grounds. The Moravians were not a unit in their opposition to war, though in the earlier years of the movement they held that true followers of Christ were bound to obey the six "least" commandments found in the fifth chapter of Matthew's gospel. This meant that they were forbidden to participate in government; could not serve as jurymen or judges, or as soldiers.[4]

Unlike that of the Anabaptists, the Quaker position on war did not grow out of any definite theory as to the position the Christian should take toward the state. Nor were they nonparticipators in the affairs of the world or of government. Nor did they base their attitude toward war on

[4]For recent treatments of the Mennonite, Dunker and Moravian positions on war see K. G. Hamilton, *John Ettwein and the Moravian Church during the Revolutionary Period* (Bethlehem, Pa., 1940), p. 131-233; Guy Franklin Hershberger, *War, Peace and Nonresistance* (Scottdale, Pa., 1944); Rufus D. Bowman, *The Church of the Brethren and War, 1708-1941* (Elgin, Ill., 1944), Chap. II.

specific Scripture passages, but rather the Quaker simply believed and practiced a way of life that made war incongruous. They placed their faith in spiritual weapons; not in carnal. It was the spirit of the New Testament rather than the letter that guided them. Rufus Jones states that Quakers are neither "non-resisters" or "passivists" for "They do not face any giant evil with a passive attitude. Rather they always seek to organize and to level against it the most effective forces there are." They would do away with war by doing away with the causes and occasions for it.[5]

In the process of the colonization of America, all of these various attitudes toward war were transplanted to the New World.

Since none of the historic pacifist groups, except the Quakers, permitted participation in government, their influence in public affairs was slight, while the Calvinistic point of view dominated the thinking of the major colonial religious bodies. The colonial clergy was practically unanimous in their support of the Indian war. Indians pretty generally were considered the children of the devil and therefore predestined to be damned. It is true that the conversion of the Indians had been represented in the early colonizing propaganda literature as one of the principal reasons for the founding of the colonies, but taking the colonial period as a whole, colonial Protestantism was little interested in the Christianization of the "infidels." In fact, they were much more interested in getting rid of them. John Fiske's statement comparing the Spaniard with the New England Puritan in regard to their respective attitudes toward the savages is not far out of the way. The Puritan, he stated, went to church with a gun on his shoulder to keep the Indian out; the Spaniard went to church with a gun on his shoulder to drive the Indian in. In other words the Puritan did not consider the Indians as a part of society because he could not use them; the Spaniard on the other hand accepted the Indians as a part of society because the Indians with whom they came in contact were of a higher cultural status and therefore were useful to them.

Life to the Puritan was grim, and involved harshness, pain, and brutality; but his duty was to face it without shrinking. If it involved destroying Indians to protect home and family, he must go about it with grim thoroughness. When the New England church members drilled on

[5]Rufus M. Jones, *The Faith and Practice of Quakers* (London and New York), p. 108-122.

militia day and marched away against the Pequods and fought in King Philip's war, they were told by the minister that enemies beset them on every hand, and the enemies were now the Indians and they must either kill them or be killed by them. They were fighting a defensive war and therefore their actions were just and right.[6]

The attitude of the Scotch-Irish Presbyterians on the colonial frontier was identical with that of their fellow Calvinists in New England. To them the only good Indian was a dead Indian.

The peace movement in America began with the coming of the Quakers, Moravians and the German sectaries—the Mennonites, the Dunkers and the Schwenkfelders. And as bodies these groups have remained faithful to their testimony against war from that day to this. The organization of peace societies as distinct from the pacifist religious sects dates from the early years of the last century. In 1826 there were some fifty peace societies throughout the several states. During these years the peace movement was simply one of many benevolent enterprises which flourished during the "Sentimental Years." Though the peace societies were nonsectarian, they were mainly carried on by ministers and pious laymen such as Lewis and Arthur Tappan, and David Low Dodge, successful merchants in New York and devoted to the advancement of every good cause. Dodge was the founder of the New York Peace Society in 1815 and was the presiding officer at the formation of the American Peace Society in 1828. The Dodge family continued their interest in advancing the cause of peace and other reforms through several generations.

The *Harbinger of Peace* was the official organ of the Peace Society and during its first year had a circulation of 1,500. Later the paper took the name the *Advocate of Peace* and has remained the organ of the society to the present time. William Jay, a stanch Episcopalian and a liberal supporter of many benevolent enterprises, the son of the first Chief Justice of the United States, was one of the founders of the American Peace Society and in 1842 published a most influential pamphlet entitled, *War and Peace: the Evils of the First, and a Plan for Preserving the Last*. One of the suggestions made in the pamphlet was that in every treaty there should be a provision that all future international differences should be referred first to arbitration, to attempt a peaceful settle-

6Perry Miller, *The New England Mind* (New York, 1939), Chap. II, "The Practice of Piety."

ment before the nations involved resorted to arms. In the treaty closing the Crimean War this suggestion was actually followed.

The churches began to give increasing attention to the cause of peace after 1830, and in the forties it was not uncommon for Congregational, Baptist and Methodist bodies to place themselves on record favoring international peace. The Mexican War was the occasion for much "deploring of war" in general and of the Mexican War in particular, especially among New England religious bodies.

In the midst of the war (1847) the New England Conference of the Methodist Episcopal Church urged its members to apply the precepts of the gospel of peace to the end that all wars may cease, declaring that "all war is and ought to be denounced by Christians." On the other hand the Baltimore Conference of the same church in the same year passed resolutions pledging to the President of the United States their sympathy, and promised to support the administration in the conflict with Mexico. In 1848 the Quakers sent to the government a petition bearing nine thousand signatures asking that peace be made with Mexico at once, while the Unitarians sent another petition of similar import with three thousand signatures. Previous to the Civil War the peace movement in America was largely tied up with the antislavery movement and **other reforms**. With the coming of the Civil War, involving as it did the great moral issue of slavery, the northern churches generally supported the war, as the only way to destroy the great evil. As a result the peace movement waned. In other words, the peace movement prospered when the churches gave it aid; when they withheld their support it declined.

With the close of the Civil War the peace movement revived. The Peace Society renewed its activities, and the Woman's Christian Temperance Union established a peace department in 1889. But the period of greatest activity was from the close of the Spanish-American War to the outbreak of World War I. The peace workers had avoided discussion of Spanish-American War issues and had concentrated on practical means for the settlement of future international disputes. Among the important new peace agencies arising were the Lake Mohonk Conferences which began in 1895 and to which clergymen of all denominations were invited. A direct outgrowth of the Mohonk Conferences was the Conference of Friends held in Philadelphia in 1901 which brought together for the first time the foremost leaders of a religious body to speak solely for the cause of peace. In 1902 the American Association of Ministers was founded in New York for the promotion of peace. In 1899 the Inter-parliamentary Union had been organized in Paris and began at once to spread propaganda for a permanent court of arbitration, and just ten years later th? first Hague Conference was held, to which twenty-six nations, including the United States, sent representatives. In the early years of the new century Andrew Carnegie began to devote a part of his great fortune to the promotion of world peace, and the most prominent leaders in both church and state were enlisted in the great cause. In 1910 the Carnegie Endowment for International Peace was established with $10,000,000. In 1909 the Peace society doubled its membership, and throughout the country ministers were more outspoken on the question of peace than at any other time. In 1905 it was stated in the report of the Department of Peace and Arbitration of the W.C.T.U. that more peace sermons had been preached that year than ever before. It was now completely respectable to condemn war as barbaric, and to advocate peace as an enduring ideal, and many good people all over the land came to believe that "humanity was finally nearing the goal of universal peace."

A typical example of a church pronouncement on peace and arbitration, on the very eve of World War I, is that found in the Episcopal Church in 1912. The people, it states,

have balanced the ledgers of the centuries and they have found that the honors and spoils of war have never been equitably divided. Save in the wars of the people for freedom, the thrones and the honors have gone to the few, and thorns and horrors to the many. In the awful arithmetic of war it takes a thousand homes to build one palace, ten thousand lives of brave men to lift a pedestal for one man to occupy in lonely grandeur.

The people also, the address states, have

learned the secrets of financial diplomacy, and the day is not far away when monarchs and plutocrats must shed their own blood in their own battles, or settle their accounts at the Hague. Ink is cheaper than blood. Law is better than force, and patience is a wiser diplomat than threat and bluster.

During the trouble on the Mexican border following the Mexican Revolution of 1911, when the Hearst papers particularly were impor-tuning our government to intervene, one minister stated that he could not get very enthusiastic about sending his boy to Mexico to fight for Mr. Hearst's oil wells and his other Mexican properties.

Many, if not most, of the Christian people of America were fully

convinced that the world was entering upon a new and glorious age in
which ballots, not bullets, were to be the weapons in a new kind of warfare, to bring in the reign of justice and right. Most thought a big war
impossible. For everybody was saying no nation was rich enough to bear
the cost of maintaining for any length of time the burden of modern warfare. The optimism of these years blinded most Americans to the fact
that across the Atlantic was a veritable powder mine ready to explode
at any moment. And so when the war began America stood aghast.

President Wilson's policy of maintaining neutrality announced at
the opening of the war found general support at first among church
people. But in the face of the skillful propaganda of the Allies, and
especially of Great Britain, together with the large influence exercised
by such leaders as ex-Presidents Theodore Roosevelt and Taft, William
Allen White, Presidents Harry Pratt Judson of the University of Chicago
and William Greer Hibben of Princeton, and Lyman Abbott and many
others who had joined in the formation of the Security League, the
neutrality policy was doomed. More and more the war began to be interpreted in spiritual terms. It was a war to save civilization; a "war to
end war." It was believed that H. G. Wells spoke as a prophet when he
said, "Every sword that is drawn against Germany is a sword drawn for
peace. . . . The defeat of Germany may open up the way to disarma-
ment and peace throughout the earth." Such spiritualization of the war
made it easy for people who were firm believers in peace to advocate the
United States' entrance into the war. And for many, even before our
entrance, it had already become a holy cause.

III

Ray H. Abrams in his *Preachers Present Arms* has told in all its em-
barrassing detail the story of the part played by Christian leaders and
the American churches in World War I. "The war is religious," said
Joseph Fort Newton as he sailed for England to become the minister of
City Temple, London. "The war for righteousness will be won! Let the
Church do her part," said Frank Mason North, president of the Federal
Council. The minister of John Street Methodist Episcopal Church in
New York in answer to the question, "Was Jesus a pacifist?" answered,
"Christ was the greatest fighter the world has even seen." And there were
plenty of texts to prove that Christ could be a mighty warrior. He drove
the moneychangers out of the temple; he said, "render unto Caesar the

things that are Caesar's." One minister got around the text on turning the other cheek, by saying that Jesus certainly never meant it literally for there is no record of his having done it himself. Lyman Abbott proved that Jesus was no anarchist because he told Peter in the Garden of Gethsemane to put up his sword. Professor Ernest De Witt Burton, later to become the President of the University of Chicago, urged that the defeat of the Germans was for the best interest of Germany, and therefore our entrance into the war was in accordance with the Golden Rule. Even the American Peace Society through its organ *The Advocate of Peace* argued that the bayoneting of a normally decent German soldier is justified on the ground that it was helping to free him from a tyranny which he at present accepts as his chosen form of government. All details of the war were glorified in a booklet, *The Practice of Friendship,* circulated by the Y.M.C.A., the authors stating, "The American nation . . . is engaged at this hour in an attempt . . . to Christianize every phase of a righteous war waged to save the very life of democracy." The joint authors of this booklet, one of whom was Henry B. Wright, a professor in the Yale Divinity School, urged the lads as they enter upon their training as soldiers to be able to "see Jesus himself sighting down a gun barrel and running a bayonet through an enemy's body." Nor were the Catholics behind the Protestant ministers in supporting the war. "Remember," said Cardinal Gibbons addressing a military mass at Camp Meade, "such wounds as you may receive will be honorable. . . . Go forth to battle and victory, and God be with you."

With the nation bending all its great energies to the winning of the war, the churches became little more than government agencies carrying out the will of the state. Churches were busy with war activities. Local units of the Red Cross met in church parlors, as did other wartime agencies. Contributions to the numerous funds, the sale of Liberty bonds and war saving stamps, the raising of quotas for this and that organization, were urged from the pulpits of the land. Ministers preached sermons from outlines sent them by government propaganda agencies, and believed and did their part to circulate stories of enemy atrocities. Preachers went to training camps as chaplains, or volunteered to go as workers, to help carry on the great task which the government had placed upon the Young Men's Christian Association in the camps both in the United States and overseas. All the churches created War Commissions to direct their special wartime activities, while a General Wartime Commission was formed by the Federal Council, made up of one hundred members representing not less than thirty-five denominations. This body raised $300,000 during the course of the war, its chief work consisting in helping the government secure efficient men to serve as chaplains. The Catholics also, through their National War Council, carried on a similar work. At least for the period of World War I the separation of church and state was suspended.

Paradoxical as it may seem, the ministers of all denominations did more than their share in propagating wartime hatred. The popular preacher and lecturer, Newell Dwight Hillis, outstripped all others in his denunciation of the Germans and in his promulgating of war atrocity stories. So effective were these tactics that the American Bankers Association called upon Dr. Hillis to assist in the second Liberty loan and sent him to Europe to gather first-hand information about the German atrocities. When he returned with his fresh ammunition he lectured 400 times in 162 cities in the interest of the drive. So pleased was Theodore Roosevelt with Dr. Hillis that he wrote, "I would rather have Dr. Hillis as chaplain than any other man." "Billy" Sunday was in his prime and very much in his element during these years and he took full advantage of the opportunity. Here is a good example of his wartime eloquence:

I tell you it is Bill against Woodrow, Germany against America, Hell against Heaven. . . . Either you are loyal or you are not, you are either a patriot or a black-hearted traitor. . . . All this talk about not fighting the German people is a lot of bunk. They say that we are fighting for an ideal. Well, if we are we will have to knock down the German people to get it over.

It is instructive also to learn to what extent ministers were willing to put a limit upon the freedom of speech. Father John A. Ryan, a liberal Catholic, held that the authorities were "justified . . . in preventing obstructive criticism, and that no citizen could justly complain if the government restricted his freedom of speech for the sake of winning the war." The I.W.W., the German-Americans, the conscientious objectors, and the pacifists were all lumped together for widespread ministerial denunciation and condemnation. Even the Quakers did not escape. "Quakerism is sixteen hundred years too late to be entitled to the epithet Christian," declared *The Living Church*; while *Zion's Herald* said, "God's employment of War as a means of dispensing with useless and harmful material is too conspicuous a feature of Scripture

to allow standing room to Quakers and men with a quaking disposition."
"Wolves in sheep's clothing," was the way in which the Canon of the
Cathedral of St. John the Divine characterized the conscientious objectors; while John Timothy Stone, the chaplain of Camp Grant, tried
to convert all the conscientious objectors confined there into accepting
military service.

It is an important fact that the war produced practically no heroes
of high military rank, as did the Civil War. To a large degree it was a
sergeants' and second lieutenants' war and there were many Sergeant
Yorks. But undoubtedly among the greatest heroes produced by the war
were the conscientious objectors. Some of them may not have been sincere, but there are enough of the older variety to warrant an appraisal of
the part they played. Abrams has listed seventy ministers who were out-
and-out pacifists, the Unitarians leading with sixteen.

What happened to the ministers who steadfastly set their faces against
war? John Haynes Holmes' congregation walked out on him and a
strange assemblage, representing all shades of opinion and all races
took its place. Bishop Paul Jones of the Episcopal diocese of Utah, rather
than cause a disturbance in his church, resigned. Norman Thomas, at
that time a Presbyterian minister in New York, joined in all movements
in helping to preserve essential liberties. Several others resigned under
pressure; some were mobbed and whipped; others were victims of tar
and feathers; one minister having refused to participate in a Liberty
Loan Drive had his house painted yellow by the patriots. Altogether
there were some fifty-five ministers representing various religious bodies
who suffered arrest. One Episcopal minister, Irwin St. John Tucker, was
sentenced by Judge Landis to twenty years in Leavenworth prison. A
convention of Christian pacifists meeting in Los Angeles in 1917 was
attacked by a mob, urged on by businessmen and ministers, and three
of the leaders were arrested. When brought to trial they were found
guilty of unlawful assembly and disturbing the peace and were sentenced
to pay fines of $1,500 each and to serve jail sentences of six months.

IV

What effect had World War I on vital religion in America? If the
average minister had been asked this question while the war was in
progress he doubtless would have said, "The war has been a vitalizing
influence in the work of the church." For never were the churches more

fully occupied than during these years. Church attendance left little to be desired. The churches were utilized for all sorts and kinds of meetings, most of them having some bearing on the war. The ladies met in the church parlors to knit socks and sweaters for the soldiers, or to engage in Red Cross activities. Leading laymen helped organize the endless campaigns, for the selling of Liberty bonds and war-savings stamps, for the Y.M.C.A. and Salvation Army drives. There were special services for the dedication of service flags, and numberless patriotic meetings of all sorts. Many felt that the war was bringing the churches closer together, and Robert E. Speer and many others believed that the net result of the war "will probably be found to be good."

It was this feeling of optimism among Christian leaders which led to the launching of great campaigns, in the very midst of the war, to raise vast sums for Christian advance throughout the world. The Methodists planned their drive to celebrate the centenary of the beginning of Methodist Missions and set the amount to be raised at $40,000,000 to be paid over a period of five years. Skillful propaganda was prepared setting forth the Christian needs of every nook and corner of the world. The campaign seemed to be a huge success and $115,000,000 was actually subscribed. But it was a period of extravagance and the machinery created for the raising of this vast sum was foolishly lavish, and the speedy deflating of the war idealism brought reaction among the church people generally, and only a relatively small percentage of the amounts subscribed were ever collected. The Presbyterians, the Methodists, South, the Baptists and the Disciples also launched similar drives, though their askings were more modest. Perhaps the most dismal failure of these years was the Interchurch World Movement, a grandiose scheme to coördinate the work of all the churches, which called for the raising of a large sum based on the askings of the various coöperating denominational agencies. The campaign for money, however, coming as it did in the beginning of the period of postwar disillusionment, fell completely flat and the debts which had been incurred in the preliminary surveys were left for the supporting denominational agencies to pay. This they honorably did. By this time the Protestant churches had learned their lesson, and there have been no more attempts at bringing in the Kingdom by the raising of vast sums of money.

Here, I think, is the place to make this generalization: No war has ever helped the cause of vital religion. Religion always slumps as a result. At

no time in the history of organized religion in America has it been at
such low ebb as after our great wars. How could Christianity be expected to thrive in an atmosphere of hate? Hate is horrible anywhere—
but hate in actual war is hate at its worst. The realization of this fact, on
the part of many Christian leaders, brought their speedy repentance for
the part they had played in the whole war business, and many vowed
that they would never "bless war again," while many have taken an
out-and-out pacifist position.

V

The peace movement as it developed out of postwar disillusionment
was very different from the peace movement of the prewar days. The
older movement was negative and more or less passive, the newer movement was positive and aggressive. There were many shades of pacifist
opinion, however, but all were rooted in a distrust of armaments, a
conviction that nothing is worse than war. In 1931 *The World Tomorrow* sent out a questionnaire on war and peace to more than fifty
thousand clergymen of all denominations, and received more than nine-
·een thousand replies. Sixty-two per cent gave it as their conviction that
the church should refuse to sanction or support any future war, while
more than ten thousand gave it as their purpose to refuse to sanction any
future war or to take any part as an armed combatant. What took place
after Adolf Hitler's rise to power, his ruthless treatment of the Jews and
his destruction of the liberties of such peoples as the Czechs caused many
of the ministers who thought themselves out-and-out pacifists to modify
their position. In March, 1939, a hundred prominent ministers signed an
Affirmation of Christian Pacifist Faith, which stated "that the gospel of
God as revealed in Jesus Christ" leaves them no other choice "but to
refuse to sanction or participate in war." On the other hand there were
such pacifists as Bishop F. J. McConnell who declined to "be put on the
spot as to what he should do" if he should come home and find a mur·
derer attempting to kill the members of his family.

By the time of the presidential campaign of 1920 the idealism with
which the United States had entered the war was pretty badly shattered.
The grand crusade was at an end. In one of his campaign speeches in the
summer of 1920, Mr. Harding stated we did not enter the war "proclaiming democracy and humanity," but "we asked the sons of this republic to defend our national rights." Theodore Roosevelt, Jr., in his

campaign speeches for the candidates opposed to the League of Nations also repudiated the idealism of the war years, and it was found to be good politics in that campaign to denounce any further participation in the affairs of the Old World with its "accumulated ills of rivalry and greed." The change in American opinion regarding the responsibility of the United States in European affairs was well illustrated by a contemporary cartoon, picturing General Pershing mounted on a very large elephant, riding rapidly away from the tomb of Lafayette, and calling back over his shoulder, "Lafayette, we've quit." The results of the election of 1920 left little doubt but that the people of the United States had quit and were in no mood to further risk their necks for any other people. Accordingly there was a return to strong nationalism, while the Republican party, now returned to power, did its best to isolate the nation economically as well as politically by building absurdly high tariff walls.

This period of declining idealism and growing nationalism was characterized by the multiplication of organizations devoted to the creation of larger loyalties to local communities and national enterprises. Rotary, Kiwanis and Lions' Clubs sprang up all over the land. Once a week their numbers dined together where there were much hilarity and a great deal of speechmaking on every conceivable subject. Each of the clubs had at least one clergyman in its membership and as a whole they sponsored many worthy enterprises.

Belonging to an entirely different category was the Ku Klux Klan, a fanatical anti-Catholic, anti-Jewish, anti-Negro and anti-Alien, secret oathbound organization which reached the zenith of its influence during the nineteen twenties. William J. Simmons of Atlanta, Georgia, was its founder (1915) and first Imperial Wizard. Modeled after the organization of the same name which arose in the South during the reconstruction years, it had little significance until 1920 when it began to spread throughout the nation, due to the high-pressure drive for members organized by a professional publicity expert, E. Y. Clarke, who received a large percentage of the $10 initiation fee as his reward. Clarke's method of winning members was to play up the anti-Catholicism, anti-Semitism and white supremacy, a sure-fire method of arousing latent American prejudices. His campaign has been described as selling "Hate at ten dollars a package."

The organization found a large following among fundamentalist Protestant groups throughout the country. John M. Mechlin, who has made the most penetrating study of the whole movement, holds that the greatest appeal of the Klan was the fear on the part of many among Protestant bodies of Roman Catholic domination and of the eventual overwhelming of Protestantism itself. In the presidential campaigns of 1924 and 1928 the Klan became politically important and was a large factor in defeating Governor Smith for the Democratic nomination for the Presidency in 1924 and in defeating him at the polls in 1928. Many ministers became actively identified with the Klan organization, some even leaving their pulpits to become Klan organizers.

During this period of postwar reaction, what is known as the Fundamentalist movement also gained great momentum. Indeed, students of society have recognized in the Ku Klux Klan and Fundamentalism identical types of reactionism. The Fundamentalist movement may be said to have begun in 1910 with the publication of a series of little books entitled *The Fundamentals: A Testimony to the Truth*, which professed to set forth the five fundamental Christian truths. More than 2,500,000 copies of the twelve volume series of these booklets were published and circulated with money furnished by two wealthy laymen. The doctrines set forth as fundamental were the virgin birth of Christ, the physical resurrection, the inerrancy of the Scriptures in every respect, the substitutionary theory of the atonement, and the imminent, physical Second Coming of Christ. Those who supported these views did not hesitate to denounce as "no Christian" any who denied any of them. In a broader sense Fundamentalism may be defined as an organized attempt to preserve the authoritarian position of historic Protestantism, against the rising tide of "Modernism." The Modernist position may be stated as the "use of the methods of modern science to find, state and use the permanent and central values of inherited orthodoxy in meeting the needs of a modern world." In other words the Modernist of the postwar years was what might be termed an upholder of liberal Christianity, as over against the conservative.

The controversy between these two types of Protestant Christianity became increasingly vocal and active during the early postwar years and affected every evangelical denomination. The issues in the several churches, well set forth by S. G. Cole in his *History of Fundamentalism*

(1931) were not always the same, but the attitudes engendered were in every case similar. The Baptists and Presbyterians were the ones most affected by the controversy, though among the Disciples and the Methodists the issues were clearly drawn. Among the Methodists the program of the conservatives was twofold: first, to compel the Commission on Courses of Study for young ministers to choose only those books which the conservatives considered in harmony with Methodist doctrinal standards; second, they urged the General Conference to declare "the binding authority of our articles of Religion and other established standards of doctrine." The conservatives also fought to retain in the *Discipline* of the church the specific rule on amusements which had been adopted in 1872. The struggle continued from 1916 to 1924, and at each successive General Conference the issue was raised and bitterly fought. Gradually the conservative party lost its strength and the issue gradually disappeared.

For several successive years in both the Northern Baptist Convention and in the General Assembly of the Presbyterian Church in the United States of America the Fundamentalist-Modernist controversy occupied the center of the stage, though in both churches the extreme Fundamentalists were eventually defeated. Shailer Mathews, who was in the thick of the controversy among the Baptists on the Modernist side, has told the story in his *New Faith for Old* (Chapter XVII). Not having any machinery for trying heretics, the Baptist Fundamentalists were driven to the expedient of roundly denouncing the Modernists and in the name of the Lord said things little short of libel. Among the Presbyterians the attempt of the Fundamentalists to control Princeton Theological Seminary finally resulted in the withdrawal of the conservative members of the faculty and the formation of a new institution in the city of Philadelphia, which took the name, the Westminster Seminary, and began operations in 1929 with fifty students. The leader of the Conservative party was John Gresham Machen, who later headed a movement to form a separate Presbyterian body which has taken the name, the Orthodox Presbyterian Church.

Among the Disciples the controversy was similar to that among the Baptists, since their loose organization made heresy trials an impossibility. The issues were given ample airing in the columns of *The Christian Century* which supported the liberal viewpoint, and in the *Christian*

Standard which stood stanchly for the old standards. Among the Episco-palians the most exciting event was the struggle between Dr. Percy Stickney Grant, rector of St. Mark's Church in New York, and his Bishop, Dr. William T. Manning, who demanded the rector's resigna-tion if he did not disavow his denial that Jesus had the power of God.

The two most advertised events in the controversy were the attempt on the part of the Presbytery of Philadelphia to bring Dr. Harry Emer-son Fosdick to trial for heresy, and the trial of John T. Scopes, a teacher of science in the public schools of Dayton, Tennessee. Scopes was accused of teaching evolution in violation of the Tennessee antievolution law which had been passed by the legislature of that state in 1925. Fosdick, a Baptist minister and a professor in Union Theological Seminary in New York, was invited by the First Presbyterian Church of New York City to be its minister. This invitation he accepted with the understand-ing that he be permitted to remain a Baptist. Recognized as perhaps the leading modernist preacher in America, Fosdick in his Presbyterian pulpit soon aroused the Fundamentalists among the Presbyterians, espe-cially after he had affirmed that, "Creedal subscription to ancient con-fessions of faith is a practice dangerous to the welfare of the Church and to the integrity of the individual conscience." When the matter came to the General Assembly in 1924 that body saw fit to invite Dr. Fosdick either to enter the ministry of the Presbyterian Church or vacate his Presbyterian pulpit. He chose the latter alternative and became the minister of the Riverside (Baptist) Church in New York, adjacent to Union Theological Seminary, where he continued to exercise perhaps the largest influence of any preacher of his generation in America.

The trial of John T. Scopes attracted world-wide attention. The fact that William Jennings Bryan and Clarence Darrow were on opposite sides made the happenings in the county-seat town of Dayton, Tennessee, front page news. The trial was opened by prayer offered by the presiding judge, to which the defense objected on the ground that it was likely to prejudice the case against the defendant. The nation divided over the issue. Bryan said evolution was the eternal enemy of Christianity. It made God unnecessary, denied the Bible and destroyed all belief in the super-natural. Darrow attempted to make Bryan ridiculous and submitted him to a mocking examination. It was Fundamentalism's last stand, and the whole affair did the cause of religion no good. Scopes was fined and his case was appealed. A week later Bryan was dead; the heat and the excitement of the trial had brought to an end his great career as a leader in an epoch of moral idealism.

VI

These years also saw the culmination of a long struggle to bring about the adoption of an amendment to the Constitution of the United States prohibiting the manufacture and sale of intoxicating liquor, a struggle very largely carried on by revivalistic churches which had fought whiskey since the frontier days. The very year the United States entered the war (1917) the Eighteenth Amendment to the Constitution was adopted by Congress and submitted to the States for their ratification. It went into effect on January 16, 1920. Preston W. Slosson in his *The Great Crusade and After, 1914-1928* has analyzed the factors which were responsible for bringing prohibition about, as follows: First, the spread of state prohibition, which by 1918 had won thirty-three states to the dry column; second, a growing conviction in the South that alcohol to the negro, as to the Indian, was an incitement to crime, and that the abolishment of the liquor traffic was therefore a matter of establishing safeguards against increasing crimes of violence; third, the growing conviction that as a people we must choose between liquor and machinery. The two would not mix. This had already been shown by the well-nigh universal imposition of teetotalism upon the employees of factories and railroads. And fourth, the final and the most important single factor was the Anti-Saloon League, and its energtic and resourceful work.

The formation of the Anti-Saloon League, characterized as the "Church at work against the saloon," was the culmination of temperance and prohibition agitation and organization, backed almost entirely by the membership of the revivalistic churches, which had been carried on in the United States since the Civil War. In 1865 the National Temperance Society was formed at a convention in Saratoga Springs, New York. In 1873 the Women's Crusade against the saloon began at Hillsboro, Ohio, when seventy-five women gathered at a church, sang and prayed, and then marched to the saloons of the town and appealed to the saloon-keepers to give up their business. This was front-page news, and was the beginning of an awakening to a new consciousness in the country of the ruin caused by drink. The Hillsboro crusade was responsible for arousing in Frances E. Willard, a red-headed teacher and Dean of Women of

Northwestern University, an interest in what might be done by American women to close the American saloons. On November 13, 1874, the National Women's Christian Temperance Union was formed at Cleveland, Ohio, and from that time until her death in 1898 Frances E. Willard was the recognized leader of its expanding work.

The Anti-Saloon League was formed at Oberlin, Ohio in 1895, marking the beginning of the most formidable attack upon the liquor interests which the country had yet witnessed. Refusing to ally itself with any political party, it supported those candidates in state and nation which stood for the "dry" program. During the period of its greatest effectiveness it was generally admitted that "there were no shrewder politicians in America than the veteran leaders of the Anti-Saloon League." By 1907 a great wave of "dry" legislation began in the country, which by 1918 had resulted in the passage of prohibition laws in thirty-three states. The fact that the Eighteenth Amendment was enacted during World War I led to the assertion on the part of its enemies that it was put over by a fanatical minority taking advantage of war psychology. But any student of the long struggle with the liquor interests dating back a hundred years will not be easily convinced.

We are all familiar with the dismal failure of constitutional prohibition and the agitation that finally brought about the repeal of the Eighteenth Amendment. The saloons went out of business, and there was without doubt a decided decrease in the comsumption of liquor. Even antiprohibition estimates placed the consumption of liquor in 1926 at about half what it was in 1918, and the year 1920 was the soberest in the history of the United States. But the ways of getting illegal liquor were so many, and the disreputable bootleggers and rumrunners found it so easy to win protection from corrupt politicians and law-enforcing officers, and the crimes resulting from these activities became so notorious that the sentiment of the country, under the skillful propaganda of the wet metropolitan press, soon began to show signs of favoring the repeal of the enforcement acts and eventually of the constitutional amendment itself. The churches which had been largely instrumental in bringing in the prohibition regime stood officially in favor of retaining the amendment, but there can be no doubt but that many of their members were won over to the side of repeal. Mr. John D. Rockefeller, Jr.'s position is typical of that of a great many churchmen. After many years of liberal support of the Anti-Saloon League and of the dry cause, he finally came out openly in favor of repeal, in the interest of temperance itself.

The campaign for repeal reached its culmination in the presidential campaign of 1932. The Temperance Boards of the Methodist Episcopal Church and the Methodist Episcopal Church, South were the victims of most vicious attacks on the part of both the "wet" press and the so-called liberal congressmen who displayed an astonishing disregard of facts and developed a fanaticism, in most instances surpassing anything that could be found among the advocates of prohibition. It was a foregone conclusion that repeal would come regardless of which party should win the election. But it was generally understood that the saloon was never to come back, that the evils of bootlegging and rumrunning would almost automatically disappear, while the government, State and Federal, was to reap a golden harvest in liquor taxes. But of course these things did not happen. The saloon came back, and at once, with women drinkers at public bars in addition. Bootlegging showed little signs of declining, and the country was soon in a veritable orgy of license.

John Haynes Holmes in articles in *The Christian Century* on the first three anniversaries of repeal attempted an appraisal of what it had accomplished. He concluded that repeal had been a failure. In the first place the ills of prohibition are still with us; second, the saloon came back with only its name changed to tavern. Contrary to "wet" promises, drinking had not diminished but had greatly increased, while the toll of traffic deaths steadily mounted. The liquor interests have done their best to disgust decent public opinion by their methods of advertising and their unwillingness to submit to decent regulation. To quote Westbrook Pegler, who is no friend of prohibition, "The United States having given the cold turkey treatment (of prohibition) a half-hearted and poorly administered trial, is now trying saturation." And it seemed that the saturation point had almost been reached, for the year 1938 showed a slowing up on liquor consumption, and results of local option elections displayed a steadily increasing "dry" territory. In the midst of the third year after repeal Harry Emerson Fosdick declared in a widely quoted sermon, "The repeal of prohibition did not solve our problem. It simply plunged us back to the *status quo ante,* plunged us once more into the intolerable situation which our fathers faced two generations ago when they rose up in indignation against the liquor traffic. Once more we face that traffic, everywhere antisocial, not to say criminal in its consequences.

. . . This present, tipsy, cocktail-party generation cannot be the last word in the story of alcoholism. As sure as history repeats itself a revolt is due, a change of public attitude born out of disgust with a fear of the intolerable estate we now are in." In his third article John Haynes Holmes is led to say, "Repeal is a failure, a fraud—and the people are beginning to find it out."

VII

The easy money of the prosperous twenties affected the religious bodies, both Catholic and Protestant, just as it did business; they over-expanded. An example is that of the Methodist Book Concern in New York, which in the years of easy borrowing built a great manufacturing plant at Dobbs Ferry, New York. With the general decline in business throughout the country; the falling off of subscriptions to church period-icals and of book buying, and with the other factors, only too familiar in the depression years, this magnificent business with a reputation for good management covering more than a century, has been distressingly near disaster. Congregations all over the country built more costly churches than they were able to carry financially and when the period of stress came, foreclosures were necessary in many instances. Denominational colleges likewise overbuilt, and with declining student bodies and de-creased income from endowments after 1930, literally scores were com-pelled to suspend, many of them permanently. Others were forced to cut faculty salaries to the starvation point and to dismiss a large proportion of their instructional staffs.

But the period of expansion and prosperity was not entirely without permanent gains. More beautiful and costly churches were built during the ten years after 1920 than at any time in our history. In 1916 the value of church buildings was $1,676,600,582; by 1926 their value had more than doubled. In the year 1921 the amount spent for new church structures was $60,000,000; in 1926 the amount expended for the same purpose was $284,00,000; and this lavish expenditure continued well into the depression period. While in many instances church build-ing was inspired by nothing more lofty than a reckless zeal for expansion, yet the net result was undoubtedly an extraordinary aesthetic improve-ment over anything America had ever had before in the way of church architecture. Many of the new churches were of cathedral proportions— as was the Riverside Church in New York, and the great Gothic chapels at Princeton, the University of Chicago and at Duke University. The Gothic style of church architecture largely predominated among the finer churches until about 1920. After that date a trend to a more varied architecture is discernible. The new churches arising in New England tended to preserve the Colonial tradition of that region. In the Southwest the Spanish and Italian Renaissance most frequently has been followed, while in the prairie states, as in Oklahoma and Nebraska, the open country has inspired the architect to inaugurate a new tradition "consonant with its openness."

These new stately church buildings arising in every section of the country, but especially in the cities and larger towns had a decided influence upon the conduct of worship. Generally speaking, the interiors of these new church edifices were planned for a more formal service, while the sanctuaries were more worshipful than the type of the former generations. Pulpit gowns and choir robes came into common use, together with a more dignified type of church music. As a natural consequence of robing the choir, lending it a larger dignity, the processional and recessional naturally followed, as did also music responses and chorals. The urge to dress up the service to fit the building, however, was not the only one contributing to the gradual changing of worship in American Protestantism. It has been suggested that a larger familiarity on the part of the better trained ministry with historic Christianity has exercised its influence. Even the liberal minister, familiar with the rich historic heritage of the Christan Church could find use for the ancient symbols, the creeds, the hymns and the canticles. To him they would not be "shackles that bow men's spirits, but memories that bow men's heads in reverence for earnest souls who sought truth, and with the insight at hand, formulated their faith." In reciting the ancient formulations the worshiper is not necessarily accepting the ideas he utters, but is cherishing the passion for truth implied in the ancient utterances. He does not seek to conform his belief to theirs, but is seeking communion with believers of all ages. And thus doing he brings all that the past has to contribute to the enrichment of his worship.

But even more fundamental than the influences emanating from the factors mentioned above in changing Protestant worship has been the growing feeling that Protestantism must "recover the art of objective worship if it is to invoke in its worshipers awareness of reality." The emphasis upon the social gospel has turned many a Protestant pulpit into a "soapbox" for the proclaiming of social issues, and a reaction was inevitable. All these influences have produced in recent years a growing body of literature on Christian worship, among them, W. L. Sperry, *Reality in Worship* (1926); G. W. Fiske, *The Recovery of Worship* (1932); and more recently Bernard E. Meland, *Modern Man's Worship* (1934) and Von Ogden Vogt, *Modern Worship* (1927).

Still another development related to the changing church architecture and worship has been the increased utilization of religious drama in developing religious appreciation among young people particularly. Professor Fred Eastman of the Chicago Theological Seminary has been one of the principal pioneers in this movement. In a survey made of the religious drama activities in the United States in 1936 Professor Eastman found that the reasons for its increasing use were, first, that it ministered to the definite need of an emotional interpretation of religion in life, to young men and women emotionally starved; second, that it does not argue about goodness, "it walks goodness on two legs"; and third, because the American people have become increasingly drama-minded. His survey showed that of the 451 churches which replied to his inquiry, 91 per cent of them had presented a total of 1,518 plays during the year.

VIII

A notable change in the missionary situation came about as a result of the revolutionary movements throughout the world which had been taking place since the turn of the century. These changes were not particularly observable in 1918 or for a few years thereafter. In fact, both Catholic and Protestant missions continued to expand in both the amounts contributed and in the missionary personnel beyond 1918. But suddenly a decided decline both in missionary giving and in general missionary interest set in, which continued to the outbreak of World War II. In the first place the people in the mission fields underwent a decided change in their attitudes toward Christian missions. The so-called "heathen" were not so sure they wanted our Western religion, as they once were. Growing nationalism the world over made the presence of the alien missionary more and more unacceptable, and there were strong movements, as in India, to preserve the national culture and to resist westernization. At the same time there was going on, as in China, an active antireligious movement, which not only denounced Christianity, but also Buddhism, Taoism, and every other religion. In Turkey not only was every attempt to win converts to Christianity forbidden, but even Mohammedan activities were limited.

Kenneth Scott Latourette in his *Missions Tomorrow* (1936) thus summarized the reasons for the declining support of missions on the part of the American churches. The first of these was the depression since 1929, unequaled in the world's economic history. As the incomes of church people declined, naturally their missionary contributions likewise decreased, though he points out that the actual percentage of giving to income did not seem to have greatly changed. World War I, of course, was another cause of unsettling the foreign missionary enterprise. As has already been noted, the attempt of the churches to capitalize on the lavish giving which characterized the war years, for the purpose of advancing a world missionary program, proved abortive, largely because of the revulsion of the American people against further participation in world affairs. This was heightened by the extravagant building programs and the expense of maintaining increased staffs on the part of many churches throughout the country. It was the period when directors of religious education were coming into vogue, greatly increasing local budgets and financial demands on congregations. The growing tax burden further discouraged large giving on the part of many who had formerly been most generous givers.

More serious and disturbing than these economic reasons for the decreased support of missions were the changing attitudes of young people toward the missionary enterprise. As has been noted, to the generation before the war, foreign missions were generally considered to offer the best opportunity "of expressing the fullest commitment to the Christian life." Following the war the Student Volunteer Bands which had flourished in all the colleges began to disappear, especially from the larger institutions, where the appeal of foreign missions as a life work more and more gave place to an increasing interest among college youth in world peace, in economic injustice and in the race problem.

Missionary zeal in the past had grown largely out of the great religious awakenings which periodically swept the country. Indeed the Student Volunteer Movement itself was the direct outgrowth of the Moody influence, having had its birth at Northfield in 1886. The question upon which the future of the old type of foreign missions seemed to hang was, "Can a renewed interest in missionary work be revived without a revival of the old emphasis in religion?" On the other hand, others believed that a complete revamping of the whole foreign missionary enterprise in both motive and method was long overdue.

So disturbing were these facts and so evident was it that the whole missionary enterprise was in a state of crisis, that in 1930 a group of laymen of one denomination which had gathered in New York to consider some of these problems came to the conclusion that it was a matter of far more than one denomination's concern. As a result an interdenominational men's missionary inquiry was inaugurated to make an independent and comprehensive study of the whole missionary situation from the standpoint of the mission fields. Accordingly a commission consisting of fourteen members, representing seven denominations, was selected to make a study of missions as they were being conducted in China, Japan, Burma and India. In order to insure a completely impartial report no one having any official connection with a missionary board was asked to serve on the commission. After many months of painstaking work, preceded by elaborate surveys by experts in the various fields in the Orient, the commission through its chairman, Professor William E. Hocking of Harvard University, published in 1932 their report under the title, *Rethinking Missions.* The report, while sympathetic with the missionary enterprise and appreciative of what it had accomplished in the past, did not spare criticism where it seemed deserved. It recommended that foreign missions should be continued and strengthened for the sake of ourselves and the world, but under changed methods and with modified motives. There was also a growing insistence that Protestant missionary effort throughout the world be unified to a much larger degree than ever before. Though sharply resented by many missionaries, the report as a whole was well received by the executives of the missionary boards represented on the commission, and steps were soon being taken to put many of the recommendations into operation.

IX

At no period in the history of American Christianity has there been more rapid change in the theological scene than has been witnessed within the past generation. The principal reason for this fact is the radical revolutionary changes which have been taking place in the whole political, economic, social and religious climate of the world. For after all, theology is not final truth handed down from above, but grows out of man's condition; it comes out of a human background. It is what men think about God and their relationship to Him; and that is conditioned on man's feeling of need. In times of prosperity we are liable to over-emphasize man's part in salvation and we tend to think of ourselves as self-saviors; when all human efforts fail and wars, famine and pestilence sweep the world, then we tend to emphasize the need of a great God who can do things man has found himself unable to do. During the last thirty years men have moved from one position to another in their theology, not because they are fickle, but because the winds of doctrine have blown in so many different directions, and at such varying velocities. Of course there are many who have not changed their theological position. Many who hold to hard and fast creeds such as the Westminster or Augsburg Confessions or who are Catholic in their views have generally clung to their historic positions, but there are indications that even some of these have been affected by the variant theological winds which have been blowing these last two decades.

At the start of the century American theology was more or less sterile and the theological crop thin. In all the theological seminaries the courses in systematic theology had become more or less stereotyped, according to each seminary's denominational pattern. The old controversies between the various schools of New England Calvinism had faded into the past while the terms Arminianism and Calvinism were seldom mentioned in the average Protestant pulpit, and then not without explanation. Baptists and Disciples here and there were still defending their immersionist faith, but even that was failing to "get a rise" out of the average loyal churchgoer. Generally it had come to be held that no one group had a monopoly on Christian truth. The distinctive social backgrounds of the denominations were gradually fading out. Several congregations of Baptists, Disciples, Congregationalists, Episcopalians, Methodists and Presbyterians had come to be made up of much the same kind of people, leading much the same kind of lives. It was the general opinion that theology only served to keep Christian people apart, and "a religion *of* Jesus rather than a religion *about* Jesus" became the great vogue. It was in this period of theological sterility that religious education stepped into the limelight and, perhaps for this reason, got an unfortunate start.

A rebirth of theological interest was soon noticeable as the weary length of World War I wore on. The terrible holocaust which was drenching the battlefields of Europe with human blood seemed to presage to many the speedy end of the world. As a result premillennialism flourished as it had not since the days of William Miller himself. Premillennial propaganda had become increasingly undenominational and great quantities of literature were spread broadcast throughout the country. Small sects which made premillennialism central in their teaching, of course, flourished, but it became increasingly also "the rallying point for various reactionary elements" within the larger denominations, especially among those who held to literal inspiration and verbal infallibility. This was true particularly among the Baptists and Presbyterians, though none of the churches escaped being affected by it. The Moody and the Los Angeles Bible Institutes were among the principal schools where this doctrine was being disseminated.

The appalling loss of young lives in World War I also gave rise to a new interest in spiritualism, due partly to the wide publicity given to the possibility of communing with the departed spirits of dear ones by such reputable men as Sir Oliver Lodge and Sir Arthur Conan Doyle. The National Spiritualistic Association almost doubled its membership between 1916 and 1926. This increase, however, does not show the widespread acceptance of spiritualism on the part of people who were members of the regular churches, since spiritualism is a system of thought and knowledge, as it advocates state, which can be reconciled with any religion.

From the standpoint, however, of the great Protestant bodies, the emphasis in theology during the immediate postwar years was of an entirely different kind than that noted above. There was much talk of the scientific approach to religion and "scientific religion" was much extolled from many a cultured pulpit. Those were the days when every branch of learning coveted some tie-up with the word science. It was indeed the charmed word. Belonging to this emphasis upon scientific religion was the emergence of the new humanism. The extreme new humanist abolished the supernatural and denied "the existence of any God other than the God resident in the human-will-to-goodness." A recent interpreter of current theology has suggested that this was a natural reaction to the experiences through which the present generation had passed, and that it grew out of "a certain healthy impatience and indignation with too easy cures for the pains of the world." In other words, the humanist was not willing to trust any other cure for the world's evil and pain than "the will-to-goodness" in the soul of a man.

In the nineteen twenties this antitheistic and antisupernatural emphasis seemed to be gaining wide acceptance among liberal ministers of all denominations, but even at the time of its greatest vogue it failed to win the vast body of moderately liberal religious opinion. This bringing God down to man's size had its main chance during the prosperous nineteen twenties. It was a "fair-weather" theology, at least as far as the average liberal minister was affected by it. But with the coming of the depression years it soon lost its attraction to the moderate liberal who had given it after all only partial acceptance. His hope that it held promise for a more adequate program for religious reconstruction was soon dissipated, having found, as one such liberal stated, that "its effervescent enthusiasm bubbled from the surface rather than from the depths," and he turned away to try to find what those depths were.

The name of Karl Barth was introduced to America during the last year of the prosperous era with the appearance of his *Word of God and the Word of Man* in an American translation. And within two years it was becoming evident that the seed had fallen on good ground. Characterized as the greatest thinker since Schleiermacher and as the savior of Protestantism in Germany, Barth was soon to find in America devoted disciples and able expounders. It would be impossible to attempt a full exposition of the Barthian theology here, even if the writer thought himself capable of doing it, but it is necessary to understand its general implications. At its center stands a transcendent God, high and lifted up, "totally other" from man. The wide acceptance of this exalted view of God was but a natural reaction against a watered-down God, a God reduced to an impersonal process, or to the human-will-to-goodness, especially at a time when things in general were getting to be very much in a mess.

The wide acceptance of the Barthian view of God even on the part of non-Calvinist groups is illustrated by the acclaim which greeted the appearance of Professor Edwin Lewis' *Christian Manifesto* among the Methodists. Lewis inveighed against the softness in religion which had crept in during the comfortable years, and showed little patience with the "sentimental theism which the Fatherhood of God too often is supposed to mean." Still another example of Barthian influence in Arminian circles was the attempt on the part of a Methodist professor of church history, the late George Croft Cell, to make a Barthian out of John Wesley, in his book, *The Rediscovery of John Wesley*. Both the above books were written out of the conviction that unless something be done and done quickly to check the sliding of Protestant teaching and preaching into humanistic paths that it was doubtful whether the Protestant Church had a future.

More important, however, is the Barthian teaching, that may be equally well characterized as the European view, which holds that this transcendent God is primarily concerned about saving individuals *from* the world, but allows "the world for the most part to shift for itself." "God alone," it holds, "can transform the structure of society;" but he is not interested in society, his concern is to attend and assist the individual soul in its pasage "through time into eternity," for the victory of God is achieved "not in history but beyond history."

The attempts of the Christian liberal to make a better world finds little encouragement in the Barthian views, which considers every attempt to correct outrageous conditions and right wrongs in human society as not only "futile but presumptuous." Likewise the liberal's doctrine of Divine Imminence is at the opposite pole from the unknowable God of the Barthians.

It is revealing to note the background of the principal protagonists of Barthian theology in America. Princeton Theological Seminary, with its reputation for stiff-backed Calvinism, is perhaps its strongest center. Among the individual Barthians the most vocal are those who have a German background and training. The Barthians have been proclaiming that the social gospel has been completely discredited and has already been largely abandoned. Even such a stanch propagandist of the social emphasis as the editor of *The Christian Century* seemed to have lost a good share of his fervor.

X

Some of the effects of the depression on religion in America have already been noted. In 1937 Professor Samuel C. Kincheloe prepared a *Research Memorandum on Religion in the Depression* primarily for the purpose of furnishing a plan for further study. It is too soon, of course, to reach any definite conclusions, as the author clearly indicates. He does, however, present some generalizations, which seem to contain a modicum of truth, one of them being that this depression, contrary to the predictions of many ministers, did not drive men to God, as have depressions in the past. At least church membership does not so indicate.

That it has not produced a revival of the old type seems perfectly clear, at least among the older revivalistic churches. But this type of religious revival was hardly to be expected since the revivalistic method was gradually being discarded by these bodies during the last twenty-five years. But there has undoubtedly been a revival of the familiar type going on among the Pentecostal and Holiness sects, ministering to the people who have been, perhaps, the most disastrously affected by the depression. "Religion and Hard Times," a study of the Pentecostal and Holiness sects in three localities by Dr. A. T. Boisen, presents an excellent cross-section picture of the expanding activities of what are often termed the "Holy Rollers."

Statistics of some of these bodies in the depression years will indicate the rapidity of their growth. The Assemblies of God, formed in 1914, had in 1926, 48,000 members; in 1937 they reported 3,470 churches and 175,000 members. The Pentecostal Assemblies of Jesus Christ, while no figures are available on membership, listed in 1935, 827 ministers and evangelists, and Mr. Boisen estimates that their membership cannot be less than 35,000. The Church of God with headquarters in Tennessee had in 1926 some 23,000 members; in 1937 the two branches had not less than 80,000. In 1937 the Church of the Nazarene reported 127,649 members, a more than 100 per cent increase since 1926. According to the *Yearbook of the Churches* for 1937 there are 15 Church of God bodies, ministering to the people occupying the lower economic levels. The pentecostal, premillennial and holiness emphasis has also had a large appeal among Negroes, and there are numerous Negro bodies of this type.

Largely produced by hard times, the growing membership in these bodies, seeing little chance for better times in this life, look to the future where injustices and poverty shall be no more. In other words they are otherworldly in their outlook. Their God is a God of love, who cares for their condition, and with whom they can walk and talk. This relationship with God is established through a conversion experience, which means the getting rid of the sense of sin. In their daily lives they are highly moral and puritanical in all their relationships with one another and the world. And the fact that they have increased so rapidly is indication enough that they are supplying needs which are not being met on the part of the "enlightened" churches.

With much the same religious emphasis as the "Holy Rollers," but belonging to the opposite economic extreme are the Buchmanites, a movement which has had its especial appeal to college students, intellectuals and the economically prosperous. Their emphasis is upon God's guidance and God's power. They insist that God has a plan for every man's life, but when through sin that plan is spoiled "God is always ready with another." But guidance is only possible with complete surrender of everything, "will, time, possessions, family, ambitions." Theologically they are entirely orthodox, but it is "orthodoxy galvanized into new life in modern conditions." The cardinal problems of modern life they hold—at least among the people where the Buchman movement has had its principal success—are sex and money. But they disappear with their sublimation, that is when instinctive emotions are "diverted from their original ends, and redirected to purposes satisfying to the individual and of value to the community."

The founder of this movement, Frank Buchman, is a Lutheran minister, and began his ministry some forty years ago in Philadelphia where he formed a new congregation made up principally of the less favored class of people. He also established a settlement house modeled after Toynbee Hall. Resigning his pastorate because of disagreement with his officials, Buckman sailed for Europe for a period of rest. It was while he was in England and worshiping in a little chapel near Keswick that he had the experience that set him about the work of becoming the leader of the Oxford Group Movement. His early disciples were won by personal talks with students at Cambridge and Oxford, where the movement has had a striking influence. Later, on a trip around the world, converts were made on shipboard, and wherever he and his party stopped.

Much of the work of the group is carried on through what are known as house parties. The first was held in China where some eighty persons gathered in the house of a Chinese diplomat, and the movement has left its stamp upon Christian Chinese leadership. They meet informally anywhere, in hotels, in universities, private houses, but never in church hours. They have no organization; each group is a separate unit, linked to the others only by the Holy Spirit. The great historic churches are their only organizations, where they worship. In America their principal influence has been exerted among the Episcopalians, though it is by no means confined to any one Christian body. Though much criticized because of its sentimentality and its overemphasis upon sex, nevertheless it has achieved some notable reformations among the "ups and outs" particularly.

A new phase of the movement was inaugurated stemming from a phrase in a speech made by Buchman in London in 1938 in which he declared that only by moral rearmament could the world be saved from destruction. It was either "guns or guidance". This declaration launched a new phase of the movement known as "Moral Rearmament". The coming of World War II killed the movement, and since that time Buchmanism waned. Though still alive and directed by Buchman from the new headquarters in Switzerland it has evidently passed its peak.

XI

Our one great defence against the rapidly increasing immorality of our nation, and the consequent drain upon the strength of the people, is Christianity. Enormous sums are given to this holy cause and the waste of money by the preachers and managers of the Church in perpetuating their differences—which the Church as a whole agrees are of no importance—is the greatest economical crime of the age. The spiritual and moral consequences are disastrous beyond calculation. The Church itself is breaking down under it. Our national moral collapse is a direct result.

These words are not the official pronouncement of any religious group; they are found in an American novel, *God and the Groceryman*, popular some twenty years ago, but they express as well as anything I know the situation so far as the American churches are concerned. Our divisions are indeed the "scandal of Christendom."

But there is hope for a better day. An increasing number of leaders representing all the major denominations have been engaged for the past three decades, especially, in efforts to heal the divisions in the Church of Christ. Many are making this their principal task. That hopeful progress has been made in this direction is shown by the following summaries of what has taken place in the United States and throughout the world in the last two decades.

Between 1906 and 1940 twelve church unions were accomplished in the United States. In 1906 the Cumberland Presbyterians in the North united with the Presbyterian Church in the U. S. A., the more conservative among the Cumberland body, however, preferring to remain an independent church; in 1911 the Northern Baptists and the Free Baptists united, though a Free Will Baptist group continued in the South. In 1917 the Norwegian Lutheran Church of America was formed by the uniting of three formerly independent bodies; while in 1918 the great United Lutheran Church was created by the merging of the General Synod, the General Council and the United Synod of the South, to form the largest Lutheran church in America. A second great unification accomplished by the Lutherans was the formation of the American Lutheran Church in 1931, composed of the former Ohio, Iowa and Buffalo Synods. The United Lutheran and the American Lutheran bodies are now engaged in negotiations looking toward the immediate uniting of their two bodies. In 1920 the Welsh Calvinistic Methodist Church which came out of the Whitefield tradition became a part of the Presbyterian Church in the U. S. A., and two years later (1922) the two Evangelical bodies, which had been a part since 1891, united to form the present United Evangelical Church. The Reformed Church in the United States (German) has been blessed with having had a part in two union movements; the first in 1924 with the Hungarian Reformed Church; the second in 1934 when they united with the Evangelical Synod, to form the Evangelical and Reformed Church, creating a great body with nearly a million members. The Congregationalists likewise have enjoyed unification with two bodies: that with the Evangelical Protestant churches, of German antecedents, in 1924, and in 1931 with the Christian Churches, the latter one of the bodies which had come out of the New Light movement on the frontier.

The largest unification movement ever to take place in the United States is that between three Methodist bodies—the Methodist Protestant, the Methodist Episcopal Church, South, and the Methodist Episcopal Church. A general plan of unification, carefully formulated by the commissions representing these three bodies, was officially adopted in 1938 and all that remained to bring about its consummation were administrative adjustments. This was accomplished at a Uniting Conference, made up of 900 delegates, which convened in Kansas City, Missouri, April 26, 1939. The new Methodist Church—for the word "Episcopal" has been omitted from the name of the new church—contained nearly 8,000,000 members. Though commissions representing the Universalists and Unitarians voted in 1932 to unite to form the "Free Church in America," the union has not yet been consummated. It would seem from

recent experience that those churches which are the more loosely organized have greater difficulty in consummating unions than have those
bodies with a more highly centralized organization. The most recent
important union accomplishment was that between the Evangelical and
United Brethren Churches, two German churches, which now form a
body of some 800,000 members. Numerous other union movements are
under way, the one nearest completion being that of the Evangelical
and Reformed with the Congregational-Christian.

Christian leaders in America were not alone interested in drawing
together the numerous religious bodies in the United States, but they
have taken the lead in recent years in trying to bring about a world-wide
unity. The first international gathering of Christian leaders was the
Edinburgh Conference held in 1916. So great was its success that it immediately inspired the General Convention of the Protestant Episcopal
Church to propose to call together "representatives of all Christian
bodies throughout the world which accept Jesus Christ as God and
Saviour, for the consideration of questions pertaining to the Faith and
Order of the Church of Christ." This met immediate favorable response
on the part of world-wide Christendom with the exception of Roman
Catholicism. World War I interrupted the immediate carrying out of
this plan, but with its close negotiations were resumed, and in August,
1927, there was convened at Lausanne a World Conference on Faith and
Order. All the great Protestant denominational families in the United
States were represented, while the cost was met by generous con-
tributions of American laymen, among whom J. Pierpont Morgan rates
particular mention. There had been held at Stockholm in 1925 a World
Conference on Life and Work, which was devoted to the study of applied
Christianity. The Lausanne Conference studied the infinitely more difficult problems of doctrine and worship. The topics discussed were: the
Church's Message to the World; the Nature of the Church; a Common
Confession of Faith; the Ministry; the Sacraments; and the Unity of
Christendom. On only one of the above topics was there anything like
agreement and that was the first, the Message of the Church. The archbishops from the Eastern Church withdrew, much to the disappointment
of the Conference as a whole. The majority opinion as to the results of
the Lausanne Conference was that it had accomplished something of
permanent value, which would warrant the carrying on for the eventual
achievement of Christian unity throughout the world.

Ten years later, in the summer of 1937, there met at Oxford and Edinburgh two other ecumenical conferences where the work begun at Stockholm and Lausanne was continued. At the Oxford Conference the theme for discussion was Life and Work, at Edinburgh it was Faith and Order. At Edinburgh there were 122 religious communions represented, which included nearly all the leaders of the Eastern, or Orthodox Churches. Oxford was almost as widely representative. As at the earlier conferences in 1925 and 1927 the Roman Catholics were not represented. Though in neither nothing definitive was decided, "the right road," to quote the editor of the *Christian Times*, "has been reached at last. Christians can talk together, and listen with interest to one another, and pray together; and if they go patiently on, God who has begun his good work, will one day perfect it."

CHAPTER XXIV

THROUGH A DECADE OF STORM TO THE MID-CENTURY

DURING the period of disillusionment following the World War I it became popular to disparage the idealisms of the war years, and to refer to the phrases "the war to end war" and "making the world safe for democracy" as deliberate fraud. The fact of the matter is, however, that it was not the idealism of the war years that was at fault, but rather the lack of any idealism in the years following the war. Indeed the idealism of the war years is as valid today as it was then, and the fact that none of the war ideals were achieved was not due to the war leadership, but to the type of American leadership which gained control immediately on the end of the war.

I

From the year 1920 to the opening of World War II a powerful peace crusade was sweeping the English-speaking world. Almost at once many of the outstanding American religious leaders put on sackcloth and ashes and repented their part in World War I, and vowed never again would they have any part in any war. Harry Emerson Fosdick led the procession of the penitents. In a great sermon, "My Account with the Unknown Soldier,' he gave eloquent expression to that position, and many others of lesser note followed. The American pacifists accepted the revisionist position of the historians, led by Harry Elmer Barnes and Professor Sidney B. Fay[1] of Harvard, which excused Germany from much of the blame for the war. The unjust character of the Treaty of Versailles was much overstressed. In the process of whitewashing Germany the Ameri-

[1]Sidney B. Fay, *Origins of the World War* (New York, 1928). See also Harry Elmer Barnes, eleven articles in *The Christian Century*, Oct. 8-Dec. 9, 1925.

can pacifists pretty generally made Britain the scapegoat. Indeed pacifist opinion in America was almost 100 per cent anti-British, stressing British imperialism as a major cause of many of the world's ills.

The pacifist movement was strong in all universities and colleges in the country, particularly in the denominational institutions. It was promoted by youth organizations of all sorts, most of them leaning strongly to leftist opinions. Many of these youth organizations had church connections, under the leadership of professional "youthers," who were behind the scenes in the great youth conventions which were held all over the nation, and where flaming antiwar resolutions were passed. Also feeding the pacifist movement among students was the stress placed upon the futility of war in the teaching of modern European history. Pretty generally the teachers of modern European history in the colleges and universities accepted the revisionist position in regard to the causes of the World War and they too exercised a strong influence in developing anti-British feeling.

Umphrey Lee, in his *The Historic Church and Modern Pacifism*[2] holds that modern pacifism as it manifested itself among the great evangelical bodies stems from the social gospel. This is supported by the fact that the outstanding social-gospel preachers became the recognized leaders of modern pacifism. The Christian pacifism, however, with which the church has long been familiar and which rejected the right of the Christian to take part in any war, differs from the modern pacifism in that the latter "is quite likely to admit coercion in restricted spheres."[3] The pacifists also urged nonresistance as a strategy and exalted Tolstoy, St. Francis and particularly Gandhi. Gandhi's nonresistance program for India became the pattern for much of modern pacifism. Nonresistance, however, as has been pointed out, is after all a form of resistance, intended to secure political power, and has as little relation to the teachings of Jesus as has any other form of resistance.

The coming of Hitler to power in 1933 and the putting into immediate operation of his ruthless anti-Semitism, together with the unleashing of the ambitious and cruel Japanese plan for the conquest and exploitation of her peaceful neighbors, caused many ministers, who had considered themselves out-and-out pacifists, to reconsider the con-

[2]Umphrey Lee, *The Historic Church and Modern Pacifism*, (New York and Nashville, 1943) Chapters IX, "Modern Pacifism."

[3]Sherwood Eddy and Kirby Page, *The Abolition of War* (New York, 1924), pp. 183, 186, 187.

sequences of their position. Many, however, expecially the most vocal leaders, had made such sweeping protestations of their pacifist position, and had put themselves so decidedly "on the spot" as to what they would or would not do under any and all circumstances, that they found themselves unable to change their position.

II

The outbreak of World War II in September, 1939, brought the American churches once again face to face with the fact of war. The question of American participation in the war speedily became the principal issue both before the nation and in the churches. Could Americans stand by and see the world crushed under the heel of ruthless totalitarianism, or should she give assistance to those nations that were resisting? The Christian pacifist almost to a man lined up on the side of nonintervention, though they did not like to be considered isolationists. The logic of events, however, threw them into the arms of the isolationists of the *Chicago Tribune* type, together with the Roosevelt haters, the anti-British, the pro-Nazi, the pro-Fascist, and numerous others, who for one reason or another wanted to keep America either from helping the Allies or from active participation in the war. It was indeed a motley crowd which lay down together in the "America First" organization. *The Christian Century* and *The Chicago Tribune* for a time saw eye to eye and took pains to congratulate one another on their united stand. Perhaps nothing was more disastrous to modern pacifism than its willingness to compromise itself with such an organization as America First. It is added proof that modern pacifism of the social-gospel type cannot be classed with Christian pacifism of the older type. It is significant that the historic pacifist bodies kept clear of the American Firsters.[4]

The extent of this type of pacifism among the American clergy in the period from September, 1939, to December 7, 1941, is revealed in numerous polls taken in the churches of all denominations. The Methodists, Baptist, Disciples, and Congregationalists furnished the largest proportion; Presbyterians, Episcopalians and Lutherans a much smaller proportion. A poll taken by the Catholic journal *America* in November, 1939, among students in 182 Catholic institutions revealed that of the 50,000 who responded, 18,164 stated that they were pacifists. Of the 3,076 Episcopalians who responded to a poll in July, 1941 (*The Living*

[4] *The Christian Century,* December 6, 1939 and numerous other issues.

Church), 293 stated that they were pacifists. The Disciples Convention meeting in St. Louis in May, 1941, voted two to one in support of a res-olution addressed to the President of the United States imploring him to "adopt no further policy in aid of Britain which will carry the hazard of involvement in the war," and further stating that "The American people are overwhelmingly opposed to belligerent participation, and we look with grave foreboding upon any action by the Government which will plunge a divided nation into war." Later a leading Disciple declared that President Roosevelt might carry the nation into the war, but it would be a divided nation, which later proved to be a mistaken prophecy.[5]

The historic pacifist churches, such as the Quakers, the Dunkers and the Mennonites, were doing very little talking. Their position was well known and recognized by government. But the pacifists in the ranks of liberal Protestantism were insistent and voluble. The program for peace advanced by them was for the League of Nations to repudiate the Treaty of Versailles, abandon imperialism and nationalistic capital-ism, while the United States was to relinquish her holdings in the Orient, and withdraw within her own boundaries. Such a program, they de-clared, would undoubtedly bring peace at once.[6]

The columns of *The Christian Century* became the sounding board for the pacifist position, although the editorial policy of that influential journal was not out-and-out pacifistic. It did, however, take a strong position against participation in the war. In order to gain a hearing for the interventionist point of view Reinhold Niebuhr and a group of associates began the publication of *Christianity and Crisis* in February, 1941. The editorial position of this periodical was that while all men on both sides of the struggle were tainted with sin, and all stood in need of repentance, yet relatively speaking, in that particular conflict, one side was right and the other wrong. They held that triumph of the wrong could only be prevented by a United Nations' victory, which, to be sure, would not insure all of the ideal ends for which Christianity stands, but on the other hand a victory of the Axis powers would make any achieve-ment of Christian ends absolutely impossible. To say, as did the pacifists, that the war was simply a conflict between two rival imperialisms mani-fested both ignorance and moral confusion. And they pointed to the basic distinctions between civilizations "in which justice and freedom

[5]*Ibid.*, May 21, 1941.

are still realities and those in which they have been displaced by ruthless tyranny . . . ." for this reason "Christians in neutral countries cannot evade the ethical issues involved. . . ."[6]

III

Pearl Harbor transformed most of the American pacifists of the social-gospel type into reluctant participants. *The Christian Century* declared after Pearl Harbor "that our entering the war now had become an un-necessary necessity." Church bodies which before Pearl Harbor had passed strong antiwar resolutions, now came over to a position in which they recognized the necessity of the defeat of the Axis powers if there was to be any just and durable peace. In no instance, however, did any church body bless war as such, and none attempted to make a holy cause out of it. Daniel Poling[7] of the Philadelphia Baptist Temple, who had been a consistent supporter of American participation from the start, refused to call the war holy, although, he stated, the cause for which we fight is holy. John C. Bennett, then of the Pacific School of Religion, called the war just, but not holy, although much that is holy is at stake. Dean Sperry in an article in *Christendom*[8] on "The 'Feel' of the War" noted the lack of emotional response to the war on the part of the American people, as compared to World War I. To the people in general and to the church people in particular there was noth-ing glorious about it at all; it was simply a grim business that needed to be done.

Like the Protestants, the Roman Catholics were divided into two camps on American participation in the war. The Irish situation was one of the main factors in determining American Catholic opinion, and there was widespread feeling among American Catholics of Irish origin that England should be humbled, and they were therefore opposed to giving any assistance to the Allies. Two Catholic bishops, however, of Irish origin, came out strongly for all-out aid to England and the Allies. Dr. Henry Sloan Coffin, who took the position of all-out aid in the pre-Pearl Harbor days, was defeated for Moderator of the Presbyterian General Assembly (U.S.A.) in 1941 by Herbert Booth Smith who took a less aggressive position. The Protestant Episcopalian clergymen were also divided, and in a poll taken by *The Living Church* on the question of

[6] *The Christian Century*, January 31, 1940.
[7] Daniel Poling, *A Preacher Looks at War* (New York, 1943).
[8] Autumn. 1943, pp. 473-483.

American participation in the War, 1,084 voted yes, and 1,900 voted no. Seventy two per cent of the members of the Congregational Christian Conference in May, 1941, voted for resolutions calling upon the government to stay out of the war.

The mood of a large proportion of American Christians, Protestants and Catholics alike, as they faced a warring world is well summed up in this brief prayer by Dean Sperry:

> Save us, O Lord, from letting our righteous anger ever become unrighteous hate, and from all presumptuous desire to take upon ourselves the office of that vengeance which is thine alone.

The Methodists at their Uniting Conference in May, 1939, claimed exemption from all forms of military service for all Methodists who were conscientious objectors, although they recognized the right of individuals to answer the call of government "in any emergency according to the dictates of his Christian conscience." The United Lutherans in 1940 asserted that the conscience of the individual, informed and inspired by the Word of God, is the final authority in determining conduct. They also asserted the individual's right to be a conscientious objector. The Federal Council in May, 1940, created a committee on conscientious objectors which was responsible for securing a change in the draft bill recognizing all conscientious objectors, not only in the well-recognized pacifist sects, but also those who were members of any well-recognized communion. The draft act, the Burke-Wadsworth Bill, contains the following statement:

> Nothing contained in this act shall be construed to require any person to be subject to combatant training and service in the land and naval forces of the United States who, by reason of religious training and belief is conscientiously opposed to participation in war in any form.

All persons of military age, however, were required to register. A considerable number of conscientious objectors, however, defied the law and refused to register. Among these were eight students at Union Theological Seminary who took this stand. They were indicted, pleaded guilty and were sentenced.

Several prominent ministers opposed the draft law in its entirety, as did Harry Emerson Fosdick, Ralph W. Sockman and Charles Clayton Morrison, editor of *The Christian Century*. President Coffin of Union Theological Seminary probably expressed the opinion of the great majority of clergymen in the nation in the following statement, issued at the time the Union Seminary students had gained nation-wide publicity because of their stand.

> . . . we are sad at heart that these young men, whose Christian characters and devotion we admire, have persisted in their defiance of the law. We have told them that we recognize that there have been times when governments have enacted statutes which violated Christian consciences. But we have pointed out that this Selective Service Act was framed with careful regard for conscientious objectors to military training and that to refuse to register was to refuse what any government had a right to ask. In my judgment their course in this matter is prejudicial to democracy, that form of government under which the Christian Church enjoys utmost liberty, and I am sure that the last things these young men wish is to injure democracy, consequently one hopes that having made their position clear they will see that no further purpose can be served by persisting in this course.

In some instances ministers refused to register and in every case they were sentenced by the courts to prison terms, though there were few if any cases where the court did not express reluctance in imposing the sentence. In 1946 there were several hundred conscientious objectors still confined, which has brought numerous protests from the church press throughout the nation.

IV

An outstanding contribution made by the Christian forces in America during the war was that of furnishing chaplains for the armed forces. In the fall of 1940 the government announced that the requirement of one chaplain for every twelve hundred men would be carried out, and that he should have full charge of all spiritual interests in camps and posts. All workers representing such agencies as the Y.M.C.A., and the Knights of Columbus were to be barred from erecting special buildings in the camps for their work, since it seemed best to the authorities to concentrate all religious responsibilities in the nonsectarian agencies. The Chief of Chaplains was the Most Reverend William R. Arnold, a broad and spiritually-minded Roman Catholic of long experience, and widely respected by all groups, and all chaplain affairs were channeled through his office. Training schools for chaplains were opened, with interdenominational staffs of instructors, and each chaplain was trained to minister to soldiers and sailors of all religious faiths, Protestants, Catholics and Jews. The various denominations set up their own commissions for the selection of chaplains, but all had to conform to the requirements laid down by the Chief of Chaplain's office. An A.B. degree was the minimum educational requirement, and also from one to three years pastoral experience. The age limit of Army chaplains was at first fixed at forty-two, but later lowered to forty; the Navy age limit was from twenty-four to thirty-three, and required both college and theological degrees.

An interesting example of church-state coöperation was the appropriation by Congress in the spring of 1941 of $12,816,880 for the building of 604 chapels in Army posts, camps and other places where there were American troops. These chapels were designed to serve all faiths, and were equipped for all type of worship, with the appropriate symbols. Thus the altars were reversible, and could be adjusted to suit the occasion. Each chapel was designed to seat about four hundred and the estimated cost of each was $21,220. This large and interesting program was launched and carried through with little if any protest.

In World War I the Y.M.C.A. was given the responsibility for looking after the recreational welfare and activities of the armed forces both in the United States and overseas. Later the Knights of Columbus and the Young Men's Hebrew Association shared in that work. In the Civil War this work was carried on by the United States Christian Commission, a voluntary agency largely supported by the churches. In World War II this type of service was placed under the direction of an agency called the United Service Organization (USO) which was related to the government through the Federal Securities Administration in coöperation with the chief morale officers of the armed services. A Board of Directors was created composed of six representatives each from the Y.M.C.A., the Salvation Army, the Jewish Welfare Board, the National Catholic Community Service and the National Travelers Aid Societies. USO units were established all over the nation—there being in 1942, 1,027 clubs and lounges in the United States and 88 abroad. Each separate USO unit was managed by coöperative local agencies including churches. The USO attempted to provide a "home away from home", and, as religion is a part of life and of the American home, religious services were carried on in the camps under the direction of chaplains in co-operation with the churches of the community. The activities and services of the clubs were open to all regardless of race, color or creed. The USO clubs were financed by popular subscriptions, although the government provided the equipment. The budget the first year was $12,000,000; the second year, $32,000,000.

The Army and Navy authorities recognized the importance of Bibles, hymnbooks and other aids to worship, and a publication called *A Song and Service Book, Army and Navy for Field and Ship* was prepared by the Chaplains' Association, which included both Army and Navy chaplains. The book contained hymns, selections from the Scriptures, and prayers, in three sections, for Protestant, Catholic and Jewish use. The office of the Chief of Chaplains also provided special Bibles for Protestants, Roman Catholics and Jews. The American Bible Society was the most active agency in distributing Bibles and Testaments to the armed forces. A pocket testament had the following *Foreword* by President Franklin D. Roosevelt:

As Commander-in-chief, I take pleasure in commending the reading of the Bible to all who serve in the armed forces of the United States. Throughout the centuries men of many faiths and diverse origins have found in the Sacred Book words of wisdom, counsel and inspiration.

The Catholics and Jews, of course, did not coöperate in the distribution of Bibles and Testaments by the American Bible Society, but both, through their own agenecies, distributed Bibles and other aids to worship, to their own distinctive groups. Christian Science agencies placed in the hands of all professing Christian Scientists in the armed forces copies of *Science and Health* as well as *Bibles*. The Missouri Synod attempted to keep a complete mailing list of all Missouri Synod Lutheran soldiers and sailors in order to supply them with a devotional leaflet entitled "Loyalty." As noted above the military and naval authorities gave full coöperation to all the religious bodies in their attempts to serve the religious needs of American men and women wearing the uniform of the United States. All this was done with little or no criticism from the country. By pursuing this policy our government made clear its concern for the religious needs of all in the armed services.[9] It further testifies to the fact that the government of the United States is not antireligious, and that the principle of the separation of church and state can be maintained, and at the same time the government may do much

[9]See Ray H. Abrams, "The Churches and the Clergy in World War II" in *Organized Religion in the United States, The Annals of the American Academy of Political and Social Science,* (Philadelphia, 1948), pp. 110-119.

actively to further the cause of religion entirely apart from any sectarian participation.

V

The American churches took a prominent part in shaping public opinion during, and following, World War II. The church press and the many utterances of official church bodies testify to the churches' awakened interest in world affairs. Soon after the United States entered the war the Federal Council of the Churches of Christ in America appointed a commission to study the *Bases for a Just and Durable Peace,* and their report was considered and approved at a National Study Conference of the Federal Council held in Delaware, Ohio, in March, 1942. This report was circulated widely throughout the nation, and exercised a powerful influence in postwar thinking. The preamble of the report was called the *Six Pillars of Peace,* which may well be compared in its effect upon national and world policy with President Wilson's Fourteen Points in World War I.

The Six Pillars of Peace stated:

I. The peace must provide the political frame work for a continuing collaboration of the United Nations, and in due course, of neutral and enemy nations.

II. The peace must make provision for the bringing within the scope of international agreement those economic and financial acts of national governments which have widespread international repercussions.

III. The peace must make provision for an organization to adapt the treaty structure of the world to changing underlying conditions.

IV. The peace must proclaim the goal of autonomy for subject peoples and it must establish international organization to assure and supervise the realization of that end.

V. The peace must establish procedures for controlling military establishments everywhere.

VI. The peace must provide in principle, and seek to achieve in practice, the right of individuals everywhere to religious and intellectual liberty.

The National Catholic Welfare Conference held in November, 1942, also issued a notable statement which served to undergird the government's endeavors to promote a just and Christian peace. Among the pronouncements were the following:

. . . we shall seek not vengeance but the establishments of an international order in which the spirit of Christ shall rule the hearts of men and of nations.

Secularism cannot write a real and lasting peace. Its narrow vision does not encompass the whole man, it cannot evaluate the spirituality of the human soul and the supreme good of all mankind.

Exploitation cannot write a real and lasting peace. Where greedy might and selfish expediency are made substitutes for justice there can be no security nor an ordered world.

Totalitarianism, whether Nazi, Communist or Fascist, cannot write a real and lasting peace. The State that usurps total powers by that fact becomes a despot to its own people and a menace to the family of nations.

The spirit of Christianity can write a real and lasting peace in justice and charity to all nations, even those not Christian.

In the Epochal revolution through which the World is passing, it is very necessary for us to realize that every man is a brother of Christ.[10]

The Christian forces in America were particularly fortunate in the leadership furnished by John Foster Dulles, a Christian statesman, upon whom the Federal government placed large responsibilities in shaping the foreign policy of the nation, and who at the same time also was taking a leading part in the activities of the Federal Council of the Churches of Christ in America. At no other time in the history of the nation was the Federal government more willing to listen to and to heed what the churches had to say on international affairs. More and more the thinking people of America had become aware of the fact that those leaders who were most efficient in using the implements of destruction were not equipped to lead the nations into paths of peace.

VI

Between August 22 and September 4, 1948, there gathered at Amsterdam representatives of 135 church bodies from 40 nations to form a World Council of Churches. John R. Mott, whose work through the years had done more to prepare the way for world Christian unity than that of any other individual was chosen honorary president, while vice-presidents were chosen from England, France and the United States. Dr. Visser 't Hooft of the Dutch Reformed Church, the general secretary of the World Council thus explains the purpose behind the formation of this world-wide Christian agency:

The World Council is not to be a new center of ecclesiastical power to compete with those already in existence. There is no plan to form a unified world church. There will be no centralized authority to speak and act in its name. The intention is much simpler than that. The Council is to provide a means of continuing relationship between the member bodies throughout the world

[10] *The Catholic Mind*, January, 1943.

so as to be able to collaborate regularly in matters of common concern, and to render a common witness wherever possible. . . .

As Professor Latourette has pointed out, this movement for world unity had its origin in the most divided branch of Christianity—Protestantism, while the most divided Protestantism—that of the United States—has played the largest role in its promotion. Although several branches of Eastern Orthodoxy have been drawn into the movement, yet it is still predominately Protestant, the most flexible branch of Christianity. And in this fact lies much of the hope for the final success of the movement. The primary incentive back of the movement was not to achieve unity of doctrine and organization, but rather to make more effective the proclaiming of the gospel and to bring all men everywhere to Christian discipleship. The World Council of Churches is simply bringing together the Christian forces of the world for joint planning and action.[11]

The movement toward building a world Christian community has stemmed from two great nineteenth-century influences; the first was the vast missionary expansion of Christianity into every corner of the world; the second was the migration of Christian people into unoccupied areas, especially the great trans-Alleghany West, and the occupying of the south Pacific areas, Australia, New Zealand and South Africa. This movement of Occidental people into these new areas was largely a Protestant movement; thus there came to be large islands of Protestant people throughout the world, living in contact with non-Christian people. Out of this situation there arose an increasing concern for cooperation among the Protestant churches in dealing with the great task of bringing Christianity to every land and every people.

Some of the principal steps in the development of Christian unity in world Protestantism were the formation of the Evangelical Alliance in 1846; the Lambeth Conferences begun in 1867 in which the Anglicans from all over the world have periodically assembled; and in more recent years the forming of world organizations by the Baptists, Methodists, Lutherans, Congregationalists and the churches adhering to the Presbyterian system of polity. The numerous unifications that have taken place within denominational families, which have been increasing in recent years, are another factor in creating attitudes favorable to larger

[11]Kenneth S. Latourette, *The Emergence of a World Christian Community.* (New Haven, 1949), pp. 1-29.

unity. Both British and American Methodists are now more fully united than at any time since the death of John Wesley; the Lutherans are now in process of bringing into closer relationship the numerous Lutheran bodies into the United States; the formation of the Congregational and Christian fellowship and the successful unification of the Evangelical Synod and Reformed Church, both within the last decade, and the still more recent union of the United Brethren and the Evangelical Church, are not only notable achievements in themselves, but are also indications of trends everywhere evident both in American and in world Protestantism. Ecumenicity is the most compelling word today in Christianity.

In 1938, a representative body chosen by the churches met in Utrecht and there drafted a constitution of a World Council of Churches. The coming of World War II delayed further action. The world Christian leadership, however, even in the midst of the war did not relax their endeavors to promote Christian unity. Indeed the imperative need for Christian unity was never so clearly evident as at the end of the war. If the Christian forces of the world cannot work more closely together for the building of a better world how can we expect the United Nations to carry on successfully! The World Council of Churches, to use the words of Professor Latourette, "is the most inclusive body that Christianity has ever possessed."

Its program embraces not only the fields dealt with by Faith and Order and Life and Work, but also relief to the victims of war and plans for giving the Christian Gospel to the entire world. It officially represents a larger number and a wider confessional and geographic range of Christians than any other organization which the centuries have known. . ."[12]

The Roman Catholics and the Russian Orthodox and two of the large American Protestant communions, the Southern Baptist and the Missouri Synod Lutherans, were not represented at Amsterdam, and none of these bodies have had any part in the movement toward world Christian unity. The Roman Catholic position is well known. It professes to be a perfect unity in itself, and any attempts at adjustment to other communions, instead of achieving a real unity would only destroy the only perfect Christian unity, that of the Roman Catholic Church.[13]

[12]Latourette, *op. cit.*, p. 51.

[13]John LaFarge, "*Roman Catholicism*," Chap. 2, in W. L. Sperry (Ed.), *Religion and our Divided Denominations* (Cambridge, Mass, 1945). For a Catholic any "process of adjustment, conference, organization, or reconciliation . . . between the points of view of different churches is something entirely out of agreement with his concept of unity of the Church itself."

The refusal of the Russians to participate was undoubtedly due to the present state of world politics. The position of the Southern Baptists and the Missouri Lutheran Synod presents the most baffling enigma.

VII

Never before have the Roman Catholics in the United States been so confident of their power and importance as since the end of World War II. This is due to a number of factors. The first is that the United States is now the principal Roman Catholic nation in the world; it has become the very center of world Catholicism since there is no longer a first rate Roman Catholic power in Europe. The second is that American Roman Catholicism has become the most closely knit and the most powerful pressure group in the nation. Although Roman Catholic membership constitutes only about one-sixth of the total population of the United States, yet the control which the hierarchy exercises over the thought and action of loyal Catholic people is so potent that any program which the Church promotes has behind it the unquestioning support of a large block of American Catholic citizens. For the first time, also the Roman Catholic Church has now definitely entered politics as a church, and has created efficient and powerful agencies to carry out the political desires of the church. In other words, there has been transplanted from the Old World to the New that bane of European politics, clericalism. It is out of this situation that a very definite anticlericalism is developing in the United States, which has become exceedingly vocal.

The Roman Catholics now feel perfectly at home in America, and think of themselves as one of the principal, if not the principal, bulwark of American freedom. Since World War I, the Catholic universities in the United States have turned out a long list of doctrinal dissertations on American Roman Catholic history to bolster their claim of the important part Catholics have played in the building of the nation. The American Catholic University in Washington alone has sponsored more than fifty dissertations in American Catholic history since 1918, all of them properly censored and published by the Catholic University.[14]

The first great Roman Catholic leaders in America, Bishops John Carroll, John England, John Hughes and John Ireland, with Cardinal Gibbons, had much to say about American Catholics being in full accord with all the great American freedoms, and there was much fraternizing

[14] John Paul Cadden, *The Historiography of the American Catholic Church 1785-1943* (Washington, D. C., 1944).

between Protestants and Catholics. It was not uncommon for Roman Catholics to share the same building with a Protestant congregation while Jesuits served as trustees of Protestant colleges, and priests not infrequently preached from Protestant pulpits. When the Catholics were a much smaller minority than they are today, their policy was one of accommodation rather than aggression, and they told their Protestant neighbors that there was not much difference between them after all. It was quite generally assumed that American Catholicism was different from that of the Old World or the South American types. All this, however, has changed, and American Roman Catholics have become more and more distinctly a separated group. There is, of course, a mingling of Catholic laymen with their Protestant neighbors in the affairs of business and nonreligious community affairs, but when the Catholic crosses the threshold of his church he puts an almost impassable barrier between himself and his Protestant neighbors. The good Catholic never enters a Protestant church; in many instances he is forbidden to do so by his priest. Thus there has been created a broad and impassable cleavage in American society which inevitably creates suspicion, if no open enmity.

The fact that official Roman Catholicism came to terms with both Fascism and Nazism when they rose to power in Italy and Germany, together with the Papal endorsement of Italy's brutal conquest of Ethiopia and the support and endorsement given the Franco regime in Spain, besides the tendency of the Catholic hierarchy to take the side of absolutist governments, as Vichy, France, has aroused a growing fear on the part of an increasing number of American non-Catholics that Roman Catholicism, wherever it has gained numbers and power, is a threat to basic freedoms. These several factors have been responsible for a greatly worsening relationship between Protestants and Roman Catholics in the United States since the end of World War II. This rising tide of resentment and suspicion of growing Catholic power, is unlike any other anti-Catholic movement in American history. It is not another crude outbreak of anti-Catholic hysteria, such as the American Protective Association of the latter years of the last century, or the Ku Klux Klan in the 1920's, but rather back of the movement are some of the most responsible, thoughtful and well-informed Protestant leaders in the United States. All are careful to say that they are not attacking Roman Catholicism as a religion, and they recognize that as a religion

Roman Catholicism has equal rights with all others. But they are aggressively opposed to Roman Catholicism in politics, with its attempts to secure special consideration for the Catholic Church.

The principal issue which has brought growing tension is the attempt of the Roman Catholic hierarchy to gain government support for their parochial schools. The cost of maintaining the increasing number of parochial schools is undoubtedly becoming a burden too great for Catholic people to bear, even though the teaching is carried on by Catholic nuns who receive no salary other than a mere subsistence as members of an order. If the Catholic parochial-school program, promulgated in 1884, which is that every Catholic child must receive its education under church auspices, is to be carried out, the number of schools must be doubled, since only about half of the Catholic children in the nation are at present enrolled. Until recent years, the Roman Catholics have opposed federal aid to education, and have exerted their influence in defeating numerous attempts of Congress to pass such legislation. But since the end of World War II, the Catholic hierarchy have centered their support on Federal bills which give some hope of government aid to parochial schools. The Taft bill was one such measure, which passed the Senate but failed in the House. This bill provided for allotted sums to the states to be used as the states determined. The bill, however, which has brought forth the bitterest opposition from the Roman Catholic hierarchy is the Barden bill, which provides for a Federal grant of $300,000,000 to be used for subsidizing public schools only, especially in the most needy states. Representative Lesinski, a Roman Catholic Democrat from Michigan, the Chairman of the House Committee on Education, denounced the Barden Bill as anti-Catholic and dissolved the subcommittee on aid to education when it voted ten to three to let the Barden bill come up for debate.

The controversy over the measure came to a head during the summer of 1949 when Mrs. Roosevelt stated in her column, syndicated in many newspapers throughout the nation, that she was in favor of the Barden Bill and gave reasons for her position. She also stated that she disagreed with Cardinal Spellman of New York in his stand for federal funds for Catholic schools. This public statement by Mrs. Roosevelt regarding her stand brought the most astounding blast from Cardinal Spellman, recognized as the most influential Catholic official in the nation. He stated that she had written from "misinformation, ignorance or prejudice."

He continued: "Even if you cannot find it within your heart to defend the rights of innocent little children and heroic helpless men like Cardinal Mindszenty, can you not have the ordinary charity not to cast upon them another stone," and his letter ends, "I shall not again publicly acknowledge you. . . . Your record of Anti-Catholicism stands for all to see . . . documents of discrimination unworthy of an American mother." Nothing could have awakened the nation to the seriousness of the issues involved as did this exaggerated denunciation of the former first lady of the land by the principal Roman Catholic prelate in America.

It soon became apparent that the Cardinal's heated denunciation had backfired, for many Catholics, as well as non-Catholics, deplored his unjust and uncalled-for accusations of bigotry against Mrs. Roosevelt. Ex-Governor Lehman of New York, in a long statement in the New York Times (July 24, 1949) came to Mrs. Roosevelt's defense. He stated that he was shocked at Cardinal Spellman's attack on Mrs. Roosevelt, since he had always believed that "in our American democracy every responsible citizen is entitled to express his or her view on public issues without being subjected to the accusation of being against any religion or any race." The real issue, he further stated "is not whether one agrees or disagrees with Mrs. Roosevelt on this or any other public question—the issue is whether Americans are entitled freely to express their views on public questions without being vilified or accused of religious bias."

The short-tempered Cardinal was quick to see his mistake, and a few days later held a telephone conference with Mrs. Roosevelt—whom he had promised never again to recognize publicly—suggesting that they issue a joint statement setting forth their respective positions. To this Mrs. Roosevelt graciously agreed, though a Catholic writing in the Chicago Sun-Times stated that he believed he echoed the feelings of many good Catholics "when I say that Cardinal Spellman should have apologized to Mrs. Roosevelt." These two statements, each restating his own views, were issued through the chancery office of the Archbishop of New York. The Cardinal stated that Catholics were only asking for what he called auxiliary aid to parochial schools, such as transportation, school lunches, the furnishing of nonreligious textbooks, and health service. He was also careful to affirm his belief in the right of free speech, which he states "not only upholds but encourages differences of opinion," a right which the whole tone of his first letter to Mrs. Roosevelt seemed to deny. Mrs. Roosevelt restated her position, in which she declared that she had no anti-Catholic bias, and closed her letter with:

I am firm in my belief that there shall be no pressure brought to bear by any church against the proper operations of the government, and that there shall be recognition of the fact that all citizens may express their views freely on questions of public interest.

Later the Cardinal called on Mrs. Roosevelt at Hyde Park, evidently hoping that such an act on his part might help allay the criticisms for his former ill-tempered attack.

Two Supreme Court decisions since 1946 on school issues have had wide publicity and have been much discussed. The first was the New Jersey School Bus case in which the court by a five to four decision affirmed the constitutionality of the use of public funds to pay bus fares of Catholic children attending parochial schools. This case brought forth two notable dissenting opinions—the first, by Justice Jackson, the other by Justice Rutledge, both of whom warn the American people of the dangers inherent in making even the slightest breach in the wall which separates church and state.

Justice Jackson points out that:

Catholic education is the rock on which the whole structure rests and to render tax aid to its church school is indistinguishable to me from rendering aid to the church itself.

while Justice Rutledge asserted that:

Transportation is an essential feature in modern education so why select this item "as not aiding, contributing to, promoting or sustaining the propaganda of beliefs which is the very end of all to bring about." It is no more or less important than other items.

The second was the Champaign, Illinois, case having to do with the teaching of sectarianism in the public schools of that community. In this instance the court decided by an eight to one decision that the Constitution forbade the use of either public school buildings or school machinery in the furthering of sectarian teaching. Both decisions have been strongly resented. The decision in the school bus case pleased the Roman Catholics, but has been strongly opposed by many non-Catholics on the ground that it but paves the way for more and greater demands on the part of Catholics for aid to their parochial schools and breaches the wall of separation of church and state. The second decision has been bitterly opposed by Roman Catholics and Protestants alike, on the ground that it results in completely secularizing the public-school system. On the other hand, the Court has gone on record as declaring that Christian principles and Christian ideals are basic in our civilization.

The large number of books and articles in leading American periodicals, both secular and denominational, which have appeared in the past year (1949), denote the widespread public interest in the issues mentioned above. Paul Blanshard's *American Freedom and Catholic Power* has brought reverberations from both sides. Some of the chapters had previously appeared in the *Nation,* which led the Superintendent of the Public Schools of New York to ban that periodical from the schools, which caused nation-wide comment. Replies to Blanshard's charges have appeared in the Jesuit weekly *America* as well as in the liberal Catholic *Commonweal.* Blanshard affirmed that his book was not an attack upon Roman Catholicism as a religion, but was aimed solely at the Roman Catholic Church in politics and its attempts by censorship and other types of pressures to direct the whole of American life into channels favorable to Roman Catholicism. *The First Freedom by* Father Wilfred Parsons, S.J., presents the Catholic argument for government support for parochial schools. He bases his contention on the fact that the First Amendment to the Federal Constitution does not provide for separation of church and state, nor did the constitutional fathers envisage such an outcome. This is doubtless true, but Father Parsons fails to note that the Constitution is not a static instrument, but has been interpreted by the courts to meet new situations such as those presented by the public school and the railroads, and numerous other matters as they have arisen. He denounces the implementing of the First Amendment by the Fourteenth, as has been done by the courts in numerous recent decisions, and declares that the highest court has no constitutional basis for declaring that the wall of separation between church and state must be kept high and wide, if our freedoms are to be secure.

Another recent book advancing the same argument is *Religion and Education under the Constitution* (1949) by J.M. O'Neill, which is aimed at the decision of the Supreme Court in the Champaign, Illinois, case. His arguments are the same as those advanced by Father Parsons. Indeed, it has now, seemingly, become more or less the official Roman Catholic position to deny the constitutionality of the separation of church and state, since the Roman Catholic bishops at their national conclave in 1948 declared that they intended from then on, by all peaceful and legitimate means to work for the overthrow of that principle. *The American Mercury* in the September, 1949, issue presented two articles on the growing Protestant-Roman Catholic tension. The first by Dean W.R. Bowie of Union Theological Seminary was entitled "Protestant Concern over Catholicism" and the Catholic reply was made by Father J.C. Murray, S.J. Father Murray largely by-passed all the issues raised by Dean Bowie and concluded his piece by stating that the real cause for Protestant concern was that they were "wounded and angry because the Catholic Church considers Protestantism to be a second-class religion," and that what they really want is for the Catholic Church to repudiate its claims of being the only true church of Christ and for the Pope to "take his seat as an equal among equals at the table of the World Council of Churches."

In the light of the above occurrences it was inevitable that an organized effort should arise among non-Catholics to combat the Catholic crusade to break down the principle of separation of church and state. This took place in 1948 with the formation of "Protestants and Others United for Separation of Church and State," spearheaded by some of the most prominent and influential Protestant leaders in the country. It has established headquarters in Washington with a permanent staff and publishes a church and state newsletter which circulates widely throughout the nation. Its immediate objects are set forth under the following heads:

To enlighten and mobilize public opinion in support of religious liberty. . . .
To resist every attempt by law or administration to widen the breach in the wall of separation of church and state.
To demand the immediate discontinuance of the ambassadorship to the papal head of the Roman Catholic Church. . . .
To work for the repeal of any law now on the statute books of any state which sanctions the granting aid to Church schools from the public treasury. . . .
To invoke the aid of the courts in maintaining the integrity of the Constitution with respect to the separation of church and state. . . .
To unite public opinion to prevent the passage of any law by Congress or by the States to use public money for church schools. . . .
To give aid to citizens of any community or State in protecting their public schools from sectarian domination. . . .

In carrying on these objectives they declare they are not anti-Catholic or motivated by anti-Catholic bias. Though recognizing profound differences between Protestants and Catholics, they declare that these differences have no relevancy in the pursuit of the objectives named above.

The final statement in the above declaration seems to mean very little to the Roman Catholic Archbishop Cushing of Boston, who recently declared before a Catholic audience that Protestants and Others United for Separation of Church and State was nothing but "a refined form of the Ku Klux Klan" and cautioned his Catholic hearers against being daunted by slogans about separation of church and state and similar "glittering generalities." He recognizes, however, that the Catholics are in a precarious position: because of what he terms the evil work of anti-Catholics. Thus the issues seem to be definitely joined and, unfortunately, we are quite evidently entering upon a period of bitter controversy, the end of which no one can foresee.

VIII

The radio has become increasingly important as a medium of religious propaganda. In 1938 a survey conducted by the Federal Communications Commission found that religious and devotional programs constituted 5.15 per cent of the total radio time. In 1934 the Communications Commission established the policy that the listening public had the right to have their tastes, needs and desires met in programs given over the air, and among these religion was to have its fair proportion. All the large broadcasting companies have adopted similar policies in regard to religious broadcasts. The National Broadcasting Company does not permit attacks upon religious faiths to be made over the radio, nor will it permit sectarian propaganda. It requires that a religious message must be nonsectarian, interpreting religion at its highest "so that it may bring to the listener a realization of his responsibilty to the organized church and to society." N.B.C. makes no charge for religious broadcasts of responsible representatives of the three major faiths—Protestant, Catholic and Jewish. In a pamphlet published by the National Broadcasting Company in 1948, entitled *Twenty-Five Years of the National Radio Pulpit,* it is stated that up to that time 6,625,000 pieces of mail had been received by the Federal Council of the Churches of Christ in America from listeners, expressing appreciation for the help and guidance received from these religious broadcasts. The Columbia Broadcasting Company maintains much the same type of religious policy as N.B.C. "The Church of the Air," conducted each Sunday, is divided among the three major faiths. Another program conducted by the Columbia Broadcasting Company is called "Wings over Jordan," and is made up of talks by negro leaders and spirituals.[15]

Besides the national radio religious broadcasts noted above there are many local broadcasts over stations owned and operated by religious bodies. The radio programs sponsored by the various denominations now number more than a thousand. While some of these programs are narrowly propagandist, sectarian and fundamentalist, yet in their total effect they are an influence for the creation of a wider tolerance. These programs reach for people of all faiths. Through them Protestants may listen in on Roman Catholic and Jewish broadcasts, while Jews and Catholics may tune in on a Protestant service and hear a Protestant sermon. These denominational broadcasts may lead to the conversion of a listener to another faith, but most often they serve to bring home to the listener the fact that the messages of any one of the three faiths may be found helpful.[16]

The production and use of religious films[17] has lagged behind religious radio largely because of the greater expense involved in their production and distribution. The serious production of films for use in religious instruction began in the nineteen twenties, and the churches were becoming increasingly motion-picture conscious. The early attempts, however, to form interchurch film-producing companies all failed. The first successful religious films were produced through the promotional boards of the large Protestant churches, particularly the Presbyterian Board of Missions and the Missouri Synod Lutherans. The Harmon Foundation, an independent philanthropic agency founded in 1925, undertook the production of religious films. Though the project soon ran into difficulties, the foundation has continued its interest and has aided in the organization of the Protestant Film Commission, formed in 1946 through the coöperation of eighteen of the major Protestant bodies in America. The commission is now actively engaged in the production of religious pictures. In 1949 the commission produced five films

15*Broadcasting and the Public* (Federal Council of the Churches of Christ in America, 1938), and M. L. Ernst, and A. Lindley, *The Censor Marches On* (New York, 1940).

16For an excellent treatment of religious radio see Anson Phelps Strokes, *Church and State in the United States* (New York, 1950), Vol. III.

17For a brief historical survey of the development of religious films see William L. Rogers and Paul H. Vieth, *Visual Aids in the Church* (Philadelphia and St. Louis, 1946), Chap. I.

and others are in the planning process. Mr. J. Arthur Rank, a devout British Methodist, who now controls 60 per cent of the British moving picture industry, is the chief supporter of the Religious Film Society of Great Britain. This society had a direct influence on the formation of the Protestant Film Commission in America. The British and American agencies are now engaged in negotiations for the making of films in conjunction with Mr. J. Arthur Rank.

IX

As a consequence of the succession of catastrophic changes which have taken place throughout the world since the first appearance of this book in 1930, there has come out of western Europe a philosophy of despair now widely accepted in America which emphasizes the utter bankruptcy into which the world and man have fallen. This pessimistic philosophy consigns history to the cosmic rubbish heap, and rejects absolutely the idea of progress, so that history at best is simply the recording of man's continued failure. Nor is there any hope for anything of value to happen in history. The idea that has been so prevalent throughout our whole history here in America, from the landing of the Pilgrims until now, that man can be and is a co-worker with God in making a better world in their view is not only absurd but it is actually sacrilegious. "Goodness can only be God's gift; it can never be man's achievement": therefore it is a travesty for Christians to sing:

> Rise up, O men of God!
> Have done with lesser things;
> Give heart and soul and mind and strength
> To serve the King of kings.

Another type of pessimism which always arises in times like these is that which points the finger of scorn at Christianity and at the church with the accusation that both have failed. And in a sense that is true. The Old Testament is a record of the continuous failure of the religion of the Jews. In the same manner we can also say that democracy has failed, that education has failed, that the family has failed. But Christianity, the church, democracy and education have failed only in the sense that none of them have reached the heights which they set out to scale. In another sense they have all grandly succeeded, for humanity has profited from them all, even as they continue to fail.

This pessimistic philosophy has rendered useful service in jolting us out of our utopianism and easy complacency, in believing that "every day in every way" we are getting better and better. The calling to our attention of the mounting evils in our world needed to be done, but, after all, the world of man has been in such a state many times before, and one of the uses of history is to call that fact to our attention. He indeed is blind, however, "who cannot see and appreciate the progress of the last twenty centuries in creating a human society that approaches a little nearer to the ideal of the Kingdom of God." Every intelligent person knows that the conflict between good and evil has been continuous throughout history. History also teaches us that Christianity thrives on crises and the words of Tertullian have been proved true over and over again, that the blood of Christians is the seed of the church. Often before the state of the world seemed hopeless, but crises have furnished the occasion for needed change in the method of attack upon ancient evils.[18] The student of church history has learned that God is in no hurry and so in patience he "possesses his soul." Church history is an excellent tonic when men are disturbed and fainting because of new and confusing voices. History says the ship has weathered many another storm, so do not throw up your hands because unaccustomed waters are rushing about your ears.

As has been noted (pp. 439-44) the movement for Christian World Unity had its origin in the most divided branch of Protestantism—that of the United States—and American Protestantism has played a major role in its promotion. The principal motive which lies back of the movement is not to achieve doctrinal unity, or organizational amalgamation, but rather to bring together the Christian forces of the world for joint planning and action.[19]

A permanent organization was formed and officers chosen at the first meeting of the World Council of Churches which met in Amsterdam in the late summer of 1948. The second meeting of the World Council of Churches convened in Evanston, Illinois, on the campus of Northwestern University on August 15, 1954, and adjourned August 31. It was made up of representatives of 161 churches throughout the world.

[18]S. J. Case, *The Christian Philosophy of History* (Chicago, 1943).
[19]Kenneth S. Latourette, *The Emergence of World Christian Community* (New Haven: Yale University Press, 1949), pp. 1-29.

Of the 1,298 individual participants, 502 were official delegates; 499 visitors; 145 consultants; 96 youth consultants; 31 fraternal delegates; and 25 observers. The World Council Staff numbered 376. Dr. W. A. Visser 't Hooft of the Church of the Netherlands, the General Secretary of the World Council since its formation, again made a statement as to the nature and purpose of the World Council. It is not, he stated, a sort of super-church; it is not based on any particular doctrine about church unity. Any church joining the World Council does not need to change its conception of the Church. The member churches all agree that the work of the Council is based on the recognition that Christ is the Divine head of the Body and that the membership of the Church of Christ is more inclusive than their own membership.

The Assembly adopted at its first session "Christ, The Hope of the World" as the main theme of the Evanston meeting, introducing a provocative note which reverberated throughout all the meetings of the Council. In answering the question "What is the World Council of Churches?" and speaking of the special tasks of the Evanston Assembly, the General Secretary stated:

We are here as men and women who are themselves bewildered, who have no ready-made solution in their pockets; who disagree with each other over many things. We have no other distinction except that we are here in the name of the Lord who is constantly gathering His people together and who uses them to proclaim His Word. We may confidently expect that in a real measure our divisions will be transcended and that beyond and above the loud voices of this world we shall hear together the eternal Word of God.

At a recent meeting of the British Council of Churches, the Archbishop of Canterbury gave the following description of the proper character of a truly ecumenical council. His statement was in answer to a question whether a certain church would feel at home in the World Council:

No member church of the Council feels at home there. A genuinely ecumenical enterprise is one where no one feels at home, where all are challenged, threatened, embarrassed, and yet remain in conversation.

A test question to ask American supporters of the World Council would be: "Do you really accept the responsibility of relating yourself positively to Roman Catholics and to fundamentalists?" Merely regional or confessional conferences are places where people "feel at home" and are in no sense ecumenical. An ecumenical movement implies the whole Church of Christ. As the General Secretary has phrased it, the best definition of the ecumenical movement is a "movement of repentance."[20]

There were thirty-one American religious bodies represented at Evanston, and 186 delegates, yet two large American Protestant churches refused to participate—the Southern Baptists and the Missouri Synod Lutherans—and both bodies took strong anti-ecumenical stands. The numerous relatively small fundamentalist bodies in the United States were generally hostile to the whole ecumenical movement. Roman Catholics by Papal decree were barred from all participation at Evanston, while only a small minority of the Eastern Orthodox churches were represented. The Church of Greece sent eleven delegates, while the several independent Eastern Orthodox churches in the United States, among them the Russian Orthodox Greek Catholic Church in North America, the Roumanian Orthodox Episcopate in America and the Syrian Antiochian Orthodox Church, sent several delegates.

[20] James Hastings Nichols, *Evanston: An Interpretation* (New York: Harper & Brothers, 1954), pp. 97-98.

BIBLIOGRAPHY

✧ ✧ ✧

CHAPTER I

GENERAL AND BIOGRAPHICAL

ABRAMS, RAY H. (Ed.), *Organized Religion in the United States.* The Annals of the American Academy of Political and Social Science, March, 1948. Philadelphia, 1948.

BACON, L. W., *A History of American Christianity.* American Church History Series, Vol. XIII. New York, 1897.

CARROLL, H. K., *Religious Forces in the United States.* American Church History Series, Vol. I. New York, 1893.

CASE, S. J., and others, *A Bibliographical Guide to the History of Christianity.* Chicago, 1931, Chapter VIII.

Dictionary of American Biography (22 vols.). New York, 1928-1936.

Dictionary of American History (6 vols.). New York, 1940.

DORCHESTER, DANIEL, *Christianity in the United States.* New York and Cincinnati, 1890.

DRUMMOND, ANDREW L., *The Story of American Protestantism.* Edinburgh and London, 1949.

HALL, THOMAS C., *The Religious Background of American Culture.* Boston, 1930.

JACKSON, SAMUEL M., *A Bibliography of American Church History, 1820-1893.* American Church History Series, Vol. XII. New York, 1894.

MECKLIN, JOHN M., *The Story of American Dissent,* New York, 1934.

MODE, PETER G., *Sourcebook and Bibliographical Guide for American Church History.* Menasha, Wis., 1921.

ROWE, HENRY K., *The History of Religion in the United States.* New York, 1924.

SPERRY, W. L., *Religion in America.* Cambridge, Eng., 1945.

SPRAGUE, WILLIAM B., *Annals of the American Pulpit* (9 vols.). New York, 1866-1869.

SWEET, W. W., *Makers of Christianity: From John Cotton to Lyman Abbott.* New York, 1942.

————. *Religion in Colonial America.* New York, 1942.

————. *The American Churches: An Interpretation*. London, 1947; New York, 1948.

The New Schaff-Herzog Encyclopedia of Religious Knowledge (12 vols.). New York, 1908-1912.

WEIGLE, LUTHER A., *American Idealism*. The Pageant of America Series, Vol. X. New Haven, 1928.

WERTENBAKER, THOMAS JEFFERSON, *The Founding of American Civilization: The Middle Colonies*. New York, 1938. *The Old South*. 1942. *The New England Theocracy*. 1938.

Year Book of the Churches (1949).

<h2 style="text-align:center">CHAPTER II</h2>

BAIRD, CHARLES W., *The Huguenot Emigration to America* (2 vols.). New York, 1895.

BRAITHWAITE, WILLIAM C., *The Beginnings of Quakerism*. London, 1912.

CHEYNEY, EDWARD P., *The European Background of American History, 1300-1600*. The American Nation Series, Vol. I. New York, 1904.

EGGLESTON, EDWARD, *Beginners of a Nation*. New York, 1896. Particularly good for the new sects arising in England.

FAUST, A. B., *The German Element in the United States* (2 vols.). New York, 1928.

HANNA, CHARLES A., *The Scotch-Irish or the Scot in North Britain, North Ireland and North America* (2 vols.). New York, 1902.

KILLEN, W. D., *Ecclesiastical History of Ireland* (2 vols.). London, 1875.

LECKEY, W. E. P , *England in the Eighteenth Century* (2 vols.). 1878-1890.

LINDSAY, THOMAS M., *A History of the Reformation* (2 vols.). New York, 1910.

WALPOLE, C. G., *The Kingdom of Ireland*. London, 1885.

WEISS, CHARLES, *History of the French Protestant Refugees*. London, 1854.

<h2 style="text-align:center">CHAPTER III</h2>

ANDERSON, JAMES S. M., *History of the Church of England in the Colonies and Foreign Dependencies of the British Empire* (3 vols.). London, 1845.

ANDREWS, C. M., *The Colonial Period of American History:The Settlements*. Vol. I. New Haven, 1934.

BRYDON, GEORGE MACLAREN, *Virginia's Mother Church and the Political Conditions Under Which It Grew, 1607-1727*. Richmond, Va., 1947.

GOODWIN, EDWARD L., *The Colonial Church in Virginia*. Milwaukee, 1927.

HAWKS, FRANCIS L., *Contributions to the Ecclesiastical History of the United States of America: Rise and Progress of the Protestant Episcopal Church in Virginia*. New York, 1836.

JERNEGAN, M. W., *The American Colonies, 1492-1750*. Epochs of American History. New York, 1929.

McCONNELL, S. D., *History of the American Episcopal Church* (10th ed.). Milwaukee and London, 1916.

MANROSS, W. W., *A History of the American Episcopal Church*. New York and Milwaukee, 1935.

PERRY, WILLIAM S., *The History of the American Episcopal Church, 1587-1883* (2 vols.). Vol. I, *The Planting and Growth of the American Colonial Church.* Boston, 1885.

———. *Historical Collections Relating to the American Colonial Church.* Vol. I, *Virginia;* Vol. II, *Pennsylvania;* Vol III, *Massachusetts;* Vol. V, *Maryland and Delaware.* 1870-1878.

TIFFANY, CHARLES C., *A History of the Protestant Episcopal Church in the United States of America.* American Church History Series, Vol. VII. New York, 1895.

WERTENBAKER, THOMAS J., *The First Americans, 1607-1690. A History of American Life,* Vol. II. New York, 1927.

WILBERFORCE, SAMUEL, *A History of the Protestant Episcopal Church in America.* London, 1844.

CHAPTER IV

ADAMS, J. T., *The Founding of New England.* Boston, 1921.

ANDREWS, C. M., *The Colonial Period of American History: The Settlements.* Vol. II. New Haven, 1936.

ANDREWS, MATTHEW PAGE, *The Founding of Maryland.* Baltimore and New York, 1933.

ATKINS, GAIUS G., and FAGLEY, FREDERICK L., *History of American Congregationalism.* Boston and New York, 1942.

DEXTER, H. M., *The Congregationalism of the Last Three Hundred Years.* New York, 1880.

HALLER, WILLIAM, *The Rise of Puritanism, or the Way to the New Jerusalem as Set Forth in Pulpit and Press, 1570-1643.* New York, 1938.

KITTREDGE, GEORGE L., *Witchcraft in Old and New England.* Cambridge, Mass., 1929.

MATHER, COTTON, *Magnalia Christi Americana: or the Ecclesiastical History of New England* (2 vols.). Hartford, 1820.

MILLER, PERRY, *Orthodoxy in Massachusetts.* Cambridge, Mass., 1933.

———. *The New England Mind.* New York, 1939.

MORISON, S. E., *Builders of the Bay Colony.* Boston, 1930.

MURDOCK, K. B., *Increase Mather.* Cambridge, 1925.

PARRINGTON, V. L., *The Colonial Mind, 1620-1800.* Vol. I of his *Main Currents in American Thought,* New York, 1927.

PRATT, W. S., *The Music of the Pilgrims.* Boston, 1921.

SCHNEIDER, HERBERT W., *The Puritan Mind.* New York, 1930.

SEWALL, SAMUEL, Diary (abridged), Mark Van Doren (Ed.). 1927. Complete Diary published as Vols. V-VIII, Series 5, Massachusetts Historical Society. Collection 1878-1882.

WALKER, WILLISTAN, *History of the Congregational Churches in the United States.* American Church History Series, Vol. III. New York, 1894.

WERTENBAKER, T. J., *The First Americans, 1607-1690. A History of American Life,* Vol. II. New York, 1927.

WINTHROP, JOHN, *History of New England* (2 vols.). J. K. Hosmer, editor. New York, 1908.

CHAPTER V

AUGUR, HELEN, *An American Jezebel: The Life of Anne Hutchinson.* New York, 1930.
BACKUS, ISAAC, *A History of New England with Particular Reference to the Denomination of Christians called Baptists* (2 vols.).
BROCKUNIER, SAMUEL H., *The Irrepressible Democrat, Roger Williams.* New York, 1940.
ERNST, JAMES, *Roger Williams: New England Firebrand.* New York, 1932.
GREENE, E. B., *The Foundations of American Nationality.* New York, 1922.
MAYNARD, THEODORE, *The Story of American Catholicism.* New York, 1941.
NEWMAN, A. H., *A History of the Baptist Churches in the United States,* American Church History Series, Vol. II. New York, 1898
O'GORMAN, THOMAS, *A History of the Roman Catholic Church in the United States.* American Church History Series, Vol. IX. New York, 1895.
(RAY) MARY AUGUSTANA, *American Opinion of Roman Catholicism in the Eighteenth Century.* New York, 1936.
STRAUS, OSCAR S., *Roger Williams, the Pioneer of Religious Liberty.* New York, 1894.
VEDDER, HENRY C., *A Short History of the Baptists.* Philadelphia, 1907.
WILLIAMS, ROGER, *The Bloudy Tenent of Persecution,* etc. London, 1848.

CHAPTER VI

BOWDEN, *History of Friends in America.* London, Vol. I, 1850; Vol. II, 1854.
CHALKLEY, THOMAS, *Journal.* London, 1851.
COLENBRANDER, H. T., *The Dutch Element in American History.* American Historical Association Reports, 1909, pp. 193-201.
CORWIN, E. T., *A History of the Reformed Dutch Church.* American Church History Series, Vol. VIII. New York, 1895.
———— *Manual of the Reformed Protestant Dutch Church* (3rd ed.). 1879.
DOBREE, BONAMY, *William Penn, Quaker and Pioneer.* Boston, 1932.
FOX, GEORGE, *The Journal of George Fox* (2 vols.). Philadelphia, 1911.
JAMESON, J. F., *Narratives of New Netherland,* In *Original Narratives of Early American History.* New York, 1909.
JONES, RUFUS M., *The Faith and Practice of the Quakers.* London, and New York, n.d.
———— *The Quakers in the American Colonies.* London, 1911.
PUTNAM, RUTH, *The Dutch Element in the United States.* American Historical Association Reports, 1909, pp. 205-218.
RUSSELL, ELBERT, *The History of Quakerism.* New York, 1942
THOMAS, R. M., *A History of the Society of Friends.* American Church History Series, Vol. XII. New York, 1894.
VAN PELT, DANIEL, *Pictures of Early Dutch Life in New York City.* 1893.

Chapter VII

Bente, F., *American Lutheranism* (2 vols.). St Louis, 1919.

Brumbaugh, Martin G., *A History of the German Baptist Brethren in Europe and America*. Elgin, Ill., 1899.

De Schweinitz, Edmund, *The History of the Church of the United Fratrum*. Bethlehem, Pa., 1885.

Dubbs, J. H., *A History of the Reformed Church*. German. American Church History Series, Vol. VIII. New York, 1895.

Faust, A. B., *The German Element in the United States* (2 vols.). New York, 1927.

Finck, W. J., *Lutheran Landmarks and Pioneers in America*. Philadelphia, 1913.

Hamilton, J. T., *A History of the Church Known as the Moravian Church or the Unitas Fratrum*. Bethlehem, Pa., 1900.

Harbaugh, Henry, and Heisler, D. Y., *The Fathers of the German Reformed Church in Europe and America* (5 vols.). Lancaster and Reading, 1857 ff.

Jacobs, H. E., *Lutherans*. American Church History Series, Vol. IV. New York, 1893.

Neve, J. L., *A Brief History of the Lutheran Church in America*. Burlington, Iowa, 1916.

Reichel, William C., (Ed.) *Memorials of the Moravian Church*. Philadelphia, 1870.

Sachse, Julius E., *The German Sectarians of Pennsylvania, 1708-1742*. Philadelphia, 1899.

Smith, C. Henry, *The Mennonites*. Berne, Ind.

Wentz, A. R., *The Lutheran Church in American History*. Philadelphia, 1933.

Winger, Otto, *History and Doctrine of the Church of the Brethren*, Elgin, Ill., 1920.

Chapter VIII

Alexander, Archibald, *Biographical Sketches of the Founder and Principal Alumni of the Log College*. Philadelphia, 1851.

Blaikie, Alexander, *A History of Presbyterianism in New England*. Boston, 1881.

Briggs, C. A., *American Presbyterianism, its Origin and Early History*. New York, 1885.

Gillett, E. H., *History of the Presbyterian Church in the United States of America*, Vol. I. Philadelphia, 1864.

Hanna, Charles A., *The Scotch-Irish or the Scot in North Britain, North Ireland and North America* (2 vols.). New York, 1902.

Hodge, Charles, *The Constitutional History of the Presbyterian Church in the United States of America*. Part I. 1705 to 1741. Philadelphia, 1839.

Klett, Guy S., *Presbyterians in Colonial Pennsylvania*. Philadelphia, 1937.

Records of the Presbyterian Church in the United States of America, etc. Philadelphia, 1904.

THOMPSON, R. E., *A History of the Presbyterian Churches in the United States.* American Church History Series, Vol. VI. New York, 1895.

TRINTERUD, LEONARD J., "Presbyterianism in Colonial New England," *Journal of the Presbyterian Historical Society.* Vol. XXVII, March, 1949, pp. 1-20.

WEBSTER, RICHARD, *A History of the Presbyterian Church in America from its Origin until the year 1760* Philadelphia, 1857.

CHAPTER IX

ALLEN, A. V. G., *Jonathan Edwards.* Boston, 1890.

CUNNINGHAM, CHARLES E., *Timothy Dwight, 1752-1817: A Biography.* New York, 1942.

DAVENPORT, F. M., *Primitive Traits in Religious Revivals.* New York, 1905.

EDWARDS, JONATHAN, *Thoughts on the Revival of Religion in New England, to which is prefixed A Narrative of the Surprising Work of God in Northampton, Mass., 1735.* New York, n.d.

FAUST, CLARENCE H., and JOHNSON, THOMAS H., *Jonathan Edwards.* New York, 1935

LUNN, ARNOLD, *John Wesley.* New York, 1929.

MILLER, PERRY, *Jonathan Edwards.* New York, 1949.

SWEET, W. W., *Revivalism in America: Its Origin, Growth and Decline.* New York, 1944. chaps. I, II.

TRACY, JOSEPH, *A History of the Revival of Religion in the time of Edwards and Whitefield.* Boston, 1842.

TYERMAN, LUKE, *The Life of the Rev. George Whitefield* (2 vols.). New York, 1877.

WALKER, WILLISTON, *Congregationalists.* American Church History Series, Vol. III, especially Chapter VIII. New York, 1894.

————.*Ten New England Leaders.* Chapters VI, VII, VIII. Chicago, 1901.

WINSLOW, OLA ELIZABETH, *Jonathan Edwards, 1703-1758.* New York, 1940.

CHAPTER X

BRONSON, WALTER C., *The History of Brown University, 1764-1914.* Providence, 1914.

CHEYNEY, EDWARD P., *History of the University of Pennsylvania. 1740-1840.* Philadelphia, 1940.

FOOTE, W. H., *Sketches of Virginia.* Philadelphia, 1850.

GEWEHR, W. M., *The Great Awakening in Virginia.* Durham, N. C., 1930.

HODGE, CHARLES, *The Constitutional History of the Presbyterian Church* (2 vols.). Philadelphia, 1851.

JARRATT, DEVEREUX, *Life of Devereux Jarratt.* Baltimore, 1806.

LEE, JESSE, *A Short History of the Methodists in the United States of America.* Baltimore, 1810.

MACLEAN, JOHN, *History of the College of New Jersey* (2 vols.). Philadelphia, 1877.

MAXSON, CHARLES H., *The Great Awakening in the Middle Colonies.* Chicago, 1920.

MURPHY, T., *The Presbytery of the Log College*. Philadelphia, 1889.

SEMPLE, R. B., *A History of the Rise and Progress of the Baptists in Virginia*. Beale, G. W., editor. Richmond, 1810; Philadelphia, 1894.

SWEET, W. W., *Men of Zeal; The Romance of American Methodist Beginnings*. New York, 1935.

TRACY, JOSEPH, *The Great Awakening: A History of the Revival of Religion in the Time of Edwards and Whitefield*. Boston, 1842.

TRINTERUD, LEONARD J., *The Forming of an American Tradition: A Reexamination of Colonial Presbyterianism*. Philadelphia, 1949.

CHAPTER XI

BARCLAY, WADE CRAWFORD, *History of Methodist Missions* (6 vols.). Vol I., *Early American Methodism, 1767-1844*. New York, 1949.

BROWN, WILLIAM, *The History of Missions; or of the Propagation of Christianity among the Heathen, since the Reformation* (2 vols.). Philadelphia, 1820.

CHURCH, LESLIE F., *Oglethorpe: A Story in Philanthropy in England and Georgia*. London, 1932.

DE SCHWEINITZ, EDMUND, *The Life and Times of David Zeisberger, the Western Pioneer and Apostle of the Indians*. Philadelphia, 1870.

EDWARDS, JONATHAN, *Life of David Brainerd*. 1749.

GILLETT, E. H., *History of the Presbyterian Church in the United States of America*. Vol. I. Philadelphia, 1864, Chapter X.

HARBAUGH, H., *The Life of Reverend Michael Schlatter*. Philadelphia, 1857.

HARE, LLOYD C. M., *Thomas Mayhew, Patriarch to the Indians (1593-1682)*. New York, 1932.

JERNEGAN, MARCUS M., *Laboring and Dependent Classes in Colonial America. 1607-1783*. Chicago, 1931.

KEITH, GEORGE, *A Journal of Travels from New Hampshire to Caratuck, on the Continent of North America*. Collections of the Protestant Episcopal Historical Society. New York, 1851.

KLINGBERG, ARTHUR J., *Anglican Humanitarianism in Colonial New York*. Philadelphia, 1940.

LENNOX, *Samuel Kirkland and his Mission to the Iroquois*. Typed Ph.D. Thesis. Univ. of Chicago, 1933.

LOSKIEL, GEORGE HENRY, *History of the Mission of the United Brethren among the Indians in North America*. Translated from the German by Christian I. Latrobe, London, 1794.

LOVE, W. D., *Samson Occom and the Christian Indians of New England*. Boston, 1899.

Massachusetts Historical Collections. Vols. I-III.

MATHER, COTTON, *Magnalia Christi Americana: or the Ecclesiastical History of New England* (2 vols.). Hartford, 1820.

MAYHEW, EXPERIENCE, *Indian Converts*. 1727.

NORTH, ERIC M., *Early Methodist Philanthropy*. New York, 1914.

PARKMAN, FRANCIS, *The Jesuits in North America*. Boston, 1925.

PASCOE, C. F., *Two Hundred Years of the S. P. G. An Historical Account of the Society for the Propagation of the Gospel in Foreign Parts 1701-1900.* Based on a Digest of the Society's Records. London, 1901.

RICHARDSON, LEON BURR (Ed.), *An Indian Preacher in England.* (Letters and Diaries relating to the Rev. Samson Occom and the Rev. Nathaniel Whitaker, etc.) Hanover, N. H., 1933.

SMITH, BAXTER P., *The History of Dartmouth College.* Boston, 1878.

SHEPARD, THOMAS, *The Clear Sunshine of the Gospel Breaking Forth upon the Indians of New England.* Reprinted, New York, 1865.

TYERMAN, LUKE, *The Life of the Reverend George Whitefield* (2 vols.). London, 1876.

WIESHIP, GEORGE P. (Ed.), *The New England Company of 1649 and John Eliot.* Boston, 1920.

WOODSON, C. G., *The Education of the Negro Prior to 1861.* New York, 1915.

CHAPTER XII

BALDWIN, ALICE M., *The New England Clergy and the American Revolution.* Durham, N. C., 1928.

BREED, W. P., *Presbyterians and the Revolution.* Philadelphia, 1876.

BRIGGS, CHARLES A., *American Presbyterianism, its Origin and Early History.* Especially Chapter IX. New York, 1885.

CROSS, ARTHUR LYON, *The Anglican Episcopate and the American Colonies.* New York, 1902.

HUMPHREY, EDWARD FRANK, *Nationalism and Religion in America, 1774-1789.* Boston, 1924.

JAMESON, J. FRANKLIN, *The American Revolution Considered as a Social Movement.* Especially Chapter IV. Princeton, 1926.

JONES, RUFUS M., *The Quakers in the American Colonies.* Especially Chapter IX, "Friends in the American Revolution." London, 1911.

MILLER, JOHN C., *Origins of the American Revolution.* Boston, 1943.

SWEET, W. W., "John Wesley, Tory." *Methodist Quarterly Review,* 1922, pp. 255-268.

THORNTON, JOHN W., *The Pulpit of the American Revolution.* Boston, 1860.

VAN TYNE, CLAUDE H., *The Causes of the War of Independence.* Especially Chapter XIII. Boston, 1922.

WEIGLE, LUTHER A., *American Idealism.* Vol. X, *The Pageant of America,* especially Chapter V. New Haven, 1928.

CHAPTER XIII

BACKUS, ISAAC, *An Appeal to the Public for Religious Liberty, against the Oppressors of the Present Day,* etc. Boston, 1773.

COBB, SANDFORD H., *Rise of Religious Liberty in America.* New York, 1902.

FORTENBAUGH, ROBERT, *The Development of the Synodical Polity of the Lutheran Church in America, to 1829.* Philadelphia, 1926.

GREENE, M. L., *The Development of Religious Liberty in Connecticut.* Cambridge, 1905.

Hodge, Charles, *The Constitutional History of the Presbyterian Church in the United States of America* (2 parts). Philadelphia, 1840.

Humphrey, E. F., *Nationalism and Religion in America*. Boston, 1924.

McIlwaine, H. R., *Struggle of the Protestant Dissenters for Religious Toleration in Virginia*. Johns Hopkins University Studies in History and Political Science, 10th Series, No. 4, Baltimore, 1894.

Meyer, Jacob C., *Church and State in Massachusetts from 1740 to 1833*. Cleveland, 1930.

Minutes of the Warren Association.

O'Gorman, Thomas, *A History of the Roman Catholic Church in the United States*. American Church History Series, Vol. IX. New York, 1895.

Purcell, Richard J., *Connecticut in Transition, 1775-1818*. Washington, 1918.

Stevens, Abel, *History of the Methodist Episcopal Church* (3 vols.). New York, 1864.

Sweet, W. W., *Natural Religion and Religious Liberty* (Dudleian Lecture, Harvard University, 1944). *Harvard Divinity School Bulletin*, March, 1945.

Tiffany, Charles C., *A History of the Protestant Episcopal Church in the United States of America*. American Church History Series, Vol. VII. New York, 1895.

Chapter XIV

Benedict, David, *A General History of the Baptist Denomination in America and other Parts of the World* (2 vols.). Boston, 1813.

Bishop, Robert H., *An Outline of the History of the Church in the States of Kentucky during a period of forty years: containing the Memoirs of Rev. David Rice*. Lexington, 1824.

Brunson, Alfred, *A Western Pioneer* (2 vols.). Cincinnati, 1872.

Cartwright, Peter, *Autobiography*. New York, 1865.

Chase, Philander, *Reminiscences: An Autobiography* (2 vols.). Boston, 1948.

Davidson, Robert, *History of the Presbyterian Church in the State of Kentucky*. New York, 1847.

Dunning, Albert E., *Congregationalists in America*. Chapter XXI, "Congregationalism in the Northwest." New York, 1894.

Finley, J. B., *Sketches of Western Methodism*.

Guilday, Peter, *Life and Times of John Carroll*. New York, 1922.

McMaster, J. B., *History of the People of the United States*. Vols. I-IV. New York, 1903.

Mathews, Lois Kiball, *The Expansion of New England*. Boston, 1909.

Mattingly, Sr. Mary Ramona, *The Catholic Church on the Kentucky Frontier 1785-1812*. Washington, 1936.

Paxson, F. L., *History of the American Frontier, 1763-1893*. Boston, 1924.

Riegel, Robert E., *America Moves West*. New York, 1949.

Rusk, Ralph L., *The Literature of the Middle-Western Frontier* (2 vols.). New York, 1925.

Shea, G. S., *History of the Catholic Church in the United States*. Vol. II, 1763-1815.

SMITH, JOSEPH, *Old Redstone, or Historical Sketches of Western Presbyterian-ism.* Philadelphia, 1854.

SPENCER, J. H., *A History of Kentucky Baptists* (2 vols.). Cincinnati, 1885.

SWEET, W. W., *Religion on the American Frontier.* Vol. I, *The Baptists.* New York, 1931.

————.*Religion on the American Frontier* Vol. II, *The Presbyterians.* New York, 1936.

————*Religion on the American Frontier.* Vol. III, *The Congregationalists.* Chicago, 1939.

————.*Religion on the American Frontier* Vol. IV, *The Methodists.* Chicago, 1946.

————.*The Rise of Methodism in the West.* New York, 1920.

————.*The American Churches: An Interpretation.* London, 1947.

TAYLOR, JOHN, *The History of Ten Churches* Frankfort, Ky., 1823.

WALKER, WILLISTON, *Congregationalists.* American Church History Series, Vol. III, Chapter IX.

WEBB, BENJ. J, *The Centenary of Catholicity in Kentucky.* Louisville, 1884.

CHAPTER XV

ALBRIGHT, RAYMOND, W., *A History of the Evangelical Church.* Harrisburg, 1942.

CLEVELAND, C. C., *The Great Revival in the West, 1797-1805.* Chicago, 1916.

DAVIDSON, ROBERT. *History of the Presbyterian Church in the State of Kentucky.* Chapters V-IX. New York, 1847.

DRURY, A. W., *History of the Church of the United Brethren in Christ.* Dayton, Ohio, 1924.

GARRISON, W. E., *Religion Follows the Frontier: A History of the Disciples of Christ.* New York, 1931

————and DEGROOT, A T., *The Disciples of Christ: A History.* St. Louis, 1948.

GATES, ERRETT, *The Disciples of Christ.* New York, 1905.

HOTCHKIN, JAMES H., *A History of the Purchase and Settlement of Western New York and of the Rise, Progress, and Present State of the Presbyterian Church in that Section.* New York, 1848.

MCDONNOLD, BENJAMIN W., *History of the Cumberland Presbyterian Church* Nashville, 1893.

POSEY, WALTER B., *The Development of Methodism in the Old Southwest, 1783-1824.* Tuscaloosa, Alabama, 1933.

RICHARDSON, ROBERT, *Memoirs of Alexander Campbell* (2 vols.) 1868.

ROGERS, JOHN, *The Biography of Elder Barton Warren Stone,* etc. Cincinnati, 1847.

SPEER, WILLIAM, *The Great Revival of 1800.* 1872.

SWEET, W. W., *Revivalism in America.* New York, 1944.

————.*Religion in the Growth of American Culture, 1765-1840* (In preparation.)

Chapter XVI

Anderson, Rufus, *History of the Missions of the American Board of Commissioners for Foreign Missions in India.* Boston, 1874.

Babcock, R., *Memoir of John Mason Peck.* Philadelphia, 1864.

Brown, A. A., *History of Religious Education in Recent Times.* New York, 1923.

Carroll, B. H., *Genesis of American Anti-Missionism.* Louisville, 1902.

Cox, F. A., *History of the Baptist Missionary Society, 1792-1842* (2 vols.). London, 1842.

Elsbree, O. W., *The Rise of the Missionary Spirit in America, 1790-1815.* Williamsport, Pa., 1928.

Gatke, Robert M., *Chronicles of Willamette.* Portland, Oregon, 1943.

Goodykoontz, Colin B., *Home Missions on the American Frontier.* Caldwell, Idaho, 1939.

Green, Ashbel, *Presbyterian Missions.* Reprinted, New York, 1893.

Kirkpatrick, John E., *Timothy Flint, Pioneer, Missionary, Author, Editor, 1780-1840.* Cleveland, 1911.

McCoy, Isaac, *History of Baptist Indian Missions.* Washington, 1840.

Memorial Volume of the First Fifty Years of the American Board of Commissioners for Foreign Missions. Boston, 1862.

Mills, Samuel J., and Smith, Daniel, *Report of a Missionary Tour through that part of the United States which lies west of the Alleghany Mountains performed under the direction of the Massachusetts Missionary Society.* Andover, 1815.

Morse, Jedediah, *First Annual Report of the American Society for Promoting the Civilization and General Improvement of the Indian Tribes in the United States.* New Haven, 1824.

Reid, J. M., *Missions and Missionary Society of the Methodist Episcopal Church* (2 vols.). New York, 1879.

Schermerhorn, John F., *Report respecting the Indians inhabiting the western parts of the United States.* Massachusetts Historical Society Collections, Series 2, Vol. II. Boston, 1814.

Strickland, W. P., *History of the American Bible Society from its Organization to the Present Time.* New York, 1849.

Sweet, W. W., *Circuit Rider Days Along the Ohio.* Chapter IV, "The Wyandot Mission." New York, 1923.

————.*Religion on the American Frontier.* Vol. I, *The Baptists,* Chapter IV. New York, 1931.

————."The Rise of Theological Schools in America," *Church History,* Sept., 1937.

Tewksbury, D. G., *The Founding of American Colleges and Universities Before the Civil War,* etc. New York, 1932.

Chapter XVII

Arbaugh, George B.. *Revelation in Mormonism.* Chicago, 1932.

BLEGEN, THEODORE C., *Norwegian Migration to America, 1825-1860*. Northfield, Minn., 1931.

CHORLEY, E. CLOWES, *Men and Movements in the American Episcopal Church*. New York, 1946.

FERM, VERGILIUS, *The Crisis in American Lutheran Theology*. New York, 1927.

FISH, CARL R., *The Rise of the Common Man*. Vol. VI, *A History of American Life*. Chapters VII, IX, XII. New York, 1927.

GADDIS, M. E., *Christian Perfectionism in America*. Especially Chapter IX, "Experimentalism and Experimentation: Oberlin and Oneida." Ms., Ph.D. Thesis, The University of Chicago, 1929.

GILLETT, E. H., *History of the Presbyterian Church in the United States of America*. Vol. II. Chapter XXXVI, XXXVII, XXXVIII. Philadelphia, 1864.

HARKNESS, R. E. E., *Social Origins of the Millerite Movement*. Ms., Ph.D. Thesis, The University of Chicago, 1927.

LINN, W. A., *The Story of the Mormons*. New York, 1902.

LOCKWOOD, GEORGE B., *The New Harmony Movement*. New York, 1905.

LOUD, GROVER C., *Evangelized America*. Chapters XI-XIV. New York, 1928.

McCONNELL, S. D., *History of the American Episcopal Church* (10th ed.). Chapters VII-X. Milwaukee, 1906.

MEAD, SIDNEY E., *Nathaniel William Taylor, 1786-1858: A Connecticut Liberal*. Chicago, 1942.

NICHOL, FRANCIS D., *The Midnight Cry; A Defense of the character and conduct of William Miller and the Millerites* etc. Washington, D.C., 1944.

NIEBUHR, H. R., *The Social Sources of Denominationalism*. Chapters VI and VII. New York, 1929.

NOYES, G. W., *Religious Experience of John Humphrey Noyes*. New York, 1923.

QUAIFE, M. M., *The Kingdom of St. James; A Narrative of the Mormons*. New Haven, 1930.

SCHNEIDER, CARL E., *The German Church on the American Frontier*. St. Louis, 1939.

SELDES, GILBERT, *The Stammering Century*. New York, 1928.

SHEA, JOHN G., *History of the Catholic Church in the United States*. Vols. III, IV. New York, 1890.

SWEET, W. W., *Religion on the American Frontier*. Vol. II, *The Presbyterians*. Chapters IV and V.

WEIGLE, LUTHER A., *American Idealism*. Vol. X, *The Pageant of America*. Especially pp. 170-186. New Haven, 1928.

WENTZ, A. R., *The Lutheran Church in American History*. Chapters XIII-XVII. Philadelphia, 1933.

WERNER, M. R., *Brigham Young*. London, 1925.

YEAKEL, REUBEN, *History of the Evangelical Association* (2 vols.). Cleveland 1909.

CHAPTER XVIII

APTHEKER, HERBERT, *American Negro Slave Revolts*. New York, 1934.

BARNES, GILBERT H., *The Antislavery Impulse, 1830-1844*. New York and London, 1933.

BARNES, G. H., and DUMOND, DWIGHT L., *Letters of Theodore Dwight Weld, Angelina Grimké Weld and Sarah Grimké, 1822-1844* (2 vols.). New York and London, 1934.

BASHFORD, JAMES W., *The Oregon Missions*. New York, 1918.

BIRNEY, JAMES G., *The American Churches the Bulwarks of American Slavery* (2d ed.). Newburyport, 1842.

CRAVEN, AVERY O., *The Coming of the Civil War*. New York, 1942.

DE SMET, P. J., *Western Missions and Missionaries*. New York, 1863.

DODD, WILLIAM E., *The Cotton Kingdom*. Chronicles of America Series, Vol. 27. New Haven, 1921.

DUMOND, DWIGHT L., *Letters of James Gillespie Birney, 1831-1857* (2 vols.). New York and London, 1938.

HART, ALBERT BUSHNELL, *Slavery and Abolition 1831-1841. The American Nation: A History*, Vol. 16. New York, 1906.

HUTCHINSON, WILLIAM T., *Cyrus Hall McCormick 1809-1856* (2 vols.). Vol. II. New York, 1930.

MCNEILLY, J. H., *Religion and Slavery, A Vindication of the Southern Churches*. Nashville, 1911.

NORWOOD, J. N., *The Schism in the Methodist Episcopal Church, 1844*. Alfred Press, Alfred, N. Y., 1923.

PHILLIPS, U. B., *American Negro Slavery*. New York, 1927.

PILLSBURY, PARKER, *The Forlorn Hope of Slavery*. Boston, 1847.

PUTNAM, MARY B., *The Baptists and Slavery, 1840-1845*. Ms., Master's Thesis, The University of Chicago, 1910.

STRINGFELLOW, THORNTON, *Scriptural and Statistical Views in favor of Slavery* (4th ed.). 1856. Proslavery views presented by a Southerner.

SWANEY, CHARLES B., *Episcopal Methodism and Slavery*. Boston, 1926.

THOMAS, A. C., *The Attitude of the Society of Friends toward Slavery in the 17th and 18th Centuries*. Papers of the American Society of Church History, Vol. VIII.

CHAPTER XIX

ALEXANDER, GROSS, *A History of the Methodist Episcopal Church, South*. American Church History Series, Vol. II. New York, 1894.

CHESHIRE, JOSEPH B., *The Church in the Confederate States; A History of the Protestant Episcopal Church in the Confederate States*. New York, 1912.

FITE, EMERSON D., *Social and Industrial Conditions in the North during the Civil War*. New York, 1910.

JOHNSON, T. C., *A History of the Presbyterian Church in the United States*. American Church History Series, Vol. II. New York, 1894.

JONES, J. WM., *Christ in the Camp*. Richmond, 1887.

McPHERSON, EDWARD, *The Political History of the United States of America during the Great Rebellion.* Especially a chapter in the Appendix, "The Church and the Rebellion," pp. 461-554. Washington, D. C., 1882.

NICOLAY, J. G., and HAY, JOHN, *Abraham Lincoln: A History.* (10 vols.). Vol. VI contains a chapter on Lincoln and the Churches. New York, 1890.

STANTON, R. L., *The Church and the Rebellion.* New York, 1864.

SWEET, W. W., *The Methodist Episcopal Church and the Civil War.* Cincinnati, 1912.

VANDER VELDE, L. G., *The Presbyterian Churches and the Federal Union, 1861-1869.* Cambridge, Mass., 1932.

CHAPTER XX

ABEL, ANNIE H., *The History of Events Resulting in Indian Consolidation West of the Mississippi River.* Annual Report Am. Hist. Ass'n, 1906. Washington, 1908.

BRADFORD, GAMALIEL, *D. L. Moody, a Worker in Souls.* New York, 1928.

CHENEY, MARY BUSHNELL, *Life and Letters of Horace Bushnell.* 1880, 1903.

Department of the Interior Bulletins; Office of Indian Affairs, *Indian Missions of the United States,* Bulletin 8, 1928; *Education of the Indians,* Bulletin 9, 1927.

DOUGLASS, H. PAUL, *Christian Reconstruction in the South.* Boston, 1909.

DuBois, W. E. B., editor *The Negro Church.* Atlanta University Studies, Atlanta, 1903.

EDWARDS, MARTHA L., *A Problem of Church and State in the 1870's.* Mississippi Valley Historical Review, Vol. XI, pp. 37-53.

FARISH, H. D., *The Circuit Rider Dismounts: A Social History of Southern Methodism, 1865-1900.* Richmond, Virginia, 1938.

GATES, ERRETT, *The Disciples of Christ. Story of the Churches.* Chapters XII, XIII, XIV. New York, 1905.

LANAHAN, JOHN, *The Era of Frauds in the Methodist Book Concern at New York.* Baltimore, 1896.

LUCCOCK, H. E., HUTCHINSON, PAUL, and GOODLOE, R. W., *The Story of Methodism.* Especially Chapter XXIV. New York, 1949.

MAYS, BENJAMIN E., and NICHOLSON, JOSEPH W., *The Negro's Church.* New York, 1933.

McCONNELL, S. D., *History of the American Episcopal Church* (10th ed.). Milwaukee, 1916.

MOODY, W. R., *D. L. Moody.* New York, 1930.

NIEBUHR, H. RICHARD, *The Social Sources of Denominationalism.* Especially Chapters VIII and IX. New York, 1929.

NEVENS, ALLAN, *The Emergence of Modern America, 1865-1878. History of American Life,* Vol. VIII. Especially Chapters VII and XII. New York, 1927.

PHILLIPS, C. H., *History of the Colored Methodist Episcopal Church.* Jackson, Tenn., 1925.

PLATT, WARD, *The Frontier.* Missionary Education, New York, 1911.

SWEET, W. H., *History of Methodism in Northwest Kansas.* Kansas Wesleyan University, Salina, Kan., 1920.

SWEET, W. W., "Negro Churches in the South: A Phase of Reconstruction." *Methodist Review,* May-June, 1921, pp. 405-418.

SWEET, W. W., *Methodism in American History.* New York, 1933. Chapter XV, "The Trying Years of Reconstruction."

THOMPSON, CHARLES L., *The Presbyterians. The Story of the Churches,* Chapters XI, XII. New York, 1903.

WENTZ, A. R., *The Lutheran Church in American History.* Part V, Chapters XVIII to XXIII. Philadelphia, 1933.

WOODSON, C. G., *The History of the Negro Church.* Washington, 1921.

CHAPTER XXI

ABELL, A. I., *The Urban Impact on American Protestantism,* 1865-1900. Cambridge, Mass., 1943.

ATKINS, GAIUS GLENN, *Religion in Our Times.* New York, 1932.

BEARD, CHARLES A., and MARY R., *The Rise of American Civilization* (2 vols.). Vol. II. Chapter XXV. New York, 1930.

BRADEN, CHARLES S., *These Also Believe.* New York, 1949.

CARLSON, MARTIN E., *A Study of the Eastern Orthodox Churches in Gary, Indiana.* Typed M.A. Thesis, the University of Chicago, 1942.

CARLTON, FRANK TRACY, *The History and Problems of Organized Labor.* New York, 1920.

CLARK, ELMER T., *The Small Sects in America.* Nashville, 1937; Revised edition, 1949.

ELY, RICHARD T., *The Labor Movement in America.* New York, 1905.

EMHARDT, C. W., *The Eastern Church in the Western World.* Milwaukee, 1928.

FARISH, H. D., *The Circuit Rider Dismounts: A Social History of Southern Methodism, 1865-1900.* Richmond, Virginia, 1938.

FAULKNER, HAROLD U., *American Economic History.* New York, 1924.

————. *The Quest for Social Justice.* History of American Life, Vol. XI. New York, 1931.

FREEHOF, SOLOMON B., *Reform Jewish Practice and its Rabbinic Background.* Cincinnati, 1944.

GADDIS, MERRILL E., *Perfectionism in America.* Typed Ph.D. Thesis, The University of Chicago, 1929.

GILL, C. O., and GIFFORD PINCHOT, *The Country Church: The Decline of its Influence and the Remedy.* New York, 1913.

GOODSPEED, THOMAS W., *The Story of the University of Chicago, 1890-1925.* Chicago, 1925.

GRIFFITHS, C. W., *Attitudes of the Religious Press toward Organized Labor,* 1877-1896. Typed Ph.D. Thesis, the University of Chicago, 1942.

GRAYZEL, SOLOMON, *A History of the Jews, from the Babylonian Exile to the End of World War II.* Philadelphia (1507), 1947.

HOOKER, E. R., *The Hinterlands of the Church: A Study of Areas with a Low Proportion of Church Members.* New York, 1931.

HOPKINS, CHARLES H., *The Rise of the Social Gospel in American Protestantism, 1865-1915.* New Haven, 1940.

JOHNSON, ROY. H., *Western Baptists in the Age of Big Business.* Typed Ph.D. Thesis, the University of Chicago, 1929.

KARRAKER, W. A., *The American Churches and the Spanish-American War.* Typed Ph.D. Thesis, the University of Chicago, 1939.

MALCOM, M. VARTAN, *The Armenians in America.* Boston and Chicago, 1919.

MATHEWS, SHAILER, *The Church and the Changing Order.* New York, 1907.

MAY, HENRY F., *Protestant Churches and Industrial America.* New York, 1949.

————. "The Development of Social Christianity," in Smith, G. B., *Religious Thought in the Last Quarter Century.* Chicago, 1925.

MATHEWS, B. J., *John R. Mott, World Citizen.* New York, 1934.

MILLIS, WALTER, *The Martial Spirit.* Cambridge, Mass., 1931.

NIEBUHR, H. RICHARD, *The Social Sources of Denominationalism.* New York, 1929.

SCHWARTZ, CHARLES, and BERTIE G., *Faith through Reason: A Modern Interpretation of Judaism.* New York, 1946.

SPINKA, MATTHEW, "The Eastern Orthodox Churches in America." *Encyclopaedia Britannica,* 1950.

TARTAKOWER, ARIEH, and GROSSMAN, KURT R., *The Jewish Refugee.* New York, 1944.

'T HOOFT, W. A. VISSER, *The Background of the Social Gospel in America.* Haarlam, The Netherlands, 1938.

CHAPTER XXII

ALLEN, A. V. G., *Life and Letters of Philips Brooks* (2 vols.). New York, 1900.

ATKINS, GAIUS G., *Religion in Our Times.* New York, 1932.

BRIGGS, C. A., "The Salvation Army," *North American Review,* 1894, pp. 697-710.

CARROLL, H. K., *The Religious Forces of the United States.* New York, 1893.

DAKIN, E. F., *Mrs. Eddy: A Biography of a Virginal Mind.* New York, 1929.

DEHEY, ELINOR T., *Religious Orders of Women in the United States.* Hammond, Ind., 1930.

EISENACH, GEORGE J., *A History of the German Congregational Churches in the United States.* Yankton, S. D., 1938.

————. *Pietism and the Russian Germans in the United States.* Berne, Ind., 1948.

GARRISON, W. E., *Catholicism and the American Mind.* Chicago, 1928.

GIBBONS, JAMES, CARDINAL, *A Retrospect of Fifty Years* (2 vols.). Baltimore and New York, 1916.

GORDON, GEORGE A., *My Education and Religion, an Autobiography.* Boston and New York, 1925.

HARLAN, ROLVIX, *John Alexander Dowie.* Evansville, Wis., 1906.

HERRON, SISTER MARY EULALIA, *The Sisters of Mercy in the United States*. New York, 1929.

KARPF, MAURICE J., *Jewish Community Organization in the United States; An Outline of Types of Organizations, Activities and Problems*. New York, 1938.

KINCHELOE, SAMUEL C., *The American City and its Church*. New York, 1938.

KUHN, ALVIN B., *Theosophy; A Modern Revival of Ancient Wisdom*. New York, 1930.

MATHEWS, SHAILER, *New Faith for Old*. New York, 1936.

MEAD, G. W., *Modern Methods of Church Work*. New York, 1897.

MOEHLMAN, C. H., *The Catholic-Protestant Mind*. New York, 1929.

MOORE, JOHN F., *Will America Become Catholic?* New York, 1931.

POWELL, L. P., *Mary Baker Eddy*. New York, 1930.

QUALEY, CARLTON C., *Norwegian Settlement in the United States*. Northfield, Minn., 1938.

RYAN, JOHN A., and MILLAR, MOOREHOUSE F., *The State and the Church*. New York, 1922.

SANFORD, E. B., *Origin and History of the Federal Council of the Churches of Christ in America*. Hartford, Conn., 1916.

SCHLESINGER, A. M., *The Rise of the City, 1878-1898*. Vol. X, *A History of American Life*. New York, 1933.

SHAFER, M. R., *The Catholic Church in Chicago: Its Growth and Administration*. Typed Ph.D. Thesis, the University of Chicago, 1929.

SHAUGHNESSY, GERALD, *Has the Immigrant Kept the Faith?* New York, 1925.

SHUSTER, GEORGE N., *The Catholic Spirit in America*. New York, 1927.

STEPHENSON, GEORGE M., *The Religious Aspects of Swedish Immigration*. Minneapolis, 1932.

STRONG, JOSIAH, *Religious Movements for Social Betterment*. H. B. Adams (Ed.), *Monographs on American Social Economics*, XIV. New York, 1900.

SWIHART, ALTMAN K., *Since Mrs. Eddy*. New York, 1931.

THOMAS, WENDELL, *Hinduism Invades America*. New York, 1930.

WILBUR, SIBYL, *The Life of Mary Baker Eddy*. Boston, 1907.

WILLIAMS, MICHAEL, *The Shadow of the Pope*. New York, 1932.

CHAPTER XXIII

ABRAMS, RAY H., *Preachers Present Arms*. New York, 1933.

ALLEN, DEVERE, *The Fight for Peace*. New York, 1930.

ATKINS, GAIUS GLENN, *Religion in Our Times*. New York, 1932.

AUBREY, EDWIN E., *Present Theological Tendencies*. New York, 1936.

BARTH, KARL, *The Word of God and the Word of Man*. Boston, 1928.

BATE, H. N., *Faith and Order: Proceedings of the World Conference, Lausanne, August 3-21, 1927*. New York, 1927.

BELL, G. K. H., *The Stockholm Conference, 1925. The Official Report*. Oxford and London, 1926.

BOWMAN, RUFUS D., *The Church of the Brethren and War, 1708-1941*. Elgin, Ill., 1944.

BROWN, WILLIAM A., *The Church in America: A Study of the Present Conditions and Future Prospects of American Protestantism.* New York, 1922.

CADOUX, C. J., *The Early Christian Attitude toward War.* London, 1919.

CHERRINGTON, E. H., *The Evolution of Prohibition in the United States of America.* Westerville, Ohio, 1920.

Christian Century, Nov. 7, 1934; Dec. 2, 1935; Nov. 25, 1936.

COLE, STEWART G., *History of Fundamentalism.* New York, 1931.

DARROW, CLARENCE, and YARROS, VICTOR, *The Prohibition Mania.* New York, 1927.

DOUGLASS, H. PAUL, *Church Unity Movements in the United States.* New York, 1934.

EASTMAN, FRED, "Religious Drama in the United States." *The Christian Century,* Jan. 22, 1936.

EISTER, ALLAN W., *Drawing-Room Conversion: A Sociological Account of the Oxford Group Movement.* Durham, N. C., 1950.

FISHER, IRVING, *Prohibition at Its Worst.* New York, 1926.

FLEMING, D. J., *Ethical Issues Confronting World Christians.* New York, 1935.

GARRISON, W. E., *The March of Faith.* New York, 1933, Chapters XVI-XIX.

HAMILTON, K. G., *John Ettwein and the Moravian Church during the Revolutionary Period.* Bethlehem, Pa., 1940.

HERSHBERGER, FRANKLIN, *War, Peace and Non-resistance.* Scottdale, Pa., 1944.

HOCKING, WILLIAM E., *Re-thinking Missions: A Layman's Inquiry after a Hundred Years.* New York, 1932.

HOVEY, AMOS ARNOLD, *A History of the Religious Phase of the American Movement for International Peace to the Year 1914.* Typed Ph.D. Thesis, The University of Chicago, 1930.

JONES, RUFUS M., *The Faith and Practice of the Quakers.* London and New York, 1927.

KINCHELOE, SAMUEL C., *Research Memorandum on Religion in the Depression.* New York, 1937.

LATOURETTE, KENNETH S., *Missions Tomorrow.* New York, 1936.

LEE, UMPHREY, *The Historic Church and Modern Pacifism.* New York and Nashville, 1943.

LEWIS, EDWIN, *A Christian Manifesto.* New York, 1934.

LUCCOCK, HALFORD E., *Contemporary American Literature and Religion.* Chicago, 1934.

MACFARLAND, CHARLES S., *Trends of Christian Thinking.* New York, 1937.

————. *The Christian Faith in a Day of Crisis.* New York, 1939.

MACGREGOR, K. C., *The New Testament Basis of Pacifism.* London, 1936.

McNEILL, JOHN T., *Christian Hope for World Society.* Chicago, 1937.

MATHEWS, SHAILER, *New Faith for Old.* New York, 1936.

MECKLIN, JOHN M., *The Ku Klux Klan.* New York, 1924.

MELAND, BERNARD E., *Modern Man's Worship.* New York, 1934.

MILLER, PERRY, *The New England Mind.* New York, 1939.

ODEGARD, PETER, *Pressure Politics; the Story of the Anti-Saloon League.* New York, 1928.

OLDHAM, J. H., *The Oxford Conference* (Official Report). Chicago, 1937.

RALL, H. F., *Modern Premillennialism and the Christian Hope*. New York, 1920.

RUSSELL, A. J., *For Sinners Only* (The Oxford Group Movement). New York, 1932.

SLOSSER, GAIUS J., *Christian Unity: Its History and Challenge in All Communions, in All Lands*. London, 1929.

SLOSSON, PRESTON W., *The Great Crusade and After*. History of American Life, Vol. XII. New York, 1930.

SMITH, GERALD BIRNEY, *Current Christian Thinking*. Chicago, 1928.

SOPER, EDMUND D., *Lausanne: The Will to Understand*. New York, 1928.

STEUART, JUSTIN, *Wayne Wheeler, Dry Boss*. New York, 1928.

TITTLE, ERNEST F., *Christians in an Unchristian Society*. New York, 1939.

TROWBRIDGE, LYDIA JONES, *Frances Willard of Evanston*. Chicago, 1938.

WARE, EDITH E., *The Study of International Relations in the United States: Survey for 1937*. New York, 1938.

WHITE, WILLIAM ALLEN, *A Puritan in Babylon; the Story of Calvin Coolidge*. New York, 1938.

CHAPTER XXIV

ABRAMS, RAY H., "The Churches and the Clergy in World War II." *Annals of the American Academy of Political and Social Science*. Philadelphia, 1948.

BATES, M. SEARLES, *Religious Liberty: An Inquiry*. New York and London, 1945.

BLANSHARD, PAUL, *American Freedom and Catholic Power*. Boston, 1949.

BLAU, JOSEPH L., *Cornerstones of Religious Liberty in America*. Boston, 1950.

JOHNSON, ALVIN W., and YOST, FRANK H., *Separation of Church and State in the United States*. Minneapolis, 1948.

LAFARGE, JOHN, "Roman Catholicism," Chapter II in Sperry, W. L. (Ed.), *Religion and our Divided Denominations*. Cambridge, Mass., 1945.

LATOURETTE, KENNETH SCOTT, *The Emergence of a World Christian Community*. New Haven, 1949.

LEE, UMPHREY, *The Historic Church and Modern Pacifism*. New York and Nashville, 1943.

MACFARLAND, CHARLES S., *Steps toward the World Council: Origins of the Ecumenical Movement*, etc. New York, 1938.

MACGREGOR, H. C. *The New Testament Basis of Pacifism*. London, 1936.

MCNEILL, J. M., *Religion and Education under the Constitution*. New York, 1949.

MANHATTAN, ARVO, *The Vatican in World Politics*. New York, 1949.

Man's Disorder and God's Design (Various authors). Addresses given at Amsterdam. New York, 1948.

PARSONS, WILFRED, S. J., *The First Freedom*. New York, 1948.

POLING, DANIEL, *A Preacher Looks at War.* New York, 1943.

RYAN, JOHN A., and BOLAND, FRANCIS J., *Catholic Principles of Politics.* New York, 1940.

STOKES, ANSON PHELPS, *Church and State in the United States* (3 vols.). New York, 1950.

'THOOFT, W. A. VISSER (Ed.). *World Council of Churches,* 1st Assembly, Amsterdam, August 22nd to September 4th, 1948. *Official Report.* New York, 1949.

INDEX

Abbott, Lyman, 343, 401
Abolition societies
  early, 290, 294-297
  Garrisonian, 294
Abrams, Ray H., *Preachers Present Arms*, quoted, 400, 403
Adams, John, quoted, 173, 179
Adopting Act, the, 124
Adventists, 278, 279
African Methodist Episcopal Church, 328, 330
African Methodist Episcopal Zion, Church, 330
Agriculture, Department of, 353
Alabama Baptist convention of 1865, action on condition of colored population, quoted, 328
Alaska, reindeer in, 361
Albright, Jacob, 240
Alva, Duke of, 20-21
America, discovery of, 8
American Anti-slavery Society, 290 ff.
American Bible Society
  established, 253
  in the Civil War, 319
  in World War II, 436
American Board of Commissioners for Foreign Missions, formed, 247, 248, 250
American churches and slavery, 290 ff.
American Colonization Society, 293
American Federation of Labor, 354
American Home Missionary Society, 250, 251, 261
American Missionary Association (Congregational), work of, for Negroes, 360
American Orthordox churches, 365
American Peace Society, 397, 398
American Protective Association, 379, 380
American Pulpit, the, 385, 386, 390
American Revolution and the churches, 172-188

American Tract Society, 254
American Sunday School Union, 254, 255
Ames, Bishop, 321
Amos, William, 50
Amsterdam, classis of, 11, 84, 85, 90, 146
Anabaptists, 16, 70
  and war, 395
Andover Theological Seminary, 241, 244, 251
Andrew, James O., 304, 305
Anglican Bishop for the Colonies, question of, 173-174
Anglican Church. *See* Established Church
Anti-British feeling, 429
Anti-Catholic legislation in Maryland, 41
Anti-Catholic movements, 379-380
Anticlericalism growing in the United States, 441
Anti-Mission Baptists, 256-257
Anti-Saloon League, 410, 411
Anti-Semitic persecutions, 368, 369
  in Nazi Germany, 371, 429
Antislavery
  after 1830, 294-297
  before 1830, 289-293
  conventions, 297
  societies, 290 ff.
Anti-Trinitarian controversy, 240-242
Architecture, Church, 413, 414
Armenian churches, 366
Arminianism, 130
Arminius, 15
Arnold, William R., Chief of Chaplains, World War II, 434
Asbury, Bishop Francis
  during the Revolution, 184, 193, 194, 195, 226, 238
  Journal of, 154
"Associates of Dr. Bray," 167
Associate Reformed Presbyterian Church, 144

475